the weakness of a simple pluralistic analysis is recognized by political scientists themselves.

MEN AT THE TOP

see p 17
25, 27, 29,

What happens in a community is microcosmic analysis for the larger national problem. Elitist vs pluralist models in a community can be for the purposes of a nat question perhaps a bit of the nat scene where they become the much discussed + ancient debate which goes back at least to Madison's admonitions against the alleged evils of faction.

The question is — how widespread is elitism or pluralism in Ami's cities — how can one measure this when one can't agree on the instrument to use?

MEN AT THE TOP
A Study in Community Power

ROBERT PRESTHUS

WITH A CHAPTER BY
L. VAUGHN BLANKENSHIP

New York   Oxford University Press   1964

For Jeffrey

Copyright © 1964 by Robert V. Presthus
Second printing, 1965
Library of Congress Catalogue Card Number: 64-11236
Printed in the United States of America

PREFACE

A frequent criticism of survey research is its failure to place its findings in some significant theoretical framework. In this study, my primary interest has been to consider the viability of political pluralism in an era of large-scale organization and concentration of political and economic power. This question is important on a normative basis of democratic values, but it also seems vital to analyze in some systematic way the conditions under which pluralism exists. If the meaning of pluralism has been transformed in our society, with its increasingly complex, technical problems, the free intellectual is obligated to face up to this condition, and perhaps to bring democratic ideology more in line with reality. While idealized conceptions of our system may inspire both higher aspirations and performance in the real world, it is also true that too great a gap between democratic ideals and reality may inspire fanciful expectations whose frustration breeds cynicism. Perhaps one counterpoise is to document existing conditions, the better to provide a basis for alternatives that can make our political system more democratic.

ROBERT PRESTHUS

Ithaca, N. Y.
June 1963

CONTENTS

Acknowledgments, ix
1. Theoretical Framework, 3
2. Power Structure Analysis, 33
3. Edgewood and Riverview: Community and Issues, 64
4. Power Structure in Edgewood, 92
5. Power Structure in Riverview, 140
6. Power Structure and Community Resources, 175
7. Elite Politics and Power Structure, 204
8. Pluralism: An Empirical Test, 239
9. Community Social Structure and Political Behavior, 282
10. Community Values and Consensus, 321
11. Power Structure and Organizational Effectiveness
    BY L. VAUGHN BLANKENSHIP, 368
12. Continuities in Power Structure Theory and Research, 405

Appendix, 434

Index, 477

ACKNOWLEDGMENTS

A great many individuals and organizations have contributed to this book. My deepest obligation is to the people in Edgewood and Riverview who, with rare exception, gave us every help in carrying out the study. On those occasions when our findings prove disenchanting, I hope they will be accepted in the spirit of disinterest and objectivity which makes research possible. From our side, we have tried to present the facts as fairly as possible.

I am also greatly indebted to Vaughn Blankenship, who participated closely in the study during its design and field research phases, criticized the manuscript in its final stages, and whose mercilessly compressed doctoral dissertation appears as Chapter 11 of the book. During the data analysis and write-up stages, Ben Vosloo, Josephine Musicus, and Ruth Swithenbank helped mightily. Susan Gaemares of the Cornell Computing Center was especially helpful in scale construction and design of tables.

Several colleagues, among them William Delany, Ray Elling, William Glaser, V. O. Key, Delbert Miller, and Aaron Wildavsky, read all or part of the manuscript. Their criticism has made this a better book.

For generous financial support for the field research, I am indebted to the Social Science Research Center and the Ford-sponsored Public Affairs program of Cornell University, and to the National Institutes of Mental Health.

My secretary, Betty Kjelgaard, did a most thorough job in what must have often seemed an endless task of typing the manuscript. The Cornell Graduate School kindly made available a grant to finance this work.

Finally, I want to thank my wife, Anita, for her help and understanding during the time the research and writing were underway.

R. P.

MEN AT THE TOP

1
THEORETICAL FRAMEWORK

Two questions dominate contemporary research on community power structure. One is the question of the meaning and the proper measurement of power. Ironically, empirical field-research in this area has not been guided by any consistent conceptualization or theory about the nature of power. The second germinal question is the extent to which existing systems of community decision-making approximate democratic values of pluralism, of widely shared power and participation in major community issues. It seems necessary at the outset to spend some time on these two questions and to set down the operating definitions that will guide the following analysis. In this way we can provide a theoretical framework that will make our findings more meaningful.

Some Observations on Community Power

Theoretical conceptions of power are notoriously unsatisfactory. The concept of power is central to social analysis, yet it remains vague and abstract, with the result that empirical research has suffered from a lack of direction and agreement upon the nature of the phenomenon being studied. A good example of this is seen in the differing approaches of political scientists and sociologists to the question of power. As Dennis Wrong has noted, the latter tend to envisage power as an attribute of social or collective relationships, whereas the former tend to define it in highly individual terms, as if it were an absolute quality possessed by a leader with much less reference to the situation in which his power is brought to bear.[1]

These divergences result in a good deal of polemical talking-past-each-other, often seeking to justify one or another approach rather than moving toward more rigorous theoretical formulations that can provide better guides for empirical research. We hope to avoid this posture. Armed with the accumulated research of community power studies, with existing methodological experience, and realizing the need to get beyond data-free debate, we will try here to take a small step forward. Our first task is to set down a theoretical approach to community power that will help us explain our findings.

Max Weber defined power as the chances of "a man or group of men to realize their own will," even against opposition.[2] He did not, it should be noted, include the capacity to gain one's ends all the time on every issue. Instead, he speaks of the "chance," the probability of such, thus avoiding what seems to be an unduly stringent requirement that even the most arbitrary and powerful elite could not meet. Weber's emphasis upon *opposition* is also a critical factor; it not only sharpens the test of power, but postulates an essential condition of pluralism,

---

[1] Review of *Power and Democracy in America*, eds. W. V. D'Antonio and H. J. Ehrlich, 28 *American Sociological Review* (February, 1963), pp. 144-5; for attempts to conceptualize power systematically, see R. A. Dahl, "A Critique of the Ruling Elite Model," 52 *American Political Science Review* (June, 1958), pp. 463-9; and F. Oppenheim, "Degrees of Power and Freedom," 54 *American Political Science Review* (June, 1960), pp. 437-46.

[2] *From Max Weber: Essays in Sociology*, eds. H. H. Gerth and C. W. Mills (New York: Oxford University Press, 1946), p. 180.

namely that opposition to an elite is the best test of the existence of competing centers of power.

However, one shortcoming of Weber's definition is that in focusing upon the individual aspect of power, it neglects, to some extent, its more important *social* dimensions. This is a crucial omission, for even though the power of individuals *qua* individuals can be empirically determined, such an emphasis overlooks two vital characteristics of power. One is that individual power is always worked out within some larger framework of institutional power. Even Robinson Crusoe's relations with Friday faced this imperative. Men are powerful *in relation* to other men. The other fact is that the power of any given individual is in large measure a result of his ability to manipulate this larger system.

In this study, we shall conceptualize power as a system of social relationships. This presupposes in every community a certain ongoing network of fairly stable subsystems, activated by social, economic, ethnic, religious, and friendship ties and claims. Such systems of interest, values, and power have desirable consequences for their members to the extent that they satisfy various human needs. In a sense, however, such subsystems are suprahuman, in that they tend to persist indefinitely and, more important, that their members may change but the underlying network of interrelated interests and power relations continues. The United States Senate provides an example of such an institutional system. It is a body with venerable customs, traditions, expectations, and rules that provide a given structure *within which* its members must learn to act. If they achieve and retain power as individuals, they do so within and through this larger social apparatus. Without the ability to form coalitions with like-minded colleagues, to avoid fracturing the prestige aspirations, seniority-based assignments and prerogatives, as well as the latent political commitments of their fellow members, no individual Senator can become powerful. In a word, his own power and effectiveness are inherently bound up in a social interpersonal system, with its own complex rules and expectations.

In community political life it seems that a similar conception of power may help us give order and meaning to our mass of empirical data. We will look for discrete, yet overlapping, constellations of power, each with a major *raison d'être*, comprising individuals who share common social interests and attributes institutionalized in a given subsystem. We shall not, of course, find that such a subsystem is composed of homogeneous members fully committed to its norms, but rather that individuals have several overlapping group memberships, each of which tends to meet one or another of their varied interests—political, economic, ethnic, cultural, and so on. Simply put, individuals of similar interests combine to achieve their ends, and such combinations of interlaced values and interests form subsystems of power. The community is composed of a congeries of such subsystems, now co-operating, now competing, now engaged, now moribund, in terms of the rise and fall of local issues. Some subsystems are more powerful than others; some are transitory; others persist, one supposes, because the interests which they institutionalize are persistent.

Such a concept should help us understand why systems of power based upon mutual economic interests seem more durable than most, and hence have a greater power potentiality than purely "political" organizations, which are less likely to inspire the sustained interest and identification of their members. As political scientists, we would like to think that political issues and elections are equally compelling, but a review of the relative number of organizations, i.e. subsystems of power, that serve the two interests suggests the futility of this preference.

The empirical implications of such a theory of community power include the need to redefine the meaning of the variables upon which research focuses. Thus the power disposed of by any given individual must be viewed less as an index of *personal* power than as an indicator of the existence of the social subsystems of power to which he belongs and from which, in some such manner as outlined above, he derives "his" power. As Hunter concludes, the "power of the individual must be structured into associational, cliques, or institutional patterns to be effective."[3] If individuals typically attribute great power to economic leaders in the community, we may assume that this is because such leaders personify an on-going system of power and interest relationships that are vital in the total apparatus of community life. Today the *primary* factor in assigning class status is typically occupational role. Class status is not mainly differentiated according to individual attributes of age, charm, political values, or any of a battery of other conceivable indexes; but instead one's role in the occupational arena is critical.

Obviously, power is attributed to individuals in any community on other bases than economic or occupational role, but it is interesting to note how often the bases for such attributions are honorific legitimations of economic status. A nice continuity often exists between an individual's official role in service, welfare, school board, and hospital board organizations and his economic role in the community. Such continuities emphasize the centrality and durability of power based upon this sector of community social systems.

As we present the data from our study, we will try to point up the relevance of this essentially social or institutional, as distinct from a purely individual, conception of community power. We shall probably find that individuals form coalitions with those of similar social and economic character and that the power of any given leader is in good part a function of the extent to which he is integrated into such coalitions. At the present time, the ability to command such resources often rests upon access and alliances that a local leader has with state and national systems of political and economic power. His "personal" resources, in this sense, become the commitments he can

[3] Floyd Hunter, *Community Power Structure* (Chapel Hill: University of North Carolina Press, 1953), p. 6.

make of the economic, organizational, and prestige resources of one or another of such systems. His own power rests essentially upon his associations with various collective systems of power; without such alliances and reservoirs, he would not be deemed powerful.

In this context, we shall look for the social and economic bases upon which individual power rests. We will analyze community power through individuals, but we must go beyond this level of analysis to determine the larger, more permanent structure of *social* power within and outside the community. This should enable us to provide a more comprehensive explanation of power at the community level.

Community Power Structure and Pluralism

As noted earlier, community power structure research has been characterized by opposing assumptions and findings. Whereas sociologists have usually found an "elitist" leadership structure, political scientists have often found a "pluralistic" system in which power is shared among several competing groups. Where the former have assumed and found that economic resources provide the critical basis of community power, the latter have assumed and found that power has many bases, each of which tends to be decisive in a given substantive area. In both cases, it seems, ideology is at work, with sociologists finding that political behavior often fails to conform to traditional social and political values, and political scientists supporting the view that mobility, equality, and pluralism are characteristic of current political systems. Both believe in democratic values and procedure per se, but they often differ as to the extent to which contemporary institutions honor them.

One of the aims of this study is to determine the extent to which the political process in two small communities may be called pluralistic. To those concerned with both the analysis of the real and the achievement of a more ideal political community, this is a vital question. The first two chapters provide a framework for the analysis by a discussion of pluralism and elitism and the orientation of the study. The present chapter is composed of a number of *hypotheses* about pluralism and the political system in our society. Neither the justification for nor the criticisms of pluralism are offered as conclusive generalizations. Our objective here is to provide a tentative theoretical framework which will give meaning and order to the findings presented in subsequent chapters.

The small community is a useful point at which to test assumptions about the democratic political process.[4] Barriers of size, complexity, and organization that characterize state and national politics are largely absent, or are certainly less formidable. Here, at the "grass roots," meaningful participation would seem to have the best chance to occur. Indeed, the German sociologist Tönnies uses the very term "community," *Gemeinschaft*, to define a type of society based primarily upon the values of friendships, neighborliness, and blood relationships, all of which are ingredients of the "natural will" which he contrasts with the "rational will" found in *Gesellschaft*.[5] The latter is characteristic of modern bureaucratized societies, and there seems little doubt that Max Weber's later conceptions of "patrimonial," "patriarchal," and "bureaucratic" types of organization were inspired by Tönnies's dichotomy. In sum, the community level provides the most favorable environment for the realization of democratic values of participation and pluralism. The opposing ideology of elitism with its pessimistic themes of mass powerlessness and alienation has usually been

---

[4] The "political process" is defined throughout to include *all* community decisions that involve the allocation of important resources. Thus the bringing in of a new industry, even though it primarily involves economic values, is viewed as a political transaction. We are concerned more with the *process* of negotiation, bargaining, compromise, and conflict whereby decisions are made, than with their substantive content.

[5] F. Tönnies, *Community and Association*, trans. by C. P. Loomis (London: Routledge and Kegan Paul, Ltd., 1955), pp. 37-9.

an urban phenomenon. For elitism connotes huge size, impersonal relationships and violent individualism, with every man seeking his own limited ends.

Democratic theory has always been concerned with these matters. From the time of the Greeks on, philosophers have set limits to the size of their ideal political communities. Aristotle insisted that "In order to do civic business properly, the citizens of a state should know one another personally."[6] Only then were a consensus and a constitution possible. Early critics of "mass democracy" rested their case in part upon the sheer size and numbers of modern society, and the consequent difficulty of achieving a feeling of community among its members. A similar concern persists in the United States today, symbolized by anti-trust legislation and the ambivalence with which huge organizations are regarded.

THE MEANING OF PLURALISM

There has been a curious reluctance on the part of scholars precisely to define "pluralism." Perhaps it is one of those terms one takes for granted. It is defined here as a sociopolitical system in which the power of the state is shared with a large number of private groups, interest organizations, and individuals represented by such organizations. The ultimate philosophical justification for pluralism lies in natural law, in the belief that the individual's right of free association emanates from God. In brief, pluralism is a system in which political power is fragmented among the branches of government; it is moreover shared between the state and a multitude of private groups and individuals. "Elitism," which we may define as its antithesis, is a system in which disproportionate power rests in the hands of a minority of the community.[7] No invidious connotation need

---

[6] *Politics*, Chap. IV.

[7] Technically, the antithesis of pluralism is "monism," which from Aristotle to Bentham has meant that the state is the highest sovereign power, to which all its constituent associations are legally and ethically subordinate.

THEORETICAL FRAMEWORK

be attached to the term. As E. H. Carr has noted, elites are in part a product of full-blown democracy: "Mass democracy has, through its very nature, thrown up on all sides specialized groups of leaders—what are sometimes called elites. Everywhere, in government, in political parties, in trade unions, in co-operatives, these indispensable elites have taken shape with startling rapidity."[8] The traditional problem of controlling the power of such leaders in a *political* context has been magnified in modern society by this proliferation of power centers, which again makes clear why students of politics cannot confine themselves to "purely" political forms of power.

The more highly differentiated structure of modern society results in elites, which tend to become separated from the members of their various groups both by their interest in maintaining themselves in power and by the demands of technology and strategy which require secrecy, dispatch, flexibility, and skills generally not characteristic of mass behavior. Although the opposite is frequently implied, elitism is not limited to arbitrary forms of government or politically underdeveloped societies, but is more likely to occur under such conditions. As Pareto said, "every people is governed by an elite."[9] The crucial matter is the openness of the elite, the ends to which its power are devoted, the means used to achieve them, and the methods available to the mass for changing and controlling it. In this study, we shall conceptualize elites as minorities of specialized leaders who enjoy disproportionate amounts of power in community affairs.

At the outset, a brief definition of "participation" is also required. This concept means more than mere voting; it includes

---

For our purposes, however, it is more useful to use the term "elitist" since it relates less to the legal and institutional aspects of the state and more to the leadership processes by which it is governed. And, of course, it has become part of the vocabulary of community power research.

[8] *The New Society* (London: Macmillan and Co., Ltd., 1956), p. 77.
[9] V. Pareto, *Mind and Society* (New York: Harcourt, Brace, and Co., 1935), p. 246.

playing an active, though not necessarily direct, role in community decisions, some knowledge of local issues, attendance at public meetings, and related attempts to influence proposed measures through individual and group action. In research terms, "participation" is viewed here as an *indicator* of pluralism, as an instrument by which pluralism in a community may be measured, however roughly. Participation, in turn, is defined by several indicators, including voting, attending public meetings, and belonging to groups and committees.

Since the ideal and the reality of "pluralism" are our major concern, we must first trace its historical antecedents. We will find that the meaning of pluralism has changed over time and, indeed, that it is used in a somewhat traditional sense in this study which attempts to retain some of its historical emphasis upon the individual.

Modern democratic societies are generally believed to be pluralistic to the extent that governmental power and influence over important public decisions are broadly shared with a great number of private organizations. Many of these organizations are "extra-official." They have neither legal nor constitutional status but instead exercise their influence on government informally. Using many paths of access, they apply pressure in an attempt to shape proposed actions to their own design. Obviously, no group succeeds in achieving its preferences all the time, nor are all groups equally concerned with all issues. Instead, each bargains and marshals its resources to do battle on those issues that impinge upon its own interests. A myriad of tactics is used in such struggles, including exchange, in which one group supports another on one issue, in return for which it receives support on another issue of vital importance to itself. We are told, for example, that in 1962 the American Medical Association offered its support to the National Chamber of Commerce against federal aid to education, in return for which the Chamber agreed to back the Association in its opposition to federal medical care legislation.

Such activities of voluntary organizations are widely viewed as the essence of democratic pluralism. Moreover, it is not only proper but *necessary* for private groups to influence public policy. As Durkheim maintains,

> Collective activity is always too complex to be able to be expressed through the single and unique organ of the state. Moreover, the state is too remote from individuals, its relations with them too external and intermittent to penetrate deeply within individual consciences and socialize them within. When the state is the only environment in which men can live communal lives, they inevitably lose contact, become detached and society disintegrates. A nation can be maintained only if, between the state and the individual, there is intercalated a whole series of secondary groups near enough to the individuals to attract them strongly in their sphere of action and drag them, in this way, into the general torrent of social life.[10]

Through their leaders, such groups mediate between individuals and all organized forms of power. In this way, government is kept close to the people, and decisions benefit from the skill and interest which such groups provide. The resulting atomization of governmental power is usually regarded with approval. It ensures the "representation" of affected interests, gives pri-

---

[10] *The Division of Labor* (Glencoe: Free Press, 1947), p. 28; this conception of pluralism as a system in which membership in politically relevant subgroups is essential to the preservation of democratic processes, is central in a careful study of the typographers union. "Democratic rights have developed in societies largely through the struggles of various groups—class, religious, sectional, economic, professional, and so on—against one another and against the group which controls the state. Each interest group may desire to carry out its own will, but if no one group is strong enough to gain complete power, the result is the development of tolerance." S. M. Lipset, M. Trow, J. Coleman, *Union Democracy* (New York: Doubleday and Co., 1962), pp. 15-16. A similarly positive conception of voluntary groups was expressed by A. F. Bentley in his early classic, *The Process of Government* (Chicago: University of Chicago Press, 1908). He believed that government represented "absent or quiescent" groups, and that the usurpation of "objectionable" power by any constellation of group interests brought the formation of new group interests to oppose them, pp. 454-5. This rationale is similar to the current "countervailing power" thesis.

vate citizens a voice in government, eases consensus, and so on. As Harold Laski, a sophisticated (although temporary) advocate of pluralism, said: "we have found that a state in which sovereignty is unified is morally inadequate and administratively inefficient."[11] The only remedy for this monistic state, which "results in apoplexy at the center and anaemia at the extremities," is widespread participation in governmental affairs by individuals and groups of many kinds regardless of their property interest. There must be competing organizations that challenge the power and authority which the modern Leviathan has gathered to itself. Pluralism is characterized by the changing alignments of such groups on changing issues. In effect, the constant structuring and restructuring of power ensure that the political process will be marked by considerable fluidity and variety.

Laski's views are based upon historical political theory, and particularly upon a well-known sixteenth-century tract, *Vindiciae Contra Tyrannos*. Perhaps the clearest expression of Laski's own views on pluralism is set down in his introduction to this noted work, which denied the omnipotence of the state and its rulers in order to make possible some measure of religious freedom for Huguenots in Catholic France.[12] From a modern perspective, the *Vindiciae Contra Tyrannos* appears aristocratic and quite unconcerned with individual rights, but it had wide contemporary repercussions on the Continent and in England as well. Although the author's main concern was for religious toleration, he made a case for the contract theory of government, which in turn was incorporated in the later writings of Rousseau and Locke, and through them, in the political values of those who wrote the American Constitution.

The origins of the pluralist rationale probably lie far back in

---

[11] *Foundations of Sovereignty* (New Haven: Yale University Press, 1931), p. vi.
[12] S. J. Brutus (pseudonym), *A Defense of Liberty Against Tyrants*, Introduction by H. J. Laski (London: A. Bell and Sons, Ltd., 1924).

history. Pluralism is inspired by the ancient fear of government, which results from impersonal, arbitrary rule, and by the reluctant conclusion that power corrupts in geometric progression as it grows. The possibility of curbing government's excessive demands by fragmenting its power was recognized as early as the Greek city states. Aristotle, for example, believed that revolutions were caused by narrowing too much the circle of government; in effect, they followed when power and its prerequisites were limited to a single circle. He noted, too, that stability, the aim of every form of government, requires balance among its various parts.[13]

This fearful conception of governmental power which underlies pluralism is clear in our own Constitution and in the American tendency to interpret it *negatively*, as a limitation upon government rather than as an instrument which grants great power to it. The Founding Fathers' pervasive fear of government is explicit in their efforts to limit its power. As a result, Madison, who was almost surely influenced by the *Vindiciae Contra Tyrannos*, set down a classic defense of pluralism in *The Federalist*, No. 10. The institutionalization of this view is seen in our "separation of powers" system and its checks-and-balances which doubly ensure that government can act expeditiously only in crises. Power is shared among the three great branches, each of which, in turn, exercises some portion of the specific power mainly allocated to the others.

Modern conceptions of pluralism, however, reflect the rise of industrial society, in which every other interest tends to be subordinate to *raisons d'état*. This rationale suggests that power is highly fragmented, that it is so amorphous, shifting, and tentative that few can be said to have more power than others over any period of time. Power is broadly shared among a congeries of competing public and private groups; those in high places may appear to have great power, but in reality they are only mediators among conflicting interests, for whose power

[13] *Politics*, 1306-13.

and support they must continually bargain. Things get done by compromise; to get along, one goes along. Government and the bureaucracy may be viewed as disinterested umpires in the struggle among private groups for larger shares of desired values.

Normatively, such an interpretation meets the liberal belief that great concentrations of power are inherently evil. Since the Constitution says that power is separated and since it is clearly shared by a plethora of interest groups, our system is seen as one in which practically every interest can affect public decisions. Widespread group memberships, plus his vote, give every man the opportunity to make his will felt in the political and economic decisions that concern him. Certain paradoxes, compromises, and exceptions may apply to the generalization, but they do not vitiate the essentially pluralistic interpretation.

Another corollary holds that even if industrial and political integration and technological demands have made power more concentrated, the competition among fewer, but larger, interests results in a "countervailing" mechanism that works in the public interest. Happily, competition among big business, big labor, and big government keeps each interest from misusing its power. That the majority of citizens and consumers affected by these giants remains unorganized is not vital, since they too could organize if they had the will. Thus some 40,000,000 unorganized workers in retail trade and other marginal occupations, and 4,500,000 small-business enterprises have only themselves to blame if the CIO-AFL and the NAM dominate their respective fields. Inequities in power, education, skill, wealth, and other such resources are recognized, but, customarily, the mere fact that vast numbers of associations obviously do exist is accepted as conclusive evidence of pluralism. However, the uncomfortable question of the practical effects of serious power disequilibria among them is often avoided.

But it would be wrong to suggest that pluralism is interpreted only in this negative context, as a barrier to concentrated governmental power. Once again, necessity proves to be a virtue. The dominant conclusion is that pluralism ensures, for both groups and individuals, the access and participation that make democracy viable.[14] Pluralists insist that government is not merely the responsibility of politicians and officials, but that individuals and social groups of many kinds have their part to play and make their influence felt in indirect ways.

IRONIES OF CONTEMPORARY PLURALISM

In order to bring pluralism into a modern context and suggest why its meaning has been modified somewhat to meet present social conditions, some criticisms of pluralism must be outlined. First, however, a brief note is required on its changing historical emphasis. Whereas historically the need and rationale for pluralism were largely of English or European origin, based upon conditions in which the supreme state was an actuality, the theory was apparently not really needed in America where from the start the state had been a "broker of competing wills," rather than an idealized monolith.[15] Given these conditions, American pluralism tended to shift its emphasis toward ensuring the institutional means, through such devices as federalism and functionalism, for the "conditions of individuality." As Kariel concludes, "The principal driving impulse behind American pluralism has always been our commitment to uphold the dignity of the individual person."[16] Yet, by its emphasis upon group and corporate hegemony, the theory has contributed to the decline of individualism. "The demand of traditional plu-

[14] Among others, D. Truman, *The Process of Government* (New York: A. Knopf, 1951); D. Boorstein, *The Genius of American Politics* (Chicago: University of Chicago Press, 1953). Obviously, pluralists recognize the costs and the limitations of popular participation, and the tendency for only the few to participate *directly* in political affairs. Nevertheless, their *conclusion*, on balance, is that our system remains a pluralistic one in which power is widely shared.
[15] H. Kariel, *The Decline of American Pluralism* (Stanford: Stanford University Press, 1961), pp. 146-7.
[16] *Ibid.*, p. 180.

ralist theory for individual participation in the policy-forming process through primary voluntary groups has been made sentimental by modern organizational conditions."[17] This individualistic drift of pluralism underlies our focus on individual participation in community decisions as a test of pluralism. In order to accommodate the contemporary shift of pluralist attention to *group* behavior, without abandoning its historical emphasis on the individual, we have also included individual membership in groups (the major remaining means of individual influence) and group participation per se among our criteria of pluralism.

A critical assumption of pluralism is that it provides for the broadest possible representation of private interests vis-à-vis the state. But a problem arises in that such interests often achieve their ends at the expense of a broader, unorganized public, usually composed of individuals in their role as consumers. On any given social issue, the voice of this majority often goes unheard, while those with an immediate interest speak loudly. That the claims of the latter are usually rationalized in the "public interest" is of tactical interest, but hardly changes the essential dilemma. This inequality of bargaining power, which reflects the reality of inequitable access and power disequilibria between organized interests and the unorganized majority, may be recognized; it does not, it seems, vitiate the normative appeal and assumed consequences of pluralism.

A related question is how functional for democratic processes are the group divisions characteristic of pluralism? Can this system provide the commitment to the larger community interest that a democratic polity requires? V. O. Key, for example, asks "whether the conditions precedent to the existence of a pluralistic order may not include a relative absence or weakness of attachment among the mass of people to group causes."[18]

[17] *Ibid.*, p. 182.
[18] *Public Opinion and American Democracy* (New York: A. Knopf, 1961), p. 530.

Moreover, after a careful survey of the conditions of political consensus, and some sobering evidence on the limits of public knowledge, he concludes that the main requirement of our system is an interested, talented elite rather than consensus among the mass of citizens. "The critical element for the health of a democratic order consists in the beliefs, standards, and competence of those who constitute the influentials, the opinion-leaders, and the political activists."[19]

The pluralist case also rests on the argument that the essential thing is competition and participation among organized *groups*, not among individuals. That is, it may be argued that pluralism requires access and participation by *organizations*, which are necessarily directed by the few. One logical problem here is the organismic fallacy which imputes to organizations an existence apart from their members. Another assumption is that leaders do, indeed, represent their constituents and that merely by joining an organization, the individual makes his will felt. In the sense that group leaders derive their legitimacy and power from their role as representatives of large numbers of like-minded individuals, the extension of the pluralist rationale to include members of the organization as well as its elite may be valid.[20] I stress this point because in this study group membership per se is assumed to be a valid criterion for measuring pluralism. In the United States, where the separation of powers system gives private organizations an unusually broad degree of access and influence over the use of public power, and where those with political power tend to listen mainly to those who command organized power, it seems that individuals must be-

---

[19] *Ibid.*, p. 558.
[20] In congressional committee hearings, for example, one is impressed by the frequency with which the first question asked the witness is some variant of "What organization do you represent, and what is the size of your membership?" Congressmen, themselves, similarly reinforce their legitimacy and points of view vis-à-vis witnesses by noting that they represent the "people" of X state or district. In both cases, the representation of substantial numbers of organized individuals provides a normative basis for legitimacy, access, and influence.

long to organizations if they are to gain the share of power promised them by pluralism.

An aspect of pluralism, which gives it a somewhat quaint character, is the changing popular attitude toward the modern state. On balance, and with many qualifications, what we have seen in the United States is the gradual erosion of the negative conception of the state, which is part of the classical pluralist view, in favor of a happier definition of its role. Today, the state is often seen as the only viable means of *ensuring* economic and civil liberty, as in the case of the Negro. This changing perspective may reflect a growing recognition that, among all social entities, the state alone possesses both ability to recognize and the resources to meet growing demands for security in industrial societies. As a result, many interests now look to the state for welfare bounties, subsidies, and the arbitration of competing group interests, rather than regarding it as a monolithic threat. In this normative sense, the pluralist conception of the state has been turned upside down.

Traditional conceptions of pluralism have changed in another way. Such reassessments may be based upon the changing nature of many groups which, instead of remaining *bona fide* instruments of pluralism, have become oligarchic and restrictive insofar as they monopolize access to governmental power and limit individual participation.[21] As one observer notes, "the voluntary organizations or associations which the early theorists of pluralism relied upon to sustain the individual against a unified omnipotent government, have themselves become oligarchically governed hierarchies."[22] Such groups have so "collectivized" the individual member that, although he re-

[21] It is interesting, for example, that despite the length of the 1963 New York City newspaper strike, with its economic losses and frustrations, it was difficult for anyone to adopt a punitive attitude or impugn the motives of the typographers union, mainly because this is one of the very few American unions which has maintained an ideal democratic system of internal government.
[22] Kariel, *op. cit.*, p. 2.

mains vital to the extent of providing the numerical base upon which the group's power rests, he has little influence on its policies. Often using democratic forms, its leaders maintain oligarchic control of the organization's resources. They *are* the organization, representing it before other publics, personifying its major values. A not too subtle rationalization follows whereby rank-and-file members are defined as somehow not true representatives of the group. Their role and judgments remain "unofficial." The effects on participation are generally restrictive, since the rank and file often accepts such limitations.

Viewed as independent systems, then, the private groups that give meaning to pluralism are rarely pluralistic, in the sense of having competing power centers *within* them. Such groups no longer meet traditional pluralist assumptions, because of the great inequality of bargaining power that characterizes them. The pluralism that exists is too often restricted to the few powerful organizations that monopolize most social areas. Producer groups, linked fundamentally by an economic interest, dominate, and the less disciplined voluntary associations rarely compete successfully with them in the struggle for access and influence.

Such developments underlie the changed conditions and meaning of pluralism, which continues nevertheless to be defined and defended in traditional terms. An example of recent efforts to accommodate pluralism to its new environment is seen in the area of community power structure research. *Its advocates now argue that pluralism exists if no single elite dominates decision-making in every substantive area.* In effect, if bargaining and opposition among three or four elite groups (who usually make up something less than 1 per cent of the community) persist, pluralism remains viable. The existence of competition among elites, so to speak, has become the essential criterion. This is obviously a realistic theory in an age of superorganization, but whether by itself it provides a valid measure of "pluralism" remains questionable. Certainly this is a much more restricted definition than that traditionally associated with the concept.

SOME CONDITIONS OF PLURALISM

Such qualifications suggest that the concept of pluralism must be made more specific if it is to serve as a framework for systematic field research. Some necessary conditions of pluralism must be set down, against which research findings can be interpreted. Such conditions can provide empirically testable propositions which enable us to avoid a retreat into faith insofar as the documentation of the viability of pluralism is concerned. While the following propositions do not include every facet of pluralism, they do include several of its basic contemporary tenets:

1) *That competing centers and bases of power and influence exist within a political community.*

To meet the pluralist standard, lively competition among several individuals, elites, or groups is required. Moreover, in a pluralistic community, the *bases* upon which power rests will be variable, i.e. money power would be challenged by other bases of power, including class, expertise, access, and the control of the media of communication. To some extent, such power bases overlap; in a capitalistic society, for example, personal wealth and the control of the means of production often enable their possessors to co-opt several of the others. But viable competition among many elites possessing *different* bases of power is a critical factor in the pluralist equation, and it is related to the notion of "countervailing power," i.e. the assumption that a built-in stabilizer exists whereby the rise of highly organized centers of power inspires opposing centers which tend to bring the system into equilibrium.

2) *The opportunity for individual and organizational access into the political system.*

Access is vital because it provides an instrument by which support and opposition toward a proposed measure may be expressed. Penetration of the formal political system must be possible if decisions are to be rational and equitable, i.e. if they are to benefit from opposing points of view and to satisfy the demands of opposing interests. A panoply of constitutional and procedural guarantees makes such access possible. Yet, it remains necessary to determine empirically the extent of individual and group access by an analysis of specific decisions. It is important to note here that individual participation has been undercut by the complexity of issues and the growth of group representation as the typical means of political negotiation and influence. We shall, therefore, not expect to find very high levels of individual participation in the decisions analyzed here. Despite this, the amount of such participation provides a useful index of *comparative* levels of pluralism in the two communities analyzed in this study.

3) *That individuals actively participate in and make their will felt through organizations of many kinds.*

In this study, as noted earlier, the dichotomy between organizational leaders and their members is denied; unless groups are given some organic reality beyond that based upon their members, it seems that the group thesis must assume that individuals turn to collective action mainly to gain their individual desires. Certainly, voting, the most characteristic form of political participation, is in the last analysis an eminently individual behavior. Not that the individual's political values and electoral preferences are not influenced by his group associations, but rather that the political parties must evoke his participation on an individual basis.

4) *That elections are a viable instrument of mass participation in political decisions, including those on specific issues.*

Two facets of this proposition are important. Not only do elections presumably provide a meaningful method of generalized mass influence over political leaders, but the assumption is that most adult citizens do, in fact, *use* their electoral power when referenda are available on specific issues. This assumption is especially vital because the electoral instrument is more accessible than other media of influence and access, such as legislative hearings, officeholding, organizational leadership, etc. In this sense, it is the most practical weapon in the pluralist armory.

5) *That a consensus exists on what may be called the "democratic creed."*

The importance of this consensus lies in the motivation to participate inspired by the belief that the democratic creed of the community is, in fact, operational. That is, voting, organizational membership, and other political activity are activated by an acceptance of the validity of the normative propositions underlying the social system. To some extent, these values provide the cement that holds society together. The absence of this consensus, which may culminate in alienation, seems to result either in a withdrawal from active participation or in somewhat indiscriminate efforts to defeat all community proposals.

These five propositions encompass several of the basic premises of pluralism; an attempt will be made to test them in following chapters.

Conditions of Elitism

We can now consider the nature of elitism. We shall use this term to define the condition that exists when the propositions above are not operational. Elitism is a pattern of decision-making characterized by limited mass participation in community issues, and their domination by small groups of specialized or general leaders. This term suits the main drift of the analysis in the sense that it seems to define the conditions sometimes found in community power structure research; for example, the tendency for decisions to be initiated and directed by one or a few leadership groups. "Elitism" also enables us to speak of change, "competition among the few," and differential bases of power according to the substantive character of a decision.

Elitism, in sum, connotes rule by the few, and when it occurs, we may assume that the five conditions of pluralism outlined above are rarely met.[23]

In a community context, we assume that a decision-making continuum exists, ranging from a high degree of pluralism at one end to a low degree (i.e. elitism) at the other. Empirically, the position occupied by any given decision along this continuum will vary according to the combination of factors that characterize it, as well as according to the criteria used to define pluralism. This problem will be discussed below. For the moment, let us merely say that community decision-making is viewed here as occurring along a *continuum*, and is characterized by varying degrees of rank-and-file participation in major decisions and competition among the elites who play a direct, *initiating* role in them. Elitism connotes domination of the decisional process by a single group or a few men, limited rank-and-file access, little or no opposition, and a failure on the part of most of the adult community to use their political resources to influence important decisions. It refers to the tendency of power, defined as the chances of a group to achieve its ends despite opposition, to rest in relatively few hands.

It is not assumed here that those who have power can achieve their ends all the time, or that they constitute a single, impenetrable, monolithic entity, or that the locus of power does not change historically (formal political power passed from Democratic to Republican hands in the two communities we studied during the time of our research), or that community power rests entirely upon the possession or control of economic resources. Such requirements, it seems, are a caricature of power relations, if not a mere straw man.

[23] Here, it should be noted, we are specifically rejecting the revisionist notion that pluralism is adequately defined when competition or specialization exists among the elites participating in community decisions. Our definition, which we believe is more in keeping with the historical spirit and meaning of the concept, requires as necessary conditions some measure of "rank and file" and organizational participation in such decisions.

We do assume that a power elite, if found, will constitute a very small proportion of the community, and that it will not be representative in social terms of the larger community. It will be made up largely of middle- and upper-class people, who possess more of the skills and qualities required for leadership, and who tend to share certain values about politics, mobility, and requirements of leadership that differentiate them to some extent from others. However, the most critical basis of differentiation will probably be found in class status and leadership resources, rather than in attitudinal differences.

A corollary of these assumptions is that such elites are subject to relatively little influence from the rest of the community. Their power may rest upon expertise, class, status, or wealth, but its distinguishing feature is a decisive control of such resources. Elitism connotes limited numbers, limited consultation with affected groups, disproportionate control of scarce resources of money, skill, and information, and a certain continuity and commonality of interest. While political elites in Western society will typically operate through nominally "democratic" forms, i.e. through public meetings, elections, referenda, and so on, these media are sometimes manipulated to achieve a democratic "consensus" that has little substance. For example, when presidential primary elections are made the target of vast and unequal expenditures of funds, organized like advertising campaigns, and carefully selected to ensure certain desired consequences, there is some doubt that the essentials of democratic participation have been met, even though technically its procedures have been followed. Elitism, as a political instrument, often rests upon similar highly differentiated and unequal access to valued resources.

A characteristic revealed in the community research of Hunter and the Lynds is the tendency for the power of a given elite to extend horizontally, as it were, across several decisional areas. That is, the elite's will may be decisive in economic, political, and social contexts; it cuts across various substantive areas of health, education, housing, urban redevelopment, tax policy, and recreation. It is sometimes argued that specialization of interest and knowledge makes such "cutting across" unlikely, but one explanation for this pattern of influence is that specialists are available as consultants or hired-hands to those with economic and political power. Experts are aligned on either side of most technical issues, such as the effects of atomic radiation or the destructive capacity of 100-megaton bombs. The possibility of genuine disagreement among them, as well as the availability of some whose judgments nicely coincide with "official" policy, means that political leaders, allied with resourceful economic interests, may often make their will felt in several discrete and highly technical areas.

Empirical Analysis of Pluralism

Historically, much of political discourse has centered on the question of pluralism. The extent to which the political process in a given context meets pluralist expectations of participation and competition has been of continuing concern. In dealing with such questions, it has often been fashionable to categorize entire nations as being pluralistic or nonpluralistic on *all* issues, as when one speaks of "totalitarian" versus "democratic" political systems. At the community level, empirical research makes it possible to move toward more selective judgments, in part because the smaller universe permits more rigorous analysis.

If one is to verify the proposition that decision-making in a given community tends toward the "low" (elitist) end of the continuum, it is presumably necessary to demonstrate by some generally acceptable indexes of participation that a single elite group has exercised determinative influence across several policy areas.[24] Some such criterion has been set by pluralists

[24] A problem of criteria arises here. Any researcher must establish cut-off points to differentiate categories that are not always intrinsically quantita-

who have either made such studies, or have made critical judgments about the research of others.

This criterion, however, seems unduly demanding, and to some extent unfair, because it puts the burden of proof squarely on the researcher to demonstrate that "elitism," so defined, exists. He must not only prove that a monolithic community power structure exists, but if he should find instead that, say, three or four distinct elite groups share power among different types of decisions, the case for pluralism presumably remains viable. I am not sure, however, that pluralism (any more than elitism) should be accepted as a given; it should be equally incumbent upon advocates of pluralism to demonstrate by equally careful research that the community political system is indeed pluralistic. Otherwise, the debate remains essentially normative, with the pluralist enjoying most of the advantages of tradition and normative preference. More important, there is little incentive for the pluralist to do additional field research, which might reinforce his claims.

In any event, the major object of this study is to determine the structure of power among different types of leaders in two communities, and to use the data on both elite and rank-and-file participation in certain decisions to test the viability of pluralism, as defined here. We make no assumptions as to the nature of the power structure, or about the motives of those who participate. We intend to go where the data lead us. It may be that conditions of leadership will differ widely in the two communities. Power may be widely shared throughout the community; on the other hand, a small group of interested,

---

tive. Such categories include not only "elitism" and "pluralism," but the distinction between "decision-makers," "influentials," and those "rank-and-file" members of the community whose participation has often been found to be mainly limited to *referending* decisions made by others. In the next chapter, we will set down the criteria used in this study; they will provide an important basis for judgments about participation in the communities studied here. Obviously, if the criteria are regarded as invalid, it will be impossible to accept the conclusions.

talented leaders may "run" things. Such a condition will not be regarded as evidence of conspiracy. Indeed, communities that have dedicated leaders are fortunate. Some types of leaders may dominate all or most kinds of decisions. Economic leaders may monopolize "private" types of decisions, but have no influence in governmental areas. Such a pattern may occur in one community, but not in the other. We may find that economic elites dominate all types of decisions, while political elites, i.e. those playing formal political roles, may be mere figureheads. We may find no consistent pattern in either community. However that may be, the study should throw light on the political process and political values in two New York State communities during 1960-1962. Whether one feels it possible to generalize from our research is perhaps as much a function of the temperament of the reader as of the data. If the findings prove to be comparable with those of similar studies in communities of similar size, ethnic, and economic character, some gains will be possible.

Conclusions

In this chapter, a theoretical framework for an empirical study of power and pluralism has been suggested. Power has been conceptualized as a social phenomenon, as distinguished from the primarily individualistic view of power as an absolute quality possessing comparable utility regardless of the situational context in which it is invoked. Instead, the power attributions of individual leaders are conceptualized as *indicators* of their role and status in one or more social subsystems. These subsystems, in effect, provide the bases of individual power, and the substantive issues to which they direct themselves provide the boundaries within which such power is effective. It is hypothesized that the centrality and continuity of *economically* oriented subsystems give their members an inside track in community power relationships. By contrast, *politically* oriented systems tend to provide relatively less viable bases of power, subject as they are to the ebb and flow of political fortune and changing electoral loyalties. In sum, we will try to look beneath individual attributions of power to their underlying social contexts.

Pluralism has been broadly defined as a sociopolitical system in which power and influence are widely dispersed and shared. Pluralism honors the fear of government and of all forms of power—a fear which motivated the founding fathers, as well as the English and French philosophers whose values they reflected. They reasoned that if power could not be eradicated, at least its bad effects could be eased by spreading it about.

A belief of pluralism is that most citizens are wise enough to make judgments about public affairs and to help manage them. Pluralism has meant more than the control of political affairs by organizational leaders. As Jackson maintained, the duties of public office are so simple that any man of ordinary intelligence can exercise them. This conception is important in the distinction made here between "pluralism" and "elitism." So defined, pluralism seems opposed to the belief that government works best when its leaders are selected from among the "elite," however this might be defined at a given time and place. It is opposed to this Burkian view in which parliaments are a necessary safeguard against the often ill-advised aims of the majority.

Nevertheless, sophisticated observers have concluded that some variant of elite rule by highly educated and interested groups is the essential requirement of our political system. Such assumptions are based upon research in public opinion and political behavior which indicates that apathy, ignorance of complex issues, and a certain alienation from "politics" are often characteristic of the "unpolitical man." The tension between "elitist" and "pluralist" conceptions of government has not been reduced. They remain as the visible manifestations of complex residual assumptions about man, society, and government.

Despite pluralist assumptions, the empirical question of the extent to which voluntary organizations participate in community decision-making remains. It is important to determine whether such organizations are active, if they are really among the principal means by which individuals gain access to the political system. The answer to this question becomes critical in making judgments about the position of any community along the pluralist continuum.

Clearly, many private organizations compete and co-operate with government in determining the allocation of governmental largesse. Pluralists maintain that bargaining among such organizations culminates roughly in the "public interest." However, this rationale has one rather pressing shortcoming, namely, that all interests are not equally represented in the bargaining arena.[25] Real competition on any specific issue is limited to relatively few powerful groups. The weakness of the *consumer* interest is one glaring example of existing inequities in bargaining power. The organizations that have most influence vis-à-vis government are producer groups, galvanized into action by a focused and compelling economic interest.

These structural facets of contemporary pluralism mean that bargaining often proceeds among a presidium of elites, which disadvantages unorganized segments of society. This condition is reinforced in turn by organizational imperatives such as the demand for leadership, power, and dispatch which makes for a tendency toward oligarchy *within* organizations.

Given the challenge to pluralism brought by technological change and organizational necessity, perhaps one must shift

[25] Among the few books by Americans which consider this unhappy theme are H. Kariel, *op. cit.;* C. Wright Mills, *The Power Elite* (New York: Oxford University Press, 1956); and K. Loewenstein, *Political Power and Governmental Process* (Chicago: University of Chicago Press, 1957).

the argument away from expectations of widespread participation toward some less sanguine but more reasonable criterion, such as the opportunity for those who *disagree* with the decisions of the governing minority to make their voice heard. If this were done, Michels's proposition, "He who says organization says oligarchy," might prove less disenchanting. Perhaps democracy could be made more viable by a more candid recognition of the limitations upon pluralism brought about by economic realities, apathy, and disparities in power among different elements of the community.

In sum, field studies of the political process at the community level are needed to test pluralist assumptions, for it is here that widespread participation has the best chance to occur. One would expect to find the closest approximation between pluralist ideals and the realities of social and political organization. Barriers of size, distance, and organization are minimal. Access to the politician, the press, and economic leaders is relatively open. The issues are neither so complex nor so far-removed that one feels ineffectual. Politics, and, hopefully, power, is less a mystery.

2
POWER STRUCTURE ANALYSIS

While many community power structure studies have been made, mainly by sociologists, very few have been much concerned with the political institutions and processes that characterize American communities. As a group, sociologists have often been concerned with social and economic power, and those who have studied community power have tended, conceptually and ideologically, to operate in an elitist or Marxist context.[1] Politics has often been regarded as a mere handmaiden of economic and class interests. Political scientists, on the other hand, despite Charles Merriam's axiom that politics is the study of power in all its forms, have been reluctant to accept the notion of concentrated power which underlies the elitist point of view. They have often had a romantically pluralistic conception of American society, which has stressed equality, the fragmentation of power, and the role of public

---

[1] There is evidence that some sociologists now entertain a more positive view of contemporary society, as exemplified by one who remarked in a review of C. Wright Mills's work how "pitiful" it was that Mills criticized his own society! This reminds one of Freud's charge the Jung wanted to remove sexuality from psychoanalysis in order to make psychoanalysis more acceptable to the layman.

opinion and elections in influencing community leaders.[2] Although inequality of power may be subsumed under the pluralist rubric, there has been little concern with empirical tests of the extent to which the local political process approximates traditional values of pluralism and "grass roots" participation. Often this condition is assumed. We shall attempt in following chapters to analyze the extent of "pluralism" and "elitism" in community decision-making, and to focus on both political and economic power.

This emphasis requires a note on the term "political." The term is used throughout in a broad sense to include what might sometimes be defined as "social" or "economic" factors or processes. This definition follows from a working conception of politics as the study of power in all its contexts. We assume that values cannot be neatly divided into compartments, that our political and economic systems are inextricably bound together, and that the process by which each allocates desired values is essentially "political."

A survey of major community studies reveals that they have often regarded political power mainly as a by-product or a residual category of economic power.[3] This orientation marked

---

[2] For an analysis of the differing normative, theoretical, and methodological conceptions of sociologists and political scientists, see T. J. Anton, "Power, Pluralism, and Local Politics," 7 *Administrative Science Quarterly* (March, 1963), pp. 425-54; for a case study suggesting ways out of some existing methodological problems, see C. M. Bonjean, "Community Leadership: A Case Study and Conceptual Refinement," 48 *American Journal of Sociology* (May, 1963), pp. 672-81. For further specification of theoretical approaches and research problems in community power structure analysis, see the exchange between R. A. Dahl and T. J. Anton, 8 *Administrative Science Quarterly* (September, 1963), pp. 250-68.

[3] This view of the political system was especially characteristic of Robert and Helen Lynd's *Middletown in Transition* (New York: Harcourt, Brace, 1937), p. 77. It should be noted, however, that the Lynds also specified two other conditions for the exercise of power: interest and identification with the community, and apprenticeship in political and service organizations. In this context, it is noteworthy that R. A. Dahl, a political scientist, concluded after a careful study of community power structure, that "in liberal societies, politics is a sideshow in the great circus of life," *Who*

the most famous of community studies, the *Middletown* research of sociologists Robert and Helen Lynd. It is important in evaluating this study to recall that it was written during the great depression, at a time when faith in liberal political and economic values and systems was tested as never before. Contemporary critics of the study, who are equally influenced it seems by current historical forces, including 25 years of prosperity and a threatening international milieu (both of which encourage rather more positive interpretations of our system), tend to overlook this point. Yet, when we abstract ourselves from contemporary influences, we must admit the relevance of such historical forces in shaping intellectual perspectives. Indeed, the truly seminal works have usually been those that interpret and give meaning to the major trends of an age. Adam Smith, Durkheim, Tönnies, Locke, Marx, Weber, and Veblen—all were inspired by existing economic and social systems, their transmutation into capitalism, and the resultant impact upon politics, community, religion, and other aspects of social life. To expect that the conceptual apparatus of the Lynds would not have included a somewhat pessimistic economic determinism seems as visionary as to expect that Marx would have drawn mainly upon pre-capitalistic data to sustain his thesis, or that Veblen would have turned to a subsistance agriculture to illustrate the triumph of the financiers.

The Lynds, accordingly, found an elitist system, in which the famous X family dominated social and economic life in Middletown. The depression made economic considerations larger than life since unemployment and attending dislocations were the dominant characteristics of the community and the times. Those who could ease these strains by providing jobs naturally enjoyed great influence. Noting that "the nucleus of business-class control is the X family,"[4] the Lynds found that education, religion, leisure, politics, philanthropy, and public opinion in

---

Governs?: Democracy and Power in an American City (New Haven: Yale University Press, 1961), p. 305.

[4] R. and H. Lynd, *op. cit.*, p. 77.

the city were greatly influenced by this family's economic hegemony. Despite the fact that Middletown was not a "one-industry" town (in 1925 Middletown had 100 manufacturing establishments; in 1933, 81), the apparent existence of a monolithic power structure is theoretically important in view of later attempts to fashion a typology of power structure in terms of economic domination of a city by a single large industry.[5]

Some of the community studies since *Middletown* have found a less rigidly elitist system in which competition exists between traditional economic elites long resident in the community and an "organization-man" elite comprising executives of absentee-owned corporations. Competition between political and economic coalitions has also been found. The sociologist Robert Schulze, for example, discovered a bifurcation of economic and political power between local-firm economic dominants, the executives of national corporations located in Cibola, and a local "public leader" group which was found to be most widely perceived as being influential in community affairs. This latter group stood between the other two leadership groups in terms of age, education, vocational status, and social mobility.[6] The executives of absentee-owned corporations were found to be singularly uninterested in local affairs. The "local-firm economic dominants," children of men "who had once run Cibola," were also relatively inactive, although considerably less so

[5] C. Wright Mills and M. Ullmer, "Small Business and Civic Welfare. Report of the Smaller War Plants Corporation," U. S. Senate, Document No. 135, Washington, D. C., 1946; William H. Form and D. C. Miller, *Industry, Labor and Community* (New York: Harper & Bros., 1960); D. C. Miller, "Industry and Community Power Structure," 23 *American Sociological Review* (February, 1958), pp. 9-15; R. J. Pellegrin and C. H. Coates, "Absentee-Owned Corporations and Community Power Structure," 61 *American Journal of Sociology* (March, 1956), pp. 413-19. For a study suggesting that economic leaders, mainly because they now often represent nationally owned corporations, tend to *withdraw* from active participation in community affairs, see R. Schulze, "The Role of Economic Dominants in Community Power Structure," 23 *American Sociological Review* (February, 1958), pp. 3-9.

[6] "The Bifurcation of Power in a Satellite City," in M. Janowitz (ed.), *Community Political Systems* (New York: Free Press, 1960), pp. 19-80.

than the executive group.[7] Others have found that political elites are less influential because increasing concentration of power in labor, business, and political affairs at the national level has made political decisions relatively less strategic in local economic and political matters.

The most influential of post-Lynd studies is undoubtedly Floyd Hunter's analysis of Atlanta.[8] Using mainly a "reputational" method of determining power, whereby a panel of knowledgeable heads of community organizations were asked to nominate leaders who then ranked themselves, Hunter concluded that some 40 "influentials," over half of whom were in business, finance, and industry, made the key decisions affecting the entire community. It is important to note that Hunter *began* his research by defining social power as being structured, the result of social and institutional alliances; his empirical findings indicated that this structure was activated by the 40 influentials. By sociometric analysis, Hunter found that this group tended to interlock socially, culturally, and, to a lesser extent, economically. A nice distinction was found between this inner elite and its lieutenants who in carrying out its policies tended to be viewed by the rank and file as the "real" holders of power. Defining power operationally as "the acts of men going about the business of moving other men to act in relation to themselves or in relation to organic and inorganic things,"[9] Hunter concluded that those who "really" have power possess financial resources and occupy or control the formal economic and governmental roles.

Sometimes forgetting Mr. Dooley's admonition, "you can't beat something with nothing," and, more important, forgetting that knowledge proceeds by accretion, some political scientists[10] have criticized severely both Lynds' and Hunter's

[7] *Ibid.*, pp. 42-3.
[8] *Community Power Structure*.
[9] *Ibid.*, p. 44.
[10] For critiques of Hunter's work, see H. Kaufman and V. Jones, "The Mystery of Power," 14 *Public Administration Review* (Summer, 1954), pp. 205-12; the Lynds and Hunter have been assailed by R. A. Dahl, "A

method and conclusions, particularly their elitist conception of power and their relegation of the political system to a mere artifact of the economic system. As a result, community power structure theory and analysis exhibit an intellectual and ideological schizophrenia. Beginning with an assumption that social power is structured, sociologists conclude, on the basis of considerable empirical research, that power is shared to some extent but that economic power is the dominant force in community affairs. Meanwhile, reasoning from a pluralist ideology, believing that power is highly diffused, and working from a rather limited amount of field research, many political scientists maintain that community power structure and decision-making are characterized by widely shared power, made good by political ceremonials, and influenced by a public opinion expressed by an electorate highly organized into voluntary groups. One of the objectives of the current report is to throw some light on this interesting dichotomy. At the same time, it seems that such conceptions as Mannheim's concerning the "situational determinism" of social observation and interpretation, may prove as relevant as field research in its resolution.

Political scientists have usually found pluralistic, specialized leadership structures. Robert Dahl, for example, concludes in

---

Critique of the Ruling Elite Model," 52 *American Political Science Review* (June, 1958), pp. 463-9; N. W. Polsby, "How to Study Community Power: the Pluralist Alternative," 22 *Journal of Politics* (August, 1960), pp. 474-84; and R. E. Wolfinger, "Reputation and Reality in the Study of 'Community Power'," 25 *American Sociological Review* (October, 1960), pp. 636-44. It is interesting that some of Hunter's and Lynds's critics were apparently uninhibited by experience in systematic community power structure research. Some of them have remedied this shortcoming, but others continue to equate the elegance of abstract epistemology, grand language, and a purely logical rigor with the untidiness of field research. Cf. L. J. R. Herson, "In the Footsteps of Community Power," 55 *American Political Science Review* (December, 1961), pp. 817-30. For comments on this immaculate conception of the theory-research nexus, see J. Bensman and A. Vidich, "Social Theory in Field Research," 45 *American Journal of Sociology* (May, 1960), pp. 577-84; and E. Shils, "Primordial, Personal, Sacred, and Civil Ties," 8 *British Journal of Sociology* (June, 1957), pp. 130-45.

his New Haven study that very little overlap exists among leaders, as measured by three key issue areas.[11] He did find, however, that the proportion of the total electorate playing an active role in each decision area was extremely small. Despite this, and despite the limited proportion of the electorate who voted in local elections in New Haven, he maintains that rank-and-file influence is greater than one might assume since those in positions of power are subjectively and objectively influenced by mass opinion as expressed through the vote, and by leaders' judgments about the assumed reactions of citizens to their policies.[12] This proposition may be valid, but no strong evidence is provided for it. Indeed, securing such evidence is among the most challenging of research enterprises. Whether generalized political preferences registered in periodic elections have much influence on specific political issues remains a moot point. Insofar as the "anticipated reaction" thesis—this holds that the assumed reaction of voters is an important factor in the decisional calculus of political leaders—is concerned, one is impressed by the professional politician's reliance upon the forgetfulness of the typical voter.[13]

In his study of Bennington, Vermont, Harry Scoble concluded similarly that "no single power structure existed in the city."[14] Only in the case of a hospital decision area did he find the "monolithic, flat-surfaced pyramid, with . . . a small num-

[11] Dahl, *Who Governs?* p. 169.
[12] Related discussions of the method and pluralistic conclusions of Dahl's study include: D. Rogers (review), 48 *American Journal of Sociology* (September, 1962), pp. 271-2; A. H. Birch (review), 40 *Public Administration* (Autumn, 1962), pp. 341-2; P. Bachrach and M. Baratz, "Two Faces of Power," 51 *American Political Science Review* (December, 1962), pp. 947-52; M. Goldstein (review), 27 *American Sociological Review* (December, 1962), pp. 860-62; F. Hunter (review), 6 *Administrative Science Quarterly* (March, 1962), pp. 517-19.
[13] For evidence that voters neither know nor (apparently) care very much about their political representatives' voting record on programmatic issues, see D. Stokes and W. Miller, "Party Government and the Saliency of Congress," 26 *Public Opinion Quarterly* (Winter 1962), pp. 531-46.
[14] "Leadership Hierarchies and Political Issues in a New England Town," in M. Janowitz, *op. cit.*, p. 141.

ber of power-holders, acting in predetermined concert, and with wealth as the dominant power base . . ."[15]

Despite such findings, a by-product of post-Hunter research has been a modification of traditional pluralist assumptions concerning the extent of rank-and-file participation in community affairs. Essentially, it seems, pluralism has now been redefined to mean viable competition among elites and organized groups, whereas historically it included as a necessary condition active citizen participation in local and national affairs and a reasonable equity of bargaining power among interested groups. As noted earlier, we shall hold to this traditional conception of "pluralism" in this analysis. Researchers may, of course, define their terms as they will. However, not much is added to clarity if old words are given new connotations.

In sum, the historical conception of pluralism seems to have been constricted, if not redefined. As Dahl's conclusions indicate, a system may now be called pluralistic if there is competition among the leaders representing several substantive areas. *Within* each specialized group, decisions are dominated by the few: "in origins, conception, and execution, it is not too much to say that urban redevelopment has been the direct product of a small handful of leaders";[16] "the bulk of the voters had virtually no direct influence on the process of nomination";[17] "the number of citizens who participate directly in important decisions bearing on the public schools is small . . .";[18] "a few people, the leaders, evidently exerted great direct influence on a series of decisions about teachers' salaries, appointments, appropriations, buildings."[19] Yet, because the *same* set of leaders does not exercise influence across all substantive areas and because of an unverified and perhaps unverifiable

[15] *Ibid.*
[16] Dahl, *op. cit.*, p. 115.
[17] *Ibid.*, p. 106.
[18] *Ibid.*, p. 151.
[19] *Ibid.*, p. 161; also, "Only a tiny group, the leaders, exerts great influence," p. 164.

assumption that citizens exercise "very great" (p. 159) and "a good deal of" (p. 106) *indirect* influence on their political leaders, we are said to have a "pluralistic" system.

Although it is true that pluralism has traditionally meant the dispersal of power among many groups, it has surely meant more than bargaining and compromise among a few leaders. A fundamental problem of Dahl's analysis is that he demonstrates empirically that participation in political decision-making is limited to a minority, but he is unable to demonstrate similarly the indirect "rank-and-file" influence which *is said to be exerted* through elections and the anticipated reaction mechanism which conditions leaders as they weigh decisional probabilities. Moreover, this concern with rank-and-file influence indicates that Dahl's conception of pluralism encompasses more than mere competition among elites. He is indeed concerned with demonstrating the influence of "followers," as expressed through "critical elections." The analysis does not always distinguish between empirical fact and value theory, between a careful methodological concern and judgments that seem to reflect the subjective preferences of most of us who received a traditional political science education.

Generally, then, on the theoretical and normative side community power structure research has been characterized by a discontinuity between sociological elitist assumptions and political scientist expectations of a pluralistic universe in which social power is elusive, atomized, transitory, and variegated. It seems fair to conclude that both the collection and the interpretation of empirical data have been influenced accordingly. The biases are undoubtedly unconscious, but the consequences seem clear enough. In this context, the words of Harry Stack Sullivan seem useful:

> But how curiously opaque we are to our own scotomata. How easy it is to overlook things which do not fit into our tentative explanation. How more than difficult it is to see evidence of an unpleasant theory. It is sad indeed that medical men are so

human as to find theories pleasant and unpleasant. There is no scientist but should blush at an accusation that he liked or disliked an hypothesis, on the basis of either ethics or aesthetics, or—and this is the important ground—on the basis of his own early training.[20]

Community power structure analysis, on the whole, has benefited from these normative and methodological conflicts. Researchers have begun to use specific *decisions* as means of determining power, in contrast to earlier studies such as Hunter's, which relied mainly upon a "reputational" index to define those who were influential; also sociologists have further tested the reputational method. An apparent advantage of the decisional method is that it enables one to conceptualize and to measure power more empirically, in Weber's terms, as the chances of "a man or of a number of men to realize their own will in a communal act even against the resistance of others who are participating in the action."[21] However, one result of the present research is the conclusion that the decisional method by itself cannot isolate all the subtle manifestations of community power. By the same token, neither can the reputational method discriminate among leaders in terms of the operational use of their imputed power, nor in the relative weight they exercise in given decisions.

Despite criticisms of the reputational method and its findings, several recent studies generally reinforce Hunter's conclusions. Form and D'Antonio, for example, found an elitist variant of power structure in their Texas city, but a pluralistic one in the compared Mexican community.[22] Miller also found

[20] *Schizophrenia as a Human Process* (New York: Norton and Co., 1962), p. 148.
[21] Max Weber, *From Max Weber: Essays in Sociology*, trans. by H. H. Gerth and C. W. Mills (New York: Oxford University Press, 1946), p. 180.
[22] "Integration and Cleavage among Community Influentials in Two Border Cities," 24 *American Sociological Review* (December, 1959), pp. 804-14. One of these authors was also involved in a check of the reputational method, which concluded that although imperfect, the technique was highly reliable. W. V. D'Antonio and E. Erickson, "The Reputational

an elitist structure in a comparative study of community power.[23] His conclusion that American leadership is more likely to rest upon economic bases, while in England it is more diversified, suggests the centrality of the economic system in American culture. Insofar as parliaments are representative of dominant national values, it is interesting that, compared with Congress, the British Parliament is much more diversified in terms of the social and occupational backgrounds of its members. The huge costs of political campaigning in the U.S. suggest that the economic question may be increasing in importance as a criterion of political leadership.[24] However, at the community level, one would assume that this factor was relatively less germane. By suggesting that politics is likely to be an epiphenomenon of economics, such assumptions challenge the neo-pluralist belief that political elites are an important element in community decision-making.

On the other hand, as we saw earlier, a careful study by Schulze found little overlap between political and economic leaders.[25] Similarly, in a study of 39 decisions in Syracuse, Freeman, *et al.* found little overlap among leaders in a variety of substantive areas.[26] The specialization that characterized modern community life was offered as a major explanation. In only one issue area, mental health, were "two decisions involv-

---

Technique as a Measure of Community Power," 27 *American Sociological Review* (March, 1962), pp. 362-76; the reputational method has also been used, with good results, to *predict* the outcome of a specific decision, R. C. Hanson, "Predicting a Community Decision: A Test of the Miller-Form Theory," 24 *American Sociological Review* (October, 1959), pp. 662-71; see also, L. C. Freeman, *et al.*, *Metropolitan Decision-Making* (Syracuse: University College, 1962), pp. 12-18.

[23] "Industry and Community Power Structure: A Comparative Study of an American and English City," 23 *American Sociological Review* (February, 1958), pp. 9-15.

[24] A. Heard, *Costs of Democracy* (Chapel Hill: University of North Carolina Press, 1960).

[25] "The Bifurcation of Power in a Satellite City," *op. cit.*

[26] *Local Community Leadership* (Syracuse: University College, 1960).

ing similar content bound together by a common core of people."²⁷ On a city-wide basis, a pluralistic leadership structure seemed to exist, reflecting "the dispersion of power in the metropolitan social structure and the complexity of an urban industrialized community."²⁸ However, when the authors consider the *total* proportion of individuals who participated actively in the gamut of decisions, an important qualification is made: "in fact, the doctrines of local democracy are incorporated into the pieties rather than the practices of the Syracuse municipal and metropolitan communities. *Less than three-tenths of one per cent* of the adult citizens participated in a direct way in the making of these 39 community decisions."²⁹

In the context of elitism-pluralism, we often find that similar empirical data are subject to opposing interpretations. Dahl finds that the proportion of citizens actively participating in three issue areas in New Haven is very small, yet concludes that the political structure is pluralistic. "We shall discover that in each of a number of key sectors of public policy, a few persons have great *direct* influence on the choices that are made; most citizens, by contrast, seem to have rather little direct influence. Yet it would be unwise to underestimate the extent to which voters may exert *indirect* influence on the decisions of leaders by means of elections."³⁰ Dahl, of course, is very cautious in this contention; nevertheless, as he himself concedes, it is extremely difficult to demonstrate empirically the character and extent of undifferentiated electoral influence upon any given issue. On the other hand, it is possible to demonstrate the power that key individuals exert upon community decisions. In this sense, insofar as its advocates define pluralism as a system of broadly shared power, they seem fundamentally disadvantaged.

[27] *Ibid.*, p. 26.
[28] *Ibid.*
[29] *Ibid.*, italics in original.
[30] Dahl, *op. cit.*, p. 101, italics in original. See also, pp. 139-40, 161-2.

As we have seen, Freeman found little overlap among elites in several substantive areas, yet he concluded that when one looks at the small total proportion of individuals involved in all the decisions, pluralism is more mythology than fact. Such conflicting judgments, all based upon careful research, suggest that generalizations about community power structure may be exceedingly hard to achieve. Perhaps discrete ecological factors and historical experiences differentiate each community to the extent that no generalizations are possible. It is of course too early for this conclusion, since insufficient research returns are in.

In addition to specialization and economic structure, it may be that the size factor is critical in determining the structure of community power. If we assume that a pluralistic leadership structure requires a fairly large reservoir of individuals with leadership skills, it may well be that smaller communities just do not possess enough potential leaders to make possible a lively competition among organized groups. In a city of 50,000-100,000, the variety and complexity of social and economic relations may provide experts of many kinds who possess the raw material commonly required for leadership. In such a context, a pluralistic form of power structure might be more likely than in the small communities analyzed here. Communities of, say, 5,000-20,000 people, by virtue of a less differentiated economic system and the absence of several large banking and industrial interests with their skilled officials who could provide countervailing elites, might be characterized by an elitist type of power structure. In effect, the limited number of people possessing leadership skills would mean that influence was thrust into their hands. In this context, it seems useful to think in terms of a pluralist continuum, along which communities may be ranged in terms of the degree to which power is concentrated or dispersed among their members.

Another related explanation of varying power structures is that smaller towns may have a more "organic" social structure. Following Durkheim, we may assume that when the various areas of community life are less institutionalized, leadership is less specialized and the demands upon it less intense. In this *Gemeinschaft* milieu, control, motivation, and direction are largely achieved through traditional norms and customs. In this condition, there may be less need for organized leadership. This hypothesis which links the effectiveness of community adaptation to value consensus and social integration will be examined in detail in Chapter 10. For the moment, we merely note that this hypothesis is an important factor in explaining the discrete capacities for adaptation found in the two communities.[31]

But, even with size held constant, such factors as industrial structure and community wealth may be crucial in shaping the local power structure. Wealth in the form of industry and financial institutions requires and attracts such skilled groups as lawyers, engineers, and accountants who have the education, interest, and time required for participation in local affairs. This may result in a rather more pluralistic system as such highly-skilled "cosmopolitans" compete with old-family "locals" for influence. This hypothesis is reinforced by the fact that the children of local elites, as well as of the rank and file, often leave small communities where educational and job opportunities are limited. When this occurs the "circulation of elites" must proceed by transfusions from external sources. Moreover, there is no guarantee that the son of a distinguished, old-family leader will inherit his father's energy, wit, or sense of civic responsibility. The resulting leadership vacuum may be filled by skilled "hired hands" of the one or two large industries that characterize many small communities. Despite Schulze's findings, national corporation executives and their skilled entourages may assume an active community role, since they and their families have a direct stake in better schools, hospitals, libraries, and so on.

[31] Parenthetically, this orientation also explains why this study is concerned to a greater extent than most community power analyses with the *entire* community rather than only its leaders.

One advantage of a comparative study such as that reported here is the opportunity to test such hypotheses. Although both Edgewood and Riverview fall into the "small" community category, one of them is considerably more wealthy than the other, and as a result the reservoir of potential leaders plus the "outward mobility" phenomenon vary considerably between the two communities. Again, as we shall see in the following chapter, marked class, ethnic, religious, and educational differences exist. We shall assume that such factors shape community leadership patterns, and we shall try to demonstrate the effects of such relationships empirically. Such findings should help isolate the peculiar social conditions associated with discrete kinds of community power structures.

Method

BASES FOR SELECTING THE TWO COMMUNITIES

Edgewood and Riverview were selected for analysis for a variety of reasons. Other Cornell researchers had carried out an earlier survey which provided considerable general information about the two communities. They were similar in several important respects, yet dissimilar in others; this provided a basis upon which any differences in leadership structure might be explained. Such differences, it appeared, were especially pronounced in the ethnic, religious, political, and economic character of the two communities. One community was dominantly Republican, the other had a slight Democratic-Liberal party majority. One community was substantially more wealthy than the other and had a somewhat more diversified industrial base, which we thought would have far-reaching effects.

On the other hand, the communities were similar in being located in the same area of the state. Both were in an economic area which had declined over time as natural resources were exhausted and technological change affected their industrial bases adversely. One town had reacted to these changes with considerable élan, whereas the other had been somewhat less innovative. This again seemed to provide an opportunity to discover the social factors underlying such differential capacities to respond to serious challenges.

The communities were also similar in being located astride a major interstate highway, and in being the major shopping and cultural center for regional hinterlands. Both were far enough from larger cities to preserve to some extent their independence and to evoke some measure of citizen loyalty. However, this latter quality differed substantially in the two communities. Finally, both had faced similar problems in recent years which meant that each had made similar decisions in at least four substantive areas, namely, health, education, flood control, and new industry. Here again, a common empirical experience —the formal effort to overcome long-standing local problems— made the communities ideal for comparative purposes.

Earlier Cornell surveys had found that the hospitals in each community were quite different in their operational effectiveness. This provided an opportunity to include a novel element in the analysis, namely, an attempt to test an "exchange" or "support" theory of organizational capability; this hypothesized that the relative ability of an organization to carry out its mission was essentially a function of the extent to which it was "tied into" the community power structure. Thus, any organization's ability to secure the necessary resources of personnel, money, publicity, and prestige was proportional to the extent to which it was able to co-opt groups and individuals in the community who either possessed or had access to such resources. The extent to which the boards of the two hospitals were articulated, socially, politically, and organizationally, with the members of the power structure, and were thus able to co-opt necessary community resources, became the major empirical test of this proposition.

Another rather mundane yet strategically important reason for selecting these particular communities was their geographical proximity to Cornell University and to each other. Given the high cost of survey research and the length of time the interviewers would have to be maintained in the field, it was economical for the research team to be able to visit the communities several times during the academic year, as well as to commute expeditiously from one to the other during the interviewing stage.

In sum, these two communities were selected because our foreknowledge of their general character suggested that they were well suited for comparative research. They shared both important similarities and differences which facilitated the task of differentiating their leadership structures and the manner in which important decisions were made in each community.

We must now define several terms which will be used in the following chapters. First, a broad dichotomy is established between individuals who are directly active in community affairs and those whose participation is limited mainly to voting or perhaps discussing community issues with their neighbors. This latter group, which comprises the great majority of citizens, is designated as the "rank and file."

The leadership group is placed into three main categories, namely, "decision-makers," those who proved to be directly involved in vital community decisions; "influentials," those who were nominated as powerful using the "reputational" method; and "organizational leaders," who comprised a sample of presidents, chairmen, etc., of voluntary organizations in the community.

"Decision-makers," in turn, have been placed in three subcategories: "political," "economic," and "specialist." It is important to note that these are merely descriptive, *post hoc* categories, based upon a preliminary analysis and differentiation of the entire leadership group. The three categories were not established as hypotheses, to be tested by data from the study. They are merely analytical constructs that seem useful in differentiating those who make up the local power structure. The definitive social characteristics of such subgroups are not regarded as "proving" anything, but are merely used further to differentiate the three types.

Political leaders are those who held political office during the time of our study, who are defined by others as being essentially political in orientation as evidenced by direct and long participation in party affairs, and whose major basis of power is political. *Economic* leaders are those whose primary local role is in business, commerce, industry, or finance and whose bases of power rest essentially in their economic status or role. *Specialist* leaders are a residual category, characterized by participation in only a single decision, usually of an educational or welfare character, a marginal position in the power structure, and a substantial proportion of women members. One other term, "leg-man," is used to accommodate a well-known phenomenon in political behavior whereby those in positions of "potential" power often delegate to their subordinates an active role in community affairs. This phenomenon explains why the decisional method by itself is unable to provide a complete taxonomy of community power.

One final comment about the use of the term "significant." Whenever it seems useful, we have used tests of significance in interpreting our quantitative findings. For this reason, whenever the term "significant" appears in the text, it indicates *statistical* significance.

Major Objectives of the Research

Building upon earlier research, the design attempts to make both substantive and methodological contributions to community power structure analysis. For example, a common criticism of such research has been its essentially *static* nature. With rare exceptions, such as the work of Dahl and Scoble, community analysis has been ahistorical, a slice of discontinuous material, which may be valid for one point in time, but fails to provide the depth and understanding made possible by a historical perspective. As a result, little is known about *changes* in the community power structure. Have the social characteristics of elites changed over time? Have local power structures evolved from a period in which economic factors provided the major bases of power to one in which other resources such as politics, skill, or class compete with these factors?

Our use of a panel of decisions covering a decade gives the study some historical continuity. We are able, to some extent, to report how the composition of the power structure has changed as a result of geographical mobility, advanced age, and the changing political fortunes of its members. We learn how the dominant political complexion of the two communities has evolved, and how their economic base has changed in response to technological change and the depletion of natural resources.

Another element often absent from studies of community power is a consideration of the recruitment process. How is the "circulation of elites" effected? What is the process by which elites replace themselves? How do they identify and co-opt new recruits into leadership positions? Also related here is the previous question of the changing *bases* of leadership. Do the communities seem to shift from domination by economic groups to control by political groups? Also, do the *kinds* of skills required for leadership change? Has, for example, the proportion of "lions" to "foxes," to use Pareto's terms, in the groups which enjoy power changed over time? Here, we find that leaders select their successors after an initiation period in which the new recruits have proved themselves in highly visible, ministerial roles in local civic organizations. Among the criteria of selection is the latent expectation that recruits in each leadership category will personify the value perspectives of their predecessors.

A second substantive area which has been somewhat neglected is the question of the political and social values of elites. Are these relatively uniform within a given community or among leaders from a given socioeconomic context? This question is important in bridging the gap between attitudes and overt behavior. It is often assumed that elites share a constellation of values which guide their behavior in leadership roles. It is also assumed that their value structures are more consistent and possibly different from those of ordinary men. An effort to test these hypotheses is made by including a schedule of normative items in the questionnaires, including some from the Adorno "authoritarian personality" scale.

Another effort at innovation is a systematic comparison of the decision-makers with the community rank and file in terms of political values, alienation, perceptions of such aspects of leadership as recruitment, required skills, bases of power and influence, and consensus upon the relative salience of various community problems and the best ways of solving them. A representative sample of each community was used to elicit such information.

On the methodological side, the work of earlier researchers was especially helpful in suggesting possible contributions. We noted earlier that the reputational method of identifying leaders has been severely criticized on the ground that it fails to differentiate *potential* or assumed power from exercised or overt power. While this method may provide a reasonably accurate index of power, a presumably more active and precise method of measuring power by actual participation in selected decisions or issues has been recommended and used. We decided therefore to use *both* the reputational and the decisional methods to identify power in the two communities. The degree of consensus achieved by the two methods regarding the distribution of power would add to existing methodological knowledge.

Identifying the Community Power Structure

THE DECISIONAL METHOD

Essentially, three discrete methods of measuring community power have been used in the research, each of which has certain advantages and disadvantages.[32] There have been firstly attempts to identify individuals who have a *potential* for power because of their statuses in community organizations.[33] Other researchers have focused on individuals who have a reputation for power and influence.[34] And finally, the roles played by different individuals and organizations in selected community decisions have been used as the basis for identifying power.[35] Power in Edgewood and Riverview was determined using a combination of the second and third methods.

To measure overt power, five important decisions were selected in each community and active participation in one or more of these became the basic criterion of individual power. Insofar as the decisions were concerned, the criteria of "importance" included the sum of money involved in the decision; the number of people affected by the decision, i.e. whether it engaged the attention and interest of most citizens, or it was germane to only a segment of the community; and the need to obtain a roughly "representative" and comparable panel of decisions.[36] After initial interviews which identified a number of recent community issues, we selected a panel of decisions that

[32] These methods are discussed by W. H. Form and D. Miller, *Industry, Labor and Community, op. cit.,* pp. 517-33.

[33] Examples include R. J. Pellegrin and C. H. Coates, "Absentee Ownership and Community Power Structure"; R. O. Schulze and L. U. Blumberg, "The Determination of Local Power Elites," 63 *American Journal of Sociology* (November, 1957), pp. 290-96; and C. Wright Mills, *The Power Elite* (New York: Oxford University Press, 1956).

[34] For example, Hunter, *op. cit.;* and A. Fanelli, "A Typology of Community Leadership Based on Influence and Interaction Within the Leadership Subsystem," 34 *Social Forces* (May, 1956), pp. 332-8.

[35] For example, Dahl, *op. cit.;* Freeman, *et al., Local Community Leadership, op. cit.;* and C. Banfield, *Political Influence* (Glencoe: Free Press, 1961).

[36] Strictly speaking, the ten decisions are not "representative" of all decisions made in the two communities during the recent past. They are too important to occur very frequently and consequently are unusually salient and visible. For these very reasons, however, they are most likely to evoke the interest and participation of the most powerful members of the community.

best met these criteria. In the end, we were confident that all the decisions were in fact "important," partly because the number of decisions involving community-wide interests and expenditures of from $100,000 to $1,000,000 was so few that there was a virtual consensus about them. A survey of local newspapers indicated that our panel included almost all the important decisions made by the communities during the last decade. The five decisions in Edgewood included a new school building program; a flood control project; a new industry; a new hospital building program; and a new community center. All but the last of these also occurred in Riverview, whose unique issue was the construction of a public housing project.

Our conception of a "decision" requires comment. Obviously, any important decision has several dimensions. Each is typically composed of a number of *stages*, some of which are relatively more crucial than others. Different individuals may participate at various stages as the strategic and skill requirements of the decision evolve. Making a theoretical distinction between the *initiation* and the *implementation* of the various decisions, we assumed that the most critical of these stages was the *initial*, to-do or not-to-do stage. For example, the action of one or a few prestigeful men in lending their names and their support to a project is usually a critical element in this "take-off" stage. Once this commitment has been secured, participation broadens to include the "leg-men" and the activists required to carry out the decision. We found that this process characterized almost every decision in both communities. A nice example is seen in the comments of a prominent Edgewood influential who, in explaining his corporation's contribution to a community hospital fund drive, said, "We made an early contribution at a level [$50,000] which would avoid a situation where other people might be inclined to give less than they should." Such a commitment was secured during the initial stage of this particular decision, and was a necessary step in the decision to launch the fund drive. Here, an analogy with the human reproduction process seems useful: we focused mainly on the act of conception and were somewhat less concerned with the period of gestation. Our "decision-makers," however, include those who were directly active in either stage, including those in opposition. As seen in Chapter 6, the "veto power" is built into our criteria of the relative power exercised by leaders.

Participation and power were determined mainly by an individual's activity in one or more of these decisions. The following criteria were used to define "participants" in the ten decisions, and hence to determine who had power in terms of its *overt* use.[37]

1) Those who a) were named as being "active participants" or "opponents" in a decision by others who were themselves active participants in response to the question, "Could you give me the names of several other people in the community whom you know of first-hand who also participated in (or were actively opposed to) the _____ decision?" and b) nominated *themselves* as being active participants or opponents.

2) Those who were nominated as having been "active participants" by at least three other individuals selected in

---

[37] Some community researchers have included *formal membership* on boards, councils, and committees as a criterion of "participation" and power. Although we initially planned to do the same, it soon became apparent that this criterion lacks discriminatory power, in the sense that several members of such boards did not play an active role in some of the decisions for which their boards were nominally responsible, nor were they nominated by participants as having been active. Although many decision-makers are in fact members of such boards or committees, to have defined *all* their members as "powerful" would have been unwarranted. This procedure was used by Dahl in establishing leadership "pools," i.e. membership was based upon formal office rather than upon demonstrated activity. Unfortunately, this useful preliminary classification was subsequently used as the basis of an attempt to demonstrate the limited *power* of New Haven's social and economic "notables," despite the fact that the "pools" themselves were initially based on essentially "reputational" rather than upon "decisional" criteria. See Anton, "Rejoinder," 8 *Administrative Science Quarterly* (September, 1963), pp. 260-61.

terms of 1) above, *whether or not* they also nominated themselves.

A "decision-maker," in effect, was an individual nominated by another active participant as having been active in a given decision and who, when interviewed, also nominated himself as an active participant. Alternatively, he could have been nominated by three or more other participants, whether or not he nominated himself. Each individual so nominated was interviewed and asked for additional nominations. Initially, a tentative list of individuals who were active in each decision was prepared, based upon an analysis of newspaper accounts of each decision and preliminary discussion with such local figures as the mayor and the director of the Chamber of Commerce. Each individual was then interviewed and asked to name the decisions in which he had played an "active" role. Specific questions asked to ascertain the timing and extent of his participation included the following: *How and when did you become aware of this problem? In what specific ways did you participate?* Criteria of participation included active membership on a committee selected to handle the problem; contacting others on behalf of (or against) the proposed decision; speaking before interested groups about the decision; and contributing funds to publicize or otherwise support (or defeat) the proposed decision. Respondents were also asked to indicate how they became aware of the decision, how it evolved, and how they evaluated the outcome. This helped us specify the time, extent, and weight of their involvement.

All interviews with those nominated as "decision-makers," as well as those with our sample of organizational leaders, were carried out by the author and his colleague, Vaughn Blankenship. The interviews took place either in the respondent's office or in our hotel rooms. Each interview with those nominated as decision-makers lasted from one-and-one-half to three hours. A structured interview schedule was used in each case.[38] After a brief explanation of the objectives of the study and a guarantee

[38] All interview and questionnaire schedules are in the appendix.

of confidence as to answers, the respondent was handed five cards, each listing one of the five decisions. He was then asked to read through the cards and indicate which decisions he had played an "active" part in. Often, we were asked to define "active," but in most cases individuals were able to specify the character of their participation without difficulty. We gradually became so well-versed in the background and evolution of each decision that we felt confident in our ability to judge accurately the extent of the respondent's participation. We did not, however, determine participation on this basis.

Each participant was asked to name "several" individuals who had played an active role in the decision. Every effort was made to avoid prompting or any reaction to such nominations. Finally, each respondent was asked to name the two or three persons who, in his opinion, were "most influential" in determining the outcome of the decision. He was then asked to specify exactly why he attributed so central a role to these nominees. Every individual nominated as having played an active part in the decision was interviewed to determine his role in the decision. In this way we cross-checked participation and secured data which helped us differentiate *relative* degrees of participation and influence in each decision. We soon found that there was a virtual consensus as to those who had been actively involved in the various decisions, and within a brief period no new names were forthcoming. When these lists were later checked against newspaper accounts of the decisions and other documents, no new names that had not appeared in the initial interviews were found.

THE REPUTATIONAL METHOD

In order to check overt power as measured above with *potential* power, we asked the following question: "Suppose a major project were before the community, one that required decision by a group of leaders whom nearly everyone would accept. Which persons would you choose to make up this group—regardless of whether or not you know them personally?" This is the "reputational" question used by Hunter, and also by Schulze to determine power by reputation in his study of Cibola, a midwestern industrial city of 20,000.[39] Our decision to identify leaders in Edgewood and Riverview by both the reputational and the decisional methods is in line with experiences which "strongly suggest the advisability of studying a community's power structure from at least two methodological perspectives . . ."[40] Every individual nominated as an "influential" was interviewed until, finally, we reached the point where no new names were being suggested. As always, a cut-off point had to be established: for an individual to be included in the "influential" category, it was decided that he must receive at least 20 per cent of the total nominations.

In the context of the criticism that Hunter's reputational method measured only potential power, rather than its overt use, it is noteworthy that Schulze found considerable difference between power measured by reputation and that measured by *formal position*. However, he found a virtual consensus as to those in "the uppermost range of community power" among three panels of judges representing the heads of voluntary associations, public leaders, and economic dominants. Our two methods similarly enabled us to compare potential with overt power, as well as to throw some light on methods used earlier. By comparing the extent of the overlap among "decision-makers" (i.e. the extent to which each leader was active in two or more decisions), as well as the degree of consensus about "influentials," we were able to make judgments about the nature of the power structure in each community. As will be shown later, extensive (and in some cases extreme) differences were found between power measured by the two methods. Moreover, as the evidence came in, we were obliged to modify our initial perspective about their relative utility and precision.

[39] Schulze and Blumberg, "The Determination of Local Power Elites," *op. cit.*
[40] *Ibid.*, p. 296.

RESOLVING THE METHODOLOGICAL ISSUE

Initially, we had assumed that the decisional method would prove to be superior to the reputational in identifying "real" community power. On the surface, it seemed highly probable that the more behaviorally oriented method would provide more accurate evidence of participation and would help solve the vexing problem of the difference between potential and overt power. The severe criticisms of Hunter's use of the reputational method by fellow political scientists also contributed to this perspective, as did my own intellectual revolt against a traditional political science education in which normative and objective analyses were often uncritically intermixed. In sum, we were conditioned to assume that the decisional method would provide a bench mark against which the reputational evidence could be checked to determine, in effect, how close it came to the revealed truth about the distribution of community power.

An analysis of all the evidence led (not without some resistance) to a reformulation of this initial perspective. *We decided that the two methods were better conceived as mutually supportive means of ascertaining power.* In Vidich's and Bensman's terms, an initial perspective was "exhausted" and modified once it no longer seemed able by itself to interpret the empirical data.[41] Each method, in effect, became a foil against which the evidence provided by the other could be tested and modified. It soon became clear that the reputational method had a great deal to contribute in refining the somewhat gross power ascriptions provided by the decisional technique. A particularly disturbing tendency of the latter (shared by the formal board membership criterion) was to assign high power ranks to individuals largely on the basis of merely formal or ministerial participation in several decisions. In the case of one political-legal official, for example, overtly active in four deci-

[41] J. Bensman and A. Vidich, "Social Theory in Field Research."

sions, we were for some time unable to account for his failure to appear on the reputational list or to receive any other empirical power ascriptions. It finally became clear that his role had been limited to the formal legitimation of these decisions as a part of his official responsibilities. Both reputational and other evidence made clear that his power ranking was inflated by the decisional method. But this insight could only occur after our theoretical commitment to the decisional method had been undercut by other empirical findings and analyses. Obviously, some safeguards against this kind of skewing are built into the decisional method, e.g. by items which ask activists to nominate the "most influential" participants. Moreover, further refinement of the decisional instrument will no doubt reduce such analytical problems.

On the other hand, the reputational method also revealed certain shortcomings, including the tendency of respondents to mix personal preferences with objective judgments in attributing power to community leaders. A related and well-known tendency was to equate potential with overt power. The reputational method, as the term nicely suggests, tends to identify individuals who by typical, marketplace criteria "should" be powerful in any community. For many reasons, however, some of them do not choose to use their power, or they use it in ways that are not picked up by the researcher who is bound to this method. The decisional instrument provided a useful check against such inadequacies of the reputational method. In effect, by playing one method against the other and by abandoning our initial assumption concerning the superiority of one over the other, we are able to obtain a somewhat more penetrating analysis of power in the two communities.

In combining the decisional and reputational techniques, we have engaged the method of *Verstehen*,[42] in contrast to com-

---

[42] For a critical analysis of the meaning and utility of *Verstehen* as a method in the social sciences, see T. Abel, "The Operation called *Verstehen*," 54 *American Journal of Sociology* (November, 1948), pp. 211-18.

plete dependence upon the rigorous application of a single empirical method. As Max Weber noted, *Verstehen*—the use of a combination of intellectual and subjective frames of thought in interpreting an actor's "state of mind" and in understanding the meaning of events from a functional point of view—is required for the analysis of social behavior.[43] In synthesizing, weighing, and modifying the evidence provided by the two methods, we have obviously brought to bear composite judgments about the meaning of events, regardless of the behavior and the intentions of certain leaders, and despite our original intention of confining ourselves exclusively to evidence produced by a single method. Nevertheless, we are confident that the final result is a truer picture of the distribution and use of power in the two communities.

Certainly, in addition to suggesting the desirability of using both the decisional and the reputational methods, we have indicated that the distinction between overt and potential power, however precise it may be logically, is extremely difficult to preserve operationally. We have also questioned whether overt power, as measured by the decisional method, is really a more critical index of community power than potential power, which may provide a situational framework that conditions greatly the exercise of overt power. The resolution of such questions will become clearer when the empirical results of the two methods are compared in Chapters 4 and 5.

Conclusions

Whereas sociologists have often found an elitist or paraelitist community power structure, in which politics has often seemed to be the handmaiden of economics, political scientists

---

[43] *The Theory of Social and Economic Organization*, trans. by A. M. Henderson and T. Parsons (Glencoe: Free Press, 1947), Chap. 2, and pp. 87-8, 94-115.

have usually found community leadership to be more dispersed, more consonant with the pluralist ideal which has long dominated American political ideology and analysis. Political systems have usually been regarded by the latter as independent of economic systems. In both political and sociological contexts, however, empirical research has led toward the evolution of distinct typologies of community power structure, depending upon the ecological characteristics of each variant. Size, economic base, class, and ethnicity have been among the determinants of the power structure peculiar to a given city. If research interest in this area can be maintained, one can assume that some taxonomy of community power systems will ultimately result. Certainly, the conditions under which variations in the structure of such systems are likely to appear will be more precisely set down.

In this study we have used both the "decisional" and the older "reputational" methods of identifying community power. Whereas we began with the theoretical assumption that the former method would provide more objective evidence as to the distribution of power, we were obliged to modify this conception in favor of the conclusion that both methods had a great deal to contribute and that neither was unqualifiedly superior to the other. As a result, we have relied upon the two methods, each of which has provided useful checks against the characteristic inadequacies of the other.

Finally, despite methodological refinements, the problem of normative preferences in community power structure research must be faced. We have seen that sociologists and political scientists tend to reach different conclusions in their empirical analyses of community political systems. It is ironic that their respective empirical findings seem to differ less than their interpretations of such data. If this suggests that normative considerations are always at work, perhaps this possibility is better recognized than muffled by a pretentious objectivity. Perhaps, as Myrdal argues, it is best frankly to acknowledge our subjective preferences, thereby reducing the chances that unconscious bias may result. In any event, in the following chapters, we shall try to stay close to the data, and make public the premises and criteria which guide the analysis.

3

EDGEWOOD AND RIVERVIEW: COMMUNITY AND ISSUES

Before turning to our findings, an introductory sketch is required of the two communities and the ten decisions used in our research. In neither case is it necessary to provide exhaustive detail since, to some extent, both the communities and the decisions are instrumental to our larger purpose of finding generalizations about the structure of community power.

Edgewood

Devon County is a hilly and still sparsely populated rural area largely occupied by farms specializing in dairying and to a lesser extent in potatoes. Settlers, who had entered the region shortly after the Revolutionary War, founded the village of Edgewood along the banks of the Cherwell river in 1831. The abundant coniferous forests surrounding the town were an early resource for exploitation. As hemlock provided an inexpensive caustic useful in treating leather, tanneries formed the early industrial base of the community.

By 1849, Edgewood had a population of only 400. In the 1850's, however, the construction of rail lines through the community enabled it to outstrip other places in the county, both in population and commerce. In 1859, Edgewood became incorporated, and a contemporary gazeteer notes that the community "contains 4 churches, 2 weekly newspaper offices, 2 flouring and 3 saw mills. Pop. 1,286." In 1854, over 50 million feet of pine were shipped to lumber mills. By 1870, there were four tanneries, the largest of which employed 75 men.

Some two centuries earlier, a Franciscan missionary had commented on the oil used for medicinal purposes by Indians in what is now the Edgewood area. Others described how the Indians, using their blankets, gathered oil from springs and wrung it out into vessels, bartering it to white settlers. In 1859, at Titusville, Pennsylvania, Colonel Edward Alfred Drake made history by bringing in America's first oil well. By the early 1860's several small wells were operating in Devon County; their product was primarily used as a lubricant, for its medicinal qualities, or as a vermin killer for livestock.

In June 1879, a major oil strike occurred in a community only 4½ miles from Edgewood, and Devon County became the site of a major boom. Overnight, several of its communities mushroomed. One soared from 200 to 8000 people in a week; another grew from 160 to over 4500 in a few months. In scenes recalling the California gold-rush, stages brought in hordes of oil-crazed adventurers. Saloons, gambling dens, and brothels sprang up; railroads were hastily constructed; and one community even built an opera house. Farmers who had had little money throughout their lives suddenly became wealthy. In some communities the oil craze ended as abruptly as it began; in others the industry stabilized. Among all the communities in Devon County, however, Edgewood was the major beneficiary of the boom. Refineries and storage tanks were constructed; pipelines from nearby fields brought the crude oil to the refineries. Gas fields peripheral to the oil deposits were also developed. Between 1880-90 some twenty brick buildings were built.

Such economic progress produced a number of families of

wealth and prominence, who formed a local aristocracy. One of the community's oil men contributed a building and land to be used for a hospital. Another contributed a magnificent library building, endowed it with a million dollars, and decreed that the entire income must be spent each year for books and maintenance. The town's daily paper has been in the hands of another old family for three generations.

By the beginning of the twentieth century, the depletion of timber had largely put an end to lumbering and tanning as major local industries. Although oil too was being depleted, new techniques prolonged the industry's profitableness. Some diversification was provided by two major, absentee-owned electrical firms, employing about 1500 workers. Today, the migrant managers and engineers of these firms compete and co-operate with local elements for community leadership.

In 1958, Edgewood experienced perhaps its greatest economic trauma when the X oil corporation closed its refinery, displacing some 600 workers and removing from the local rolls a lucrative source of tax revenue. A consequence of the refinery's closing was a considerable decrease in rail freight to and from Edgewood. The weight of economic factors in community decisions and opinion is well illustrated by this event, which was cited again and again by respondents as a critical factor in the school bond and the new industry decisions. Anxiety about the community's economic future apparently lay behind the rejection of the first school bond issue; and efforts to attract new industry were largely motivated by the loss of the refinery. A determination on the part of leaders to build a more diversified industrial base was another attitudinal by-product of this experience. As late as March 1961, however, the community was on the state's critical list for unemployment areas. From a 1950 population of 6400, the village had dropped to slightly under 6000 in 1963. However, as our analysis will show, the community had responded most effectively to this economic challenge.

COMMUNITIES AND ISSUES 67

Something must be said about local government in Edgewood, which like many other New York communities consists of a village surrounded by a larger town area. The town elects a supervisor who presides over the town board and represents the town on the Devon County board of supervisors. The town government also includes five councilmen, two justices of the peace, a town clerk, a tax collector, and a highway superintendent. Appointees of the town government include three assessors, an airport manager, a town attorney, and four constables.

The village of Edgewood, on which our study is focused, is administered by a mayor elected for a two-year term, assisted by four trustees with two-year terms. There are commissions for water and light, recreation, a hospital board, and a library board. The village staff includes a clerk-treasurer, an attorney, assessors (co-opted from among the town assessors), an engineer, and a commissioner of streets. There is also a school district government, which will be discussed in detail when the school bond issue is considered.

Although local government is nominally nonpartisan, both county and village are overwhelmingly Republican. In the last four presidential elections, Devon County voted as follows:

	Republican candidate	*Per cent of vote*
1948	Dewey	73
1952	Eisenhower	81
1956	Eisenhower	81
1960	Nixon	73

In Edgewood itself, however, the Democrats did somewhat better, getting 33 per cent of the vote in 1960.

Ethnically, the community is very homogeneous. Of 5967 persons (1960), only 708 were of foreign or mixed parentage and 175 were foreign-born. According to Devon County figures, the major countries of origin for the foreign-born (i.e. countries providing 300 or over) were the United Kingdom,

Germany, Canada, Italy, and Ireland in that order. In 1961, 75 per cent of persons over 20 were classified as Protestant. Further details regarding social and economic characteristics of Edgewood will be supplied later.

Riverview

Riverview, our second community, is located in adjacent Sussex County. The county is cut through by the Dee river and characterized by rolling hills covered by coniferous forests. In 1810 there were only ten families in the entire county. In 1816, the first permanent settler built a house near the banks of the Dee, where the city now stands.

Timber resources played a comparable, if not larger, role in the economic life of Riverview than in Edgewood. As early as 1813, a sawmill was in operation. But the community's growth was slow. According to one report, Riverview had only 453 people in 1860. The community was described in the following way: "The soil is a clay and sandy loam. A large share of the town is yet covered with forests; and lumbering forms the leading pursuit."

In the last half of the nineteenth century, however, a number of railroads converged on or passed through the community, transforming it into a major transportation center for the region. As a state historian summarizes: "It was, until 1868, little more than a logging town located in a swamp so soft that the roads were of corduroy. Its importance as a railroad town and shipping point made it grow in spite of its unusual location."

Here again the hemlock forests encouraged the growth of an important tanning industry. Unlike Edgewood, however, which limited its use of abundant timber resources to this activity, local entrepreneurs developed a major furniture industry. There were other industries, textiles, mirrors, etc., but Riverview was primarily a railroad town in which two major roads maintained a complex of maintenance shops for servicing locomotives and cars, and in which, as a result, a large number of railroad workers and their families lived.

Early in this century, the depletion of timber resources brought about the elimination of the tanning and lumbering industries. Railroad investments, however, more than made up the loss and the town enjoyed its greatest period of growth in the first three decades of this century. Population rose steadily from 4734 in 1900 to 9577 in 1930.

Since the depression, however, Riverview's population has been steadily declining. The 1930 level remains the peak reached by the community. Indeed, one can say that the community has never recovered from the depression of the 1930's during which its industries and workers suffered acutely. A further blow to the community's economic base occurred when the railroads switched to diesel engines, enabling trains to make longer trips and eliminating the need for maintenance shops at close intervals.[1] Riverview found itself midway between the longer change points made possible by dieselization. As a result of this combination of technological innovation and bad luck, several hundred workers have been laid off or transferred since 1956. One major railroad that once employed a thousand men, has reduced its work force to 300. The city's population has continued to decline. By 1960 there were 8480 persons in Riverview, nearly 1100 less than the peak year of 1930.

Today, Riverview industries are generally of a low-paying and low skill type. The labor force is made up of newer immigrant groups from Eastern and Southern Europe. Of the 8480 persons in the town, 1867 were of foreign or mixed parentage of foreign-born. In Sussex County, the major nations represented were, in the following order (i.e. groups including 100 or more persons), Poland, Germany, Italy, Canada, and the

---

[1] W. F. Cottrell, "Death by Dieselization: A Case Study on the Reaction to Technological Change," 16 *American Sociological Review* (June, 1951), pp. 358-65.

United Kingdom. City directories show a number of Polish names in various political offices, and our research includes several references to the importance of the Polish element in community affairs.

Riverview has a mayor-council form of government. Since about 1950, the city has had a slight but decisive Democratic majority, which ensured the party's control of the mayor's office. For a decade before our study, and during the period in which our sample of decisions occurred, the Democrats controlled the city administration. However, shortly after the field work phase of the study, in November 1961, the incumbents were overthrown by a coalition of Republicans and disenchanted Democrats; the latter voted for their opponents or refrained from voting. In 1961, 53 per cent of the voters were registered Democratic and 47 per cent Republican. In the Eisenhower landslide of 1956, Riverview gave him only 57 per cent of the votes cast. In Edgewood, he received over 75 per cent. In religion, Riverview is split almost equally; in 1961, 52.7 per cent of persons over 20 were classified as Protestant while most of the remainder were Catholic.

Another difference between Edgewood and Riverview is the relative strength of their trade union movements. Led by the railroad men who traditionally have been strongly organized, Riverview workers have strong union loyalties and the class sensitivity which often accompanies such loyalties. In Edgewood, unions have been weak or nonexistent, with much of the population hostile toward them. In response to the statement, "On the whole, labor unions are doing a lot of good in this country," only 30 per cent of the Edgewood community sample (N 494) agreed, whereas 51 per cent of the Riverview sample (N 704) did. Riverview is indeed a strong union town, in one or two cases even rejecting needed new industry on the ground that the companies intended to pay substandard wages.

The city lacks a similar proportion of public-spirited, wealthy philanthropists or leaders from among the old elite which has served Edgewood so well. As a result, Riverview has had to rely mainly on political action and state and federal grants to finance its major community projects. Four out of five of the decisions included in our research were publicly financed. This orientation is dramatically evident in a comparison of the relative amounts of money spent for public versus private projects: the four governmental projects involved a total of some $3,500,000; the single private decision (bringing in a new industry) required only $50,000.

The preceding descriptions indicate that the two communities have developed along different lines of economic specialization, and that such specialization has been an important "cause and effect" of their differing demographic structures. The extent of these differences can be demonstrated by New York State Commerce Department figures of 1957. Edgewood had some 2500 persons in the labor force; Riverview about 3500. Grouping these employees by industry, we find the following distribution:

TABLE 3-1 INDUSTRIAL CATEGORIES OF EMPLOYED PERSONS, IN PER CENT

	Edgewood	*Riverview*
Agriculture, forestry, and fisheries	1	2
Mining	4	0
Construction	4	3
Manufacturing	35	29
Wholesale-retail	22	17
Public administration	3	4
Transport, communication, and utilities	6	27
Finance, insurance, and real estate	3	2
Business, repairs	2	1
Personal services	8	6
Entertainment, recreation	1	1
Professional and related services	11	9
	100	100

The relatively large mining figure for Edgewood is of course attributable to the oil industry which is maintained by a number of small operators. With the important exception of transportation, Riverview tends to have a smaller proportion of its workers in the various industrial categories. Edgewood has fourteen manufacturing firms employing 1700 workers, producing goods valued at $18.1 million per year. Wages are exceptionally high, averaging $85.94 weekly per production worker; the New York State average wage per production worker is only $68.44 per week. Despite its greater size, Riverview has only 18 manufacturing establishments, employing 1025 workers at an average weekly wage of $61.10, 12 per cent below the state average. Edgewood has 15 wholesale establishments employing 112 persons with sales of about $4.2 million per year. Riverview, on the other hand, has only nine such firms, employing 33 persons and doing $1.5 million in annual sales.

By 1954 statistics, retail shops in Edgewood number 154, employ 588 persons, and sell $13.5 million in goods. Riverview contains 120 retail businesses, employing 454 with annual sales of about $10.5 million. A detailed breakdown of retail units in the two communities follows:

TABLE 3-2 COMPARATIVE RETAIL SALES

Category	Edgewood No.	Sales	Riverview No.	Sales
Food stores	28	$3.057 million	28	$3.219 million
Eating and drinking	23	.804	28	.885
General merchandise	4	1.065	4	.721
Apparel and accessories	15	.874	8	.470
Furniture and appliances	13	.618	12	.697
Automotive	13	3.605	8	2.176
Gasoline	10	.968	12	.651
Lumber, hdwr., farm	15	1.102	4	.709
Drug	6	.407	4	.273
Miscellaneous	26	Unknown	12	.671

The remarkable fact here is that Riverview has one-and-one-half times the population of Edgewood, yet contains about the same or fewer shops in most categories, and lags behind by one-quarter in annual sales.

The following occupational distribution gives some indication of the economic and class structure of the two communities:

TABLE 3-3 OCCUPATIONAL CATEGORIES, IN PER CENT*

	Edgewood (462)	Riverview (655)
Professionals	10	7
Managers and proprietors	25	13
Farm owners and managers	1	1
Sales and clerical	11	15
Service workers	5	5
Operatives	42	50
Laborers	6	9
	100%	100%

* These percentages are based on the occupation of the head of the household (1961). Excluded are housewives, N.A.'s, and unclassifiables.

The categories are scaled in roughly descending class order. Edgewood has about 45 per cent of its workers in various white-collar categories, whereas Riverview has only about 36 per cent in these categories. Again, when the relative populations of the two communities are considered, the significantly smaller proportion ($p = .01$) of managers and proprietors, and to a lesser extent, of professionals, in Riverview is noteworthy. Edgewood has fully one-third more of its labor force in these statuses.

In summary, then, the people of Edgewood are generally advantaged in regard to wealth, income, amount and quality of services, and industrial diversification compared with those of Riverview. The implications of this for community leadership structure and decision-making will be examined in subsequent chapters.

The Panel of Decisions

The methods by which we proposed to identify members of the local power structures were outlined in Chapter 2. We decided that several major decisions or issues would be analyzed to identify individuals who were *directly and overtly active at one or another stage in such decisions.* Our primary aim was to determine in objective, measurable terms, the distribution of community power. The motivating assumptions were that a study of vital community issues would reveal the nature of participation within the community and that active participation in such decisions was a valid index of power. In identifying the power structure, we decided to use both the reputational and decisional methods of analysis; that is, to measure power in overt terms by an analysis of decisions, and also, following Hunter, to attempt to identify powerful leaders through the judgments of their peers as to their ability to "move things." We were less directly concerned with *formal position,* since we assumed that the positions held by the leaders would be built into the evaluations of respondents as they attempted to specify the bases of personal power. As is well known, in contemporary society a critical basis for assigning both power and prestige is an individual's formal position or occupational role.

Five major issues in each community were analyzed. Each was selected on such criteria as the amount of funds involved, the scope of impact, and the number of persons affected. We also attempted to select a "representative" panel of decisions which would include both "private" and "governmental" programs. We now turn to a brief description of these issues.

The School Bond Issues

EDGEWOOD SCHOOL BOND DECISION

Edgewood Central School District serves the village, the town, and five other towns in the area. The various school units, all of which are located in the village, include the central high school and three elementary schools. The elementary schools contain about 1200 pupils and 49 teachers; the secondary school has approximately 1000 students and 53 teachers. The assessed valuation of property in the district is about $20 million (full valuation, $38.2 million). The tax rate is $19.00 per thousand of assessed valuation (nearby communities range between $18-45 per thousand of assessed valuation). The annual school budget runs about $971,000, of which $615,000 is provided by state aid, via equalization formulas, and the remainder is provided through local taxes.

The school district is an independent unit of government directed by an elected school board with policy-making, legislative, and tax-collecting functions. Edgewood's board consists of nine members, three of whom are elected each year for three-year terms. The board meets monthly, but the most important session is undoubtedly the board meeting on July 1, in which the annual budget is presented.

The schools are directed by a superintendent, whose administrative staff is made up of several principals, directors of guidance, health, athletics, and transportation, a business manager, a cafeteria manager, and a superintendent of buildings and grounds. Supplemental services are provided by a part-time psychologist, dental hygienist, school nurses, and special teachers for mentally and physically handicapped children.

In a recent report the superintendent of schools writes that Edgewood's salary scale "is reasonably close to the state average" (excluding the state's large metropolitan areas). The teaching staff is quite stable, 87 per cent of the teachers having five or more years of experience. The expenditure per pupil is somewhat below the state average. The tax rate is quite low. "The tax rate per $1000 of full valuation shows Edgewood to have the lowest of all 30 school districts in the county, with the exception of . . . ." The average of the schools outside the county is $13.35 as compared with Edgewood's $10.98. Other schools in the county average $13.40, while the state average is $15.00.

The reasons for Edgewood's low tax rate include "the relatively low percentage of the budget spent for debt service," as well as the school board's reduction of capital expenditures.

In an interview, the superintendent outlined the two school bond elections. Two professors from a nearby university, who were called in to survey the school's needs, had made the following observations and recommendations. The high school building, built in 1927 with additions in 1938 (cafeteria) and 1951 (gymnasium and shops), "provides adequate facilities for the present secondary school program and the present enrollment." The Pembrooke elementary school, built in 1937, with thirteen classrooms added in 1949, was considered quite "adequate." Of the Howard Street elementary school, however, the report states:

> This school, erected in 1910, is of the familiar box-like type built in many school districts at the turn of the century. Little attention was devoted to the function of such buildings to the educational program which they were to house. Classrooms were used for recitation purposes primarily, with little attention to work-study activities.
>
> Howard school is constructed of concrete and brick with a roof of wood. There are eight classrooms, one basement room for kindergarten and one for a library. Toilets are in the basement, a poor location at best. . . . A playground of three-fourths of an acre is far too small to be of any great value as a play or recreation area. . . . This building, although structurally sound, should not be used for educational purposes any longer than absolutely necessary.

Finally the report gives the following description of the Jefferson elementary school:

> Jefferson elementary school was built in 1909. It resembles its counterpart, the Howard Street school, but is in much worse physical condition. . . . This building has outlived its usefulness for school purposes, and perhaps for any purpose.

As a result of these recommendations and the expectation of increased enrollments, the school board prepared plans for a new school building program. A special bond issue was required to finance the proposed buildings. It is noteworthy that this bond issue evolved shortly after the closing of the oil refinery had inspired a great deal of anxiety about the community's economic future. The inevitable citizens' committee was formed to support the bond issue, but subsequently this committee joined those in opposition to the program. This group and those who felt the same provided a determined opposition to the proposed building program. They established a display in a downtown store window which emphasized the extravagance of the program, and distributed "boilerplate" literature provided by an anti-school-building group on Long Island, New York. The committee's arguments included the following elements:

1. That the courtyard plan of the building was too elaborate.
2. The million dollar cost in addition to the loss of the X refinery was too much for the community to sustain.
3. Opposition from the Howard Street area people who didn't want to lose 'their' school.
4. Belief that the closing of the oil refinery would cut school enrollment.
5. Speculation on the possibility of a Catholic high school being built.
6. A counterproposal to make an extension on the Howard Street school.

The opposition leaders included some individuals who were primarily opposed to closing the Howard Street school, which was located in a "better residential district" in which they had lived for a long time. Besides sentimental ties to the school, parents were concerned about the inconvenience to their children who would have to walk a greater distance if the new school were built.

The initial bond issue involved $1,230,000 for a new elementary school of 21 rooms, and the remodeling of the high school and the old Howard Street school. In the future, the latter was to be used exclusively for administrative offices, and children who had been going there would go to the Jefferson school, located near the high school. The bond election for the initial program, though held on a severe winter day, had a massive turnout of voters, who defeated the proposal overwhelmingly by a vote of 1616 to 508.

In an interview regarding the first bond issue, a city official attributed its defeat to "perennial oppositionists, composed mainly of engineers in large local industries." However, it is clear that a great many other citizens shared their view. Three Edgewood citizens, a newly elected official, the editor of a county weekly, and a business leader, cited "extravagance" as the major reason for the defeat of the initial bond issue. A more frequently expressed reason was the economic anxiety produced by the closing of the factory. The superintendent included among those supporting the first bond issue the school board (save for a single member), a prominent local banker, the editor of the daily paper, and PTA officers and members.

About a year and a half later, in December 1959, a second bond issue of $640,000 was approved by a vote of 1617 to 628. This program cut out many of the proposed elements and reduced the size of the new elementary school from 21 to 14 rooms. A substantial proportion of voters, including most of those who had opposed the first proposal, found themselves supporting the second.

RIVERVIEW SCHOOL BOND DECISION

Unlike Edgewood, Riverview is classified as a city school system rather than as a central school district. Its school needs are satisfied through a special form of state aid. To ease the consolidation of small rural districts, the state provides special financial assistance to rural districts which will combine; additional aid is made available for new buildings and transportation.

A local businessman who had served on the school board for

twelve years provided the following history of Riverview school policies. Prior to the construction of the new junior high school in the late 1950's, no school buildings had been built in the community since 1915. Some board members had tried to get a school built through the PWA during the depression, but even this largesse was voted down. The community's conservatism is suggested by the fact that "the city fathers in the past could never see fit to allow the school board any excess bonded indebtedness for a new school building." In fact, the board managed to put aside nearly a quarter of a million dollars.

A state law allowing small cities to organize themselves as central school districts was due to expire in 1955. Upon being apprised by state education officials of this situation, and particularly of the fact that failure to act would result in the loss of extensive state aid, the Riverview school board began a determined campaign for centralization. Board members spoke before numerous groups and committees, including those in outlying areas which would be included in the proposed district. The superintendent put his speeches in a financial context, attempting to convince people that tax increases would be moderate. A citizens' committee of prominent men was formed to speak in Riverview and neighboring communities in support of centralization. The PTA, Kiwanis, and Rotary clubs also co-operated. The election resulted in a 6 to 1 vote in favor of centralization. Opposition was not organized, and only a few older people opposed the plan.

Thirteen months after the approval of centralization, Riverview approved the construction of a new junior high school by a 3 to 1 margin. The community received 12 per cent additional special aid for building the school under state central school legislation, and in addition received more aid under its city district provisions, thereby enjoying the best of two worlds.

The New Industry Decisions

EDGEWOOD'S ACME MANUFACTURING COMPANY

For some time before 1958, Edgewood's political and economic leaders were aware of the imminent departure of the X refinery. Although the publisher of the town paper partly attributed the move to high labor costs, oil depletion was probably the prime reason. The move was hastened by a major fire in the plant during 1957. The town contained a number of other major plants, including the Excello plant with 774 employees and the Plate corporation with 700 employees, including manufacturing, engineering, and sales divisions. The Sheffield company, with 115 and several smaller plants specializing in buttons, novelties, and ceramics were also thriving. But the refinery was a major employer in the community, providing work for some 600 persons. It was a complete refinery, processing crude oil into gasoline, kerosene, naphtha, solvents, etc., and its loss was a sharp blow.

Following the shutdown in 1957, the refinery donated its extensive plant facilities to Edgewood for tax credit purposes. The site included about 90 acres with rail sidings, a black-top road, truck access to main highways, 28,000 square feet of office space, and total building space of 175,000 square feet. Obviously these facilities provided an attractive site for new industry. The local Chamber of Commerce had an industrial committee, but some people we interviewed felt that the committee was dragging its feet due to commitments to existing industries and a consequent reluctance to bring in rivals. In 1957, the current mayor, the publisher of the local paper, and a group of businessmen and leaders formed a new organization to attract industry. The group's policy was to encourage fairly small industries in order to avoid overdependence on any single industry. To enable them to buy and sell stores and properties, the group incorporated in January 1960. This industrialization group has been very active, and has sent out brochures and offered generous inducements to prospective firms. In 1961, over $175,000 was raised locally to bring in two small industries.

Although the members of the industrialization group included a former mayor, the incumbent mayor, most of the town and village board members, and some two hundred other persons, its executive committee was made up of about 10 men. There was some policy disagreement between members: the former mayor emphasized the desirability of diversified small industries, and he was supported by several of the other leaders. It was the members of the executive committee, however, who negotiated the industry with which we are concerned. These men arranged to meet the terms set down by the prospective entrepreneur; they made the necessary financial arrangements; they called and directed the public meeting at which these conditions were revealed. Specifically, the following arrangements were made. The village sold a $25,000 building to the industrialization group for $500; this group in turn donated the building as an inducement to the new company. Local banks and several businessmen quickly underwrote a $100,000 debenture bond issue. Edgewood was apparently in competition with a neighboring community for the Acme company, a competition in which she proved successful.

RIVERVIEW'S SKYBOLT FABRICATING COMPANY

Like Edgewood, Riverview has suffered a diminution of jobs. However, this was due not so much to industrial departure as to technological changes which drastically reduced employment by the railroads. Riverview, too, has attempted to attract new industry. Before the end of World War II, one industrial site had been intermittently occupied by a number of different firms, including two or three cookie factories. In 1945, a certain company bid for the building, guaranteed a certain payroll for a five-year period, and set up operations. One of the city bankers conceded that the plant had done well in the community, but maintained that in view of an already existing factory producing the same product, it might have been advisable to have accepted some other type of industry to ensure greater diversification. He also related how the community, through public subscription, had managed to keep a woolen plant in the community.

On the whole, however, Riverview's efforts to attract new industry have been relatively ineffective. For example, one prominent civic leader, who was chairman of a mayor's industrial development committee between 1954-55, complained that his committee had no financing and only a small sum from the mayor's budget for telephone calls, etc. He seemed to feel that local banks had retarded industrial attraction because of their investments in the existing furniture industry and attending fears that large, efficient industries would change the labor situation in the community. He maintained that there were instances where companies interested in locating in Riverview had been discouraged. He also cited as deterrents to industrial investment the lack of buildings for factory usage, and poor service facilities such as schools and hospitals.

Riverview trade unions have also exercised a veto over prospective industrial settlement when the industry concerned was non-unionized and might therefore pay substandard wages. For example, a machining company interested in locating in the city, provided it received financial aid, was kept out. As a local union leader stated, "I think it is immoral for a firm to come in and say they are going to pay substandard, non-union wages to its employees." He added that it would hardly be fair to ask for public subscriptions from union members to bring an unorganized company into town.

A local official also believed that the banks were not too cooperative in helping to bring in industry. He stated that they did not and would not put up any money without complete security. Despite its record, he maintained, Riverview was well endowed with assets which should have encouraged industrial investment. It had abundant cheap power, ample water supply, good transportation facilities, and an adequate labor supply.

In 1958 the Skybolt Fabricating Company was brought into the community after $28,000 was raised by public subscription and the banks supplied the balance amounting to $22,000. Most of this sum was used to provide a new building. Here, a leading role was played by a local banker who made a major loan in return for a first mortgage on the building. According to another decision-maker, this local leader was partially motivated by a desire to atone for his past efforts to keep new industry out of the community, or at least to overcome any local beliefs that such had in fact been his policy. The other local bank was reluctant to invest in the project. Using the rhetoric of scarcity which often characterizes economic discourse in Riverview, one of its officers commented at length on the risks involved in the proposal. The bank had bought a $1000 certificate and felt it had performed its civic duty; the chance the bank was taking in purchasing the certificate, and the untoward reaction of state examiners when informed of the investment were mentioned.

In this case, however, the banker's skepticism was well based, since the new company has not been very successful. It has undergone reorganization, and many local subscribers regard their money as lost. However, for the purposes of our research, this decision provided a useful instrument. Not only was it comparable with a similar decision in Edgewood, but it had occurred recently enough so that respondents remembered well the facts of participation.

The Hospital Decisions

EDGEWOOD'S HOSPITAL PROGRAM

During the 1920's, an Edgewood philanthropist had given the village a site and building to be used as a community hospital. This legacy, however, was a mixed blessing. The building was old and inadequate; many complained of the hospital's continuous deficits; others complained that two-thirds of the patients were from outside the community, and that many were nonpaying welfare patients; some proposed joining the county hospital. The publisher of the community's daily paper described the building as "very inadequate, a firetrap."

The Edgewood hospital, parenthetically, is a unit of local government, administered by a board of managers appointed by the mayor; it consists of two doctors (one-year terms) and nine laymen appointed every two years for five-year terms without salary. The board of managers determines policies, rates, appointments to the medical staff, and draws up the budget. There is also an advisory board of seven persons.

In 1946 the state passed legislation allowing local governmental hospitals to form hospital districts. Surrounding communities and rural townships could be included in order to provide for a wider financial base. Under this law, however, participating communities could withdraw at any time and were not compelled to provide financial support for the hospital. Edgewood sought without success to interest adjacent communities in forming such a district. Then there was a voluntary drive to raise funds locally to build the new hospital. In four months the drive netted $500,000, including contributions from the outlying communities and $10,000 from the county board of supervisors. The rising costs of the Korean War period inflated prices of building materials, necessitating a second drive in which an additional $350,000 was raised. Through its Hill-Burton program, the federal government provided about one-third of the amount required for the new building. The new hospital was completed in 1952, with provision for expansion as needed. The initiation and direction of this fund-raising campaign, in effect the decision of Edgewood's leaders to build a new hospital by voluntary contributions, was the focus of our research on this particular decision.

RIVERVIEW HOSPITAL ISSUE

Riverview's hospital was set up in 1918 in a converted school building, already outdated at the very time of the hospital's establishment. Like Edgewood's hospital, it was operating at a deficit, and local observers complained similarly of the community's subsidization of the health care requirements of those living in the surrounding area. Under the hospital district legislation of 1946, Riverview and six surrounding rural townships voted to form a district. An arrangement was made between Riverview and the participating communities whereby Riverview agreed to pay 61 per cent of any annual hospital deficit, the rest to be paid by the participating communities.

Riverview's hospital is also a governmental institution, with a board of twelve members, seven of whom are appointed by the mayor, and five by the town supervisors of communities that participate in the hospital district. The board members are selected for five-year terms. Important committees of the board are finance, personnel, new hospital building, and a joint conference group consisting of the hospital board and the medical staff.

As mentioned earlier, the building was inadequate when it became a hospital. With the passage of time, it became worse and there was a constant danger of fire. The hospital was in such a wretched condition that there was a definite possibility of state action to enforce more adequate standards. However, the community was in a poor position to improve the situation. The city had almost reached the limit of its allowable indebtedness and could not borrow additional sums. An obvious alternative was to raise the money by a voluntary fund drive. As a result, a local hospital committee was formed and soon engaged a fund-raising group to survey the possibilities of public subscription. The fund group's report was negative; its conclusion was that no more than a quarter of a million dollars could be raised by local subscription.

Leadership in Riverview's hospital project was then assumed by resourceful city attorney, Fred Morrow, who lobbied intensively at the state capitol to secure aid for the community. In a session with Governor Harriman, he was getting nowhere till he said, "Well, our hospital has been condemned and it's a fire trap. What would you do if the hospital burned down today and several people lost their lives?" This argument apparently impressed the Governor who asked the state comptroller to work out something with Morrow.

Fortunately, a 1958 law provided for the establishment of hospital authorities with the power to issue bonds up to $1,500,000 for hospital construction. Local referenda were necessary in order to establish the authority. Once incorporated, the participating units could not withdraw from the authority, and the financial assessments of the hospital board were binding legal obligations upon all participating communities. Morrow and the city leaders campaigned throughout the area, urging support for such an authority. In an election held in 1958, all but two of the towns in the hospital district agreed to join the new hospital authority, and one of them has since voted to come in.

Morrow apparently persuaded the financial institution selected to handle the bonds to establish certain conditions before they would accept. These conditions included a medical administrative audit, a survey of projected income and expenditures, and a strong recommendation to remove the present administrator. A management-consultant firm investigated the hospital and recommended several administrative improvements, including the provision that its firm should run the hospital for two years. After considerable discussion, it was decided to build a 56-bed hospital, to be completed in 1963. Approximately one-third of the necessary funds were to come through Hill-Burton aid.

Some fifteen years after the first timid steps, the hospital board announced readiness to accept bids for building the proposed hospital, and in March 1960 the ground-breaking ceremony was finally held.

The Flood Control Decisions

Edgewood has had a long experience with flood problems. The Cherwell river, which divides the town, has overflowed its banks each spring, flooding and eroding the town and rural hinterlands. A quotation from a Devon County history suggests the continuity of this problem:

> We have had three great and many lesser floods. September 20, 1861 the rapidly rising river tore out dams and bridges. Half Brooklyn was under water. Cattle and horses were drowned, Dikes Creek bridge carried away and water filled the road from Hanrahan's shop to the Advent church. The water cut a channel 93 feet in width beyond the State Street bridge. The awful flood of 1865 occurred March 17th. A warm rain melted four feet of snow. The State Street and lower bridges were swept away. Jacob Weaver lost his life trying to cross the rope and one-plank-footbridge temporarily strung across where the lower bridge had been. In June 1889, the storm that produced the Johnstown Pa. disaster caused the most disastrous flood in our history. Both our railroads were greatly damaged, crops and cattle were destroyed, numerous buildings carried away or injured and dams swept down the river. The water covered the fairground and park, marking 14 feet above the stream's bed. Edmund Fitterer was drowned in the rear of his residence.

The flood problem has thus been endemic, and has often been discussed by the county Board of Supervisors. There has always been some difficulty in persuading the Army Engineers to undertake a flood control project, however, because of a legal requirement that damage done by floods must exceed the cost of the project, and apparently Edgewood's floods were unable to meet this curious standard. In any event, building upon work done by his predecessor, the mayor began in 1953 to negotiate with the Corps of Engineers, with the support of the village board. The board pledged $50,000 of local funds to confirm the community's desire to participate. Apparently, the village attorney played a central role, handling "all the financial stuff and all the correspondence."

The dependence of local governments upon federal largesse is again shown by the efforts of the mayor and attorney to secure federal funds for a community project. An "external" factor that added weight to the mayor's plea was the fact that the flooding affected a local industry which was doing important defense work, thus providing a justification for quick action on the federal government's part. In 1955, Congress authorized $350,000 for the project, and the engineers began their work.

Riverview has had similar flood control problems. The Dee river periodically overflows its banks in Riverview, endangering valuable property in the center of the town, and threatening to dislodge the main bridge connecting the north and south sectors of the city. Parenthetically, this decision once again illustrates the similarity of problems that communities face, and in the process gives us some basis for feeling more secure about generalizations based upon our case studies. Here again, the mayor and city attorney led the campaign for federal aid. As early as January 1952, in the first of his five consecutive terms, the Democratic mayor and his Republican colleague, who holds the rank of colonel in the National Guard, wrote to the Army Corps of Engineers, asking for surveys of the river at Riverview to determine and help establish the need for a comprehensive flood control program. Early in 1956, as a result of the worst flood in the city's history, the city attorney prepared a comprehensive report and historical summary of the city's annual problem with flooding. This report, which contained a great deal of correspondence and evidence pertaining to flood dangers and damage, including pictures of a boatload of citizens rowing down one of the main streets, and a Corps of Engineers report that several girders in the main bridge seemed to have been buckled by the high flood waters, was sent to both New York Senators and the district's Congressman in Washington.

After the flood of March 1956, the mayor dramatically closed the bridge joining the two sections of the city:

> I closed the bridge even to pedestrians. I called Congressman Reed and told him what I did. I told him to get the Army Engineers up here to look at it. They'd been working on it for 12 years and never done anything. Then I appointed a flood con-

trol committee, and the Engineers came up after the flood and we went to work on it. All that remains now is for Congress to appropriate the money.

But Congress has not yet (December, 1963) appropriated the money, amounting to $1,390,000, and work has not begun on Riverview's flood control program. Although the decision, unlike the others, has not yet been consummated, it serves our purposes equally well. Not only has the critical *initiatory* stage been resolved, but city leaders have done virtually all they can do to secure federal help.

Edgewood Municipal Building

In 1955 Edgewood's ancient village hall was demolished by fire.[2] A new structure was proposed for governmental offices and recreation; the cost of construction was estimated at $376,000. A bond issue in the amount was voted and passed, the bond issue to run over a twenty-year period. At the same time, local government officials included the construction of a municipal parking lot, which resulted in a good deal of criticism. In 1956 the new community building was dedicated. The second floor of the building was to be used for recreational purposes, and a recreation director was hired at a salary of $4500 per year to handle all recreational facilities and to plan a program. A recreation commission of five members (one changes each year) was appointed by the village board and endorsed by the town board. Community members can use the building for meetings of any type, except partisan political meetings or sectarian religious meetings.

[2] One of our respondents, who had been a member of the village council at the time and a strenuous advocate of a new village hall, informed us that it was widely believed that he had started the fire. However, he stoutly maintained that he had not, although he did admit that he was "glad it happened."

Riverview Housing Authority

Riverview's experience in governmental building was of a completely different nature. Once again, the prime movers in establishing the Housing Authority in Riverview were the two city officials, Fred Morrow and Mayor Ted O'Brian. After his election in 1951, O'Brian appointed Morrow city attorney and asked him to do something about housing. Although Morrow had some ideological reservations about governmental housing ("I had been opposed to public housing, and thought it was sort of socialistic"), realism conquered ideology. Believing "the town looked terrible" and that slum clearance provisions of the housing program could improve things, Morrow contacted officials of the state Housing Agency and, with the mayor, negotiated a $1½ million housing contract.

Although both officials agreed that some opposition had developed, their perceptions of this opposition were somewhat at variance. Morrow felt that the organized Republican party was mainly involved, including realtors, bankers, and many others. "We had nobody on our side," he stated. He later conceded, however, that the local Republican newspaper had been of considerable help in pushing the decision through. The mayor, on the other hand, said there was only token opposition, mostly from people who couldn't believe the city was going to get the necessary money for nothing. He recalled that one of the city's bankers, who had opposed the project, was quite surprised to learn that his own bank had been buying state housing bonds which were used to finance projects of the type the banker opposed. Morrow, too, had great difficulty convincing local Republicans that the state housing legislation had been passed by a Republican governor and legislature and was being administered by Republicans. He cited instances in the past when a similar hostility to state and federal governmental programs had cost the community a sewage system and a school under the PWA.

In any event, the two officials proceeded to create a local housing authority and to meet other requirements of the law, including a slum clearance project. The new housing was built and some remaining excess funds were used to build a road and parking lots for the city. Both men were quite proud of the accomplishments of the authority, describing it as "the best housing authority in the state." In addition to a tastefully designed structure, its facilities included community rooms, a clinic, and a gymnasium. Among other things, the officials had been able to induce a prominent New York City architect to design the project for $38,000, instead of his usual $100,000 fee.

Conclusions

In this chapter, we have outlined the major historical, economic, ethnic, and political characteristics of Edgewood and Riverview. It is clear that their socioeconomic compositions are quite different and, generally, that Edgewood enjoys a somewhat more advantageous position. The implications of these differences for the power structure, values, and political viability of each community will be pointed out at appropriate places in the following analysis.

We have also described briefly the ten decisions around which the analysis proceeds. If the description of the decisions seems rather sketchy, it may be recalled that for our purposes they are only instrumental. We are not concerned with them as decisions per se, but rather as "critical incidents" which provide an operational index of power and a means of identifying those who possess most of it.

4

POWER STRUCTURE IN EDGEWOOD

Having examined the ecological base and the decisions studied in the two communities, we now turn to their power structures. The composition of the power structures is determined. We analyze the social characteristics of different types of leaders and compare the differences found between power measured by the decisional and the reputational methods. Although our generalizations about community power structure in Edgewood and Riverview are based upon only 81 individuals, it should be noted that we are not dealing here with a sample, but rather with a universe. We are generalizing from data on the entire local elite.

The Structure of Participation

In Edgewood, according to the criteria specified in Chapter 2, a total of 36 individuals actively participated in one or more of the five decisions, namely, flood control, municipal building, the new hospital, new industry, and the school bond issue.[1]

---

[1] Two additional decision-makers are not included in the analysis; one flatly refused to be interviewed, the other had moved away and he found it impossible to find time to be interviewed.

The school issue included two separate campaigns and elections, the first was defeated and the second, a modified proposal coming some months later, passed by an impressive majority. Our decisional index, it should be noted, includes individuals who were either actively in favor of or in opposition to one or another of the decisions. Only four individuals, however, were found in the latter category, all of them in the school bond decision. They were able to organize the defeat of the first bond referendum, which is the basis for attributing power to them.

ELITE PARTICIPATION

We turn first to the question of community power structure conceptualized in terms of an elitist-pluralist continuum. One useful index is the amount of overlapping of participation on vital decisions. If several individuals exercise their power in two or more issues, we may say roughly that elitism is relatively greater than in a situation where little or no "overlapping" exists. Theoretically, a 100 per cent overlap would have been possible, i.e. each leader could have been active in at least two of the five decisions. What is the extent of overlapping among Edgewood's decision-makers?

TABLE 4-1 OVERLAPPING AMONG LEADERS (36) IN EDGEWOOD DECISIONS, IN PER CENT

Number of decisions		
5	0	
4	6 (2)	
3	11 (4)	39% total overlapping
2	22 (8)	
1	61 (22)	

As Table 4-1 indicates, 22 individuals participated in only one decision and overlapping occurred in 14 additional cases. We find that 8 individuals, or 22 per cent of the decision-makers, participated in two of the five vital decisions. Two individuals, i.e. 6 per cent, participated in four decisions. No one participated in all five decisions. When the proportion of those participating in two or more decisions is analyzed, we find that 39 per cent of those in the local power structure overlap, that is, they participated actively in two or more community issues. Their power extends beyond a single substantive area to affect decisions in two or more areas. This proportion can be viewed as a rough *index of elitism*.

Several aspects of this distribution are suggestive. While three-fifths of the decision-makers were active in only one issue, a significantly large proportion were also active in more than one decision. By "significant" here, I refer to the fact that virtually 40 per cent of a possible 100 per cent is large enough to be deemed "significant." If, for example, we were to find that 40 per cent of all males in New York City were homosexuals, it seems that most reasonable men would agree that this was a "significantly" high proportion. Another index of "significance" is a comparative one. For example, Dahl found in New Haven that only 6 per cent of 50 leaders were engaged in more than one of three issue areas.[2] Our finding of 40 per cent is "significant" compared with this figure. Scoble, moreover, found in Bennington that 27 individuals, 39 per cent of a total group of 69 leaders, were nominated as *general,* i.e. overlapping, leaders, exactly the same proportion found by the decisional method in Edgewood. In addition, it appears that from 53 to 85 per cent of each of four types of leaders were named to one or more additional policy areas.[3] These data indicate that the overlap phenomenon in Bennington is the same as that in Edgewood, but much higher than that found in New Haven. Scoble and Alford found similarly in a study covering four decisions in each of four Wisconsin cities, ranging in size from 62,000 to 126,000, the following rates of overlap, respectively:

[2] Dahl, *Who Governs?* pp. 180-83.
[3] *Ibid.,* pp. 119-20.

29, 52, 11, and 19 per cent.[4] A comparison of these cities with New Haven suggests that Dahl's very small rate of overlap is atypical. It is interesting, moreover, to find a rough inverse association between community size and overlapping, as shown by the following data:

Community	Overlap in per cent	Population
New Haven	6	100,000 and over
Madison	19	..
Syracuse[5]	36	..
Racine	29	75,000-100,000
Kenosha	52	50,000-75,000
Green Bay	11	..
Riverview	32	10,000 and under
Edgewood	39	..
Bennington	39	..

Green Bay and, to a lesser extent, Kenosha are obviously deviant, for unknown reasons. Nevertheless, despite Michels, who concluded that size was positively associated with elite rule it seems probable that larger communities provide an opportunity for greater specialization, and hence for more pluralism within the power structure. It is also interesting that the proportion of elite as a percentage of total population is very similar in these communities, being well under one per cent in all cases. This enables us to suggest the following propositions about community power structure:

1) There is an inverse association between the size of a community and the degree of overlap on decisions among its leaders.

2) Members of the power structure will typically constitute approximately one per cent of the total population of a given community.

[4] From a forthcoming book, *Leadership and Decision Making in Urban Politics*.
[5] I am indebted to Linton Freeman for providing the Syracuse overlap figure, which must be evaluated in terms of the fact that 550 leaders provide the base. This undoubtedly increases the overlap rate considerably.

In any event, if 40 per cent is accepted as a valid index of a "significant" degree of overlap, we can probably conclude that Edgewood's leadership structure tends toward the elitist end of the continuum. This conclusion is reinforced by the fact that the entire decision-making group constitutes only one-half of one per cent of Edgewood's total population. From this, one could conclude that leadership is concentrated. Some leaders accept this conclusion. The most potentially powerful economic leader in Edgewood was asked the following question, "Some studies of other communities have shown that a small group pretty well runs local affairs and makes most of the important decisions. In your opinion, is this an accurate description of the way things are done here?" He replied, "Definitely true, about 1 per cent, and certainly not more than 2. Not too many people are willing to take time for such affairs. Only a certain number have the ability to get people to go along with them." In his view, the scarcity of organizing skills and motivation explain the tendency toward elitism. It may be that the imperatives of organization and the need for action make such a pattern inevitable, but such judgments challenge the pluralist assumption that power is widely diffused in community affairs.

We next consider the relative number of leaders active in each of the five decisions.

TABLE 4-2 ELITE PARTICIPATION IN EDGEWOOD DECISIONS (36)

Decisions	*Number of Decision-Makers*
School bond issue	16
Hospital	15
New industry	14
Flood control	7
Municipal building	5

Table 4-2 indicates that the school bond issue was the most "open" decision. Of the 16 individuals participating, 11 were specialists who were active *only* in this decision, which indicates that they are relatively less powerful than the other decision-makers.[6] This judgment is reinforced by the fact that five of the participants were women, only one of whom was active in any other issue. Another participant was the local school superintendent, also active only in this issue. Finally, in terms of the total number of decision-makers involved in the three "public" decisions, the school bond issue had a much larger number of participants. The total of 16 activists may be compared with only seven in flood control or five in the municipal building issue.

We will now attempt to differentiate the leaders in terms of the relative amount of power enjoyed by each type. Several criteria are available, but each has its limitations. Overlapping is an objective, quantifiable index, but it lacks discriminatory power. Perhaps a leader who exercised a great deal of power in only one decision should be attributed greater power than another who was marginally active in two or three issues. As we shall see in a moment, some refinement is provided by a question as to the relative influence of each participant in a given decision. Moreover, our research indicates that some decision-makers, i.e. those found to be active by empirical test, are probably less powerful than some "influentials" whose style of participation in a decision was not amenable to quantitative techniques. In view of such problems, we have decided to use evidence from both the reputational and the decisional techniques. In some cases, this will result in an apparent rejection of objective data in favor of a *Verstehen* based upon all available evidence. Such a system appears essential if we are to avoid a spurious precision.

Let us look first at overlapping as a criterion of relative power. As noted earlier, a total of 14 leaders were active in two

---

[6] Decision-makers will be differentiated later in terms of their relative power in each issue; for the present we assume that the scope of a leader's activity is a rough but valid index of his power.

or more decisions. Eight were political leaders, five were economic, and the remaining one was a specialist. The eight politicos accounted for 22 participations, while the economic group had 12. By this index, which will be refined in Chapter 6 by the use of weighted criteria, political leaders in Edgewood enjoy somewhat more power than their economic counterparts. Their average number of participations per individual is higher. When all political and economic leaders are analyzed, regardless of overlapping, we find nine politicos with 23 discrete participations confronted by 14 economic leaders with 21 participations. By this index, the two groups are almost equally powerful.[7]

We turn next to the reputational measure of power. Here we find that 11 of 14 nominees are economic leaders. Only three are political. Moreover, the first nine men on the list are business-type leaders, including three corporation managers who were not found to be overtly active in any decisions. Such men have great *potential* power, even though they do not qualify for inclusion under the decisional method. For the moment, it seems valid to add these influentials to the list of "economic" leaders in Edgewood, making a total of 17 "economic" members of the local power structure, compared with only nine political members. From such evidence, it seems that economic leaders in Edgewood are somewhat more powerful than their political rivals.

Next, evidence is presented from a question which asked decision-makers to name the "most influential" participants in the decisions in which they were active. Economic leaders received a much higher number of power nominations under this rubric.

[7] We do not assume that these "groups" are tightly knit Politbureaux who agree on every policy and strategy. In Edgewood, an impressive measure of agreement among economic leaders was observed, while in Riverview there was a patent split between an economic "old guard" and the "new men."

TABLE 4-3 NOMINATIONS FOR "MOST INFLUENTIAL" DECISION-MAKERS, EDGEWOOD*

	Leaders		
Decision	Political	Economic	Specialist
	(9)	(14)	(13)
Flood control	Dodd 6		
	Woods 4		
	King 4		
Municipal building	King 5		
	Wells 5		
New hospital	Eberhart 2	Remington 9	Stein 7
		Hughes 3	Wainwright 2
New industry	King 3	Hadwen 11	
	Eberhart 2	Prince 10	
		Remington 6	
		Williams 4	
		Dunn 4	
School bond issue			Hanson 5
			Hollis 3

* Only individuals receiving two or more nominations are included in this table. "Most influential" here means that other participants regard them as having exercised the most weight in the decision.

As Table 4-3 indicates, although there was considerable issue specialization within the elite, economic leaders received 47 "most influential" attributions compared with only 31 for political leaders. Since only one economic leader was active in the flood control and municipal building issues, the data on these issues tell us nothing about the relative power of each group. For such evidence, we must turn to the new industry and new hospital issues in which both competed for influence. By this measure, economic leaders are considerably more powerful.

The data indicate that Mayor King was the most powerful political leader, but that his village attorney, Clinton Woods, who was also active in four decisions, functioned mainly in a ministerial role. In the hospital and new industry decisions, the mayor and another powerful politician, Ben Eberhart, had important roles, but, as the distribution shows, they were not widely regarded by other participants as having been the "most influential" leaders in the issues. In sum, we conclude from this evidence that political leaders dominated the "public" flood control and municipal building decisions, and that economic leaders were most powerful in the "private" hospital and industry decisions. Three specialists, namely, a local doctor, the superintendent of schools, and a local optometrist, also had leading roles in the hospital and school issues. In the hospital decision, however, it was the firm economic base of the community and the positive collaboration of those mainly in control of its financial resources that made a successful fund drive possible. Moreover, it is important to note that the defeat of the first school bond issue by a coalition led by three economic leaders provides additional evidence of their power.

When one adds to these considerations the greater *continuity* of power potential enjoyed by economic leaders, including their superiority in such attributes as university education, high income, preferential status in local banks, business, and corporations, and attending possession or control of disproportionate amounts of community wealth, it seems safe to conclude that Edgewood's economic leaders have exercised somewhat more overt power than their political counterparts. Moreover, compared with their counterparts in Riverview, they were intensely interested in community problems; indeed, in several cases, a feeling of stewardship was evident among them.

Styles of Participation

We saw in Table 4-2 that, with the exception of the school issue, elite participation was highest in what we have called "private" as distinguished from "public" types of decisions. The hospital and new industry decisions rank in the upper ranges of participation whereas flood control and the municipal building had less than half as many individuals actively involved.

A brief survey of these decisions will indicate the styles of participation characterizing the various types of leaders. Not only was participation among the decision-makers themselves highly restricted, but the amount of community discussion and interest was relatively limited. Although a special election was required in the case of the municipal building, this occurred after a minimum of preliminary discussion, and, of our community sample, only 130 citizens, or about one-quarter, voted in the election held to approve the bond issue. This decision was monopolized by six political officials, one of whom refused to be interviewed about it, in part because of the controversy and claims of high pressure tactics that surrounded the issue.

The comments of another decision-maker reinforce this judgment. When asked to name others who were active in the decision, he found it extremely difficult to do so, saying, "We [he and one other public official] organized and pushed it through." He added that no local organizations were involved in supporting the measure, although some were *opposed* to it. The other most active leader, again a public official, commented, "I think that I alone put this thing through. I did all the campaigning, and the village attorney and I arranged all the hearings and the bond issue." Despite some organized opposition, this official refused to "back down," believing strongly that the village needed the building and the parking area proposed in the decision.

Evidence such as this raises questions about the influence of elections upon specific local issues, as well as about the validity of local bond issue election returns as an index of community participation. The municipal building decision was dominated by two or three political leaders. They knew a bond referendum would ultimately be required, yet it seems that they could and did "push it through," regardless of opposition within the town council, among some local organizations, and the prospect of an election. Certainly, when local politicians, whose sensitivity to community expectations must be assumed in view of their vocation, attach as little importance to bond referenda as this evidence suggests, the importance of "winning consent" through elections must be questioned.

Probably because it required little in the way of financial participation by the community, the flood control program was similarly restricted to a handful of public officials. The major role in the decision was played by the mayor and town attorney, who visited politicians and officials in Albany and Washington and arranged for meetings in Edgewood with the Army Corps of Engineers, which provides the major guidance and a great deal of leadership in such projects. The only official action required by the city was a commitment to appropriate $50,000 as "matching funds" for the project. Only seven men qualified as decision-makers, two of whom clearly monopolized the attending state and federal negotiations. The decision-makers may have rationalized this on the ground that the small amount of local funds required did not warrant extensive consultation. Again, and possibly for the same reason, there may not have been sufficient interest on the part of citizens to inspire them to push for alternatives. In any event, only ten per cent of the community sample participated in any way in this decision. Two hundred and eighty-seven, 58 per cent, were unable to name *any* of the public officials directly concerned in the decision. However, 126 citizens, just over 25 per cent, did name the mayor, who was indeed the person most actively involved.

A common pluralist assumption is that most important community decisions involve formal political processes. But here again, some qualifications arise. In Edgewood, the two "private" decisions, bringing in a new industry and building a new hospital, were widely regarded as among the most important decisions made in the community during the past decade. Seventy-seven per cent of the community leaders, as well as the community rank and file, placed the hospital issue at the top of the list. Although these issues were less "centralized" than the flood control and municipal building decisions, our research indicates that both decisions were initiated by a relatively small number of community leaders.

The impetus for the new industry program came from an outsider, an entrepreneur who had once lived in Edgewood. Now that he was planning to expand, he wanted to return, provided certain inducements could be offered. These included a grant of land, a building, and a $100,000 loan. The entrepreneur's major contact in Edgewood was the president of the largest local bank, a recent arrival who had previously worked in the nearby town in which the entrepreneur had his major plant. These two men contacted the members of Edgewood's industrial development committee, which in turn enlisted the aid of local financial officers and business leaders who were able to pledge to the venture both their personal and official support. After the leading banks legitimated the enterprise by pledging approximately 20 per cent of the total bond issue, bonds in $500 denominations were made available for individual purchase. Parenthetically, setting the minimum size of bond at this level has implications for the scope of participation. The Survey Research Center found in 1957 that American families with incomes between $5000-$9999 had a median of $759 in liquid capital assets. If similar conditions are characteristic of Edgewood, whose median per family effective buying income in 1960 was $6800, it would be economically impossible for a large proportion of the community to participate through this medium, unless they were prepared to deplete some two-thirds of their liquid capital resources.

After these events, a public meeting was held at which about 10 of the decision-makers explained the project to a small group of local citizens. A few days later, the industrial development committee chairman, who also owns the local paper, was able to announce that the bond issue had been fully subscribed. This expeditious venture illustrates the lively character of Edgewood's leaders. By any standard, these economic leaders and their legal aides are highly competent, enterprising men. They are clearly motivated by a sense of civic pride and responsibility. In the immediate context, their behavior suggests that some of the most vital community decisions do not require formal political ratification which might ensure a decisional process more in line with pluralist norms.

It was noted earlier that local government was involved in the new industry decision since the land and buildings for the new plant were jointly owned by the town and the village of Edgewood. The properties involved had been given to the community by the large industry that had closed its doors in 1957. Legally, the local governments were obliged to "sell" these properties; this was done for a token price, set by the village council, which owned the section of the industrial area in which the facilities were located. This action raises the question of the significance of the council members in the community power structure. Should all council members automatically be defined as decision-makers in those issues where the council's participation was required? Or was their participation a mere formality? Logical arguments supporting either interpretation can be made.

Legally speaking, formal action by the town and village councils was required before the proposed transfer of the properties could occur. Practically, however, there was little question about their decision: the town and village were urgently seeking industry. The competition among small towns and cities for new industry was exceedingly keen; concessions of this kind, and more, were the rule among small communities. The council had inherited a huge, vacant industrial area. The tax revenues lost by the departure of the area's major employer in 1957 needed to be replaced. Moreover, council members were in active competition with local economic leaders to demonstrate *their* initiative and concern for industrial development. They wanted to participate and their legal responsibility for transfer of the property provided a necessary instrument.[8] Given such considerations, it seems valid to regard the council's action as ministerial. When the alternatives to a given decision are so limited, it seems incorrect to accept the action as an indication of power.

The essentially "private" character of this decision is indicated by the fact that only six of the 14 active participants were public officials, and of these, all but two were marginal participants. Those centrally involved included a member of the town council and the mayor. The others were businessmen and their legal aides. Eight (three of whom were lawyers) of the 14 decision-makers fall in this latter category. It should be noted, however, that this dichotomy between "public officials" and "businessmen-lawyers" is to some extent artificial since (as shown in Chapter 10) the six "public officials," four of whom are small businessmen and the other two lawyers, share many of the social values of the economic leaders.

Nevertheless, political party constitutes an important basis for tension between public officials and the majority of decision-makers. Three of the six public officials involved were members of the Democratic party (called the "Square Deal" party in deference to local nonpartisan tradition), while all the business-legal participants were Republicans. This ideological split became evident in a patent competition between members of each coalition to demonstrate the superiority of its own group's contributions. Each tended to nominate its own brethren as "decision-makers" and "influentials," while neglecting those of the opposite faith who may have been equally active. This led to the "anomaly" of two of the most active leaders (as

[8] It is interesting that whereas economic leaders were probably dominant in Edgewood, political leaders actively competed with them for control of local affairs. In Riverview, we find political leaders dominant, with a noteworthy tendency during the time covered by our research for economic leaders (with only two or three important exceptions) to withdraw from such competition.

determined by the decisional method), both Democratic politicians, failing to receive enough nominations to qualify as influentials.

As noted earlier, despite the fact that the hospital is government owned, the hospital issue seems to be another case in which a decision was initiated and pushed through by a relatively small number of private citizens without recourse to formal political ceremonials, other than a pro forma approval by the Edgewood council *after* the initial decision had been made elsewhere. Although a large number of individuals (15 leaders and 229 members, about 47 per cent of the community sample) became involved in the network of committees organized to handle the fund-raising campaign, in terms of our evolutionary conception of a "decision" this participation occurred at an *implementary* stage, less critical than the decisive initial stage.

The conception of a new hospital apparently arose in the local Rotary club, and subsequently became its major civic project. Among the members of the original Rotary committee was an undertaker, who was also a politician, and whose work presumably made him well aware of the need for better facilities. According to this individual, who became very active in the fund drive, the decision to build a new hospital financed by local funds was reached at a Rotary hospital committee meeting held in one of Edgewood's banks: "We decided then to hire a company to do the fund raising."

As noted earlier, an attempt had been made to establish a regional hospital district, which would enable Edgewood to share its costs with surrounding communities who used the existing hospital, but did not contribute a "fair share" of its operating costs. After this effort failed, the decision to build the new hospital independently was made. Here again, the resourcefulness of Edgewood and its ability to take unusual steps to achieve its goals are apparent. Since, technically at least, theirs was a governmental hospital, the conventional recourse for community leaders would have been to finance the project through long-term funding as is customary with local government projects. However, the more dramatic, "private" alternative of a volunteer fund drive was selected, with excellent results. Within four months, $850,000 had been raised, a substantial portion in large amounts from a few wealthy families. Only after the money had been raised did the governing board of the hospital step in to administer the building program.

A total of 15 leaders participated actively in this decision. However, according to one decision-maker who had been directly concerned with the project from its inception, "six or eight people really carried the ball on this thing."

An interesting facet of the two "private" decisions, namely, the new industry and the hospital, is that (with the exception of the school bond issue, whose two separate bond referenda may account for the high number of participants) they had a substantially larger proportion of active community participants than the "public" or governmental decisions. *Within* the local power structure, morever, there was far more widespread participation in these two private issues than in two of the public decisions. It also seems that specific *kinds* of leaders participate in essentially "public" decisions. The school bond issue attracted a majority of specialists, whose social characteristics, and, more important, power attributes, are different from those of the economic and political leaders who dominated the remaining decisions. Fully 62 per cent of the participants in the school bond issue were specialists, only one of whom was active in any other decision. Only three specialists were involved in *both* the "private" decisions. If the decisions are defined from another point of view, namely, in terms of their substantive content, we find that all specialists are restricted to the hospital and school bond elections, i.e. to "welfare" types of activities.

The distribution suggests that there is somewhat more "pluralism" within the local power structure in essentially private decisions than in those we have defined as "public" or "governmental." That is, more leaders, representing more organizations and, potentially at least, a greater range of interests, become involved. With the exception of the school bond issue, "public" decisions are monopolized by political leaders, whereas essentially "private" decisions evoke the participation of all three types of leaders.

Insofar as relative power is concerned, this fact might be interpreted as evidence of the greater power of political leaders in Edgewood, i.e. they are able to push through their programs with less need to negotiate among various interests. This is an attractive idea, especially in those cases where referenda do not play an important part in "public" decisions. Such dominance also reflects the external origin of the resources needed to carry out some "public" programs, such as flood control and public housing. One suspects, however, that the dominance of such issues by political leaders can be attributed less to their superior power than to the fact that the community is relatively less involved in such issues, compared with new schools and hospitals. In this sense, their power is a combination of default, of specialization, and of the reliance of local political leaders upon outside sources for political and financial aid.

Perhaps the explanation lies in the political context of Edgewood during the time covered by our study. The Democratic *cum* Square-Deal village council may have alienated conservative business and legal groups who would not therefore participate in governmentally-sponsored projects, but would work hard for "private" programs that, in their view, demonstrated the ability of the community to "do things for itself." This ideology seems particularly germane in the hospital issue, and may be a residue of an earlier era in which health and charity were viewed as a private responsibility. It is also in harmony with the "local self-reliance" theme long characteristic of conservative political ideology. Moreover, this climate of opinion may have been exceptionally compelling during the period covered by our study (1952-60) when the Eisenhower Administration was stressing anti-big-government, "grass-roots" values.

In a community like Edgewood, which contains skilled, wealthy, and devoted leaders, such political values can be operationalized, although they are often honored in the breach. In Riverview, where such resources are less plentiful, we shall see that they tend to become mere platitudes.

It should not be assumed, however, that political competition between Edgewood's Democratic politicians and its Republican business-legal elite was dysfunctional. On the contrary, it stimulated both elements to outdo themselves in various ways, most of which contributed to the community's development. Despite the nonpartisan tradition of local politics and the honorific "community welfare" context in which both groups articulated their participation, it was clear that partisan political values and motivations were at work. Such values influenced the leadership perceptions of those in the community's power structure.

Reputational and Decisional Power

An intriguing methodological question in power structure theory concerns the validity of the reputational method of identifying power. As noted earlier, Hunter's landmark study of Atlanta has been criticized for its reliance upon the reputational method. Critics argue that this technique measures only *potential* power, which is, or may be, quite different from power in an operational sense. They insist that the critical test of power is its *use* to achieve desired ends. One might meet this claim with the argument that *potential* power is similar to authority in that its efficacy is greatest when it is not formally evoked. More important, local leaders do not make their judgments about reputational leaders in a vacuum, but rather base them upon long experience and (in small towns at least) intimate knowledge of those concerned.

Perhaps the reputational method tends to measure individual perceptions of power, which must always be verified by more substantial criteria. Certainly, we received the impression that the reputational method sometimes became an instrument of sociometric preference rather than one of "real" differences in power, e.g. those revealed by the decisional criteria. By itself, reputation is probably not a valid index of power, since, in positivist terms, power must be exercised in some way, however subtle or indirect, before its existence can be documented. *Behavior* remains critical because it permits empirical observation and measurement; hence the advantage of the decisional method. Obviously, sociometric choices are also empirical and subject to measurement. In *themselves,* they are objective and factual. However, whether the attributions of individual power which inspire them are valid is another question. Here, to some extent, we are differentiating between personal "beliefs" about individual power and manifestations of power observed by a disinterested researcher.

Insofar as the reputational technique rests upon *formal position,* its validity is probably enhanced. Hunter's diagnosis was partly based upon the formal position of Atlanta's leaders, as well as upon their reputation for power. Certainly, in an organizational society, we feel safe in attributing *some* measure of power to those whose formal position and authority give them control over institutionalized values and resources, a legitimate monopoly of a certain function, attending skills, and the potential and overt influence flowing therefrom. While there may be a tendency to exaggerate the power of those in high formal positions, they are certainly more powerful than men who command no organized resources. Even in this tautological sense, it seems valid to impute a large measure of potential power to those who hold high, strategic formal positions. Because exact quantitative discriminations in power cannot be made among such individuals, this is no reason to go to the other extreme of denying either that such gradations exist or that in reality one has power only in his specialized field. There is indeed plenty of evidence that power gained in any given substantive area "spills over" into other social fields; for example, there is the well-known tendency of Americans to accept judgments by eminent men in areas far removed from the one in which their prestige was achieved. In the United States, it seems that economic success is the basis for the "spill-over" phenomenon in many areas,[9] particularly in politics.

Although power often rests upon formal position in an organization and is ascribed *prima facie* to those who occupy such positions, the problem of the hiatus between potential and overt power remains. In order to test this intriguing question, we augmented the decisional method with the reputational technique. We now turn to the results in Edgewood. As Table 4-4 indicates, there are substantial differences in the two sets of results. In this table we have ranked the 14 "most powerful" decision-makers (those who were active in two or more issues) opposite the influentials, who include both active and inactive community leaders.

In general, only a rough consensus on power characterized the two measures. Overlap occurred in 43 per cent of the cases. It is especially noteworthy that the individual who received the highest number of influential nominations, Jonathan Davis, was not actively involved in any of the five decisions analyzed, i.e. he was not included in the local power structure as measured by the decisional index. However, the leader who received the second highest number of influential nominations was active

[9] Evidence on the scope of economic dominance in community decisions is reported in a study of an extended effort to build a new hospital in Syracuse. The authors conclude that their findings are consistent with those of a national study of similar programs in 218 other communities. Although these communities, unlike Syracuse, were small (7500 and less) and rural, the generalization was that the people who dominated hospital building programs were "neither farmers, social workers, nor doctors. They were people who knew about dollars and banks and bookkeeping. They were the people who knew about the wealth of the community and, for the most part, possessed it." C. V. Willie and H. Notkin, "Community Organization for Health," in E. G. Jaco, *Patients, Physicians and Illness* (Glencoe: Free Press, 1958), p. 159.

in two decisions. Two influentials who ranked ninth, George Parker and Robert King, participated in three and four decisions, respectively. They were among the top 17 per cent of those in the local power structure. Had there been a one-to-one correlation between the two methods, they should have ranked among the first three nominees on the reputational list. Similarly, politician Ben Eberhart, who ranked fourteenth, was active in two decisions and should therefore have ranked considerably higher.

TABLE 4-4 NOMINATIONS BY DECISIONAL AND REPUTATIONAL METHODS

Decision-makers*	(Decs.)	Influentials	(Noms.)	Overlap
Clinton Woods	(4)	Jonathan Davis	(20)	No
Robert King	(4)	Don Remington	(18)	Yes
Frank Moore	(3)	R. G. White	(17)	No
George Parker	(3)	Robert Williams	(17)	Yes
Robert Williams	(3)	John Wainwright	(16)	No
Joseph Wells	(3)	Henry Turner	(15)	No
Don Remington	(2)	R. F. Prince	(14)	Yes
George Albright	(2)	John Dunn	(13)	No
Ben Eberhart	(2)	George Parker	(12)	Yes
Mrs. Thompson	(2)	Robert King	(12)	Yes
R. F. Prince	(2)	Harold Carter	(12)	No
George Reeder	(2)	Anthony Hadwen	(12)	No
John Dodd	(2)	Allen Kimbrough	(12)	No
Robert Evans	(2)	Ben Eberhart	(10)	Yes

* For illustrative convenience, only the "most powerful" of the decision-makers, i.e. those active in two or more decisions, are included here.

The most glaring difference produced by the reputational method, however, is the case of Clinton Woods, a young lawyer who participated in four decisions, and ranked (by this measure) at the very top of the power structure, yet failed to receive sufficient nominations to qualify as an influential. Here, it seems, is an example of the influence of political values: Woods is a young Democratic official whose influence and activity may have been unconsciously minimized by members of the Edgewood elite, over 90 per cent of whom are Republicans. However, Woods's position in Table 4-3, which contains the nominations of the "most influential" decision-makers substantiates the reputational findings. He received only four attributions, all in the flood control decision, from a group of leaders which included nine of his political colleagues and several other lawyers among the remaining group of economic and specialist leaders. This suggests that Woods's participations were multiple, but ministerial. An uncritical acceptance of the decisional findings would give him an unjustifiably high power status. However, on the basis of other evidence, including the use of weighted criteria for ranking the power of individual leaders, we can safely conclude that Woods's participation as village attorney in four decisions was, in all but the flood control decision, essentially implementary. In effect, by a *combination* of our own knowledge of the issues, the judgments of other participants about the importance of Woods's role, and the data provided by the reputational nominations, we reach more accurate conclusions about the true extent of his power.

Evidence of respondent bias on evaluations of participation and power is seen in the answers to the question, "Who would you say were the two or three people *most influential* in determining the outcome of this issue?" In the industry case, although two Democratic decision-makers participated in initial discussions with the entrepreneur and in negotiating the token sale of the land and buildings, one was nominated by only one of 14 participants and the other by two. (In addition, each man nominated himself.) Similarly, both men ranked near the bottom on replies to a related question, "Who are several other (in addition to the respondent) people whom you know of firsthand who participated in the decision and were generally in favor of it?" One man received four nominations and the other received only one. From such evidence, we conclude that selective perception may also bias the decisional method.

The reputational instrument focuses upon economic leaders, who either possess the bases of potential power or who have put such power to use. Only one of five "most powerful" economic decision-makers was not nominated. Nevertheless, judging from the way in which Edgewood leaders are ranked, the instrument tends to discount overt power in favor of those, such as the managers of large corporations, banks, and utilities, who possess traditional, latent attributes of power.[10] At or near the top of the scale are found those who have the most "potential" power, e.g. the heads of the largest local corporations, but who are not likely to be identified by the decisional method either because they do not choose to use such power or because they use it in rather subtle ways.

The examples of Jonathan Davis, John Wainwright, and Henry Turner, who ranked first, fifth, and sixth, respectively, on the reputational scale are germane. According to our criteria, *none of these men participated directly and actively in a single decision.* Wainwright's case will receive extended comment because it seems to illustrate a common phenomenon in community leadership and political behavior: the behind-the-scenes figure whose acquiescence and support are indispensable prerequisites of action.[11] Such figures are often said to

[10] L. C. Freeman, *et al.* found similarly in Syracuse that "reputation for leadership seems to derive primarily from position, not from participation." They also found that "many of the top reputed leaders . . . , though not active participants themselves, head up the largest organizations, and those organizations are often also the most active." The reputational method thus leads us to individuals whose control of organizations enables them to exercise power in ways that are not easily identifiable by the decisional method itself. *Metropolitan Decision Making: Further Analyses from the Syracuse Study of Local Community Leadership* (Syracuse: University College, 1962), p. 16.

[11] As Vidich and Bensman report, "There is no clear relationship between technical or secondary positions in formal 'offices' or chairs and the actual control of policy within the community. The highest political leaders in the community, for example, may have no formal political positions, although they may have a position in the church. . . . Similarly, many of those who are merely technical implementers and who make no major policy deci-

enjoy high social status and wealth, and they may occupy high formal positions in community organizations. They may personify *noblesse oblige*, but are reluctant to assume an active public role, preferring to work quietly through subordinates or representatives, often called "leg-men." They may remain unknown to the rank and file (because of their muted style of participation), but politically sophisticated citizens seem well aware of their role.

From an analytical standpoint, it is unfortunate that this "behind-the-scenes" role has a conspiratorial cast, violating traditional American political values which abhor secrecy. Political corruption, moreover, has often been the result of secret machinations between officials and "invisible government." Despite such lurid evidence, this role is often used for beneficial purposes. In Edgewood, this was certainly true in John Wainwright's case. President of a large, family-owned corporation, Wainwright is an intensely public-spirited person who does his good works quietly, yet with an eye to shaping the behavior of others. As noted earlier, he made his corporation's contribution to the hospital fund early enough and large enough to "avoid a situation where others would give less than they should have." According to other decision-makers, he was often consulted informally about community decisions. Several commented, in effect, that "We felt John's thinking would be important in shaping our approach." Wainwright and his corporation contributed financially in both "private" decisions, yet by our decisional criteria he failed to qualify as a decision-maker.

A closer analysis of the hospital fund decision indicates that this is an inadequate conclusion. Several active participants informed us that tacit commitments from some two dozen potential donors in Edgewood, including Wainwright, were received *before* they launched the fund campaign. The campaign was organized in three stages, the first of which was called the "me-

---

sions may occupy what appear to be the top official positions," *Small Town and Mass Society*, p. 265.

morial" grant stage, in which several local families "bought" a room or made general memorial grants which were announced in the local paper. The second stage consisted of negotiations with the three major local industries, in which the amount of their bequests was determined by the number of their employees. Finally came the house-to-house stage, in which participation extended to include a network of committees which secured small donations from the entire community. As the chairman of the campaign, Don Remington said, "When we went into the house-to-house stage, we had our goal in sight."

Remington's role illustrates two aspects of community power structure: the power of "behind-the-scenes," reputational leaders and the "leg-man" role. When Remington was approached to become chairman of the drive, he accepted, but only *provided* that his "boss," John Wainwright, would consent, since the job would involve a great deal of work on company time. Moreover, by the very act of permitting Remington to assume the chairmanship, Wainwright was in effect commiting the resources of his own corporation to the campaign. Without denying Remington's skill and devotion, it is clear that his role in this decision was to some extent that of a "leg-man." As he noted, in differentiating between the resources and roles of "elder statesmen" and activists, "One gives what he has to give. And time is my major resource. If those people [elder statesmen] aren't with you, you just aren't going anywhere." If Remington had time and energy, Wainwright had the power to permit Remington to direct the campaign, as well as the financial resources to pledge one-fifth of the entire amount sought in the initial fund drive, and in so doing, to set a bench-mark for other large potential donors.

Had we depended exclusively upon the decisional method, we might have remained unaware of Wainwright's influence. The reputational method provided the initial clue that he was indeed powerful in this decision. Moreover, we had the impression, following current reference group theory and the "anticipated reaction" hypothesis, that it was not really necessary for less prominent leaders to communicate with him on a specific issue.[12] He seemed to be a sort of "brooding omnipresence," a model of wisdom, conduct, and probity against which activists evaluated proposed actions. This judgment is reinforced by the frequent comment that Wainwright was quietly influential in major decisions. Despite his limited activity, others in the power structure were aware of his influence. As one decision-maker, asked to name a committee of influential locals, put it, *"Do you want those whose approval is necessary to go ahead with a project or those who do the actual work?"* He included Wainwright among the former.

Henry Turner's case is different. Manager of a large, nationally-owned corporation, he travels a lot and rarely participates directly in community affairs. Although he has lived in Edgewood for 20 years, he did not feel closely identified with the community. The sense of civic responsibility which seems so prominent a part of Wainwright's ideology is almost absent. However, Turner is sensitive to the local power structure as indicated by his knowledgeable nominations to the reputational scale. His orientation seems fundamentally economic. Very sensitive to his corporation's vital role in providing employment, he defined the major problem of the community as economic. When asked "what have been the most important issues or problems which this community has faced during the past five years," he replied, "bringing new industry to Edgewood." When asked to name additional problems or decisions, he could think of no others. The difference in the community roles and power of Turner and Wainwright, despite their similarly high organizational status, is unexpected. Certainly, it illustrates the difficulty of generalizing about the influence of

[12] In small communities as in large ones, there remain, it seems, residues of that effect nicely put by Veblen whereby industrial leaders provide models of emulation for the rank and file, "to the greater spiritual comfort of all parties concerned."

industrial executives in communities of Edgewood's type.

The rationale and dynamics of the "leg-man" role are again illustrated by Turner's case. When asked about his own community activities, he replied that he was away much of the time, but that Fred Sherman, an engineer in his plant, was "very active" in Edgewood affairs. Sherman, a participant in one decision, was referred to literally as a "leg-man." He may have been viewed by Turner as a surrogate, possibly providing a rationalization for his own inactivity. Wainwright's policy of assigning subordinates as "leg-men" is again apparent in the case of Frank Thomas, who was active in one issue but was not included on the reputational scale. As in the case of Fred Sherman, Thomas's community work is occasionally done on company time, and one may assume that both men have been rewarded within their corporations for their community efforts. Here again the findings of the decisional and reputational methods are at odds. Moreover, in this case, at least, we would judge that the reputational method, which identified Thomas's boss Wainwright as an influential even though he was not active in any issue, yet did not include Thomas, who was a decision-maker, provides a more valid index of power.

Edgewood's most highly ranked influential was Jonathan Davis. Like Turner, he managed one of the town's largest, nationally-owned industries. Although he had a livelier perception of his community role than Turner did, he too relied upon "leg-men." During our interview sessions, for instance, he called in a subordinate who was introduced as being "very active" in community affairs. We got the impression that some of his work was done on company time. Another of Davis's employees, one of our specialist leaders, played an active role in the school bond issue, closely reflecting Davis's own view toward the issue. Although Davis himself was not centrally active in any decisions, he seemed quite aware of the extra-economic aspects of Edgewood's community life. Despite a marginal role in two decisions, he did not qualify as a decision-maker. Since Davis and Turner are similar in age, socioeconomic position, and occupational role, the difference in their community activity may be attributed to the policies of their parent corporations, one of which may stress community participation, while the other may encourage a laissez-faire policy. Explaining the relative degrees of participation of the three industrial leaders, it may be that Davis's and Wainwright's greater interest stem from their leading positions in *locally-owned* industries.[13] A tendency has been found for executives of nationally-owned corporations to withdraw from community affairs, and to be very circumspect about those activities in which they do engage, in order to avoid any charge of attempting to "run" the community.[14]

On the other hand, some national corporations encourage their executives to participate actively in local affairs, in order that their corporation *not* be regarded as an alien intruder. One common problem of community dependence upon such executives for leadership is their mobility. Indeed, the very qualities that make them effective leaders are the ones which earn them promotion and transfer to new positions. These changes, plus those induced by political changes, cause considerable turnover in the power structure. In follow-up interviews in June 1963, some two years after our initial research, we found that almost one-fifth of the decision-makers had left one of the communities. Moreover, the effects of executive mobility are at work *during* the time such men live in the community. As one decision-maker noted, speaking of the young manager of a branch store of a national chain, "John was always turning

---

[13] This statement must be qualified somewhat. The firm which Davis heads began as a locally-owned enterprise, but after two decades was acquired by an international combine; however, it is noteworthy that Davis began his career under local owners and worked his way up through the hierarchy. It is understandable that he would have a greater commitment to the community than Turner, who was sent in from the outside to manage a nationally-owned firm.

[14] Among others, see Schulze, *"The Bifurcation of Power in a Satellite City."*

down chairmanships of local organizations because he didn't know how long he was going to be here. Finally, he decided he wouldn't be transferred, bought a new home and started to become more active. Two months later, he was transferred to Cleveland."

In comparing Wainwright, Davis, and Turner, we conclude that Wainwright's high ranking as an "influential" despite his lack of direct participation is less anomalous than it first appears. He *is* influential and he exercises power, although in an indirect way. Our research indicates that before active participants embark upon "private" types of community projects, they solicit his advice and secure his support, as was the case in the hospital decision. In a sense, such a conclusion is an indictment of the decisional method of analysis, which in demanding overt behavior as evidence of power may overlook its more subtle manifestations.

The cases of Davis and Turner, on the other hand, suggest the danger of equating power with formal position and measuring it only by reputation. Despite his strategic economic role in the community, which gave him an effective means of access, Davis was only peripherally involved in the major decisions; we found no evidence that Turner had any influence in any of the five decisions, except insofar as he was able to delegate overt activity to his leg-men. Certainly, neither man participated *actively* in any of them. Turner's case is a classic one of an individual who possesses almost all of the attributes—save interest—of community power, yet elects not to use them. One or two similar cases were found in Riverview. Although these men are few, it is suggestive that they were "self-made" types with limited education, whereas those who participated were university graduates. There is a well-known positive association between education and participation in community affairs.

In terms of the Edgewood data, we can say that the reputational method provides a rough index of power structure in the sense that it will identify about 40 per cent of the decision-makers, and will be more likely to include "behind-the-scenes" influentials who have considerable potential power. On the other hand, it sometimes produces gross distortions, if one accepts the results of the decisional method as a more objective measure of power.

The discontinuity between the findings of the two instruments raises the question of whether the decisional method can accommodate the subtleties of community power and influence. For example, in terms of their formal organizational roles and socioeconomic status (henceforth SES), it seems unreasonable to exclude from the local power structure all of the six influentials who were not active in our five decisions. Although we believe that the decisional method is probably more reliable than the reputational method, it seems necessary to combine the two methods to achieve the most valid analysis. As noted earlier, it is relatively simple to include items in the research design that measure power reputationally. It seems best not to be hamstrung by the decisional method to the extent that judgment and *Verstehen* based upon extensive field inquiry, are completely ruled out of the analysis. So purist a conception of research undoubtedly has heuristic value, but it cannot be maintained given the untidiness of data in the "real" world.

In sum, it seems anomalous to include in the power structure decision-makers who are "leg-men" of certain influentials, who are themselves excluded. Moreover, many of our "specialist" decision-makers obviously possess fewer of the social characteristics typically associated with leadership than do the influentials. We have also seen that one member of the economic elite, Jonathan Davis, participated to some extent in three key decisions. In the new industry case, he was involved as director of the local bank which, in his words, "brought them here." Moreover, he personally bought some of the new industry bonds. In the flood control decision, his corporation, which was directly affected by the annual flood, provided considerable detailed information which helped justify the proposed program to federal authorities. He and his "leg-man" opposed the first school bond issue, which was defeated, and helped elect three new school board members who one year later supported the second bond issue. It may seem from this account that Davis should have qualified as a decision-maker, yet none of the individuals immediately involved in these decisions nominated him, nor do we feel on the basis of our own observations that he merits inclusion. Having said this, however, it is equally clear that we cannot disregard entirely the judgment of local decision-makers who ranked him first on the reputational scale, nor other random evidence of his potential and actual influence in the community.

A similar conclusion must be made about John Wainwright. Unlike Davis, who maintained that he *had* participated actively in two issues, Wainwright stated that he had *not* played an active role in any of the decisions. The only qualification we can find of this self-evaluation was in the hospital decision where he established a challenging model for subsequent contributions. As noted, a commitment from Wainwright for a large contribution was a condition for the initial decision to raise the money by voluntary subscription. Some decision-makers indicated that they had consulted informally with him on some issues. Nevertheless, he did not meet our decisional criteria. Despite this, by virtue of the perceptions of decision-makers whose own activities are sometimes influenced by their judgments of Wainwright's reactions, as well as by his critical role in the local economy, we feel justified in regarding him as a member of the local power structure.

Two of the remaining four members of the reputational elite seem to warrant similar status, namely, Allen Kimbrough, a wealthy oil producer, who was born in Edgewood and has lived in the community for over 60 years, and Henry Turner. Men who were actively involved stated that Kimbrough participated to some extent in the hospital and new industry decisions. As a director of a local bank, he supported the latter venture, including the purchase of part of the $100,000 bond issue. He also contributed generously to the hospital fund. Although not centrally or initially active in either issue, it seems clear that his support was important for the eventual success of both ventures.

Henry Turner maintained that he had not been directly active in any decisions, and this was verified by our research, including evidence such as that cited in the cases just mentioned. Nevertheless, we found evidence that he exercised some "behind-the-scenes" influence; moreover, his "leg-man" participated actively in one of the key decisions. For this reason we feel justified in attributing considerable potential and some overt power to him. The same generalization does not hold for the two remaining influentials, R. G. White and Harold Carter, both of whom played a limited role in the school bond and hospital decisions. None of those directly involved in these decisions nominated them, and no other evidence was found to support the conclusion that they should be considered members of the local power structure. Unlike the powerful individuals mentioned above, these men do not command large organizational resources nor do they have the social or financial status which might give them "behind-the-scenes" power despite a lack of active participation.

The four reputational leaders whom we have included in the power structure were similar in having high organizational positions, income, control of financial resources, and enjoyed high prestige in the community. Moreover, they were also minimally active in the decisions, and in some, as noted, they delegated an active role to lieutenants employed in their organizations. Generally, they were older than their more active counterparts in the power structure, yet in only one case could it be said that age was a major factor in restricting their overt participation. Perhaps their most common characteristic was the extent to which they remained in the background, avoiding publicity and active leadership.

The intriguing question remains: why these disparities between power measured decisionally and reputationally? Several explanations suggest themselves. One concerns leadership style. From our data, it seems that four of the six reputational leaders tend to operate quietly, delegating active participation to "leg-men" who work in their corporations.[15]

In an age when publicity has become a valued element in shoring up values of status, prestige, and security, it is worthwhile speculating further on the reasons why some individuals play this self-denying role. Undoubtedly, the desire for privacy and the prestige gains of studied remoteness that have characterized dominant Anglo-Saxon elements in American society are at work. A corollary is the contempt that such elites often have for politics and political office, particularly at the local level. *A more crucial factor may be the intriguing dynamic whereby power often seems reluctant to test itself.* It has been suggested that some community leaders are reluctant to commit themselves openly to issues which must be hammered out in public because such a role submits them to potential defeat or modification of their announced goals, with consequent losses of prestige and power. Since power must be carefully nourished, a reluctance to test it in ambiguous situations is quite understandable. Indeed, part of the bureaucratization of American society stems from the effort of elites to avoid unstructured situations, to avoid testing their power openly by the careful, preliminary marshaling of status, prestige, evidence, skill, and public opinion behind any proposed objective. Consider, for example, the "staging" employed by top organizational leaders or the exploratory maneuvers of candidates for political office.

[15] Whereas some influentials and economic leaders may work through others, political leaders in Edgewood participate directly in important decisions.

In this context, one useful basis for differentiating decision-makers from inactive influentials is leadership style and visibility. The inactive influential role may be characteristic of high status, "old-family," economic elites, who value privacy highly, take a dim view of politics and politicians, and do not wish to test publically their own power and prestige. (It is noteworthy that political leaders in Edgewood participated directly and personally in important decisions.) If this hypothesis is valid, inactive influentials should differ from decision-makers in SES terms. They should have lived in the community longer, have greater prestige, more education, and higher incomes than the decision-makers. Such a comparison is presented in Table 4-5.

TABLE 4-5 SES OF DECISION-MAKERS AND INACTIVE INFLUENTIALS, IN PER CENT

	Decision-makers* (14)	Influentials (6)
Education: 16 or more years	50	33
Time in community: over 20 years	79	100
Fathers' occupation, white collar or higher	79	67
Income: over $30,000	7	50
Membership in organizations: 3 or more	100	100
Political affiliation: Republican	71	100

* For comparative facility, we have included here only those decision-makers who were active in two or more decisions.

The data indicate that although influentials have some SES advantage over the decision-makers they are not favored on all counts. While a much higher proportion enjoy higher incomes, have lived in the community longer, and belong to the Republican party, they are comparatively disadvantaged in educational achievement and occupational level of father. What the data suggest is that high income (often associated with high organizational status) and long residence, which are highly visible in small communities, may create an *assumption* on the part of other community leaders that those who enjoy them are powerful. They may reason that these qualities "should" give their possessors disproportionate power in local affairs. On the other hand, it may be that such individuals do indeed exercise power, but in informal ways that mask their visibility and impact. Certainly, this was the case to some extent in Edgewood.

Perhaps a more useful way of isolating differences between decision-makers and influentials is to analyze SES differences between the seven powerful decision-makers who were *not* nominated to the reputational scale and the 14 members who were nominated. This might reveal more clearly the social factors that differentiate the two categories. Such a comparison is made below.

TABLE 4-6 SES CHARACTERISTICS OF SELECTED DECISION-MAKERS AND INFLUENTIALS, IN PER CENT

SES characteristics	Decision-makers* (7)	Influentials (14)
Education: 16 or more years	50	43
Time in community: over 20 years	63	93
Father's occupation, white collar or higher	63	86
Income: over $30,000	0	29
Membership in organizations: 3 or more	88	100
Political affiliation: Republican	75	86

* For comparative facility, we have included here only those decision-makers who were active in two or more decisions.

Here again, income and long residence are major differentiating factors. Residence is again crucial, with influentials continuing to enjoy a substantial advantage. Belonging to organizations also becomes a somewhat more important factor in inclusion in the reputational scale. Whereas Table 4-5 showed that inactive influentials were just as likely to belong to organizations as decision-makers, when we consider only those influentials who were *active* in our decisions, we find that they are likely to have more memberships in local organizations. Educational achievement remains unchanged with decision-makers again outranking the reputational leaders.

In sum, the two methods of ascertaining power used in this study produce somewhat different results. In over 40 per cent of the cases, the reputational method does identify individuals who by decisional test are found to be overtly powerful. It also identifies individuals who possess necessary attributes of power, but who escape the decisional net because they either do not choose to use their power, or, as in several of our Edgewood cases, use it "behind-the-scenes." However, as noted earlier, the use of both methods provides evidence of the existence and the use of the latter type of power. If one were to rely only upon the decisional method, he might well overlook these more subtle facets of community power.

Leadership Categories

Despite the small size of Edgewood's elite group, it seems that three distinct categories of leadership exist: the economic elite; the political elite; and a residual category called "specialists," a

TABLE 4-7 DISTRIBUTION OF LEADERSHIP TYPES AMONG DECISIONS (36)

	Municipal Building	Flood Control	School Bond	Hospital	New Industry
Political (9)	5	6	2	5	5
Economic (14)	0	1	3	8	9
Specialist (13)	0	0	11	2	0

group whose special competence and interest in a given substantive area give it access and influence in that area.[16] One basis for differentiating the three types is the kinds of substan-

[16] It is important to note again that these are merely descriptive, *post hoc* categories. We are not testing hypotheses here, but merely establishing a taxonomy of leadership types based upon an analysis of the major social and behavioral characteristics of all members of the power structure.

tive issues in which the majority of them participate. Although each type is active in several decisions, as the following table indicates, there is a tendency for economic and specialist leaders to be predominantly active in one or two specific kinds of decisions whereas the power of political leaders is more generalized.

The influence of specialists seems the result of a normative commitment to some "welfare" aspect of community affairs, and active participation in the organizations that institutionalize this commitment. It must be said that this is a tentative category. Whereas the political and economic elites dichotomize nicely on the criteria of formal office in local political or financial-corporate hierarchies and owner-operated businesses, the specialists are a mixed residual category. The subsequent analysis will indicate some differences between its members and those in other elite categories.

As shown in Table 4-8, the power of specialists is limited to a single issue, while political leaders typically exercise power in two or more decisions. In Edgewood, this was true of 90 per cent of political leaders. While such "overlapping" is much less

TABLE 4-8 PARTICIPATION AMONG EDGEWOOD POLITICAL, ECONOMIC, AND SPECIALIST ELITES (36)

	Number of participations		
No. of decisions	Political	Economic	Specialists
5	(9)	(14)	(13)
4	2		
3	2	3	
2	4	2	1
1	1	9	12

common among the economic elite, they too exhibit some multiple involvement, with 36 per cent of them active in more than one decision. By contrast, the specialists, with one exception, participated in only a single decision. Used independently, such data suggest that political leaders are considerably more powerful than other leaders; however, as noted earlier, such a conclusion will become unwarranted when all the evidence is considered.

We now turn to the social characteristics of each leader category. As Table 4-9 shows, specialists have several distinguishing characteristics, the most striking of which is high educational achievement. Over three-fourths of them have university degrees; in view of their marginal power status compared with other types of leaders, specialists controvert the common belief that knowledge is power. Some 45 per cent are

TABLE 4-9 SES OF POLITICAL, ECONOMIC, AND SPECIALIST ELITES, IN PER CENT

Characteristics	Political (9)	Economic (14)	Specialist (13)
Education: 16 or more years	44	64	77
Time in community: over 20 years	88	79	77
Fathers' occupation, white collar or higher	77	93	62
Income: over $10,000	88	100	77
Membership in organizations:* 3 or more	89	100	31
Political affiliation: Republican	67	93	67

* This category includes voluntary organizations, other than churches and religious groups. It has the same meaning when used in later tables.

women whose education, age, energy, and vocation enable them to be active in community organizations. All but one of these women are university graduates. Three of them have full-time secretarial, sales, or similar white-collar jobs, yet they find the time and motivation to participate in educational and philanthropic activities and organizations. Three are members of the school board. They and their husbands are in the middle-income categories, ranking lower than economic and political leaders in both income and group memberships. Their main characterization is an exceptional interest in community improvement of a "welfare" kind. One of these specialist women, however, is apparently motivated even more strongly by tax reduction considerations. Working for the manager of a local corporation who also opposed the first bond issue, she is much interested in "economy and efficiency." Publicly and vigorously, this "leg-woman" opposed the first school bond issue on the grounds that a more economical plan could be found and that, since her only interest was in "good government," it was important that people "got the facts."

The remaining seven members of the specialist group are divided among small-business and professional men. One of them opposed the first school bond issue, also for "economy and efficiency" reasons. However, three of them are school board members, suggesting their special interest and knowledge in a given area. In the main, these men are characterized by a middle position in the local prestige hierarchy, ranking below most economic leaders but above political types.

Without exception, specialists are not regarded as powerful by their fellow decision-makers. None of them was nominated to the reputational scale, although some leaders of voluntary organizations did perceive some of them as powerful. In broader social terms, this specialist group may be conceived of as a middle-class "countervailing" element within the local power structure. Pushing against the traditional dominance of local affairs by "old-family," Anglo-Saxon guardians and newer political elites who in both communities represent ethnic and religious minorities, they are mainly concerned with educational policy, health, and welfare. In Edgewood's school bond issue controversy, while the lines were not precisely drawn, specialists sometimes found themselves opposing local economic leaders and other citizens who were older both in point of age and residence. Their limited power is based upon civic interest, energy, and, less frequently, special knowledge about a given area. They are sometimes members of official bodies concerned with a decision, such as school or hospital boards. Most male specialists are independent professionals in medicine, education, engineering, or accounting. Forty per cent of them fall in these categories. Usually well-educated, having managerial and technical skills, specialists are often employees of large corporations, as were 25 per cent of those in Edgewood.

Speaking generally, Edgewood specialists are of somewhat lower class status than other leaders; they are more likely to have experienced upward mobility, as suggested by their fathers' occupational level compared with their own, and by their high educational achievement. They are much less likely to be joiners, and their incomes are lower than those of their fellow leaders. In addition to educational achievement, their principal resources are interest, energy, and community spirit. They have been in the community long enough to learn its social structure and its dominant values. By initiating some competition among elites, they contribute to the pluralist image. However, it seems that specialists have difficulty penetrating the higher political and economic strata; in the latter case, they are disqualified by their employee status and relatively lower income; and in the former they lack the important criterion of long residence. Moreover, they are somewhat alienated from "politics"; their own activities are usually described by them as "nonpolitical" or "community-oriented." Some of them dichotomize community activities between those that are done for "political" (bad) reasons over against those motivated by "community welfare" (good) aims.

These three elite categories are hardly watertight. The economic group is the most highly differentiated. Only one of its members,[17] for example, holds political office (but not locally), so this group can be nicely differentiated on this dimension from the political elite. However, the Edgewood political elite

[17] The problems of categorization are shown by this individual who has been an official of the Republican party for 25 years, yet is a corporation lawyer, bank trustee, patron of the arts, and a *bon vivant*. We decided that his major orientations were *economic*. For him, politics was something less than a vocation.

is ideologically quite similar to the economic elite; most of its members are small businessmen or lawyers who share many of the dominant values of the business community, even though they may often be members of the Democratic party. In Chapter 10, their attitudes toward government, equation of free enterprise and democracy, will show how similar they are in this respect. Political leaders in Edgewood are not usually *career* politicians, but all were either in office when this study was underway or had been when the five major community decisions were initially made. SES characteristics provide several bases of differentiation.

TABLE 4-10 SES OF POLITICAL AND ECONOMIC ELITES, IN PER CENT

Characteristics	Political (9)	Economic (14)
Education: 16 or more years	44	64
Time in community: over 20 years	88	79
Fathers' occupation, white collar or higher	77	93
Income: over $10,000	88	100
Membership in organizations: 3 or more	89	100
Political affiliation: Republican	67	93

Edgewood's political leaders obviously have less education, somewhat smaller incomes and membership rates in voluntary organizations, compared with the economic group. By two criteria used to determine class, namely, education and occupation, they are as a group of somewhat lower class status than economic leaders. Insofar as membership in the Republican party is a valid index, this measure also attests to their relatively lower status. A larger proportion has lived in Edgewood somewhat longer than the economic group, and substantially more of them are members of the minority Democratic party. They are also *better known* in the community. On the basis of a scale ranging from "don't know" to "know well," the community ranked two political leaders first, with 272 and 252 "know well" attributions. The third ranking individual, with 211, was a prominent influential, very active in voluntary organizations, and an official in a local bank. The next ranking individual had 40 fewer nominations. The impact of political change on such generalizations is shown, however, by the fact that in 1960, the entire Democratic (Square-Deal) village administration was thrown out by a young Republican organization. As a result, a survey made today would change sharply the party distribution between political and economic leaders. Nevertheless, the generalization on the relative class status of the two elites would, we believe, remain valid.

Members of the economic elite do not commonly hold formal political office. This finding is consistent with other community research which suggests that local political office and activity do not rank very highly in the value scale of social and economic elites. The common American saying, "I didn't raise my boy to be a politician," is apparently especially strong among economic elites at the local level where the stakes and the rewards of a political career are minimal.[18] When one of its members occupied political office in Edgewood, he was often a marginal type who played a "leg-man" role. Thus one influential, a junior bank official who was elected mayor in the Republican victory in 1960, ranked in social class III, compared with eleven other economic leaders on the reputational list, all of whom were either in class I or II. Two other young Republican politicians, also successful in the same election, were similarly disadvantaged in the assessment compared with Edgewood's older Republican, economic leaders. Nevertheless, the visibility of those in political office insured the new mayor's nomination to the reputational list. Like most men who are successful in local politics, he had lived in the community all his life. Moreover, the other two politicos ranked just outside the cut-off point on this list.

Insofar as perceptions of influence held by the decision-

[18] This is in interesting contrast to the national level where business success or inherited wealth is a common legitimation for political office.

makers themselves are concerned, it is noteworthy that economic leaders monopolize the highest ranks on the reputational scale. Even though the total number of economic and political leaders was somewhat different, 14 v. 9 respectively, only three political leaders were included in the 14 men nominated to the reputational scale. *This distribution means that political leaders themselves accept the dominant power position of their economic fellows.* That is, if we look at the *first three* reputational nominations made by each political leader, we find that only three of the nine *political* leaders included *any* other political leader among their selections. Moreover, the most powerful political leader ranked only ninth in the reputational scale, despite the fact that he had participated actively in four decisions. This peripetetic Democrat received the same number of nominations as a young Republican politico who did not participate in any decisions. As noted earlier, another Democratic political leader, Clinton Woods, who also participated (although marginally) in four decisions, did not receive enough nominations to qualify as an "influential."

Comparing the power of political and economic leaders on a gross "decisional" basis, we find that political leaders had a total of 23 participations, an average of just over two and one-third per individual. Economic leaders, on the other hand, had a total of 22 participations, or one and one-half per leader. Thus, although the two elites are quite similar in total participations, political leaders seem to be more powerful. This conclusion is not warranted however. As shown earlier in Table 4-3, one reason is that several political leaders, such as the village attorney, were involved in decisions mainly on the basis of their formal, legal role. The same is true of one member of the town council, who "sat in" on three decisions by virtue of his office, but was not otherwise nominated as being powerful. In sum, their membership on official boards, their formal status, tends to exaggerate the "overt" power of political leaders.

Moreover, the decisional index does not include the power

attributes of the *influentials,* all of whom were economic types. We have already noted that four of these men must be included in any discriminating taxonomy of power in Edgewood. The rationale need not be repeated, but the consequence is to reinforce the conclusion that economic leaders in Edgewood not only possess more of the social variables that provide the potential basis of power, but they are also somewhat superior in terms of its overt manifestation. Additional data supporting this conclusion are presented in Table 6-11, where the comparative, weighted power aggregates of political and economic leaders are presented.

In sum, political leaders generally and Democratic political leaders specifically are not perceived by those in the local power structure as being among the most powerful figures in Edgewood's affairs. In the case of the Democratic mayor who (along with the village attorney) was found to be the most powerful member of the community according to the decisional index, some personal and political bias is probably at work. But regardless of party affiliation, political leaders are not highly ranked on the reputational scale. Even in Republican Edgewood, neither of the two Republican political *decision-makers* was nominated to the reputational scale. We find the interesting anomaly that the men who are most powerful in terms of the "decisional" and "overlapping" criteria are not perceived as such by the most knowledgeable segment of the community. This "anomaly" may reflect the fact that political leaders are a minority among the decision-maker group, comprising only nine of 36 members. On this basis, if individuals tend to nominate people like themselves as being influential, we would expect some bias against the political group. Perhaps, too, the common bias which high status, economic leaders hold against political officeholders is at work. On the other hand, political leaders do not rank themselves highly. Finally, in objective SES terms, the political group ranks somewhat below the economic elite, although it compares favorably with the specialist group. Such findings again suggest the danger of relying on any single method of identifying those who are powerful in community affairs.

Conclusions

In this chapter on the power structure in Edgewood, we found that active participation in our panel of decisions was limited to 36 individuals, some 40 per cent of whom participated in two or more decisions. This suggests that leadership in Edgewood is quite concentrated, both in terms of the small proportion of all community adults who are involved and in terms of a substantial amount of "overlapping" among decisions by those in the power structure. We have seen that current conceptions of pluralism include the assumption that decision-making within the power structure is highly specialized, and that as a result power will be fragmented among several discrete groups of leaders, each of which dominates decision-making in its particular sphere of interest and knowledge. We have found instead that decision-making is characterized by overlapping among some 40 per cent of the more powerful decision-makers.

This condition exists in part because most decisions, regardless of their substance, seem to demand several common but different kinds of skills. This brings into the process individuals who have over time demonstrated their ability in such tasks as fund-raising, legal matters, command of mass media, political negotiations, control or possession of financial resources, organizing ability, and positions of ethnic or religious leadership in groups whose support is required for the success of a given project. The result seems to be a division of labor between *generalist* leaders, who control and direct various types of decisions, and specialized "second-level" leaders who are drawn into various types of decisions as the need for their peculiar skills arises. The generalists, who may be either political or economic types (and who may themselves exercise one or another of the required skills), tend to control the vital *initial* stage. By this measure, they are the most powerful men in the community. For even though increasing demands for technical expertise may increase the demand for specialists, they often remain "leg-men," subject to the influence of those who hire them. As Freeman *et al.*, conclude, "their participation is conditioned by their organizational affiliations. Typically, they are not totally "free agents" representing only their personal beliefs and commitments; rather, they are employed by and to some degree must serve the interests of large private and public corporate organizations."[19]

In order to test the intriguing question of the relative utility of the "reputational" and "decisional" methods of identifying powerful individuals, both methods were used in the research. Our findings indicate that the reputational method will identify something over half (including both Edgewood and Riverview findings) of the *most powerful* overtly active leaders. The reputational index seems to isolate individuals who have the qualities usually assumed to be essential for overt power, including wealth, high organizational status, and long residence. But it also seems to be subject to some sociometric bias; individuals who are well known and well liked tend to be nominated, despite some evidence of their limited activity in community decision-making.

The reputational instrument seems especially useful, however, in getting at the time-honored phenomenon of "behind-the-scenes" power. Decision-making in "private" sectors in Edgewood seems to be characterized by some dependence upon the prior support of two or three strategically placed reputational leaders. Such leaders are apparently approached by the activists in order to achieve "consensual validation" upon certain proposals, after which the latter organize and carry them out. As a result, we find the anomaly that to some extent the decisional method identifies "second-level" or "leg-man"

[19] *Metropolitan Decision-Making, op. cit.*, pp. 22-3.

types of leaders, who in some cases have been assigned active roles by their reputational masters who have only "potential" power. Because the decisional method does not always reveal the latter, we conclude that it is necessary to use both methods in power structure analysis.

Finally, although active leaders can usefully be differentiated into political, economic, and specialist types, it seems that economic leaders enjoy a favored position in Edgewood's power structure. Even the political leaders who compete with them validate this judgment, as indicated by their nominations to the reputational list. At the same time, a healthy competition for the direction of major "private" decisions, such as the new hospital and new industry, and to a lesser extent, the new school decision, exists between Democratic-political and Republican-economic leaders in the community. There was, however, no competition between them on the flood control and municipal building issues, which were virtually monopolized by political leaders.

In sum, although power was broadly shared between the two groups, we conclude that economic leaders are perhaps slightly more powerful. One explanation for their relatively greater power is *continuity:* their power tends to rest upon bases that are relatively stable, compared with the transitory role of political leaders who must often depend upon office as their major means of access to the local power structure. This condition is reinforced by the fact that economic leaders are generally advantaged in terms of socioeconomic status, which again provides them with more of the ingredients usually required for leadership, including high social and organizational status, high income, and more local prestige.

The third leadership typology is comprised of specialists, a group characterized by marginal power and participation in a single decision of an educational, health, or welfare kind. Such leaders are not regarded as highly powerful, either by other leaders or by the community at large. None of them was included in the reputational list. They do not nominate themselves. They suffer somewhat by comparison with economic leaders in social class terms, with the exception of educational achievement in which they enjoy a substantial advantage. However, in local decision-making, economic strength, high organizational position, political office, and long residence tend to be more important bases of power than extended education, insofar as this variable can be considered independently.

5

POWER STRUCTURE IN RIVERVIEW

We now turn to an analysis of power structure in Riverview. As might be expected from the discrete socioeconomic structures of the two communities, the social characteristics of their leadership groups are somewhat different. However, the physical structures of leadership prove to be quite similar. In both communities, a small proportion of the adult population dominates decision-making, as measured by their direct participation in five major issues. Indeed, we find a smaller proportion of activists in Riverview than we did in Edgewood. The pattern of leadership within the power structure of Riverview differs from Edgewood's in that a handful of *political* leaders assumed the major role in the initiation and direction of four of the five decisions. In Edgewood, although they were challenged by their political counterparts, economic leaders were probably somewhat more powerful.

The Structure of Participation

Using the same criteria of participation, we find a total of 35 individuals actively involved in one or more of the major decisions: a school bond issue, a new hospital, new industry, flood control, and a public housing authority. Unlike Edgewood, we found no individuals who were actively enough *opposed* to any issue to be designated as decision-makers on this basis. Nor did any decision-makers refuse to be interviewed, although one influential did.

We now turn to the distribution of participation; Table 5-1 shows that some two-thirds of the decision-makers were active in only one issue. Seventeen per cent were active in two issues. Six per cent were active in three decisions. Another 6 per cent were active in four decisions, and 3 per cent, i.e. one political leader, was active in all five issues.

TABLE 5-1 OVERLAPPING AMONG LEADERS (35) IN RIVERVIEW DECISIONS, IN PER CENT

Number of decisions		
5	3 (1)	
4	6 (2)	32%
3	6 (2)	overlapping
2	17 (6)	
1	68 (24)	

Table 5-1 also has implications for our elitism-pluralism question. In Riverview two-thirds of the decision-makers were active in only one decision, while the remaining one-third were active in two or more decisions. Here the proportions are similar to those found in Edgewood, with two exceptions. A higher degree of overlapping (39 *v.* 32 per cent) was found in Edgewood, and the Riverview decision-makers constitute a somewhat smaller proportion of the total population. Even though Riverview has about one-third again as many people as Edgewood, its decision-maker group[1] is virtually the same size, 35 to

[1] When we refer to the leaders as a "group," we mean that they share similar status, membership, and value characteristics that tend to increase their sense of identity. In G. E. Homan's terms, they have similar patterns of sentiment, activities, and interaction, *The Human Group* (New York: Harcourt, Brace & World, 1950).

36. Possible explanations for this condition will be offered later. For the moment, we merely note that the limited supply of leaders in Riverview was frequently mentioned by respondents, some of whom answered our reputational question with the comment: "That's just the trouble, there are too few leaders here."

Styles of Participation

Once again, if 32 per cent of overlapping is accepted as a "significant" index of elitism, we would probably conclude that power is rather concentrated in Riverview. Indeed, despite the fact that there is a somewhat smaller proportion of overlapping, it seems that decision-making is more concentrated than in Edgewood. Power tends to spread across several issues. Some one-third of Riverview's leaders exercise influence in two or more decisions, all of which are substantively different. This point is emphasized because some researchers have found that while the elite group is always a small proportion of any community, *within this group* power and participation are dispersed according to the special skills and interests of the members. Such specialization is less apparent here than in Edgewood, even though the decisions are equally disparate. Not only can Riverview's decisions be dichotomized as "public" and "private," but the content of each is quite varied. Expertise has often been cited as the basis for diversified leadership, but something else must account for overlapping among issues involving flood control, housing, a school bond issue, a new hospital, and the attraction of a new industry concerned with electronics. Indeed, the political leader, Mayor Ted O'Brian, who participated in all five issues is a generalist par excellence, having no training in law, finance, business, medicine, or similar skills which seem relevant to the exericise of power. Considerable political acumen, directed in turn by an unusual sense of civic responsibility, is the basis of his expertise. However, the other most powerful individual in Riverview, city attorney Fred Morrow, is a lawyer whose professional training is clearly a major basis of his power. In general, in addition to special knowledge or training, *any* given decision seems to require a proliferation of diverse skills for its successful resolution, e.g. almost every issue has legal, financial, and political aspects. Insofar as this brings the same individuals into several decisions, the belief that substantive differences *among decisions* ensures pluralistic leadership may require some modification. To an extent, we find that the *same* set of Riverview leaders use their discrete skills in various decisions, regardless of differences in the character of the decisions.

As noted earlier, four of the five decisions were similar in both communities. The unique decision in Riverview was a public housing authority project, financed almost entirely by state and federal funds. Dividing the decisions on a "public-private" axis, we find only one private decision—introducing a new industry. Riverview, as noted earlier, has relied overwhelmingly upon public funds from state and federal sources for its major programs. Unlike Edgewood, there is almost no viable community ideology or organization espousing the values of private initiative. Despite this, for reasons noted later, the largest number of participants in Riverview are found in the private decision to bring in a new industry. Fully 49 per cent of the entire decision-making group was active in this decision. By contrast, 40 per cent of the group was active in the most lively public decision, the high school bond issue.

Table 5-2 indicates the ranking of participation in all decisions. Again differentiating between public and private decisions, it is interesting that an essentially "private" type of decision, new industry, evoked the largest measure of participation, and that two specifically "public" decisions, flood control and housing, were at the other end. This point is stressed here in view of the assumption that governmental decisions, which often require referenda and other public ceremonials, are likely to be more pluralistic than private ones. However, mainly because it was Mayor O'Brian's policy to appoint prominent economic leaders to all his committees, there was more diversity among leaders in "public" decisions in Riverview than in Edgewood.

TABLE 5-2 DISTRIBUTION OF ELITE PARTICIPATION IN RIVERVIEW DECISIONS

Decision	Number of participants
	(35)
New industry	17
School bond issue	14
New hospital program	11
Flood control	8
Housing authority	6

Nevertheless, there is a striking similarity in the general pattern of elite participation in the two communities. In both, the high school and hospital decisions are in the middle and upper ranges of the participation scale, whereas flood control, community building, and housing are at the lower end. The major difference is the new industry issue, which ranked in the middle in Edgewood, but evoked the most participation in Riverview. One reason for this difference is that a network of fund-raising committees was used to obtain part of the money needed; moreover, unlike Edgewood, where the minimum cost of bonds was set at $500, Riverview economic leaders cast their net wider by accepting $50 contributions.

From this we can conclude tentatively that "welfare" types of issues, such as schools and hospitals, whether the latter are privately initiated or not, tend to evoke the highest measure of elite participation in community decisions. They apparently inspire the greatest degree of interest, drawing into their penumbra specialist types who help to swell the total of those actively involved. Such rates of participation also reflect community evalutions of the relative importance of different kinds of decisions. In both communities, the school and hospital decisions were ranked as being the "most important" of the five decisions.

One explanation of the low participation in such issues as flood control and public housing may be that they involve negotiations with external political systems that are outside the scope or influence of most of the community. It is doubtful whether more than a few interested individuals know very much about the specific requirements or procedures involved in a flood control scheme. The decision, so to speak, comes down from above. Negotiations are carried on by local politicians with representatives in Congress and with the Corps of Engineers. No local referendum is required and the financial commitments for most communities are small. Political and legal talents are the major skill requirement, and these are typically provided by mayors and city attorneys. Such factors probably reduce both the need and the motivation for local participation.

The character of elite participation in Riverview compared with Edgewood, and particularly the tendency for power to center in the mayor and his city attorney, may be explained in part by the greater intensity of partisan political rivalry in the latter community.[2] During the time of our research, there was considerable tension in Edgewood between local economic leaders and political officials. The importance of labor unions aggravated this tension, giving community politics a class quality. This explanation, which was advanced by several leaders, raises questions about the pluralist assumption that diversity and competition encourage interest, discussion, and superior solutions to community problems. In Riverview, at least, the evidence appears to support the contrary view that intense en-

[2] Relationships between community power structure, political party, and the values of "Main Street" business and financial leaders are explored in R. E. Egger and D. Goldrich, "Community Power Structure and Partisanship," 23 *American Sociological Review* (August, 1958), pp. 383-92.

gagement in social and political issues may be at best a mixed blessing. Surely compromise becomes more difficult. In a manner more Gallic than American, local leaders were politically engaged. Community decisions were sometimes defined and defended in partisan terms. Some competent but frustrated economic leaders withdrew from community affairs. The strains of partisan politics were stressed by some leaders as a critical factor in Riverview affairs. As one member of the local hospital board put it, "Any community project around here, no matter how small or large, is always doomed. People always think somebody is getting a rakeoff." He also spoke of a wealthy Republican state senator who had been "kicked off" the hospital board when the Democrats came in with the result that he "never left a sou. Isn't that terrible? Because of a political and personal difference between two men, the community suffers." A local Democratic politician maintained that "Whenever anything comes up, there seems to be a certain faction opposed to it and a certain faction in favor of it, and they fight like hell." In the same vein, a Republican business leader commented that he had fought most of the major decisions because they were initiated by the Democratic city administration.

Data such as these suggest the importance for a community of what might be called "psychological tone," based mainly on the extent of social and cultural integration in the community. In Edgewood, there exists a rather positive image of community potentials, which manifests itself in concrete achievements such as the fund drive for the new hospital. Even though the local administration was in Democratic hands, political and economic leaders worked together in healthy competition. In Riverview, on the other hand, competition was less productive; there was a tendency toward defeatism and disenchantment on the part of some individuals who possessed the skills and resources which might have made change easier. Of course, there is an objective basis for such disparate attitudes: Edgewood is blessed with plentiful resources of money and personal talent, while Riverview is not. Nevertheless, this psychological difference seems to be an important explanation of the different political processes observed in the two communities.

Decisional and Reputational Power

We now turn to the question of the relative validity of the decisional and the reputational methods of identifying power structure in Riverview. Table 5-3 shows that the results of the two indexes are somewhat different.

TABLE 5-3 NOMINATIONS BY DECISIONAL AND REPUTATIONAL METHODS

Decision-makers*	(Decs.)	Influentials	(Noms.)	Overlap
Ted O'Brian	5	Ted O'Brian	17	Yes
Fred Morrow	4	Richard Cavenaugh	13	Yes
Kenneth Armstrong	4	Dick Mason	13	Yes
Richard Cavenaugh	3	Robert Carr	12	No
Frank Baxter	3	Kenneth Armstrong	12	Yes
John Wolchak	2	Frank Baxter	10	Yes
Walter King	2	Fred Schwartz	9	No
Dick Mason	2	John Riley	8	No
Fred Rivers	2	Fred Rivers	7	Yes
Elmer Riddell	2	Ted Johnson	7	No
Frank Patriarch	2	Fred Morrow	5	Yes

* For comparative facility, only those decision-makers who participated in two or more issues are compared with the first eleven (of 14) influentials.

Here, with two striking exceptions, Robert Carr and Fred Morrow, we find a nice congruence at the top of both indexes. Ted O'Brian is the most powerful individual as measured by the decisional method and there is a clear consensus on this ranking among the decision-makers. Similarly, Kenneth Armstrong, Richard Cavenaugh, and Frank Baxter, who are among the top 12 per cent in the local power structure, are accurately perceived by other decision-makers as being influential. In all, almost two-thirds of the most powerful decision-makers are included in the reputational scale. This is a considerably higher ratio than the 43 per cent found in Edgewood.[3]

Some serious "distortion" however occurs.[4] Fred Morrow, the city official who was active in four decisions and ranked among the top 10 per cent of the power structure, appears at the bottom of the scale. Frequently nominated as the "most influential" participant in the housing authority and hospital decisions, member of a family that has lived in Riverview for over two generations, very well educated, and a city official for over a decade, Morrow is extremely competent, active, and highly conscious of the city's needs. However, it is not difficult to explain the disparity between his overt power and his low ranking on the reputational list; this results from interpersonal conflict, based in part on political bias.

Recall that, in Edgewood, political values appeared to have considerable influence upon perceptions of leadership and participation. Partisan political values were apparent in the interviews with leaders who tended to evaluate participation and power in terms of the respondent's political party. This tendency was aggravated in Riverview. Although the stakes of local politics may seem relatively unimportant, the intensity of partisan political feeling appears to reflect a "localization" of national party ideology. In Edgewood such political rivalry was less noticeable. In Riverview, however, more tangible elements were involved, since not only were political leaders proud of their personal rapport with state and federal political leaders, but such connections had obviously paid off in assistance for flood control, housing, roads, and bridges. Moreover, the com-

---

[3] It is useful to compare these rates with those found by Freeman in Syracuse, who informed us that the overlap rate between decision-makers and reputational leaders was 33 per cent for the top 32 men in each category. The average rate for Syracuse, Edgewood, and Riverview combined is 47 per cent.

[4] In the immediate context, the term "distortion" rests on the assumption that the decisional method produces more reliable evidence as to the distribution of power. As noted earlier, we believe that both methods are required to ensure the most penetrating analysis of local power structure.

munity is almost equally divided between Republicans and Democrats.

The major ideological split in Riverview is between a nominally Democratic city administration, of which Morrow (despite being a Republican) is the most aggressive and talented member, and a local business-professional group which is predominantly, yet not exclusively, Republican. The latter are again divided between young businessmen and an old guard of financial and mercantile leaders who remain imbued with the Protestant ethic and its somewhat anachronistic values of hard work, thrift, and saving. This split probably explains the perceptual "distortion" of Riverview's economic elite as to the relative influence of its business leaders. For example, Fred Schwartz, who is a member of the young, progressive wing of the economic community, was ranked quite high on the reputational list.[5] His values are symbolized by the physical condition of his Main Street store whose gleaming aluminum and glass facade contrasts sharply with the painted wood fronts of most Riverview stores. The department-store building at the opposite end of the block, which is owned by a member of an old, wealthy family is a monument to old-guard economic conservatism. Quaintly anachronistic, this department store is harnessed to a passing age. Change, for example, is still carried in little trolley-borne boxes that climb and descend a web of black wires radiating out from a central office on a mezzanine above the main floor. The tension between the old and the new economic elite seems to explain Schwartz's being ranked seventh in the reputational scale, despite his failure to participate in a single decision. Such a ranking may be the result of the hopeful expectations of the younger, progressive decision-makers who realize that Riverview economic leadership must pass into the hands of the "new men."

The main hiatus, however, is between the essentially politi-

[5] Schwartz's progressiveness, however, does not encompass social research since he refused to be interviewed, our only refusal among the Riverview leadership group.

cal-Democrats (plus Morrow) and the nominally economic-Republicans. This alignment produced several tensions and attending anomalies in the evaluation and motivations of the decision-makers. To some extent, the reputational instrument seemed to be used as a sociometric index: respondents tended to name as influentials those they perceived as like themselves, and with whom they enjoyed common social values. However, it also seemed that political bias might be an important and related cause, the expectation being that Republicans might nominate Morrow, while Democrats would underrate his obvious influence. The following table shows the distribution of responses regarding Morrow on the reputational question: "Suppose a major project were before the community, one that required decision by a group of leaders whom nearly everyone would accept. Which people would you choose to make up this group—regardless of whether or not you know them personally?"[6] The 31 relevant decision-makers (of the remaining four, two were independents, one refused to answer the question, and one, of course, was the decision-maker himself) responded as follows regarding Morrow:

TABLE 5-4 MORROW NOMINATIONS TO REPUTATIONAL SCALE BY POLITICAL PARTY (31)

	Decision-makers	
	Republican	Democrat
Nominated Morrow	4	1
Did not nominate Morrow	17	9

These data answer the question about the extent of political bias in Morrow's case. Such bias may have affected both Democrats and Republicans, who may have regarded him as a renegade member of a Democratic city administration. But certainly if political faith were a critical variable, it would have

[6] The qualification "whether or not you know them personally" is included to inhibit sociometric choices.

affected Republican nominations more favorably. Instead, we find that *both* Democrats and Republicans tended to exclude him. As a further test, we next compare nominations for Morrow with those for Ted O'Brian, the other most powerful political decision-maker, but of the Democratic party.

TABLE 5-5 O'BRIAN NOMINATIONS TO REPUTATIONAL SCALE BY POLITICAL PARTY (31)

	Decision-makers Republican	Democrat
Nominated O'Brian	10	5
Did not nominate O'Brian	12	4

These data suggest that political bias is not the explanation for Morrow's low ranking on the reputational scale. Compared with Morrow, a much larger proportion of Republicans, 49 per cent, nominated O'Brian. The Democratic proportion also changed substantially, from only 10 per cent in Morrow's case to 55 per cent in O'Brian's case. We conclude from this that political differences were not the major variable affecting Morrow's low reputational ranking. Interpersonal tension provides a more likely explanation. This conclusion is reinforced by other evidence, including spontaneous comments received about the two men from respondents. Despite his contributions to the community, and despite frequent testimonials to his influence and ability, several respondents expressed a lack of personal rapport with Morrow. In the case of Republican leaders, he may have been suspect for aligning himself so closely with local Democratic politicians and, perhaps worse, for contributing greatly to the success of their city administration.

Whatever the explanation for Morrow's ranking, the reputational instrument may thus sometimes be used as a sociometric index which distorts power attributions. It is hard to explain why these same leaders would, as shown in Table 5-9, ascribe to Morrow a "most influential" role in three specific decisions, yet rank him at the bottom of the reputational list. One would expect a more uniform relationship between the two evaluations. In this instance, we have two complementary bases of power ascription, namely, the reputational instrument and the decisional instrument. The latter places Morrow at the top of the local power structure; the former at the very bottom. The burden of our findings makes it reasonable to accept the decisional evidence as more accurate.

An equally glaring example of a difference between the results of the decisional and reputational method is the case of Robert Carr, who ranked fourth on the reputational scale, yet was not active in a single decision. One feels fairly sure that interpersonal influences were also critical in this case. Carr's SES is not sufficiently high to explain his reputational ranking on this basis. He has lived in the community most of his life, being an "old Riverview family" type, which might possibly explain his high rank. During the 1930's, his father was a popular mayor for several terms, and the affection for his father is undoubtedly at work in the younger Carr's community image. Personally, he is extremely appealing; he presents himself as an impressive, indeed handsome, and almost courtly man.[7] Responses to a scaled "community visibility" question indicate that fully 65 per cent of the community "knew" Carr. He was better known than eight of the decision-makers. The utility of this index is challenged, however, by the fact that Fred Morrow ranked only slightly lower than Carr on the community visibility scale. Perhaps the explanation lies not so much in merely being well known, but in what one is well known for.

On the other hand, visibility is also associated with power at the upper levels, for not only were most decision-makers well known, but the best known individual in Riverview was Ted O'Brian, probably the most powerful decision-maker.

[7] Parenthetically, our extended interviews provided a rough generalization about respondent reactions to survey research: the higher the SES of the leader, the more understanding he was about the interview, the research, and the imposition on his time.

We now turn to the inactive "reputational" leaders, i.e. those who were nominated by other leaders as being influential in community affairs, yet were not found to have participated actively in any major decisions. In Edgewood, it will be recalled, we faced the question of "behind-the-scenes" influence when four individuals who were clearly potentially powerful in terms of SES and organizational role, and who exhibited some, although limited, degrees of participation, were not included among the decision-makers, but were "merely" ranked as "influential." In Riverview, no similar discrepancy appears. Only one of the inactive influentials, Ted Johnson, who ranked tenth in the reputational scale, has the formal position and attending social or economic power to play such a role, assuming he wished to.

However, Johnson not only maintained that he had *not* participated, but his views about the desirability of participation and about the quality of local leadership were somewhat jaundiced. Indeed, the term "alienated" seems accurate to describe his position on these matters. Fred Morrow was among the few community leaders who enjoyed his respect. A self-made man of impressive appearance, Johnson was not born in Riverview. As president of one of the largest local industries, and like most highly successful respondents, he was very frank and detached in his appraisal of the community and its problems, among which he included a lack of leadership ability. He also felt that the ethnic character of the community inhibited progress since, in his opinion, many citizens of Eastern European origin were quite satisfied with a marginal economic existence. His ambivalent opinion of politicians was similar to that of other successful business executives in both towns. Although his own position, income, and directorships gave him highly preferential status, shared by very few individuals in the community, his heavy work load limited his participation to infrequent community welfare activities. He was not actively involved in any of the five decisions studied, although he did buy some of the stock sold to finance the new industry.

Here again, a disparity between the result of the decisional and reputational index appears. If true power is defined as action, verifiable by empirical test, Johnson is not powerful in Riverview. Yet he possesses all of the social attributes typically associated with power, including high occupational status, control of extensive organizational resources, high income, and personal prestige. We must conclude that he fully enjoys the *potentials* of power, but he does not choose to use them, or at least not in ways that permit verification by the decisional method. Unlike Edgewood's inactive influentials, he did not work through a "leg-man," nor was there any evidence that those who were active in the decisions consulted him at any stage.

Two other men, one of whom maintained he was active, and both of whom narrowly enjoyed being nominated to the reputational list, deserve mention. They are Frank O'Connor, Democratic lawyer-politician, and George McGuire, manager of a local chain store. O'Connor's is an interesting case because he possesses most of the attributes commonly required for leadership, yet by his own testimony and both the decisional and random information, he was not active. Born in Riverview, a lawyer, relatively young, ranked in social class I, member of 12 voluntary organizations, including the Society of Former Agents of the FBI, sometime official of both city and county Democratic Committees, ethnically and religiously affiliated with dominant elements in the community, city judge for an extended period, O'Connor obviously possesses many of the attributes of power. Indeed, one wonders how he could have avoided being active. Unfortunately, the only explanation we could find for his inactivity was his official position as city judge which fully occupied his time. There is also some evidence that Mayor O'Brian consulted informally with him on local problems and appointments, so that he did exert some indirect influence.

George McGuire's case is easier to explain. Although he indicated personally that he had been active in the new industry decision, he did not receive sufficient nominations by other activists to warrant inclusion as a decision-maker. Like Fred Schwartz, and despite his inactivity in the important decisions, McGuire was probably mentioned in anticipation of his future contributions to community affairs. This judgment is supported by an analysis of his social characteristics. About 32 years of age, social class III, resident of Riverview for less than 10 years, member of only two local voluntary organizations, understandably ranked low on the "community visibility" scale, it is clear that McGuire lacks many of the typical requisites of community leadership. However, insofar as interest and desire are themselves important bases of power, we would predict that he will become a member of the local power structure within a few years, provided he remains in the community.

Leadership Categories

Here again, the leadership group will be placed into three *post hoc* categories: economic, political, and "specialist." Their social characteristics are shown in Table 5-6.

TABLE 5-6 SES OF RIVERVIEW POLITICAL, ECONOMIC, AND SPECIALIST LEADERS, IN PER CENT

	Political (10)	Economic (19)	Specialists (6)
Education: 16 or more years	20	42	33
Time in community: over 20 years	78	95	66
Fathers' occupation, white collar or higher	80	68	67
Income: over $10,000	30	68	17
Membership in organizations: 3 or more	80	68	67
Political affiliation: Republican	50	68	67

Over half of Riverview's decision-makers fall in the "economic" category. Most of the 19 individuals are businessmen, nine of whom own small retail stores. Two are newspaper publishers, two are bankers, one is a corporation executive, another has a large contracting business, and one is a lawyer. The remaining three are salaried employees in local service organizations or businesses.

The economic elite is characterized by long residence; one-third were born in Riverview and fully 95 per cent have lived in the community over 20 years, compared with only 70 per cent of the political leaders. This finding is exceptional, since most community studies have found that nativity and long residence are more characteristic of political leaders than of their economic counterparts. The data on fathers' occupation show that the latter are largely "self-made" men, almost two-thirds having fathers who were blue-collar workers. Although less than half of them have college degrees, they rank well above other leaders in educational achievement. Only 68 per cent had incomes of $10,000 or more, contrasting unfavorably with Edgewood economic leaders, all of whom fell in this economic category. Indeed, in Edgewood, 55 per cent of the economic leaders earned over $20,000.

Riverview's leadership group includes 10 political types, two of whom were undoubtedly the most powerful of the entire group as indicated by their role in the five decisions and other evidence. Most of these leaders are designated "political" because they hold or have held political office and are perceived by other members of the community as being politicians. They include a small businessman, lawyer, railroad supervisor, retired railroad worker, local "judge," retail clerk, a public utility employee, two city officials, and (as often happens) one was a mortician. With the exception of the mayor and city attorney, who participated in four and five decisions respectively, and one individual who was active in two decisions, political leaders were limited to one decision each. There is no pattern in the kinds of decision in which they participated. Even in flood control, an obviously "public" type of decision, more economic leaders than political leaders were involved. This is because Mayor O'Brian co-opted several Republican businessmen for his flood control committee, a practice he followed in other decisions.

The extent to which political leadership is associated with high community visibility and long residence is again apparent in Riverview. Although two economic leaders rank high, political leaders dominate the "visibility" scale. John Riley, mortician and long-time Democratic committeeman, ranks at the top with fully 49 per cent of our community sample indicating that they know him "well." Richard Mason, a young Polish economic leader, is almost equally visible with 47 per cent of our community sample responding similarly. Another "home-town" political leader, Frank O'Connor, ranks a close third with 46 per cent. Next is Mayor O'Brian, with 42 per cent of the community sample testifying that they know him "well." Richard Cavenaugh, elderly member of an old, distinguished family, and president of a local bank, ranks next, followed by Fred Morrow, the mayor's energetic city attorney. (The next ranking member is again a Democratic politician and union official, who differs from all those named above in being neither an influential nor a decision-maker). The final leader in this category is also a Republican politician.

In sum, five of the seven best known leaders in the community are political leaders. To some extent, visibility is a function of age and length of residence, but neither of these nor power by itself seems sufficient. This is suggested by the case of Kenneth Armstrong, the most active economic leader, who is much less "well known" than other leaders, despite the fact that he was born in Riverview, as was his father. Both Armstrong and Mason are relatively young, in their mid-forties, so their different ranking must be due to some factor other than power, participation, residence, or age. Reverend Baxter is similarly "unknown," despite his participation in three decisions. However, of all the group, he alone has lived in Riverview less than a decade; five of the remaining leaders had lived there all their lives.

A major distinction between political and economic types is in income and education. As Table 5-6 indicated, political leaders are generally of lower SES; surprisingly, they have lived in the community, on the average, somewhat less long than the economic leaders. They are notably lower in education, and indeed, the lawyer among them is the only college graduate, compared with eight of the economic leaders. In sum, the SES differences found in Riverview between economic and political leaders are even more pronounced than in Edgewood, and suggest again an explanation for the ambivalence with which politicos are regarded by the economic elite.

The "specialist" category is rather small, comprising only 17 per cent of the elite group. Such leaders tend to be active in only one decision, and usually participate in eleemosynary activities such as education or health. We find among them a high proportion of "marginal" power figures, rarely ranked high in power by their fellow decision-makers. Only the Reverend Baxter, active in three issues, was nominated to the reputational list. Nor do they rank at the top in education or income. This segment of the power structure compares rather unfavorably with its Edgewood counterpart, particularly in education and income. Specialists also constitute a much smaller proportion of the entire Riverview leadership group, which has implications for the total supply of disinterested, "welfare-oriented" type of leaders available in the community. Once again, they tend to have lived in the community a shorter time than other leaders, and a much smaller percentage of them have incomes of $10,000 or more.

Table 5-7 shows the distribution of leadership participation. There is no firm pattern of differentiation here. Politicians dominated the housing authority decision, and provided about 40 per cent of those participating in the flood control issue. These were the most "political" of the Riverview decisions. The incongruously large number of economic leaders in the flood control issue is explained by the mayor's desire to make his flood control committee representative. Conscious of the existing split between political and business elements, and perhaps anxious to enlist the co-operation of higher-status citizens, the mayor used this means of dealing with the problem. Two of the five economic leaders on the committee ranked second and ninth in the reputational scale, and a third member also received several nominations, although not enough to meet our cut-off standard. The mayor followed a similar practice with his industrial development committee, which included members of both the economic and specialist groups.

TABLE 5-7 DISTRIBUTION OF LEADERSHIP TYPES AMONG DECISIONS

	Housing Authority	Flood Control	School Bond	New Industry	Hospital
Political (10)	5	3	3	3	4
Economic (19)	1	5	6	13	4
Specialist (6)	0	0	4	1	3

Specialists, with one exception, are confined to matters involving education and health. Dr. Baxter, the lone specialist active in other decisions, served as chairman of the industrial development committee, but there is evidence that his major role was one of symbolizing the community-wide, nonpolitical character of the new industry problem. Not only was he the only specialist active in more than one issue, but with one exception—the local school superintendent—he was the only one possessing more than marginal influence in such decisions. The remaining specialists are included in our leadership group mainly by virtue of participation based upon their membership on boards or committees concerned with one or another of the five decisions. Some researchers automatically cover such individuals into the power structure on the ground that they could have exercised a "veto power" or that their formal legitimation was a requirement for the resolution of a decision. We elected not to do so in all cases, but only where such individuals were *also* nominated on decisional criteria as having been overtly active.

In terms of the total number of issues participated in by each group, the 10 political leaders accounted for a total of 18 participations, contrasted with 29 for the 19 economic leaders, and 8 for the specialists. As in Edgewood there was thus a somewhat higher *individual* rate of participation among the political leaders. Were it not for the mayor's practice of co-opting business and professional leaders to his committees, the difference would be even more marked. Despite the preponderance of gross participations on the part of economic leaders, which is partially explained by their large representation in the local power structure, the dominant thrust in four, and possibly five, of the decisions was provided by O'Brian and Morrow. Unlike some political figureheads, whose membership on boards and committees mainly explains their power, the mayor and his city attorney clearly maintained the initiative in four of the five decisions. Here again, the problem is one of the stage and intensity of an individual's participation in a given decision. In the next chapter, when the relative power of political and economic elites is compared, we will provide systematic evidence on this point.

In the case of two of the three Riverview political leaders, *overlapping* provides one valid index of power. When overlapping is combined with other forms of evidence, we conclude that their roles were not only official or ministerial, but that they were involved in four of five decisions at the critical initial stage. The most active individual in Riverview is a political leader—the mayor. He appears in Table 5-8 as the one political leader participating in five decisions. Moreover, one of the two individuals ranking as second most active is city attorney Morrow. The other a young, "old-family" Republican, Kenneth Armstrong is very powerful in Riverview affairs, both by this measure and by virtue of being ranked fourth on the reputational list. However, he is the only leader who seriously challenged the hegemony of the two politicos. Although he was clearly involved in three decisions, the other economic challenger, Richard Cavenaugh, was vital only in the hospital and new industry issues. The dependence of the community upon state and federal resources gave the two political leaders the central role in local affairs during the time of the decisions considered here.

Table 5-8 shows the over-all pattern of participation.

TABLE 5-8 DISTRIBUTION OF ELITE PARTICIPATION

Number of Decisions	Political	Economic	Specialists
	(10)	(19)	(6)
5	1	0	0
4	1	1	0
3	0	1	1
2	1	5	0
1	7	12	5

Despite the virtual monopoly of initiative enjoyed by the two political leaders, when we look at gross overt power as measured by the total number of participations, the economic leaders enjoy a substantial net advantage.[8] If we compare the proportions of those in both categories who were active in two or more decisions, we find that the economic leaders have more power: 38 per cent compared with only 27 per cent of the political group. This conclusion, moreover, is reinforced by the composition of our reputational scale in which only three of 14 members are politicos. Ten of the remaining 11 individuals on the list are economic leaders. The other is a specialist.

Such a conclusion, however, tends to obscure the true locus

[8] A more systematic comparison of relative power between leaders in both communities is presented in Chapter 6, where power aggregates based upon weighted levels of participation are worked out.

of power in Riverview. Judged by their initiation and control of most of the important decisions, it is clear that the two political leaders had the most power in the community. Here, we are suggesting that qualitative differentiations as to the weight of power and the stage at which it is exercised in a given decision provide as valid criteria as the quantitative ones just mentioned. Overlapping among decisions and the total number of participations by each leadership segment are obviously crucial, but both must be augmented by careful evaluations of the relative power exercised by each individual involved in the decision. Like the statistician who drowned in a stream averaging 3 feet in depth, we must beware of undifferentiated quantitative judgments.

If, for example, in determining the relative power of political leaders in the two communities, we relied upon the total number of decisions participated in by each group, we would find that Edgewood's nine political leaders participated in 23, compared with their 10 Riverview counterparts who participated in only 18. From this evidence alone, one might conclude that Edgewood's political leaders were more powerful than their Riverview counterparts. Qualitative judgments, based upon a fairly intimate knowledge of both communities and the relative decisiveness of political roles in all decisions would, however, require us to reject this conclusion. The major bases for such a conclusion lie in the *centrality* and *intensity* of the roles of those who brought power to bear and in the *stage* at which their power was introduced. In Riverview, the two political leaders initiated four and possibly five of the decisions; they personally carried on negotiations with several external centers of public power. They appointed several economic leaders to relevant committees. In some cases, these leaders were undoubtedly essential in mobilizing community interest and support for such decisions, but the launching and direction of most decisions were mainly determined by the mayor and city attorney. All of those involved had power, but, as always, some were more powerful than others; in Riverview these were political leaders. The centrality of their role, as well as that of other politicos, is suggested in Table 5-9 by the attributions of relative influence in the five decisions by those who were active in each decision.[9]

TABLE 5-9 NOMINATIONS OF "MOST INFLUENTIAL" DECISION-MAKERS*

Decisions	Political (10)		Leaders Economic (19)		Specialist (6)	
Hospital	Wolchak	7	Cavenaugh	7	Baxter	4
	Morrow	7	Armstrong	4		
	O'Brian	3				
Flood control	Morrow	6	Armstrong	2		
	Riley	6				
	O'Brian	2				
Housing authority	O'Brian	5	Armstrong	2		
	Morrow	4				
New industry	Adams	5	Cavenaugh	10	Baxter	3
	O'Brian	4	Mason	4		
			Porter	4		
			Patriarch	4		
			Duncan	4		
			Armstrong	3		
School bond issue			Mason	8	Fischer	7
			Armstrong	3	Baxter	6

* Only leaders receiving two or more nominations are included.

These data show that O'Brian and/or Morrow were regarded by other activists as the "most influential" leaders in four of the five decisions. Moreover, three additional politicos are similarly perceived in one or more decisions. Overlapping of influence in decisions is a major criterion here.

Among economic leaders, Kenneth Armstrong is the only one

[9] In evaluating these nominations, it is well to recall that the attributions to political leaders are probably understated due to the ambivalent view of economic and, to some extent, specialist leaders toward those holding political office, and to some personal antipathy toward Morrow.

whose participation is as broad in scope as O'Brian's and Morrow's, although it is not as intense. The second most powerful leader, Richard Cavenaugh, is widely perceived as the most influential economic leader in the hospital and new industry decisions. It is noteworthy, however, that two political leaders, Morrow and Wolchak, match him exactly in the hospital issue. The only other instance (where political and economic leaders compete) in which an economic leader received a greater number of "most influential" nominations is in the new industry decision where Cavenaugh's financial role was indeed central. The total respective nominations are 55 for the economic leaders and 49 for the politicos. The comparable figures in Edgewood were 47 to 31. The advantage of economic leaders is partly because there are more of them in the power structure, as well as in the "most powerful" category, in which seven economic leaders face only four politicos.

When we turn again to qualitative discriminations, the two economic leaders fare less well. In Cavenaugh's case, and in much lesser degree in Armstrong's, their participation in the housing and flood control decisions was essentially ministerial. Armstrong supported the public housing decision publicly, and this was important because, as Morrow noted, such housing was regarded as "socialistic" by most leading citizens. Indeed, some organized opposition was encountered from local real estate men. Nevertheless, Armstrong's role in the issue was subsidiary to those of the mayor and his Republican legal aide, Morrow. In the new industry case, simple economic determinism seems to explain the consensus on Cavenaugh as the "most influential" leader; several respondents remarked, "We just couldn't have done it if his bank hadn't provided the money." As noted earlier, Cavenaugh's bank took a first mortgage on the new building provided for the new industry.

Cavenaugh, however, was ambivalent about the project, and it seems fair to conclude that had financial discretion been his only guide, he would not have participated. Wanting to dispel any local beliefs that he was opposed to new industry, he pledged his bank's support at the very beginning. In effect, he had a veto power, since had he refused to do so, the industry could not have been brought in. Three or four other economic leaders received three or more nominations as being the "most influential" individuals in the decision, and Dr. Baxter, the specialist leader, also ranked near the top. Two political leaders were also included among such nominations.

As might be expected from our Edgewood data, specialists are prominent in the school decision. As Table 5-9 shows, Mason, Baxter, and the school superintendent, Norman Fischer, were widely regarded as the "most influential" participants. Yet, here again, Mayor O'Brian apparently triggered the decision by encouraging state officials to make the Riverview school board aware that it risked losing extensive state aid by its inaction. He also called meetings of the school board and other interested organizations to alert them to this danger.

The specialists include one of the two female members in the Riverview power structure, a charming, old, long-time member of the school board. Born in Riverview over 70 years ago, this lady has been on the board for 17 years. On behalf of the new school, she visited Albany to interview "I don't know how many," state education officials and architects, and addressed a "great many" meetings. Delightfully frank, politically sophisticated, and a staunch Republican, she answered a routine "true and false" question naming the current mayor of Riverview by remarking that she was going to answer it as "true," but she honestly (however wrongly) believed that someone else "really ran things." Other specialists included the school superintendent and two other members of the school board. The rather limited participation among all decision-makers in the school bond issue, amounting to 34 per cent (in Edgewood the comparative figure for the same decision was 47 per cent), is surprising in view of its top ranking by Riverview leaders as the "most important" of the five community decisions.

The last of the "public" issues is the decision to build a new hospital. Here again, participation is dispersed among all types of decision-makers. And here again, a comparatively smaller proportion of all decision-makers, 31 per cent (in Edgewood the figure was 42 per cent), participated. Four of these were economic leaders, four were politicos, and the remaining three were specialists. In this decision, the major role was shared by three political and two economic leaders. The power of one of the political leaders, city attorney Fred Morrow, was based mainly upon his political office, legal skill, and connections in Albany. Since new state legislation was required to make the new hospital possible, Morrow, who was actively involved in four decisions, wrote the bill and lobbied it through the state legislature. Mayor O'Brian was also centrally involved. The other major political figure was a member of the local hospital board, whose political connections and long residence were effectively brought to bear in support of the program.

The two economic leaders involved in the hospital decision are among Riverview's SES elite; both are highly educated, with relatively large incomes. One of them, Richard Cavenaugh, has been a member of the local hospital board for 20 years. An expert in financial affairs, he felt that people in surrounding towns who used the Riverview hospital were not "paying their fair share" of hospital costs.[10] (His conservative economic values made him a somewhat reluctant participant in the flood control project, 90 per cent of which was financed by the federal government. This consistency to the principle of local autonomy and limited public expenditures was almost unique among economic leaders, most of whom felt that exceptions in their own community were acceptable for practical

[10] Although generalization from a survey of two communities is hazardous, it is interesting that this economic motivation for a new hospital system was also prominently mentioned by Edgewood citizens as a motivation for their new hospital. The fact that four of the five critical decisions in both communities over a period of a decade were the same suggests again the similarity of the problems that face small communities at this time.

reasons.) The other leader, Kenneth Armstrong, was the most active of the economic elite. A liberal Republican who participated in four decisions, he cheerfully supported all the "public" programs. Consistent with his political values and keen sense of community responsibility, he provided the major leadership of the economic group. Here again, activism was correlated with long residence; like his father before him, he was born and had spent all his life in Riverview.

On the other hand, a nice sense of community responsibility is also visible among some specialist leaders, who are often "cosmopolitan," highly educated, middle-income individuals with technical or professional skills that are not restricted to one place. Such individuals are particularly concerned with educational, medical, cultural, and recreational facilities for themselves and their families. Generally unpropertied and restricted to a marginal power position by their "hired-hand" status in the town, such men make their influence felt through public meetings and committees. It is sometimes hard for them to penetrate long-established community alliances or to meet local definitions of the qualities required for leadership, which often include long residence, property ownership, wealth, and "old-family" ties with the community. Despite this, a leading role in both the school and hospital decisions was played by one such individual, Dr. Frank Baxter, the minister of a local Protestant church. Although he had lived in Riverview less than 10 years, and was soon to be called away, he was active in three decisions, thus ranking among the top 12 per cent of the local power structure. While his activism was undoubtedly eased by the relatively large amount of free time available to those in his type of work, Dr. Baxter was mainly motivated by philanthropic values.[11] His rhetorical skills were essential in

---

[11] This point is stressed here because, whether consciously or not, many decision-makers often exhibited a nice synthesis of economic and civic values. Even new schools and hospitals were rationalized in economic terms of greater appeal to new industry, attracting tourists, increasing the

organizing and developing community support in the school, industry, and hospital decisions.[12] These skills and the widespread conception of him as a disinterested leader made him an excellent choice as president of the local hospital advisory committee. Some of the dynamics of community leadership, such as the common practice of co-opting established leadership resources, are explicit in Baxter's belief that "they asked me [to be president] because of my publicity from the school centralization and bond issue."

Another example of specialist penetration of the local power structure is the school superintendent, Norman Fischer, who had a vital role in the school bond decision. Fischer illustrates well the characteristics of the typical specialist. Highly educated, a professional administrator, with the relatively high income and local prestige which this group enjoys, he argued convincingly for the new school program. His central theme was the limited effect that the bond issue would have on local taxes, in part because a contingent centralization of school districts would permit the city to qualify for state aid (amounting to 42 per cent of the total cost) and to spread the tax burden more widely. Fischer wrote articles for the local paper explaining this aspect of the decision, and met with New York City financial agencies to secure an improved rating for the city which permitted it to incur further indebtedness. His experience with school legislation augmented his role: he met with the state commissioner of education in Albany to help push

---

economic viability of the community, etc. For example, in designating the high school and hospital decisions as the "most important" of the five issues, the head of a local corporation explained, "we can't attract industry without these two." An Edgewood leader remarked on the benefits of the summer school program. It was not only good for the children, but each of them brought with him daily fifty cents which was spent on Main Street.

[12] Here is an example of the extent to which a given leadership skill is required in several types of decisions, regardless of their substance. Such conditions tend to thrust small town leadership into relatively few hands.

through the centralization bill upon which the entire program ultimately rested. Fischer personally took centralization petitions to outlying areas and attempted to convince the "tough ones" that centralization was in their interest. Another characteristic of specialists, mobility or limited residence, is apparent in his case; once the bond issue was passed, after 12 years as superintendent, he left the community for a better job in Long Island.

Fischer's comments provide evidence for the specialization and co-optative facets of community leadership. He nominated as one of the "two or three most influential leaders" a young Polish businessman, Richard Mason, who "helped swing the Polish and Catholic citizens of the community."

The widely dispersed participation among several types of leaders noted in the school bond issue and the hospital decision is sharply modified when we consider the final, and only "private," issue, the bringing in of a new industry. Here, some 80 per cent of the participants were economic leaders. Although two political leaders were apparently quite important in the exploratory stage, they were the only ones directly involved. One specialist, Dr. Baxter, was included, again as chairman of the industrial development committee which negotiated the venture. Here again, co-optation is apparent. Baxter felt that his earlier role as head of the hospital and school committees was the main reason for this appointment. Aware of the implication that he might be viewed as a "front man," he noted, "I don't feel that I had too much to do with it, outside of being a sort of head." Perhaps such a candid expression of self-denial could come only from a minister.

Responses to the question, "Who would you say were the two or three people who were most influential in determining the outcome of this issue?" suggest that banker Richard Cavenaugh played the critical role in the new industry decision. Most respondents noted that without the financial support provided by his bank, and to a lesser extent, by two other banks, the project would have been impossible. Some also believed that several other economic leaders' contributions put them in the "most influential" category. Among them was a young Polish businessman, Frank Patriarch, who directed the fund-raising campaign in which about 40 per cent of the required funds was raised by subscription from local citizens. Born in Riverview, a self-made man with excellent personal connections throughout the community, Patriarch clearly played a vital role in the decision. As one respondent put it, "Frank got the large Polish element behind the project." This again is a case of a decision-maker playing an essentially "political" role on the basis of his long residence, ethnicity, personal prestige, and a sense of community responsibility, mildly colored by a commercial interest. Altogether, over $50,000 was raised to provide a building for the incoming industry. As usual in these cases, the land was donated by the city council.

The information and the impetus for the decision came from outside the community. A local car dealer learned from a traveling salesman that a certain Pennsylvania company wanted to relocate in a community which would provide a suitable building. As a result of this tip, Ted O'Brian went to Pennsylvania, arranged for the entrepreneur to meet with other Riverview leaders, and in effect put the decision into motion. However, the evolutionary character of decisions and the different types of skill and leadership required as an issue unfolds, are again illustrated by this case. Once the first step was taken, other leaders with different talents and resources stepped in and made their contribution by mobilizing public opinion, raising funds, and handling the legal aspects of the transaction.

Here, too, is a facet of specialization that ensures a degree of pluralism within the local structure. However, it is not the kind of specialization that ensures the monopoly of an entire decision by a single group on the basis of special skill or interest in a given *substantive* type of decision. As noted earlier, most important decisions seem to require organizing, representative, financial, political, and legal skills; leaders who possess these tend to overlap in their decisions. In Riverview's new industry case the initiative was taken by a political leader, but soon shifted to economic leaders possessing legal and financial expertise, as well as the confidence of important ethnic and religious groups in the community.

The distinctive elements in these five decisions include the following. First, contrary to several studies which have found that political leadership has been largely superseded by, or is a mere by-product of, economic leadership in community decisions, in Riverview political leadership was more vigorous than economic. Some of the potentially most powerful economic leaders had withdrawn from active participation. While a coalition between a few political and economic leaders existed, it was clear that the mayor and city attorney maintained initiative and control in four of the major decisions. To some extent, their economic and specialist colleagues were used to symbolize the community-wide implications of the decisions, and to attempt to ease the split between political and economic elements in the city.

Second, with the possible exception of the school bond issue, participation in all decisions was broadly, but unequally, shared among political and economic leaders. Excluding Dr. Baxter and Norman Fischer, the small specialist group was restricted to ministerial roles in the school, industry, and hospital issues. As in Edgewood, and as suggested by the fact that only one specialist was nominated to the reputational scale, specialists are typically marginal decision-makers; some of them included mainly through their official position on a board or committee, rather than because of demonstrated activity and power. Some of them commented on their relative lack of influence. One, briefly a member of the hospital board, said, "I wasn't reappointed and I feel they wanted—oh, let's say—more influential people on it than me." Even Dr. Baxter, despite his participation in three issues which places him near the top of the local power structure, had some question about the true extent of his influence. Certainly, our evidence indicates that he played an implementary rather than an initiatory role, and that his main function was to symbolize the "community-wide" nonpolitical nature of the decisions.

Conclusions

Our analysis of power structure in Riverview indicates that, unlike Edgewood where economic and political leaders share power rather equally, two political leaders are the most powerful men in the community. Their power is shared to some extent with three or four economic leaders and, to an even lesser extent, with one or two specialists, but they retained the initiative in most of the major decisions. This situation is due in part to the withdrawal of several potentially powerful economic leaders, including some who might have exerted a beneficial "behind-the-scenes" influence comparable to that found in Edgewood. But it also reflects the character of the community, which lacks the economic resources that enable Edgewood to rely to a greater extent upon its own initiative. As a result, political leaders who have access to the largesse of higher governments enjoy an unusual amount of power vis-à-vis other elements in the community power structure.

Politically, socially, ethnically, and religiously, Riverview is quite heterogeneous, and this diversity seems to have had some dysfunctional consequences for its ability to handle community problems. Pluralism connotes diversity of interests and competing centers of power. However, there is some evidence that these conditions are not an unmitigated blessing; they may generate tension and alienation. Such diversity and attending ideological dissonance will be treated in Chapters 7 and 10. For the moment, we will merely note that the differential capabilities of the two communities seem in part a function of variations in their socioeconomic structures, one of which is relatively homogeneous, the other quite diversified.

Power in Riverview is somewhat more concentrated than in Edgewood. Mayor O'Brian and city attorney Morrow, with the aid of three or four economic leaders, played a major role in four of five decisions. Three of the four "public" decisions were initiated and directed by the two political leaders. As noted earlier, economic and specialist leaders were co-opted by the mayor on the basis of their special skills and interest, and their support gave the decisions a patina of disinterest and participation that undoubtedly eased the problem of carrying them out. But the withdrawal and weakness of economic leaders and the combination of socioeconomic factors that made the community rely essentially upon external political systems for its resources, thrust leadership upon political leaders to an extent that seems quite unusual, compared with the findings of several other power structure studies which indicate that economic leaders tend to play the most active role in community affairs.[13]

As a result, to a greater extent than in Edgewood, political office and roles provided a means of access, power, and social mobility for a few individuals who might not otherwise have penetrated the local power structure. In Riverview, as in Edgewood, political leaders as a group (except Morrow) were of somewhat lower class status than their economic counterparts. Politics was especially essential in ensuring access to the power structure for such men. Mayor O'Brian is the most obvious example, but in addition, there were several other locals whose political orientation served this function. Although over half of the political leaders were Democrats, a few Republicans, including Morrow, also found their political roles useful in gain-

[13] Among others, R. and H. Lynd, *Middletown in Transition*, p. 74 passim; F. Hunter, *Community Power Structure*, p. 114, passim; D. C. Miller, "Decision-Making Cliques in Community Power Structure," 24 *American Journal of Sociology* (November, 1958), pp. 299-309; W. Form and W. Antonio, "Integration and Cleavage Among Community Influentials in Two Border Cities," 24 *American Sociological Review* (December, 1959), pp. 804-14. On the other hand, economic dominance was not found by R. Schulze, "The Role of Economic Dominants in Community Power Structures," 23 *American Sociological Review* (February, 1958), pp. 308; R. Dahl, *Who Governs?* pp. 69-84; and H. Scoble, "Leadership Hierarchies and Political Issues in a New England Town," in M. Janowitz, *Community Political Systems*, p. 141.

ing access to decision-making elites, both locally and at higher political levels.

In Riverview, fully 64 per cent of the decision-makers are included on the reputational list, compared with 43 per cent in Edgewood. This finding supports the judgment that power is more concentrated in the former leadership group. There are fewer members of the decisional elite, they are more clearly visible, and a greater consensus exists as to their identity. In the next chapter, we will show more systematically that power tends to cluster in the hands of some half-dozen leaders. A related explanation for the greater continuity between "decisional" and "reputational" power in Riverview is the tendency for more leaders who possess potential power to use it overtly, plus the self-disqualification of a few men who enjoy the social requisites of power but withdraw from active participation.

Unlike Edgewood, where several reputational leaders participated marginally (although not sufficiently to meet our decisional criteria) in the five decisions, in Riverview, none of the "inactive" reputational leaders was even marginally involved in the decisions. Moreover, our task was simplified by the fact that very few of them had the socioeconomic or political characteristics usually necessary for the exercise of power.

Specialist leaders in Riverview numbered only six, compared with 13 in Edgewood. (One of these leaders, however, was more powerful than any of his Edgewood counterparts.) Since specialists include citizens whose participation is in some special sense "community-service" oriented, this difference may be a commentary on Edgewood's greater leadership resources. While the motivations of political leaders may include the desire for power and prestige, and those of economic leaders include substantial elements of both power and pecuniary interest, specialists seem to be activated most strongly by civic responsibility. Such motivational differences have a self-fulfilling quality, in the sense that community welfare motives probably inspire additional civic interest and participation.

6

POWER STRUCTURE AND COMMUNITY RESOURCES

The social characteristics of members of the power structure reflect to some extent those of the larger community. Moreover, the effectiveness of the power structure is closely related to the socioeconomic structure of the community. In the end, such community resources as wealth, industrial strength, skill, energy, and value consensus tend to determine both the composition and the effectiveness of its leadership elite. As Edgewood and Riverview illustrate, a lively, diversified economy attracts individuals who possess the education, ambition, technical skill, and civic interest that make successful leadership possible. While the former has extensive resources, the latter has relatively few. While most of Edgewood's top economic leaders have participated in the major decisions, some of those in Riverview have remained inactive. Edgewood's industries have been mainly high-waged and modern; those in Riverview have often been low-waged and traditional, and they have suffered more severely from technological change. Both communities have faced similar challenges, including exhaustion of natural resources and depression, but Edgewood has reacted somewhat more effectively.[1]

[1] We are anticipating somewhat by comparing community "effectiveness" here; however, Chapter 11 will provide detailed support for the generalization.

Once leaders and communities have been compared, we will analyze more precisely the relative power disposed by members of the power structure. Until now, overlapping has been our main index of power; it is necessary, however, to specify the power exercised by each leader in each decision through a systematic weighting of the intensity of his participation. This refinement enables us to differentiate the aggregate amounts of power of political, economic, and specialist subgroups.

We begin by comparing leaders and the rest of the community in class terms. Using Hollingshead's method, class is based on occupation and education.

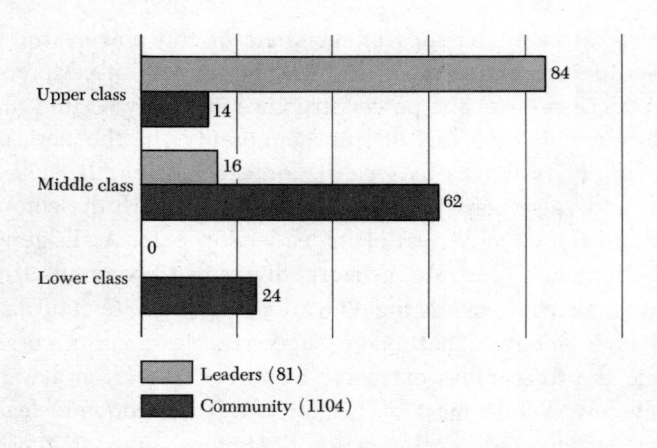

Class	Leaders (81)	Community (1104)
Upper class	84	14
Middle class	16	62
Lower class	0	24

FIGURE 6-1 COMPARATIVE CLASS DISTRIBUTION OF LEADERS AND COMMUNITY, IN PER CENT

These data show that an overwhelming proportion of leaders are of upper-class origin, compared with other members of the community. Only one-seventh of the latter fall in this category, compared with four-fifths of the leaders. This indicates the extent to which leaders command disproportionate amounts of resources, and how different they are from most of their fellow citizens. Class is determined by occupation and education, but these attributes bring with them other essential leadership resources, including prestige and visibility. Some men obviously do not choose to use these resources, but they remain potential leaders. To this extent, resources are a necessary but not a sufficient condition of leadership. At the moment, however, we are dealing with leaders who *have* used their resources. To agree that some potential leaders do not use their resources is not to say that those who are active need not possess them.

Next we compare social characteristics of the two leadership groups. If they are quite similar, our hypothesis of leader-community reciprocity will be challenged because we know that the communities themselves are quite different. On the other hand, if the two elites vary considerably, we can feel more confident about the hypothesis. Table 6-1 compares all members of both power structures. It should be noted here that we are dealing with a universe rather than a sample.

TABLE 6-1 SES OF EDGEWOOD AND RIVERVIEW DECISION-MAKERS, IN PER CENT

	Edgewood (36)	Riverview (35)
Education: 16 or more years	62†	31
Time in community: over 20 years	81	80
Respondents' occupation, white collar or higher	97	91
Fathers' occupation, white collar or higher	77	72
Income: over $10,000	89†	38
Political affiliation: Republican	76	62

† Significant at .01 level.

The two groups differ significantly in terms of education and income. Given the extreme disparity in income, which is usually highly correlated with class position, the similarity in occupational status of fathers is unexpected. Leaders in both communities seem to have started out with quite similar socioeconomic backgrounds, and were able to increase their initial advantage somewhat. We encounter here the peculiarly American phenomenon—upward mobility. This explanation, however, ignores the fact that income, a reasonably accurate index of occupational achievement, is so extremely different. Moreover, there is the striking educational difference between the two groups. Since education is associated with income, the lower educational achievement of the Riverview elite may provide an independent explanation of the income disparity.

To test further differences among the leaders, we again compare the influentials in the two communities.

TABLE 6-2 OCCUPATIONAL AND CLASS STATUS OF COMMUNITY INFLUENTIALS*

	Edgewood			Riverview	
Scale rank	Occupation	Class	Scale rank	Occupation	Class
1.	Corporation President	II	1.	Mayor-Stock Clerk	IV
2.	Corporation President	I	2.	Bank President	II
3.	Bank Vice-President	II	3.	Bank President	I
4.	Corporation President	II	4.	Small Businessman	II
5.	Corporation President	I	5.	Newspaper Editor	I
6.	Bank Vice-President	I	6.	Minister	I
7.	Newspaper Editor	II	7.	Small Businessman	II
8.	Corporation Executive	II	8.	Small Businessman	III
9.	Lawyer-Bank Counsel & Director	II	9.	Small Businessman	II
10.	Ex-Mayor-Small Businessman	II	10.	Corporation President	II
11.	Mayor-Bank Clerk	III	11.	Lawyer-City Attorney	I
12.	Bank Vice-President	I	12.	Corporation Executive	II
13.	Corporation President	II	13.	Lawyer-Judge	I
14.	Town Supervisor-Small Businessman	III	14.	Supermarket Manager	III

* This group comprises all those who received at least 20 per cent of all nominations to our "reputational" list.

These data show that Edgewood influentials tend to play dominant roles in the economic structure of the community. All of them are businessmen, but with only three exceptions they are different from the small-business, owner-entreprenurial types who make up about half of the Riverview group. Edgewood influentials, for example, include five corporation presidents, while Riverview influentials include only one. Perhaps the marginality of the Riverview group is suggested by the fact that a comparatively recent arrival like the Reverend Baxter could quickly assume top status in the local power structure. This table, as well as Tables 6-12 and 6-13, show that Edgewood leaders tend more to represent and to pull together dominant community institutions, which enables them to bring to bear upon local problems a greater sum total of resources.

Differences between the influentials are more clearly shown in the following table.

TABLE 6-3 SES OF EDGEWOOD AND RIVERVIEW INFLUENTIALS, IN PER CENT

	Edgewood (14)	Riverview (14)
Education: 16 or more years	43	46
Time in community: over 20 years	86	86
Respondents' occupation, white collar or higher	100	88
Fathers' occupation, white collar or higher	86	78
Income: over $10,000	93	80
Membership in organizations: 3 or more	100	100
Political affiliation: Republican	86	71

Political affiliation and occupational status provide the largest difference between the two subgroups. Income and education, which sharply differentiated the two decision-maker groups, no longer have this effect. Although some income difference remains, the educational difference has disappeared. A higher proportion of Edgewood influentials have incomes of $10,000 and over, and a somewhat higher proportion have fathers in white-collar or higher occupations. As might be expected from the general political structure of the two communities, more Edgewood influentials are Republicans. More of them also belong to white-collar or higher occupational groups.

In Table 6-4, the power figures identified by the decisional method (called decision-makers) are compared with those power figures chosen by the reputational method who were not active in any decisions (called inactive influentials.) Since this subgroup contains a much smaller proportion of individuals with college education, it suggests that university education is associated with active leadership. The subgroup ranks higher than the decision-makers on only two variables, Repub-

TABLE 6-4 COMPARATIVE SES OF DECISION-MAKERS AND INACTIVE INFLUENTIALS, IN PER CENT

	Edgewood and Riverview	
	Decision-makers (71)	Inactive influentials (10)
Education: 16 or more years	46	30
Time in community: over 20 years	81	90
Respondents' occupation, white collar or higher	94	90
Fathers' occupation, white collar or higher	75††	40
Income: over $10,000	64	50
Political affiliation: Republican	69	90

†† Significant at .05 level.

lican political affiliation and length of residence. Less than half of the inactive influentials had fathers in white-collar or higher positions, whereas the decision-maker group had some three-fourths. The proportion of influentials in white-collar or higher occupations, however, compares very favorably with that for decision-makers.

We suspect, however, that these data conceal some important differences between the two influential subgroups, as well as between them and the decision-makers. The following Table 6-5 considers several such differences.

TABLE 6-5 SES OF EDGEWOOD AND RIVERVIEW DECISION-MAKERS AND
INACTIVE INFLUENTIALS, IN PER CENT

	Edgewood Decision-makers (36)	Influentials (6)	Riverview Decision-makers (35)	Influentials (4)
Education: 16 or more years	62†	33	32	25
Time in community: over 20 years	81	100	80	75
Respondents' occupation, white collar or higher	97	100	91	100
Fathers' occupation, white collar or higher	77	33	72	50
Income: over $10,000	89†	100	38	75
Membership in organizations: 3 or more	100	100	90	75
Political affiliation: Republican	76	100	62	75

† Significant at .01 level.

Although the N's here are very small, Edgewood's inactive influentials, compared with those in Riverview, are advantaged in every case except fathers' occupation. They have had somewhat more education, earn more money, are more likely to be Republicans, and have lived in the community longer.

Considering each inactive influential subgroup with its decision-maker counterpart, the groups compare favorably, save on education and income. For Edgewood, however, it is important to note that four of the six influentials command the highest social and organizational positions in the community, a fact which is not revealed by the "white collar or higher" criterion. These data suggest again that community leaders who dispose the greatest amounts of resources are not likely to play *active* roles in local decisions. Their role is suggested by the following comments of an Edgewood decision-maker, "We try to pick out civic-minded, energetic leaders—you hate to put down names. We have a lot of good, hard workers. Now Williams[2] and Wain-

[2] Williams, however, was active in three decisions, and ranked fourth in the Edgewood reputational scale.

wright never do any work; they just sit down and write a check."

Finally, since economic leaders are the most numerous and potentially powerful subgroup in both communities, they are compared in the following table.

TABLE 6-6 SES OF EDGEWOOD AND RIVERVIEW ECONOMIC ELITES, IN PER CENT

	Edgewood (14)	Riverview (19)
Education: 16 or more years	64	42
Time in community: over 20 years	79	95
Fathers' occupation, white collar or higher	93	68
Income: over $10,000	100	68
Membership in organizations: 3 or more	100	68
Political affiliation: Republican	93	68

Here again, a segment of the Edgewood power structure proves to have more of the characteristics generally associated with leadership. Not only do they rank similarly or higher than their Riverview counterparts on education, fathers' occupation, and income, but they are not, as suggested by Table 6-1, very different from those in other Edgewood leader categories.

On the other hand, when economic and political leaders are compared both within and between the two communities as in Table 6-7, we find sharp differences. Here, it seems, is an important differential which helps explain the relatively greater cohesion among leaders in the Edgewood power structure. On such crucial variables as education, time in the community, income, and political affiliation, the data show that there is a wide gulf between Riverview economic and political leaders. Such differences probably inhibit close working relations. Moreover, as will be shown in Table 6-13, there is correspondingly less overlapping in social and organizational memberships, compared with the Edgewood elite.

Another striking fact here is the greater difference, found in every variable, between economic and political leaders in

Riverview, compared with those in Edgewood. These data suggest that the reason why economic leaders in Riverview were relatively inactive during 1950-60 was perhaps both that they lacked sufficient qualities of leadership and they had not organized themselves effectively. Compared with Edgewood economic leaders, they suffer in every attribute of leadership. Despite their advantages over political leaders, they have not, with only two or three exceptions, competed strongly with the former for the direction of Riverview affairs. Given their preponderance of resources, and the Republican victory in the 1961 city election, it seems safe to predict that they will assume a larger role, provided, of course, that they make the leap from potential to overt power.

TABLE 6-7 SES OF EDGEWOOD AND RIVERVIEW POLITICAL AND ECONOMIC ELITES, IN PER CENT

	Edgewood Economic (14)	Edgewood Political (9)	Riverview Economic (19)	Riverview Political (10)
Education: 16 or more years	64	44	42	20
Time in community: over 20 years	79	90	95	78
Fathers' occupation, white collar or higher	93	77	68	80
Income: over $10,000	100	88††	68	30
Membership in organizations: 3 or more	100	89	68	80
Political affiliation: Republican	93	67	68	50

†† Significant at .05 level.

Comparative SES of Edgewood and Riverview Rank and File

Following our assumption that leadership effectiveness and the quality of community resources are closely related, we now look at the social characteristics of rank-and-file members of the two communities. In general, we would expect educational, income, and occupational levels to be somewhat higher in Edgewood.

TABLE 6-8 SES OF EDGEWOOD AND RIVERVIEW RANK AND FILE, IN PER CENT

	Edgewood (494)	Riverview (704)
Education: 16 or more years	14†	8
Time in community: over 20 years	59†	68
Upper class (I and II)	17†	11
Lower class (IV and V)	52†	67
Protestant	75†	53
Family income over $10,000	14	12
Membership in organizations: 3 or more	53†	45
Political affiliation: Republican	60†	40

† Significant at .01 level.

Here, it seems, Edgewood is favored in all but time in community. The differences are significant in every case save family income. Edgewood, moreover, is shown to be a somewhat more homogeneous community. As the example of British society suggests, the shared values and sense of community which attend such homogeneity pay off in co-operative attitudes and action. In brief, the resulting value consensus may ease the strains of community life in a competitive society.[3] It seems probable that such strains are more likely to exist in communities such as Riverview where political, ethnic, and religious diversity abounds.

Another way of illustrating differences between the two communities is to compare them by certain variables that roughly measure "community viability," i.e. the degree to which each possesses certain resources necessary for effective leadership and followership. Examples include per capita amount spent for education, family income, proportion of skilled to unskilled

[3] For the moment we are merely inferring consensus on the basis of Table 6-8; in Chapter 10, we will show that Edgewood is indeed somewhat more integrated than Riverview.

workers, unemployment rates, assessed valuation of the community, economic growth, etc. Using data from a variety of sources, we have constructed a rough comparative table for the two communities.

TABLE 6-9 "COMMUNITY VIABILITY" DATA FOR EDGEWOOD AND RIVERVIEW

	Edgewood	Riverview
Assessed valuation of real property (1961)[1]	$26,124,000	$18,605,802
Per capita bank deposits (1961)[*]	$4,444	$1,179
Per family effective buying income (1960)[2]	$6,880	$6,201
Per family income over $10,000[2]	14%	10%
Educational spending, per student[3]	$490	$520
Proportion with some college	27%	15%
Public library books, per capita	9	2

[1] State Comptroller, *Special Report on Municipal Affairs* (Albany, 1962), pp. 88, 128. (These figures are corrected to meet differing assessment rates.)
[*] The disproportion is overstated because the Edgewood total includes deposits in three neighboring communities, in which one of Edgewood's two banks maintains branches.
[2] *Sales Management*, "Survey of Buying Power," May 10, 1961. This item includes: ". . . total cash actually available for spending divided by total households. It does not include . . . non-cash items such as food and fuel produced and consumed by farmers, imputed rentals of owner-occupied homes, income received by trust, pension and welfare funds and income of non-profit institutions," p. 52.
[3] *Annual Educational Summary*, New York State 1959-60 (Albany: State Education Department, 1961), pp. 151-2.

Edgewood enjoys an advantage according to most of these indexes, and most dramatically in community wealth, as indicated by assessed valuation of local property. However, in the important matter of "net current expenditure per pupil," Riverview makes a higher contribution, one which ranks only slightly below the median for all New York school districts.

Further evidence of Riverview's less-favored socioeconomic base is provided by a comparison of the occupational structure of the two communities.

TABLE 6-10 OCCUPATIONAL PROFILES OF EDGEWOOD AND RIVERVIEW, IN PER CENT*

	Edgewood (462)	Riverview (655)
Professionals	10	7
Managers and proprietors	25†	13
Farm owners and managers	1	1
Sales and clerical	10†	15
Service workers	6	5
Operatives	42†	50
Laborers	6	9
	100	100

* These data, from our 1961 survey, are based on the occupation of the head of the household. Housewives, NA's, and unclassifiables are excluded.
† Significant at .01 level.

The major differences in occupational structure occur at the critical ends of the scale. Edgewood has over one-third of its labor force in the two top categories, professional and managerial-proprietary, compared with only one-fifth in Riverview. Riverview, moreover, has a significantly higher proportion of its force in the two lowest categories—operatives and laborers. When such factors as differential income, skill resources, and occupational structure are considered, it is easier to understand why Edgewood favored "private" solutions more than Riverview during the period of our study. In a sense, without denying Edgewood's achievements, the community could afford to use private, local solutions whereas Riverview was more obliged to look elsewhere for the capital resources required to improve the community. This difference is patent in the hospital case. Edgewood was able to raise $850,000 by private subscription in a few weeks, but it took a commercial fund-raising team only three days to conclude that it was impossible to finance a hospital in Riverview by private donations. Moreover, even though both hospitals are formally governmental, during the period from 1949-60, Edgewood's hospital received only 18 per cent of its total revenues from governmental appropriations, which for Riverview constituted fully 72 per cent of its revenues. On a "dollar per bed" basis, Edgewood Memorial received $16,063, compared with only $8304 for Riverview District hospital.

Similarly, in the new industry case, Edgewood was able to raise $100,000 and provide land and a building,[4] whereas Riverview had a difficult time and considerable opposition in securing $50,000. Over half of this amount came from three local financial institutions, compared with the $90,000 of the total $100,000 raised by individual subscription in Edgewood.

Disparities in highly trained human resources are also germane. For example, although Edgewood is only two-thirds the size of Riverview, it has six lawyers among the decision-maker group, while Riverview had only two. When the communities are compared, Edgewood has a total of eleven lawyers, whereas Riverview has twelve practicing lawyers. Since lawyers tend to congregate where property and money exist, this differential provides a very rough index of the relative wealth of the communities. Lawyers, of course, are highly qualified for community leadership, possessing dialectical skill, political sophistication, and the control of their time which permits participation.[5] Moreover, political ambition often propels them into community activities.

Similar differences in education and skill are found among the communities at large. Not only do 14 per cent of Edgewood's citizens, compared with 8 per cent of those in Riverview, have college degrees, but educational achievement in Edgewood is generally higher. For example, 77 per cent of our Edgewood sample had more than eight years of education, over against 65 in Riverview.

[4] Shortly after our research was completed, Edgewood raised another $75,000 by private subscription to bring in a new industry.

[5] However, such resources are not always *used*. As a leading Riverview decision-maker and lawyer said, "We've got fourteen lawyers here in Riverview and I can't honestly tell you a thing they have done."

Combined with the economic differentials mentioned above, such factors suggest that inequality of opportunity is at work. Riverview lacks some of the raw materials from which leadership, as well as followership, springs. Even with the best will in the world, the community would have great difficulty matching Edgewood in the struggle for security and growth. The whole socioeconomic context is inapposite. Even if members of the power structure were equal in leadership qualities, a comparable substratum of wealth, skill, and an active interested citizenry does not exist. Given such disadvantages, Riverview has, during the period of our study, done more than one could reasonably expect. Indeed, had it not been for the efforts of the two political leaders, and the co-operation of the local banker and newspaper editor, the community would have suffered badly from what may fairly be called a leadership vacuum.

Such facts probably underlie the following spontaneous comments of members of the power structure about leadership and community viability in Riverview. These comments were inspired by our reputational question, which asked respondents to name several individuals whom they regarded as leaders capable of carrying out an important community project. Representative responses include the following:

"You know, we just haven't got any top leaders."

"Our lack of a good economic base makes leadership difficult. The young people leave town and the remaining citizens are old and conservative."

"With the exception of . . . all your so-called leaders are laborers; that shows you the level of leadership here."

"The town was beat when I came here; people with any ability left, and they are still going to some extent."

"The banks and newspapers are disgustingly conservative."

"Anyone trying to become a leader here would be crucified."

"We just don't have any leaders here."

In deciding how to weigh such evidence, it is noteworthy that these comments were made by men who are among the most powerful and well-educated members of the community. With perhaps two exceptions, they are not alienated by feelings of ineffectuality, interpersonal conflict, or social distance. Three rank at the top of the local SES hierarchy, and none of them has lived in Riverview less than 20 years.

Further Specification of Elite Power

Our analysis of the social characteristics of leaders is incomplete in the sense that it fails to differentiate precisely the relative amounts of power disposed by individual leaders and subgroups. In using the gross number of decisions in which each leader participated as an index of power, we neglect the fact that different men dispose different amounts of power in each decision. Decisions, moreover, have various stages, some of which are more decisive than other. It is quite possible for some leaders who participate overtly in several decisions to actually dispose less aggregate power than others who dominate a single decision. In order to meet this condition, we next differentiate three weighted levels of participation.

INITIATION, VETO, AND IMPLEMENTATION AS INDEXES OF POWER

Three levels or intensities of power are specified: *initiation* of a decision, i.e. participation in the crucial decision to go ahead on a proposed issue; the exercise of a *veto* power in a proposed issue; and the *implementation* of a decision or what we have called a "ministerial" style of participation. Initiation is assigned 5 points, veto power receives 3, and implementation receives 1. In making these assignments, we depend primarily upon our *Verstehen* as to the nature and importance of each leader's role in a given issue, and on the nominations of decision-makers as to the "most influential" participants in issues in which they also participated. The resulting distributions are presented in Table 6-11.

TABLE 6-11 AGGREGATE POWER ATTRIBUTIONS OF POLITICAL AND ECONOMIC DECISION-MAKERS

	Edgewood			Riverview		
	Political		Economic	Political		Economic
King	9	Remington	10	O'Brian	21	Armstrong 12
Woods	8	Williams	9	Morrow	16	Cavenaugh 11
Wells	7	Prince	7	Wolchak	6	Mason 10
Dodd	6	Hadwen	5	Adams	5	Patriarch 6
Moore	3	Dunn	5	Riley	5	Duncan 5
Eberhart	2	Parker	3	Plank	1	Porter 5
Ward	2	Albright	2	Smith	1	Riddell 2
Reeder	2	Thomas	1	Cohen	1	Kruger 2
Parks	1	Miles	1	King	1	Rivers 2
	—	Wilson	1	Thomas	1	King 1
	40	Sherman	1		—	Forrest 1
		Rogers	1		58	Brock 1
		Babcock	1			Morton 1
		Hughes	1			Clark 1
			—			Rowen 1
			48			Wheeler 1
						Muller 1
						Hunter 1
						Waters 1
						—
						65
Average	4.4		3.4		5.8	3.4

These data generally confirm earlier judgments about the distribution of power between political and economic elites in the two communities. In Edgewood, the economic group enjoys an advantage in total attributions. The large size of the group adds to its strength vis-à-vis political leaders. In Riverview, the economic elite also has an advantage over its political counterparts. The Riverview data, however, are strongly affected by the greater difference between the relative number of leaders in the two groups. This effect can be shown by averaging individual attributions, which gives political leaders an *individual* power index of 5.8 compared with one of only 3.4 for economic leaders.

Continuing with an individual perspective, one striking fact is the concentration of power within both political and economic elites. If, for example, we consider only the first *five* leaders in each category in each community, we find that they virtually monopolize power. Among Edgewood politicos, these five ranking members capture 83 per cent of all attributions. Among the economic group, they have 75 per cent. Among Riverview politicos, the concentration is even more pronounced: the ranking five have over 90 per cent of all attributions. Among economic leaders, the first five have 68 per cent.

Moreover, if we compare the relative power sums of the first *five* political and economic leaders in each community, we get the following results: in Edgewood, economic leaders receive an aggregate of 36 points compared with 33 for politicos. In Riverview, however, political leaders receive 53 points compared with only 44 for economic. Since, like concentrated wealth, concentrated power is more decisive than aggregate power, we conclude that economic and political leaders dispose roughly equal amounts of power in Edgewood, while in Riverview political leaders are clearly dominant.

Social and Organizational Interaction Among Leaders

In Chapter I, power was conceptualized as a social rather than an individual phenomenon. Power was seen, in Mills's terms, as "not of a man," but rather as the result of group alliances and a given leader's role within a set of social relationships. Power, in effect, is always *relational;* one does not "have" power in a vacuum, nor in every substantive context, but always in regard to another person or persons, and in a given situation. As

Hunter noted, power must always be "structured into associational, clique, or institutional patterns."

A crucial question about power structures is thus the extent to which their members share social and organizational identifications that provide an opportunity for them to influence each other and to work together. Such memberships are often a valid index of value consensus among their members, as well as an index of class propinquity. They are instruments of *Gemeinschaft,* of collective alliances, in which group norms provide the major guidelines for the behavior of individual members. Critics of sociological research in power structure have sometimes rejected the assumption that members of such groups share certain common values. Actually, of course, value consensus is one of the definitive characteristics of a group or a class. Not only are the members of such associations aware of certain objective indexes of occupation, education, and style of life that set them off from other groups, but such indexes are usually accompanied by discrete clusters of shared norms that further differentiate the group and integrate its members.

The usual psychological dynamics seem to be at work, including individual rewards of consensual validation, interpersonal sympathy, formal acceptance (via membership) by the fraternity, and personal integration with the group. Both personal and ideological ties bind members together in such associations, and the attending consensus probably encourages unified action in community affairs. Considered at a broader, community-wide level, such alliances may have bad consequences, in terms of the possible alienation of individuals excluded from membership, and whatever substance this may give to the belief that a small group "runs things." In the main, however, interlocking memberships probably enhance the ability of elites to marshall and use their power.

Group research indicates that individuals who interact frequently tend to develop shared norms.[6] The opportunity to

[6] Among others, G. C. Homans, *The Human Group,* pp. 60-61, 72-3,

communicate and interact provides a means of influencing others to accept collective norms and values. Generally, although not always, members of a group share similar values; they use rewards and sanctions to induce individual members to accept them. We will show in Chapters 9 and 10 that members of the power structure do indeed share certain basic values to a somewhat greater extent than rank-and-file members of the community. A larger proportion believe that they can influence political events; that the community is worth working for; and that private initiative is often preferable to governmental solutions to community problems. Generally, their civic morale is higher; they vote in higher proportions; and they have higher rates of membership in voluntary organizations. *The assumption here is that interlocking group memberships and attending social interactions provide valid indexes of a rough consensus among leaders on many political values and community policies.*[7] No doubt, they agree less on the strategies best calculated to achieve such policies, but organizational membership provides an important instrument for those who agree on certain objectives to work together and to influence others.

To determine the extent of overlapping memberships and social contacts, with their attending thrust toward value and behavioral consensus, we analyzed the memberships of decision-makers in both towns. Our findings are presented in Tables 6-12 and 6-13.

125-7, 417; and H. C. Selvin and W. O. Hagstrom, "The Empirical Classification of Formal Groups," 28 *American Sociological Review* (June, 1963), p. 408.

[7] Here, the common need of individuals to find "consensual validation" through group legitimation of their own values is germane, as is the concept of reference groups. Among others, see H. S. Sullivan, *Conceptions of Modern Psychiatry* (New York: Norton and Co., 1953); L. Festinger, "Informal Social Communication," 57 *Psychological Review* (September, 1950), pp. 271-92; R. Merton, *Social Theory and Social Structure* (Glencoe: Free Press, 1957), Chap. 8.

TABLE 6-12 ORGANIZATIONAL INTERACTION

	Chamber Comm. (19)	Country Club (17)	G.E.I. (15)	United Fund (13)
Political leaders (9)	King** Eberhart** Woods** Evans**	King Eberhart Moore** Reeder** Parks Evans	King Eberhart Woods Parks	King Moore Reeder Parks
Economic leaders (14)	Parker** Thomas Prince** Hadwen Sherman Miles Rogers** Williams** Remington** Albright** Dunn Hughes Wilson	Parker Babcock Prince Hadwen Sherman Williams Remington	Parker Thomas Prince Hadwen Sherman Babcock Rogers Williams Remington Albright Dunn	Parker Thomas Prince Babcock Sherman Miles
Specialist leaders (6)	Hollis Livingstone	Wilson Edison Waite		Preston Herman Waite

* Only organizations having nine or more members of the entire
** Denotes participation in two or more decisions.

EDGEWOOD

The greatest concentrated membership occurs in Edgewood's Chamber of Commerce, in which 21 of the 36 leaders are found. More important is the distribution of membership among leaders differentiated as to the type and extent of their power.

AMONG EDGEWOOD ELITE* (36)

Elks (13)	Hosp. Fund Drive (11)	Rotary (11)	School Bd. (10)	Masons (9)
King Eberhart Woods Parks Wells** Reeder Evans	Moore Eberhart Woods Dodd**	King Eberhart Woods	Wells Evans	Moore Eberhart Woods Dodd
Parker Babcock Hadwen Rogers	Remington Thomas Prince Hughes Miles	Remington Thomas Prince Hadwen Sherman Rogers	Albright Dunn	Parker Thomas Williams Hadwen Hughes Miles
Wilson Herman	Livingstone Thompson**	Hanson	Wilson Thompson Hollis Preston Kennedy Johnson	

leadership group are included in this table.

Fully 13 of Edgewood's 14 economic leaders belong to this organization, including all five of the "most powerful" economic leaders. They are joined by four political leaders and two specialists. Two of the four political leaders are active in four decisions, i.e. they are at the top of the power structure, as measured by the decisional instrument. All but one are among the "most powerful" politicos. In effect, this organization is a rallying point for many of the most powerful economic and political leaders.

Ranking second in terms of overlapping memberships is the Country Club, nominally a "social" organization, but one in which a great deal of nonrecreational activity goes on. Here, just under half of all the leaders belong. And once again, many of the same men found in the Chamber of Commerce are members. Seven economic leaders, half of the subgroup, are members here, and all but one of them are also members of the Chamber of Commerce. All are officials in local banks, industry, and publishing, or lawyers associated with such enterprises. Six political leaders also belong, and here again two-thirds of them are also members of the Chamber of Commerce.

The third organization serving as a focal point for many leaders is Greater Edgewood Industries, a special committee formed to bring new industry to the community. Fifteen leaders, just over 40 per cent, belong to this committee, almost three-fourths of whom are economic leaders. The cohesiveness of this group is shown by the fact that all 15 members were active in the new industry decision, and they were the only active participants. Four of the political leaders who belong are also members of the Chamber of Commerce and the Country Club. Among the economic elite, six of the 10 members are also members of *both* the Chamber of Commerce and the Country Club. Of the remaining four men, all are members of one or another of the latter organizations. Similar although less concentrated overlapping is characteristic of the other organizations considered here.

The membership pattern among the political leaders is fully as concentrated as that found among the economic leaders. Four of the most powerful politicos share memberships in four of Edgewood's most important organizations. Two of the most powerful political leaders, King and Eberhart, share memberships in G. E. I., the Chamber of Commerce, and the Country

Club, with eight or more of the economic leaders. Such evidence supports our conclusion that even though economic leaders probably dominate the power structure in Edgewood, there is more cohesion *within the entire elite* than is found in Riverview, as can be seen by comparing Tables 6-12 and 6-13.

In sum, there is a great deal of organizational and social contact among members of the power structure. By this index, the leadership group is highly integrated and homogeneous. This adds to its decisional effectiveness, i.e. its power, in the sense that its members not only share mutual contacts and values, but they have many opportunities to communicate formally and informally about community problems. The social consensus among the most powerful leaders, reflected and reinforced by such joint memberships, makes it possible for them to support decisions with the resources of the banks, industries, occupations, and businesses which they represent. Indeed they have usually been selected for memberships on the basis of demonstrated skill in fund-raising and organization, as well as their status in the community and the resources which they possess or control.[8] Their power rests in their ability to commit such resources to community projects.

RIVERVIEW

As Table 6-13 indicates, members of the Riverview power structure are somewhat less integrated by organizational memberships than their Edgewood counterparts. A smaller proportion of them are represented in the "most joined" organizations, and there is also less overlapping. Within the entire power structure, we do not find to the same extent as in Edgewood a tightly-knit nucleus of the most powerful leaders joined through group ties. Compare, for example, joint memberships in two important organizations, the Chamber of Commerce and the

[8] An example of such co-optation is the fact that a bank official, Anthony Hadwen who (in 1961) had lived in Edgewood only one year, is a member of six of the nine organizations included in Table 6-12.

TABLE 6-13 ORGANIZATIONAL INTERACTION

	Amer. Leg. (15)	Chamber Comm. (14)	Moose (13)	Ind. Dev. Comm. (12)
Political leaders (10)	Riley Wolchak** O'Brian** Thomas Cohen Morrow**	Riley	Riley Wolchak O'Brian Plank Adams Thomas	Adams Wolchak O'Brian
Economic leaders (19)	Armstrong** Rowan Riddell** Rivers** Muller Morton Wheeler	Armstrong Cavenaugh** Riddell Rivers Mason** Forrest Wheeler Rowan Kruger** Clark Muller Morton	Patriarch** Kruger Clark Waters Mason Wheeler King	Armstrong Cavenaugh Porter Waters Mason Forrest King Morton
Specialist leaders (6)	James Gould	James		Baxter**

* Only organizations having eight or more members of the entire
** Denotes participation in two or more decisions.

Industrial Development Committee. Within each of the three elite subgroups, moreover, a somewhat smaller proportion of the leaders participate and have overlapping memberships. This contrast is particularly evident among political leaders. For example, we find that Mayor O'Brian and his powerful lieutenant, Fred Morrow, share memberships in only one organization—the American Legion. In that organization, they are joined by four other marginal political leaders. Mayor O'Brian is also a member in Moose Lodge along with five other marginal politicos. However, in the remaining organizations

AMONG RIVERVIEW ELITE* (35)

Masons (12)	Country Club (11)	Kiwanis (8)	Hospital Bd. (8)	United Fund (8)	Elks (8)
Thomas Cohen Morrow	Riley		Riley Wolchak Plank	Plank Wolchak	Riley Cohen O'Brian Adams
Hunter Cavenaugh Riddell Rivers Muller Forrest King Wheeler	Armstrong Cavenaugh Riddell Rivers Mason Patriarch King Rowan Kruger	Armstrong Rowan Riddell Patriarch Clark Forrest Wheeler	Rivers Cavenaugh	Armstrong Kruger Riddell Patriarch Clark	Mason Forrest King Rowan
James	Fischer	Baxter	Baxter Gould Cullen	Baxter	

leadership group are included in this table.

there is very little overlapping, and the over-all pattern is one of relatively less interaction, compared with that of political leaders in Edgewood.

Among the economic elite, considerably more social and fraternal interaction exists. The Chamber of Commerce, as might be expected, is the major center for this subgroup, including some two-thirds of the entire elite. Six of the seven "most powerful" leaders (active in two or more decisions) are members. Only one marginal *political* leader, a wealthy local mortician, is a co-member. The Country Club is the second most popular organization for the economic elite, nine of whom are members. Of this group, all but two are also members of the Chamber of Commerce. Here again, the same marginal political leader joins them.

When we turn to the Industrial Development Committee, the third most popular organization, we find that eight economic leaders are joined by Mayor O'Brian and two other political leaders, one of whom is among the most powerful leaders. Only three of the economic leaders in this organization were also active in *both* the Chamber and the Country Club. However, all but two of them were active in at least one of these two organizations.

An interesting difference between the two communities is the greater tendency of Riverview leaders to interact through their memberships in fraternal and veteran groups, such as the Moose, Masons, and American Legion. In Edgewood, for example, the Moose Lodge includes only two members of the elite group, whereas in Riverview 13 members belong; similarly with the American Legion. In Riverview, 15 leaders belong; in Edgewood, only six. The only exception is Elks Lodge, which is somewhat more popular in Edgewood.

In sum, there is relatively less interaction through joint organizational memberships among the Riverview elite, compared with that of Edgewood. This conclusion is particularly germane for Riverview political leaders, who despite their relatively strong position in community affairs, do not exhibit an equal amount of group cohesion. Perhaps equally relevant is the separation between economic and political leaders insofar as membership on major "functional" committees is concerned. Although Riverview leaders interact to some extent through social and fraternal clubs, there is relatively little interaction in such organizations as the Chamber of Commerce, Industrial Development Committee, and the United Fund, which in Edgewood were among the most frequent instruments of joint political-economic memberships.

We conclude that two factors may be responsible for these divergencies. First, they may reflect the ideological hiatus between Riverview political leaders who (with the exception of Fred Morrow) have generally a "left" orientation and economic leaders who typically share small-businessman values, including anti-government spending, scarcity economics, and private initiative. While it would be easy to exaggerate this difference, when it is viewed on a comparative basis with Edgewood, the generalization seems accurate. In Edgewood, political leaders tend to share to a greater extent the dominantly conservative business values of their economic counterparts. This difference, which is one of degree, will be demonstrated in Chapter 10.

A second variable that may explain differences in organizational affiliations is social class. Divergent patterns of joint membership in the Chamber of Commerce, United Fund, and the Country Club, for example, probably reflect in part the somewhat greater social class differences between political and economic leaders in the two communities. We saw earlier that although there were some class differences between *economic* leaders in the two communities, the greatest class differences were found to exist between economic and political leaders in Riverview. United Fund, Chamber of Commerce, and Country Club are middle- and upper-middle class types of organizations, membership in which tends to differentiate to a greater extent those in the Riverview power structure, compared with those in Edgewood. In the same context, the greater preference of Riverview leaders of all types for membership in Moose, Elks, Masons, and veterans organizations probably reflects the divergent class structure of the two groups. Such organizations are relatively less prestigeful than those mentioned above; they tend to attract individuals of somewhat lower status than do the United Fund or Country Club type of organization. Such associations between class and group memberships are documented in Chapter 9; for the moment they may be regarded as hypotheses.

Conclusions

In explaining community power structure and the relative capacity of a community to handle its problems effectively, several variables are germane. The social and economic structure of the community provides the framework within which elites necessarily function. This framework may enhance elite potentials or it may reduce them. In addition, the elites themselves may possess different amounts of leadership resources. When Edgewood and Riverview are compared along these dimensions, we find that the former is advantaged in several contexts. In SES terms, its leaders enjoy somewhat higher amounts of education, occupational status, income, and prestige, and this suggests a major reason why they should be more effective in initiating and directing community affairs. In the case of economic leaders in Riverview, however, it seems that apathy and withdrawal also contribute to the comparatively less active role of this group.

Turning to community resources, both human and economic, we find a similar disparity. Social class structure in Riverview is skewed somewhat toward the middle- and lower-class sections of the scale, whereas Edgewood has larger proportions of the community at the upper and middle levels. As Table 6-8 shows, significant differences between selected social indexes occur in Edgewood's favor in seven out of eight cases. From this we conclude that Riverview leaders do not have a comparable reservoir of talented followers to draw upon, and attending differences in their performance rest in part upon this condition.

In terms of economic base and occupational structure, Riverview is again somewhat less fortunate. Although its family income is only about $600 per year less than Edgewood's, and its per capita annual spending for education is slightly higher, it is disadvantaged in several other contexts, especially in the proportion of its citizens who have had some college work. Occupationally, over one-third of Edgewood adults are in professional and managerial statuses, compared with one-fifth in Riverview. Again, as noted earlier, technological change has dealt more harshly with Riverview industries, including railroads and furniture making. Edgewood, too, has suffered important losses, as in the case of its huge oil refinery, but the remaining industries have proved more adaptable to new electronic and defense types of technologies.

Despite community studies which indicate that economic leaders tend to dominate local affairs, we found this to be most true in Edgewood, and, even there, a healthy competition existed between them and political leaders. In Riverview, political leaders controlled most decisions, and applied their skills very effectively in negotiations with higher systems of government which provided most of the financial resources for all but one of the major decisions.

One index of the viability of leadership groups is the extent to which they are integrated through social and organizational relationships. Attending interactions are means of exercising power and influence, and they probably reflect a rough value consensus among the members of an organization. In general, a higher degree of joint memberships and interaction exists among members of the Edgewood power structure. To a greater extent than in Riverview, political and economic leaders are members of the same local organizations, as shown in Tables 6-12 and 6-13. Class differences between leaders in both communities, as well as among them, are reflected in divergent patterns of membership. Elite overlapping in Edgewood is relatively higher in such associations as the Chamber of Commerce, United Fund, and Country Club, each of which tends to differentiate individuals on a class basis. On the other hand, there is a somewhat greater tendency for Riverview leaders to cluster in fraternal and veterans' organizations which are not as strategic for community development, and which characteristically do not attract individuals of equal leadership potential.

7

ELITE POLITICS AND POWER STRUCTURE

In Edgewood, the dominant thrust in community decision-making was shared by political and economic leaders; in Riverview, it came mainly from political leaders. In both communities, however, there was competition between these two groups for a major role in community affairs. In Edgewood, this competition was generally healthy, and occasionally it was vigorous. In Riverview, during the years covered by our study, it often seemed merely rhetorical and unproductive.

We will consider here some aspects of community politics and the social factors that condition political behavior. The role of political leaders in the power structure of Edgewood and Riverview will be analyzed, along with the latent ideological and power conflicts between political and economic leaders. In discussing relationships between political leaders and higher echelons of government, we will show that political office provides a fulcrum for bargaining with economic power. It provides an alternative base of local power and a means of access and mobility. By "mobility," we do not mean a permanent rise from one class status to another, but rather the opportunity to participate directly and temporarily in important decisions, and to derive, again temporarily, the attending psychic gains of publicity, influence, and interaction with prestigeful economic figures.

The degree of stability and continuity of their power is an important factor differentiating political and economic leaders. Following Pareto, we may say that there is more circulation among political elites than among economic ones. Given the vicissitudes of politics, individuals whose power is based on political office tend to be *transient* and to this extent *marginal* members of the power structure. In such cases, politics is less a vocation, to be continued after one leaves office, than an episode in a business or professional career. Unlike big city, state, and national levels, where abundant patronage or personal wealth may enable defeated candidates to run again, political office in smaller communities is more likely to be a one-shot affair. By contrast, economic leaders tend to retain their elite statuses over a long period, since the bases of their power remain undisturbed by the winds of political change. It is true that marginal economic types, often found among the specialists, are transient. However, a characteristic of the "most powerful" economic leaders was their long-established connection with major local industries, banks, and newspapers. Managers of local branches of national industries were more likely to play "leg-man" roles.

An attending condition is the inequity of access characterizing the two elites. Broadly speaking, economic leaders penetrate the local power structure rather easily, while political types find access somewhat difficult. Whereas economic success is often accepted as a legitimate basis for membership, political experience at the local level is less likely to be offered or to be honored as a necessary qualification.[1] Eisenhower's success in

---

[1] Freeman, *et al.*, for example, comparing Syracuse and six other cities, found that 58 per cent of community leaders came from business sources, compared with only 8 per cent from government, *Local Community Leadership*, p. 14-15.

1952 and Romney's in Michigan in 1963 suggest that the state of American politics is such that a candidate's most useful political stratagem is often to insist that he is "above politics" and to base his qualifications on success in some other field. Political leaders may become temporary members of the local power structure, but it seems unlikely that this role will culminate in either long-term service or an extended alliance with economic leaders.

Our major criteria for differentiating "political" leaders are two: formal political office and/or a commonly recognized active professional political role in the community. The political category is not exclusive, since most of the political decision-makers depend upon some other kind of work or business for their livelihood. Only in the case of Riverview's mayor could politics be called a vocation. Yet, there is a widely recognized dichotomy between those who view themselves (and are designated by others) essentially as politicians, and those who regard politics as something that others do. Even when the latter engage in nominally political activities, they rarely define them as "political." They tend to stigmatize as "political" certain types of activities, such as public housing, while activities that are regarded with favor, such as new schools and hospitals, are often honored as nonpartisan "community" activities.

Ambivalence Toward Political Leaders

This ambivalence toward politics and politicians is evident in both communities. It is crystallized by the natural tendency of both groups to use those kinds of resources available to them. Political types turn to governmental kinds of solutions for local problems, which often require help from state and federal governments. In this sense, they are more "cosmopolitan" than economic types who generally prefer private, "voluntary" solutions. Often regarding politics with a certain amount of distaste, the latter believe that people should "do things for themselves" rather than turn to government. When they turn to government, as they frequently do, the situation is defined in community-welfare, "nonpolitical" terms. This attitude is apparent in responses to a question which asked leaders to assume that they wanted to run for local political office and then to name individuals whose support would be critical for their success. In several cases, economic and specialist leaders objected or laughed, saying, "Of course, I'd never run for political office." Some, with an extremely literal cast of mind, refused to answer the question, saying it was not relevant for this reason. Others reported that they avoided "political" issues and participation because they were often controversial and might disrupt long-established commercial alliances. One decision-maker, owner of a store, remarked, "I had a chance to run for office and I turned it down. You can't run in politics if you're in retail business." Another leader, also in the retail trade, stated, "I just can't afford to get into controversial issues in this town."

This attitude toward political office was associated with social class. Those of higher status tended to deprecate "politics." As one powerful decision-maker of middling social status, who had played an active role in local politics, said, "Ordinarily, the very best people in a small community will never run for office because they get batted around." We noted earlier that our "influential" group included several prestigeful individuals who preferred not to display or to test their influence in the political arena. This phenomenon is of course particularly relevant in small communities where the stakes and rewards of political activism are minimal and the issues often mundane.

That such attitudes toward politics both shape and are shaped by reality is shown by Table 7-1 which compares the SES of political and economic leaders in both communities.

We find here that political leaders do in fact have lower socioeconomic statuses. They are more likely than their economic counterparts to have had less education and to earn less money in minor kinds of jobs. We also found them more likely to be salaried employees in small businesses rather than professionals or managerial types in large concerns, to belong to

TABLE 7-1 COMPARATIVE SES OF EDGEWOOD AND RIVERVIEW POLITICAL AND ECONOMIC DECISION-MAKERS, IN PER CENT

Social characteristics	Political (19)	Economic (33)
Education: 16 or more years	32	53
Time in community: over 20 years	84	96
Respondents' occupation, white collar or higher	98	100
Fathers' occupation, white collar or higher	78	81
Income: over $10,000	59	84
Membership in voluntary organizations: 3 or more	84	84
Political affiliation: Republican	58	80

the Democratic party, and to have smaller incomes. Only in organizational memberships and fathers' occupation are they equal. Moreover, the narrow line between the two groups in terms of their own occupational status is really greater than revealed here, because several political leaders have precarious white-collar jobs, such as clerks, assistant supervisors in large corporations, and small, politically appointed jobs in the post office or similar public agencies. The differences would be marked if both their own and their fathers' status were calculated solely in terms of managerial and professional criteria.

The question arises as to social differences between political leaders in the two communities. These data are presented below.

TABLE 7-2 COMPARATIVE SES OF EDGEWOOD AND RIVERVIEW POLITICAL LEADERS, IN PER CENT

Characteristics	Edgewood (9)	Riverview (10)
Education: 16 or more years	44	20
Time in community: over 20 years	90	78
Respondents' occupation, white collar or higher	95	100
Fathers' occupation, white collar or higher	77	80
Income: over $10,000	88	30
Membership in organizations: 3 or more	89	80
Political affiliation: Republican	67	50

Here again, although the differences are not always substantial, Edgewood political leaders enjoy a higher proportion of those social attributes usually regarded as desirable. More of them have university educations, more of them were born in, or have lived in, the community 20 years or longer, they are more fortunate in terms of income, and a higher proportion are Republicans, which as noted earlier, tends to be associated with higher class status. One example of the differences between the two groups is seen in the number of college graduates and lawyers who are active politically in the two communities. Whereas Riverview's political leaders include only two college graduates, Edgewood has four. Similarly, the Riverview group includes only one practicing lawyer, whereas Edgewood politicos include three.

Another index of the ambivalence with which political leaders are regarded is provided by their rankings on the reputational scale. In Edgewood, two of the three most active political decision-makers ranked tenth and fourteenth in this scale, near the very bottom. One of these men was active in four decisions, the other in one decision; both were members of the local power structure as measured by this index. *The other public official, who was actively involved in four decisions, did not receive enough nominations to qualify for the scale.* With only one exception, the remaining six political decision-makers, some of whom were active in two decisions, were similarly excluded. The exception, a young Republican recently elected to local office, was nominated, but since he was active in no decisions and did not enjoy the class status which ensured nomination in the case of other, nonactive leaders, his inclusion seems to have been based upon political visibility rather than upon performance.

In Riverview, the situation was somewhat different. Mayor Ted O'Brian, who was clearly one of the two most powerful leaders, received the most nominations to the reputational scale. However, the other most powerful political leader, Fred

Morrow, ranked near the very bottom of the scale, along with another local political figure who was not active in any decisions. This consensus on O'Brian by a dominantly economic decision-maker group may reflect a relatively greater acceptance of political solutions in Riverview by all members of the power structure. More likely, however, it is a recognition of the mayor's leadership in most of the five major decisions and his obvious devotion to the community. As noted earlier, Fred Morrow's case may be explained in sociometric terms since he was unpopular among many fellow decision-makers, and had been involved in internecine conflicts with fellow Republicans. One other local political figure was also included on the reputational scale, yet participated actively in no decisions. This assessment seems to have been based upon sociometric preferences and his long residence in the community rather than upon objective performance. In sum, with the exception of O'Brian, nominations to the reputational scale seem to support the judgment that the power and effectiveness of political leaders tend to be somewhat underestimated by other community leaders.

The Two Elites: Political and Economic

Despite the lower prestige of political roles compared with economic ones in both communities, it would be wrong to leave the matter here. Prestige is relative. Although economic elites deny prestige to local political figures, our evidence indicates that most ordinary citizens respect local office-holders. For example, one of Edgewood's political decision-makers, who was not among the "most important" leaders in the new industry issue, was nevertheless ranked by the community as the person "best known" to them as a leader in this decision. This condition is partly explained by the tendency of the community to attribute power to men who are *most visible* in community affairs, even though they may actually be marginal, "leg-man" types. However, whether such judgments are the result of inaccurate perceptions of power is not critically important in the immediate context. In other cases, community perceptions were accurate. Mayor King of Edgewood was ranked as the "best known" local figure in the flood control and municipal building decisions, in both of which he clearly played the central role.

For lower status members of the community, political office provides an instrument of mobility, power, and prestige. Such honors may be temporary since they are contingent upon officeholding, but, as seen in Mayor O'Brian's case, they may be enjoyed for several terms. The political route to prestige is critical because those who travel it tend to be excluded from the private world of committees organized by higher status corporation executives, bankers, and their legal aides. Political success compensates for disadvantages of education, ethnicity, and income. Indeed, for several local politicians who had neither the education nor the capital required to compete in the local economic arena, it provided the only avenue to mobility and influence.

Although both potentially and actually, economic influence appeared to be the major base of power in both communities, it was challenged by political influence. A kind of imperfect competition resulted in which two major contenders for influence and power faced each other. In Edgewood, as noted earlier, the resulting struggle seemed generally healthy as each element tried to outdo the other, each marshaling its major kind of resources. In Riverview, with a few notable exceptions, economic leaders were inclined to withdraw from community affairs, with the result that major decisions during the time of our study were dominated by the mayor and the city attorney. In the context of a theory of community politics as a competition among elites, a diluted pluralism results as the two elites struggle for control of local, state, and federal resources and the prestige and personal satisfaction that go to those who get things done. The resulting opportunity for social mobility provided by political office seems healthy in a society that stresses individual opportunity and raising from the ranks as strongly as ours does.

Parenthetically, it should be noted that while specialist leaders also contribute to this competitive milieu, they do not appear to be serious contenders for community power. Despite their interest in community development, they lack the comparable amounts of required social and economic resources as well as the desire to exercise influence over the whole political and decisional spectrum. As noted earlier, with rare exceptions, they are active in only one decision, usually in the areas of health, education, or welfare. Both our reputation and decisional findings document this conclusion.

The role of politics as an alternative base of community power is suggested both by the competitive posture of economic and political leaders and by the patent conflict between Republican and Democratic political ideologies. Since many local issues, such as schools and hospitals, are nominally "nonpartisan," such firmly held beliefs seem in part to reflect party loyalties that have their major source and relevance in state and national politics. One explanation for this posture may lie in the hierarchical linkages characteristic of our political system. Such linkages will become clear in a moment when we consider the crucial roles of majors and city attorneys in both communities and the bases of their power. Their behavior is partly explicable in theoretical terms of anticipatory socialization and reference group values. Local politicians repeat many of the campaign slogans of state and national leaders. They identify with politicians at higher levels; and in some cases they hope to attain similar levels. Their offices contain pictures of themselves with present and former governors, state and national congressmen, often inscribed by the latter in first-name terms of mutual respect and friendship. Such organizational and sentimental identifications help explain the rather incongruous intensity of partisan political values at the local level.

The extent to which such partisan values are strongly held is further suggested by the local elections in Edgewood in 1961. Although local politics had long been defined as nonpartisan, and candidates were not permitted to campaign under major party labels, a young Republican organization put up its own slate against the Democratic "Square-Deal" incumbents and easily won the election. Among the successful group's explanations was the belief that as the incumbents had introduced partisan politics into community government, it wanted to restore the traditional, nonpartisan system. If this rationale seems ingenuous or naïve, it should be remembered that entire states, including California, have until recently been characterized by a similar mythology. As noted earlier, a more convincing explanation was public resentment against Mayor King's forceful handling of the parking lot issue, and to a lesser extent, his leadership in the municipal building decision, which also became somewhat controversial. It also seems that any Democratic administration in Republican Edgewood is bound to live dangerously.

In Riverview, too, shortly after our field work was completed, a Republican revolt against the incumbent Democrats culminated in virtually a clean sweep (only one Democrat retained his post) of city offices. The intensity of feeling generated by the 1961 local election is suggested by the fact that the "lame duck" Democratic council cut the salaries of the three top city officials, the mayor, commissioner of taxation and assessments, and city attorney, in amounts ranging from 30 to 70 per cent. One minor position was abolished. Over $100,000 was cut from a budget of some $600,000 proposed by the several city departments.

Unlike Edgewood, Riverview is characterized by a certain measure of "class" politics. We saw earlier that some respondents mentioned the tension between the evenly divided political and religious forces in the community. Some leaders spoke almost too frequently about the "excellent co-operation" among local ethnic and religious groups. Others referred to certain leaders as "representatives" of such groups. Such individuals, they maintained, were capable of "bringing in" these groups behind one or another of the major decisions. Again, one or two of the alienated reputational leaders cited the large foreign-born element in explaining existing conditions of leadership and participation. Such people, they maintained, did not work hard to better themselves, nor were they interested in a proper education for their children. There is some basis for this belief, both in the class structure of the community and in the attitudes of its citizens. We have seen too that Riverview's power elite is less favored in SES terms than that of Edgewood. Its members have less often possessed the qualities generally associated with leadership. During the decade covered by our research, the most successful members of the economic group in Riverview, with only a few notable exceptions, tended to withdraw from local affairs.

Our data on the socioeconomic-ethnic character of the community support this "class" thesis. During 1950-60, local politics were dominated by a Democratic party which manifested a generally "New Deal" orientation, reflecting strong union elements, a relatively large proportion of Catholics, and a substantial proportion of low-income ethnic groups. Compared with Edgewood, for example, we find a substantially higher proportion of "working class" occupational groups, 30 to 19 per cent. Similarly, fully two-thirds of our Riverview sample falls in social classes IV and V, whereas Edgewood has one-half in these classes. That such demographic variables manifest themselves in differing ideological perspectives will be seen in Chapter 10.

Coalition Strategy and Economic Dominance

Efforts of Mayor O'Brian and the city attorney Morrow to solve Riverview problems support a current hypothesis about community decision-making, namely, that the dominance of local affairs by economic elites has now been eased by the emergence of new professional political types who form coalitions with relevant subgroups in discrete substantive areas in order to fashion policy.[2] What does our research tell us about this hypothesis?

In Riverview, it is clear that Mayor O'Brian used the coalition strategy to a great extent. In his campaigns for new industry, flood control, and the housing authority, he deliberately co-opted representatives from among the city's economic leaders. Among such men were three Republicans engaged in banking, publishing, and commerce. Like most other knowledgeable individuals, the mayor realized that an unproductive split existed between Republican-business and Democratic-labor elements, and that bringing leading members of both sectors into several of his committees was one way to ease its effects.

The mayor was quite explicit about the bases of his use of such coalitions. His guiding principle was to find individuals who regardless of party would "have the welfare of the city at heart." He recognized that related motivations might also be harnessed, since his criteria included the premise that certain individuals, "who would themselves benefit directly from the growth of the city," had greater stakes in participation than others. The mayor's understanding of public opinion and the co-optation of existing resources are apparent in his explanation of the appointment of publisher Kenneth Armstrong to his housing authority committee: "I appointed him in order to prevent his paper from fighting the housing plan." But the mayor gave full credit to Armstrong for his support of the program once he had become a member of the committee. Again, the mayor appointed the conservative local banker, Richard Cavenaugh, to his flood control committee, even though Cavenaugh was opposed in principle to the use of federal funds for such purposes. It appears, then, that the mayor deliberately forced

[2] Among others, see R. Dahl, *Who Governs?* pp. 200-214.

powerful local economic leaders to choose between their political preferences and the pressing developmental needs of the community. By conceptualizing city needs in nonpartisan, civic service terms, he was able to overcome the latent opposition of such leaders.

The extent of the mayor's nonpartisan policy of appointments is further indicated by his selection of Fred Morrow as his city attorney. Although potential Democratic nominees were quite limited (there were only two or three Democratic lawyers in Riverview, and one was disqualified by virtue of being city judge), the mayor might have appointed someone else. Instead, he removed the incumbent who appeared to be ambivalent about the mayor's housing authority plans, and appointed Morrow to the position, mainly because the latter was energetic and had good connections in both Albany and Washington. Whether or not the mayor was influenced by the fact that Morrow was currently at odds with the local Republican organization is moot, but the fact remains that the mayor did not hesitate to cross party lines to make his most important appointment. In this case, his strategy proved most fruitful.

The results of the mayor's coalition strategy are seen in the distribution of participation in the panel of decisions. The Republican publisher was active in four decisions and the older financial expert was active in three decisions. Three other economic leaders, all Republicans, were active in two decisions. It will be recalled that Reverend Baxter was invited by the mayor to become chairman of two relevant committees. (The mayor also included another minister on his housing authority committee, apparently hoping that such men would have a community-wide appeal.)

Insofar as the coalition hypothesis assumes that alliances will be made with representatives of discrete groups who are not themselves members of the local power structure, the preceding examples are not precisely relevant. All these Republicans were members of the "most powerful" decision-making group, i.e. all were active in more than one issue area.

It seems fair to conclude that the critical role in decision-making in Riverview remained in the hands of the mayor and his "renegade" Republican city attorney. In every decision, one or the other provided the initial impetus, and especially in the school, housing, flood control, and hospital decisions which required state and federal resources. The only exception to this generalization is the new industry decision which, once the desire of the entrepreneur to find a new site became known, was carried out entirely by local initiative.[3] The necessary economic resources were provided by local financial leaders, and most respondents specified such leaders as the "most important" individuals involved in the decision, for the very practical reason that without their consent the money needed to bring in the new industry could not have been raised. Their command of this base of power ensured a central role for local bankers and businessmen.

Although the mayor formed coalitions with local business leaders, it seems clear that such alliances were temporary and certainly could not overcome the basic divergencies in economic philosophy and social background that characterized the two elites. As the Republican banker, who had been a member of the mayor's flood control committees, noted, "I was against the flood control program. I just don't believe in taking huge amounts of federal money for such programs."[4] He also stated his misgivings about the new industry venture, saying (in the event, correctly) that it was a "shaky" proposition. Yet, like Byron's Julia, who while protesting she would never consent, consented, he played a leading role in both decisions.

Our analysis reveals, furthermore, that there were very few

[3] In mid-1961, Riverview began the expansion of a local furniture industry; in this instance, about 40 per cent of the $700,000 capital requirement was provided by loans from the New York State agency for industrial development. Moreover, community participation is ensured in such cases by a state requirement that such loans be negotiated through local industrial development committees.

[4] Here again, since the capacity to overcome opposition is a key criterion of power, we have further documentation of the mayor's power.

organizational relationships between the mayor and his lieutenants and the economic leaders with whom he co-operated in the ways outlined above. In terms of overlapping memberships in voluntary organizations and directorships in business and financial establishments, we find that the mayor and his city attorney shared only a single such relationship. The two most powerful men in the community associated in only four cases with other powerful Republican decision-makers through joint memberships or directorships in local organizations. Theirs was a strictly political association.

In terms of *social* relationships, defined as the exchange of home visits, we found similarly that the mayor and his legal aide did not associate with the three top Republican leaders with whom they had formed coalitions. Moreover, the utility of the coalition stratagem in Riverview is challenged by the competition between the mayor and attorney on the one hand and local business elements on the other. At least two of the mayor's programs—housing and new industry—were either opposed or at least not fully consented to by the latter group. In the first decision, opposition was ideological, and in the second it was a matter of competition for initiative and control of the substantive matter involved.

In sum, insofar as Riverview is concerned, it seems that if economic dominance has been characteristic of Riverview in the past, it had during the time of our research been overcome by political leadership exercised by the mayor and city attorney, whose political acumen gave them access to alternative resources from state and federal governments. The weakness of the local Chamber of Commerce and the split between the older, conservative economic leaders and their younger progressive legatees contributed to the virtual monopoly of initiative held by the two political leaders and their allies on the city council, in the labor unions, and among a few small businessmen.

The effectiveness of such coalitions is less clear. As we have seen, the mayor did attempt to enlist the support of economic leaders by bringing them into committees. And certainly, Armstrong's help in the housing issue was decisive. In most instances, however, the initiative remained in the mayor's hands. Insofar as the coalition theory requires political leaders to bring into the decision process representatives of several diverse local interests, its conditions were not met. The same leaders tended to appear in several decisions, and where local capital and legitimation from economic leaders were vital, their support was obviously essential. In the case of specialists, of course, there was more diversity. However, specialists, as noted earlier, are marginal leaders, who are almost all active in only one decision, mainly because of their formal position on a board or committee concerned with a given decision. Their marginality is documented by their failure to be nominated to the reputational scale as "influentials," as well as by their relatively small number in Riverview.

Turning to Edgewood, we find a somewhat different situation. In the first place, it seems fair to conclude that economic leaders are probably somewhat more powerful than their political counterparts. Certainly, there is no sustained competition from a new group of professional politicians whose exceptional skill enables them to build alliances with extra-economic interests in the community. A hiatus exists between political and economic leaders, but it is less on the basis of ideology than on the bases of class and power. Edgewood's politicians tend to share the dominant economic values of the community, but they are small businessmen without the social prestige and educational achievement of their economic colleagues. As noted earlier, Edgewood's small-businessman mayor expressed this view when he said that the "best people" in small communities never run for political office because they have to take too much abuse. Political leaders dominated public decisions such as flood control and the municipal building, but the initiative in the hospital project, new industry, and to some extent in the school bond issue was in the hands of economic leaders, some of whom were on the school board and one of whom, attorney Robert Williams, member of a wealthy and old Edgewood family, was widely cited as the successful leader of the opposition to the first bond issue.

A certain separatism existed between economic and political leaders, as evidenced by the tendency of each group to magnify somewhat its own role in major decisions. But this seems to have been as much the result of a power struggle as a conflict in ideology between the two groups. Insofar as coalitions were concerned, there was little effort by Mayor King to co-opt economic leaders by creating special committees as in Riverview. In none of the major decisions was there close collaboration between economic and political leaders similar to that seen in Riverview in the flood control and housing decisions. Otherwise, politicians dominated governmental decisions, while economic types dominated the hospital and new industry projects. The major role in the school bond issue was shared between economic and specialist leaders.

Mayor King's style of politics was different from that of his Riverview counterpart. He believed in operating through existing formal agencies, such as the city council, planning board, and the numerous commissions in Edgewood local government. Here, it seems, forms of government may be an important variable in the operation of the power structure. King specifically noted that the local commission form of government shaped his thinking in regard to coalitions. He felt that the appointment of outside economic leaders to handle new programs would alienate the officials formally responsible for the areas concerned. "We have so many nonpaid commissioners that they will feel I am undercutting them if I create special committees." Public hearings, he believed, were a better way of securing community opinion. Another explanation, however, is that Mayor King personally found it difficult to bring in economic leaders and the community into public types of decisions. He referred to the municipal building issue (which included an off-street parking facility) when five public meetings were held in which "most of the people there were against the proposal." They believed that merchants should pay for downtown improvements that would enhance the commercial attractiveness of the town. Here, the mayor felt, it was a case of the public not knowing its own best interest. Thus the parking lot decision was made without a referendum; funds were borrowed on a short-term note basis from local banks rather than through a bonding procedure which would have required popular approval.

In sum, the coalition hypothesis is applicable in Riverview, although initiative and control remained in the hands of the mayor and his city attorney. In Edgewood, on the other hand, the mayor preferred other stratagems. The skill, social prestige, and control of financial resources enjoyed by economic leaders enabled them to operate independently and to dominate two and probably three of the major issues. To a much greater extent than in Riverview, political and economic leaders worked independently and shared power almost equally.

The most effective strategy for political leaders in both communities, but particularly in Riverview, was to turn to higher levels of government for the resources necessary to solve local problems and to maintain their own share in community decision-making.

The External Bases of Community Power

Much more important in local political decisions than either partisan dialectics or coalition strategies are the resources that higher level politicians can deliver to local politicians, enabling them to contribute to the community on a scale far beyond what its own resources permit. In the process, their own positions vis-à-vis economic leaders are reinforced. Such prizes are perhaps especially crucial for small communities such as Edgewood and Riverview. Although this generalization applies to both, the two communities show an interesting contrast. In Edgewood, which has a tradition of wealth and philanthropy, several local projects such as the library, the hospital, and several small new industries are the products of private largesse and private effort. In Riverview, on the other hand, the absence of a philanthropic tradition means that the community must depend almost exclusively upon government for the resources it needs. Political relationships with higher level officials thus have a much more strategic function in Riverview. In such circumstances, political values and stratagems become, as Mr. Dooley said, more than "beanbag." They become the major instruments of access to the local power structure, and of community survival.

Such differences in the orientations of the two communities regarding "self-help" versus "outside" governmental aid are suggested by the editorial policies of their daily newspapers. The Edgewood paper has no editorial page. Its front page is devoted exclusively to national and foreign affairs. The news columns are confined mainly to state, national, and international affairs, and local events are often buried in the middle of the paper. In Riverview, on the other hand, local news is sometimes featured, and editorials frequently center on community affairs or on the immediate relevance of certain state and federal policies and programs for the city. Local and regional planning, federal flood control and urban redevelopment programs, state aid for sewage treatment facilities, and the availability of state aid for local industrial development were among the editorials appearing during a three-month period in 1962. In each case, the paper emphasized the importance of the proposals for the community and urged its members to inform their legislative representatives and responsible officials of their interest and support. Insofar as the daily press represents community opinion, we may conclude that Riverview has a much more positive attitude than Edgewood regarding the use of governmental solutions to community problems.

RIVERVIEW

Riverview's experience is particularly germane since four of its five decisions involved external resources allocated mainly on a political basis by state and national governments. Two of them —flood control and public housing—were almost completely so.[5] In the school issue, *state* officials (inspired by Mayor O'Brian) provided the initial impetus by a warning to the local school board that the city would fail to qualify for considerable state building aid if it did not act expeditiously. The hospital program required state enabling legislation, plus $467,333 of federal Hill-Burton funds, approximately one-third of the total estimated cost of the new hospital.

In each of these cases, the mayor and city attorney used their political skill and connections to secure resources from state and federal agencies. One might say that the only *local* resources they possessed were the electoral organization and support required to keep the mayor in office, the legal training and energy of the city attorney, and the obvious need of the community for the programs they sponsored. In effect, and similar to national legislators vis-à-vis their local constituencies, their local influence was largely based upon external sources of power; for they functioned essentially as brokers between these sources and the local community. Their specialized local political roles, moreover, enabled them to monopolize access and negotiation in these areas. This condition reflects the unbroken web existing among the different levels of our political system, and emphasizes a notable characteristic whereby the power manifested at one level often emanates from another. However, it seems that regardless of its ultimate source, if it is to anchor its holder into the local power structure, such power must pay off in concrete benefits at the community level.

The raw materials which made local political rhetoric mean-

[5] In the sense that the initial impetus and the major financial resources came from outside, the new industry decision provides a similar example in the private sphere.

ingful in Riverview were the resources allocated by higher levels of politics and government. The political alliances of its political leaders gave them access to the most strategic offices in the state and national government. The mayor's connections with Democratic Governor Averell Harriman (and his ability to deliver Democratic majorities in state and national elections) were in good part responsible for a fine new bridge and roadways in the city which helped solve a serious traffic problem in the downtown area. In the school board decision, O'Brian went to New York City to consult with the head of the state school districts' agency and urged him to put pressure on the Riverview school board and superintendent of schools to "move faster" on the building program. As a result, the mayor indicated, "He called Superintendent X while I was in his office."

City attorney Morrow was also effective with the governor. He wrote the bill which provided Riverview with the only hospital authority in New York and guided its passage through the state legislature. As noted earlier, his meeting with Governor Harriman provided the breakthrough in the city's long campaign to secure adequate hospital facilities. His work was consummated in May 1963, when Riverview's magnificent new 56-bed hospital was dedicated. Similarly, Morrow and O'Brian worked effectively with state and federal officials to secure the flood control and housing authority programs.

The hospital decision reveals clearly the extent to which Riverview and other small communities are dependent upon outside resources in meeting their local needs. The state legislature had to provide special legislation and the governor had to throw his support behind the project before Morrow could act. Federal Hill-Burton funds had to be available from a generous Congress. The numerous standards of the Public Health Service had to be followed in order that the community qualify for the grant. The original plan for a hospital of 70 beds had to be revised for one of 56 beds to meet the "recommendations" of state and federal planning agencies, which were based on the estimates of future health care needs and existing hospital beds in Sussex County. Such dependence, moreover, was not limited to public governments. In order to raise its share of the building costs, Riverview had to enlist the help of a financial house in nearby Buffalo City. This institution would not provide the necessary funds until several conditions were met. One condition was the use of an outside management consultant firm to improve the administration of the existing hospital. Another was that certain surveys be made, some of which were quite expensive. In such ways, the initiative and autonomy of local leaders were conditioned by policies determined at other points in the state and nation.

The *quid pro quo* for state and federal grants was the political support which the mayor was able to provide the Democratic ticket in state elections. In 1958 and 1960, for example, when most upstate and western areas of New York were Republican, Riverview was faithful to Harriman and Kennedy. In the 1958 gubernatorial election, despite his overwhelming defeat by fellow-millionaire Nelson Rockefeller, Harriman carried the city by 139 votes. The Liberal party, which gave Harriman a total of 147 votes, also contributed to his victory.

In the 1960 presidential election, this small Democratic enclave in a sea of upstate Republicanism gave John F. Kennedy a plurality of 532 votes out of some 4000. Meanwhile, surrounding Sussex County was giving the Nixon-Lodge ticket a plurality of almost 7000 of a total county vote of 21,749. Contrary to popular (and often valid) assumptions about the requisites of personal political power (i.e. legal skill, extended education, business success, wealth, etc.) the mayor's power rested almost exclusively upon his ability to deliver such pluralities and upon his alliances with powerful men at higher levels of government, plus, of course, the ability to be elected mayor for five straight terms.

In the city attorney's case, legal expertise was a critical source of his power, but no more so than his knowledge of state and federal politics and politicians. The political origin of most Riverview resources made such skills essential. In the housing authority decision, Morrow went to New York City to negotiate with the state public housing director. This meeting was followed by a state survey of Riverview's needs, and a recommendation to Albany for favorable action. In the hospital decision, as we have seen, Morrow personally urged Governor Harriman to find a way to help the community replace its obsolete hospital; a prerequisite was new legislation permitting the community and surrounding towns to form a special hospital authority. Morrow wrote this legislation and helped push it through the state legislature. Again, in the flood control project, Morrow's active role as a National Guard Colonel was often cited by respondents as a factor in negotiations leading to Army Corps of Engineers' approval. His Guard status, it was felt, gave him access to the Engineers, upon whose recommendation Congress acts in such projects. We have already noted that he prepared a dramatic report in 1956 on the city's need for flood control.

Similarly, although the project was not included among our five decisions, Morrow and O'Brian also influenced a state decision to provide, at a cost of $350,000 a new highway access to the huge state park which lies south of Riverview. Since the city benefits economically from the tourists who use the park during the year, this project was of direct local concern. Securing this appropriation was no mean feat, since it had been cut out at the committee stage, and a direct personal appeal from O'Brian to Harriman at a conference in Albany was required to reinstate the appropriation. Morrow, meanwhile, wrote to the governor's secretary outlining in painful detail the traffic congestion at a 1956 ski meet, when some 10,000 spectators resented the considerable delay caused by the inadequate roads to and from the park. These representations resulted in a generous appropriation.

Unlike the case in Edgewood, the political acumen and connections of the two city officials were recognized by other leaders, as the following evidence indicates. In response to the question, "If a decision were to be made in Albany affecting this community, who would be the best contact man to get in touch with state officials, not including local members of the legislature?" Morrow ranked at the top with 13 nominations, while O'Brian was second with 11. The individual ranking third received only five nominations. On a similar question relating to Washington, D.C., Morrow ranked at the top with 13 nominations; the mayor was again second, but with only six nominations. It is interesting to consider why Morrow would rank so low on the reputational scale, yet be so accurately perceived in this political context, since both instruments seem to measure rather similar attributes. Certainly, the link between his state and federal influence and concrete local benefits seems obvious enough. We can only assume that the personal and political preferences of other leaders influenced their choices.

EDGEWOOD

On the basis of the five decisions, it can be said that Edgewood's leaders relied less upon state and federal echelons of government as a basis for their local power. However, although the rhetoric of local autonomy is strong, the community exhibits considerable dependence upon higher sources of government. This situation is similar to that found by Vidich and Bensman in Springdale.[6] In return for their subsidies, state and federal agencies demand certain building standards and modes of operation that undercut the discretion of local leaders. Even though Edgewood's economic leaders minimized this facet of modern political reality for the small community, they were often obliged to work within the broad framework of policies determined in Albany and Washington.

The major example of political largesse at the state level was

[6] *Small Town and Mass Society* (Princeton: Princeton University Press, 1961).

the school decision where 60 per cent of the funds were provided by the state. Federal grants included the flood control project, for which Congress appropriated $350,000 in July 1955. Here, Mayor King, his predecessor, and village attorney Clinton Woods carried on negotiations with the Corps of Engineers and local Congressmen. As Woods noted, "The mayor and I, over the sometimes strenuous opposition of the [village] board, went directly to Washington and got the funds. Senator Lehman was our greatest help."[7] Two Republican leaders believed that Representative Dan Reed, "a man of exceptional ability," had also provided vital help.

The critical role that strategically placed leaders play in public decisions is indicated by the attorney's reply to a question which asked, "Who were the two or three most influential people in this decision?" Mayor King, he said, had been the main force. This was followed by the question, "Do you think the outcome would have been different if he (they) had not participated?" Woods replied, "Oh, yes, it was his tenacity in the face of the [board's] opposition that made it possible." Note here that the mayor was able to override the frustration-born opposition of his local council. Such questions differentiate leaders in terms of their relative influence in a given decision, as well as their relative power in the community.

The other Edgewood decision involving outside governmental aid was the new hospital. Approximately one-third of the hospital building fund was supplied by the federal government. Yet, leaders invariably conceptualized the decision as a private venture, depending upon local, voluntary contributions. Only three of the 15 leaders directly involved in this decision even mentioned the federal grant, which must have provided a major stimulus to the initial decision to build a new hospital, and

[7] The nature of this "opposition" must be specified. Follow-up interviews in mid-1963 revealed that the board's opposition was not to the principle of securing a flood control program, but rather to the continuation of the mayor's efforts which were not only expensive, but seemed futile in view of the community's long but unsuccessful attempts to secure help.

without which the community probably could not have carried out the project.

Similarly, even though the hospital is a unit of local government, it is regarded by its board as a personal undertaking.[8] The privatization of public office is, of course, a common political phenomenon. Despite the penetration of state and federal agencies into almost every local area, and such concrete benefits as flood control, school subsidies, the Hill-Burton hospital grant, and power from the New York State Power Authority, the psychology of Edgewood's most powerful leaders remains essentially private. Even when the fruits of governmentally financed projects are accepted, they are usually regarded by economic leaders as a violation of principle, often rationalized on grounds of practicality. Thus when one extremely active and conservative economic leader was questioned about his endorsement of the proposal that the community become part of the New York State Power Authority system, he replied, "We would have been damn fools not to accept the offer from the power authority."

Another example of the essentially "private" orientation of Edgewood's leaders, as well as of the competition between economic and political elites, is seen in the make-up of its industrial development committee. During its first year the committee included two political decision-makers, the Democratic mayor and a Democratic town supervisor. But, as a powerful economic leader said, "I found that politics just doesn't mix in these things, so I personally asked them to get off, and they weren't re-elected the second year."

This "private" orientation deserves further comment because it touches upon the pluralist assumption that major community decisions often involve formal political processes. In Edgewood, the two "private" issues, bringing in a new industry and building a new hospital, were among the most important decisions made

[8] This orientation toward the hospital is developed more fully in Chapter 11.

by the community during the past decade. Although the new industry issue was not highly ranked among the five critical issues, 77 per cent of the community leaders placed the hospital issue at the top of the list. This issue was similarly ranked at the top by the community rank and file. Although these decisions were less "centralized" than the flood control and municipal building decisions, our research indicates that both were initiated and pushed through by a small number of community leaders.

As noted earlier, impetus for the new industry came from an entrepreneur who had once lived in Edgewood and wanted to return, providing the community would give him a grant of land, a building, and a $100,000 loan! His major contact in Edgewood was the president of a local bank, a recent arrival who had previously worked in the nearby town where the entrepreneur had his major plant. These men contacted Edgewood's industrial development committee, which in turn enlisted local bankers and business leaders who gave their personal and official support to the venture. After the leading banks underwrote 10 per cent of the total loan, bonds in $500 denominations were made available for individual purchase.

After these events, a public meeting was held at which about 10 of the decision-makers explained the project to a group of some 35 local citizens. A little later, the industrial development committee chairman, who also owns the local paper, was able to announce that the bond issue had been fully subscribed. This expeditious venture symbolizes the lively character of Edgewood's leaders. By any standard, these economic leaders and their legal aides are highly competent, enterprising men. They are clearly motivated by a sense of civic pride and responsibility. In the immediate context, their behavior indicates that vital community decisions do not always require formal political ratification which might ensure a decisional process more in line with pluralist norms.

It was noted earlier that local government was involved in

the new industry decision since the land and buildings for the new plant were jointly owned by the town and the village of Edgewood. The properties involved had been given to the community by the refinery that had closed its doors in 1957. Legally, the local governments were obliged to "sell" these properties; this was done for a token price, set by the village council which owned the section of the industrial area in which the facilities were located. This action raises the question of the importance of the council members in the community power structure. Should all its members automatically be defined as decision-makers? Or was their participation a mere formality? Logical arguments supporting either interpretation can be made.

Legally speaking, formal action by the town and village councils was required before the proposed transfer of the properties could occur. Practically, however, there was little question about their decision: the town and village were urgently seeking industry. The competition among small towns and cities for new industry was exceedingly keen; concessions of this kind were the rule among small communities. The council had inherited a huge, vacant industrial area. The tax revenues lost by the refinery's departure in 1957 needed to be replaced. Moreover, the council members were competing with local economic leaders to demonstrate *their* initiative and concern for industrial development. They wanted to participate and their legal responsibility for transfer of the property provided a necessary instrument. Given such considerations, it seems valid to regard the council's action as ministerial. When the alternatives to a given course of action are so limited, it seems incorrect to accept the action as an indication of power.

The essentially "private" character of this decision is indicated by the fact that only six of the 14 active participants were public officials, and half of these were marginal participants. Among those centrally involved, one was a member of the town council, one was the mayor of the village, and the other was the village attorney. A majority of participants were businessmen and their legal aides. Eight (three of whom are lawyers) of the 14 decision-makers fall in this latter category. It should be noted, however, that this dichotomy between "public officials" and "businessmen-lawyers" is to some extent artificial since the six "public officials," four of whom are small businessmen and the other two lawyers, share many of the politico-economic values of the economic leaders.

However, between public officials and the majority of decision-makers there existed one important cause of tension—political party. Three of the six public officials involved were members of the Democratic party, while all the business-legal participants were Republicans. This ideological split became evident in a kind of competition between members of each coalition to demonstrate the superiority of their group's contributions. Members of each party tended to nominate their own brethren as "decision-makers" and "influentials," while neglecting those of the opposite party who may have been equally active. As noted earlier, this led to the anomaly in Edgewood of an extremely active decision-maker (as determined by the decisional method), attorney Clinton Woods, failing to receive enough nominations to qualify as an influential.

Despite Edgewood's preference for private sources of funds, its philosophy of self-reliance, and the strength of its economic leaders, local politicians played important roles in some essentially "private" decisions. Mayor King, for example, described at length his administration's part in attracting the new industry. The refining properties, it will be recalled, were deeded to local government by the oil company. As a result, the village and town boards were necessarily involved in negotiations for the new industry. As the mayor put it, "We stuck out our necks a bit and sold the building for $500." He then outlined the expeditious way in which the $100,000 bond issue had been subscribed to: "You can see we haven't had to tap any of the smaller sources yet to raise this money." Despite the mayor's collaborative "we," however, it was clear to us from direct observation that the fund-raising campaign was designed and monopolized by local economic leaders in legal, banking, and publishing fields.

Liaisons between local and state politicians are again seen in a decision to install a new parking lot in downtown Edgewood. Despite some local opposition, Mayor King worked vigorously for the parking addition, which cost about $100,000. The mayor financed the program from village funds. Since such projects usually require a bond issue election, the mayor consulted the State Attorney General, who reputedly said to the mayor and his council, "Don't pass your decisions on to the people. If you have to do that, get out of office!" The Attorney General explained further that he believed the decision was within the prerogative of the board, and that, in his opinion, to ask the people in the community to pass on it would be shirking their duty. However, another participant said of this issue, "We tried to railroad it through. We knew damn well if we held a referendum we would be voted down on it."

This rationale and the decision which it honored have interesting implications for pluralism, including again the assumption that important *governmental* decisions are usually amenable to popular influence through local elections. In this case, no election occurred, and decisive state influence took the form of legal expertise and psychological reinforcement for aggressive local action. At the same time, however, the mayor's somewhat arbitrary behavior became an important factor in his subsequent defeat and the replacement in 1960 of his "Square Deal" administration by a group of young Republicans. In this situation, the avoidance of the bond referendum may have provided the impetus for a reaffirmation of public control, expressed through the electoral process. However, although the mayor is gone, the parking lot and the indebtedness remain.

The general community's perceptions of leadership differ from those of leaders. For example, Mayor King's role in the flood control and municipal building decisions was widely recognized by those in our community sample. Insofar as the perceptions of the *leaders* themselves are concerned, however, we have seen that none of Edgewood's political leaders was highly ranked on the reputational scale, and that one of them, active in four decisions, was not even nominated to the scale. Corroborative data is provided by responses to our question on political liaison between Edgewood, Albany, and Washington, D.C. With respect to Albany, Mayor King, the most likely candidate of the three most powerful political leaders, received only a single nomination! However, the Democratic town supervisor ranked second with nine nominations. The village attorney received only one nomination. The strength of Republican political values in Edgewood is suggested by the fact that the most highly nominated individual was a former Republican state legislator who was not active in any major community decisions.

In connection with political liaison with Washington, the mayor received only three out of 23 nominations, which indicates a somewhat greater inclination to recognize his influence, but still underrates considerably his relative influence. The village attorney received four nominations, which is again a patent underestimation. The third of the most active Democratic political officials received no nominations. However, this is less incongruous since his main activity was at the county and state levels.

Politics as an Instrument of Mobility

It is well known that in the United States politics has often provided a means of social and economic mobility for members of marginal ethnic and religious groups. This latent function of politics is nicely illustrated in Riverview in the case of Mayor O'Brian. The conditions of his success include the tendency of Riverview's economic leaders to withdraw from active participation, and the relatively limited economic resources of the community. Nevertheless, the case is clear. As indicated earlier, the mayor's tangible assets included only his sincere devotion to Riverview, the political acumen that enabled him to retain office for a decade, and his personal connections with high-ranking Democrats at state and federal levels. Neither in terms of education, business experience, professional success, nor income did he possess the common attributes of political influence, except insofar as his Irish-Catholic background may have provided the basis for political effectiveness in a community in which roughly half of the citizens shared these characteristics.

In the specific context of Riverview affairs, politics also provided an avenue of mobility for city attorney Morrow, not in terms of social status, because he was a secure member of the upper-middle class, but rather in the sense that local political office provided an access to state and federal leaders. Such access not only reinforced his local influence, but gave him considerable personal satisfaction in the knowledge that he was also making his will felt in community affairs. Since economic leadership in Riverview, with the notable exception of newspaper editor, Kenneth Armstrong, was relatively moribund, a local alliance with the Democratic mayor was the most effective way that Republican Morrow could use his legal talent as well as his state and federal military *cum* political associations in the community's interest. In effect, the dominantly legal and political nature of Riverview's major decisions provided a natural environment for a lawyer with these skills and connections.

The utility of politics as an instrument of mobility and access to the local power structure was less pronounced in Edgewood where economic groups not only enjoyed disproportionate resources, but were also strongly committed to participation. As noted earlier, nine of Edgewood's 36 leaders were political types, most of whom were active in one or more of the five major decisions, but were mainly concerned, as might be expected, with governmental decisions such as flood control and the building of a new community center. They were generally of lower SES than economic leaders. Nevertheless, two, and perhaps three, of them illustrate the mobility generalization. In two cases, their leadership in some decisions and the participation necessitated by their official status (e.g. the new industry decision required deeding over public property to the incoming entrepreneur) projected them into the local power structure. Such participation gave them a place in the sun. Not only was Mayor King cited as being vitally concerned with the flood control and community building projects, but despite reluctance by some members of the leader group to include him, he was included, albeit in the lowest quartile, in the reputational scale. Another political figure, active in two decisions, was similarly included, although at the very bottom of the scale. The remaining member of the political trio who was nominated to the reputational list was not a decision-maker, but was apparently included by virtue of his political ability and activity. He, too, could not have penetrated the local power elite on any other basis. Neither in terms of income, education, long residence, formal status, nor social prestige, did he possess the required characteristics.

The difference between the two communities in terms of the efficacy of political roles as a means of mobility and access is suggested by the fact that twice as many political types (who were also decision-makers) were nominated as influentials in Riverview as in Edgewood.

Conclusions

In this chapter the characteristics and behavior of political leaders have been analyzed. We found that political leaders were generally regarded with some ambivalence by their economic colleagues, and that there was, particularly in Edgewood, a tendency among other leaders to underestimate their power in local decisions. Within the community at large, however, political leaders were regarded as the most powerful participants in several decisions. We assume this is because they are more visible than other types of leaders and have lived in the community longer. In both communities, political leaders ranked somewhat lower on the class scale than economic leaders. They were disadvantaged in point of education, occupational status, level of fathers' occupation, and income. At the time of our study, they tended to be fairly evenly divided between the major parties, even in Edgewood which is overwhelmingly Republican. Here political leaders enjoyed somewhat higher class status than those in Riverview, although the differences were not nearly as great as those found between political and economic leaders as a whole.

In both communities, tension and competition existed between political and economic elites. In Edgewood, this posture seemed generally functional, resulting in more participation within the leadership group. In Riverview, on the other hand, such competition often seemed dysfunctional, mainly because it culminated in dissention, and a withdrawal from community affairs by several men who could otherwise have contributed a good deal to the solution of the community's problems. This result was aggravated by the existence of a split between the economic "old and new guard."[9] In both communities, politics and political office seemed to provide a means of mobility for some members of the community. In several cases, it provided the *only* means of access to the local power elite for men whose education, occupation, and ethno-religious characteristics would otherwise have disqualified them.

Political leaders in both communities, but especially in Riverview, relied upon connections with politicians at the state and

---

[9] This internecine conflict within the economic elite contrasts interestingly with the cohesion found among members of the Edgewood economic group. On the one hand, this condition signalizes pluralism within the power structure; on the other, it suggests that cohesive elites are more effective.

federal level for the major resources that solidified their power at the local level. In Riverview, the major *quid pro quo* was the ability of the mayor to deliver Democratic majorities in a dominantly Republican county. Although such liaisons brought both communities important grants for health, education, housing, and flood control, they also undercut their autonomy. In return for state and federal largesse, as well as for financial aid from private sources, local governments were obliged to meet various standards and conditions imposed from the outside. In effect, the initiation and control of local decisions was to a considerable extent shared with external sources of power. In Riverview, this phenomenon was patently recognized, while in Edgewood the rhetoric of local autonomy remained somewhat more viable. Nevertheless the dependence of both communities upon external governments was a major condition of decision-making in almost all of the areas analyzed.

8

PLURALISM: AN EMPIRICAL TEST

The viability of political pluralism in Edgewood and Riverview, measured in terms of community participation in ten major decisions, is our next concern.[1] Pluralism was defined earlier as a political system in which the power of government is broadly shared with a plethora of private groups. Writing some four decades ago, the Beards said: "The tendency of Americans to unite with their fellows for varied purposes—a tendency noted a hundred years earlier by de Tocqueville—now became a general mania. . . . It was a rare American who was not a member of four or five societies."[2] This generalization has been accepted wholeheartedly by most political scientists. Multiple membership is assumed to be the mode, and great advantages for the stability of our political system are attributed to this phenomenon.[3]

During the 1930's, however, Komarovsky surveyed some

[1] Obviously, "pluralism" is an extremely complex matter, and this chapter deals with only one set of its hypotheses, however crucial.
[2] C. and M. Beard, *The Rise of American Civilization*, vol. 2 (New York: Macmillan, 1927), pp. 730-31.
[3] D. Truman, *The Governmental Process* (New York: A. Knopf, 1953), pp. 508-16.

239

2200 citizens of New York City and found that 60 per cent of working-class members and 50 per cent of white-collar workers belonged to *no* organizations, with the possible exception of church membership which she did not define as an organized group affiliation.[4] Multiple membership was characteristic only of business and professional men, who were a minority of the community. She concluded that "the majority of citizens remain completely outside the stream of organized social life."[5] A 1958 survey concluded similarly that "voluntary association membership is not a major characteristic of Americans. Nearly half of the families (47 per cent) and almost two-thirds of the respondents (64 per cent) belong to no voluntary associations. . . . These findings hardly warrant the assumption that Americans are a nation of joiners."[6]

Since these data are from metropolitan areas or from national surveys, differences between more and less urbanized areas are obscured. However, when such differences are checked for "other urbanized counties," which include communities of the size of Edgewood and Riverview, the differences prove to be very small. For example, whereas 42 per cent of families in urban areas in metropolitan counties belong to no organizations, the comparable figure for those in urban areas in "other urbanized counties" is 46 per cent.[7]

These findings suggest that organized groups may be both prolific and active, but they do not necessarily engage a majority of citizens. Yet, pluralist theory offers an image of a far-reaching and pervasive bargaining among groups and individuals as a foremost characteristic of our political system.

[4] "Group Membership among Urban Dwellers," 11 *American Sociological Review* (December, 1946), p. 687; on the rationale for excluding religious organizations as voluntary organizations, see G. Lenski, *The Religious Factor* (New York: Doubleday and Co., 1961), pp. 17-19.

[5] Komarovsky, *op. cit.*, p. 698.

[6] C. R. Wright and H. H. Hyman, "Voluntary Association Memberships of American Adults," 23 *American Sociological Review* (June, 1958), p. 286. This study was based mainly upon national survey data of 1953.

[7] *Ibid.*, p. 290. Only when one turns to rural farm residents are membership rates substantially lower.

Obviously, pluralism is an extremely complex phenomenon, about which reasonable men may differ. However, if it is to be more than a normative preference, mere "mind stuff," it must be made amenable to operational definition and systematic inquiry. We cannot merely assume its existence, nor argue abstractly that the electorate and groups in the political system exercise their influence in mysterious ways beyond demonstration.

According to pluralist theory, voluntary groups play a critical role in a democratic system. Linchpins between government and the individual in a complex society, they become the most important means of direct access to those with political power. In the sense that they help shape public policy they are parapolitical. By hammering out a consensus among their members, which then becomes part of the raw material from which political parties manufacture their policies, they become part of the political system. Such groups ensure that their interests are articulated before political leaders and the bureaucracy by delegating to their elites a monopoly of organizational control. These elites may be regarded as political and economic brokers, some of whose products are bought by government, while others are rejected. Successful brokers and groups are those who maintain a favorable balance of value payments.

But more than mere self-interest is involved. On its side, government needs help in ordering the congeries of attitudes and interests existing in a vast and heterogeneous society. Groups share this task with political parties. Such contributions are augmented by the ideological justification that the competition among them prevents dangerous clots of power by spreading wide the net of participation.

In sum, voluntary organizations are essential instruments of pluralism because they make possible citizen influence on government. Group elites, speaking for their members, make pluralism viable by contributing to the shaping of public policy. Pluralism honors both functional necessity and normative preference.

This group hypothesis will be tested here by an analysis of

political behavior in Edgewood and Riverview. As noted in Chapter 2, three criteria will be used to test pluralism: the extent of individual *participation* in our panel of community decisions; widespread *membership* in politically relevant voluntary groups; and *direct participation* by such groups in these decisions. Obviously, a critical question is the meaning of "widespread." Following democratic tradition, one might define it roughly in terms of *majority*. For democratic government is majority government, plus a decent respect for the opinions and rights of minorities. Yet, this is obviously too demanding a standard. We know that participation in local elections rarely rises above 50 per cent, and that, at any level, only about one-third of respondents say that they are seriously concerned with politics or feel that they can make their will felt in political affairs.[8] We would not therefore expect a very large proportion of our sample of community adults to participate individually in vital decisions. However, if pluralist theory is accurate, a substantial proportion should be members of politically relevant voluntary groups; and organizations *qua* organizations should play a lively part in most of the decisions. It should be informative to determine precisely the proportion of the community belonging to such groups, and participating to some extent in the major decisions that affect them.

Such a test required some bench-marks for "pluralism." *Here, the best solution seems to be to conceptualize pluralism as a continuum, along which each of the major decisions can be ranged as being "more" or "less" pluralistic.* In this way we can compare the communities in terms of their relative position on a scale of participation or pluralism. We can begin the task of

[8] Among others, see P. F. Lazarsfeld, *et al.*, *The People's Choice* (New York: Columbia University Press, 1948); A. Campbell, *The Voter Decides* (Evanston: Row, Peterson, 1954); R. Dahl, *Who Governs?*; A. Campbell, *et al.*, *The American Voter* (New York: John Wiley and Sons, 1960); S. M. Lipset, *Political Man* (New York: Doubleday and Co., 1960); and V. O. Key, *Public Opinion and American Democracy* (New York: A. Knopf Inc., 1961).

differentiating issues according to the rates of participation they typically evoke in communities with similar demographic characteristics. In this context, the "absolute" level of pluralism is less important than its relative dimensions in the two communities.

In considering levels of participation, it is not necessary to consider the limitations prescribed by the internal structure of groups. Even if groups are oligarchic, one may still argue that their elites represent the true interest of their members and provide an effective medium for expressing their will.[9] Like politicians, they play a representative role in the public sector of government. One can sensibly argue that in a mass society the demands of organization, time, and knowledge inevitably exclude most individuals from an active role. Because of this condition, pluralism often rests its case on the fact that competition exists among such groups and between them and public government. Thus, to meet the group participation criterion, one need only show that organizations *qua* organizations are active in our panel of decisions, and that some substantial proportion of citizens belong to them.

We will attempt to test both this criterion and the more demanding standard that some direct *individual* participation is required, to determine the point at which a decision falls on the pluralist continuum. As noted earlier, several types of political participation are available to individuals whether or not they are members of organizations. Moreover, individual participation is a direct measure, while group participation can only be inferred from organizational membership. Voting, for example, provided a means of direct personal participation in

[9] While some observers may find debatable the proposition that conflict and bargaining among oligarchically run voluntary groups culminate in pluralist democracy, it is a basic tenet of contemporary pluralism. Among others, see S. M. Lipset, M. Trow, and J. Coleman, *Union Democracy* (New York: Doubleday, 1962), p. 461; F. Neumann, "Approaches to the Study of Political Power," 65 *Political Science Quarterly* (June, 1950), pp. 161-80; D. Truman, *op. cit.*, pp. 503-24.

six of our ten decisions. Our remaining indicators include membership on boards or committees concerned with one or another of the ten decisions; attending public meetings regarding a proposed decision; discussing a decision with a friend or neighbor; and contributing time or money.

These criteria are not strictly comparable. In most cases, committee or board membership is a highly restricted type of participation, limited to members of the power structure. In most decisions, only 10 to 20 individuals could possibly be active in this way. However, the remaining media are freeways of participation; attending a meeting, discussing a decision with friends, contributing money, and voting are open to all interested citizens. In sum, while all these media of participation are not available in each of our ten decisions, and while committee membership is an especially demanding criterion, the others seem to provide a fair test of the pluralist hypothesis. Similarly, if (as pluralism holds) individuals today must usually make their will felt through alliances with others of similar interest, membership in voluntary organizations is often a necessary condition of participation. We turn first to this question.

Membership in Voluntary Organizations

In order to summarize our findings, Table 8-1 presents comparative membership rates for several kinds of organizations.

Social organizations, which attract the highest proportion of members, are dominated by fraternal associations such as the Elks, Masons, and Moose. Riverview has a significantly larger proportion of its members in such lower-middle-class organizations. As we have seen, such memberships are also characteristic of her leadership group; a fact which again suggests the different class structures of the two communities.

Regarding service organizations, we find a significant difference in the proportion of respondents active in each community. In Edgewood, 39 per cent of the community sample belongs to one or more service organizations; in Riverview, only 30 per cent do. Among the various types of service organizations, a significant difference exists in terms of PTA membership in Riverview. Riverview's advantage is probably explained by her large Catholic PTA organization. Service club memberships are especially important because they have a "community-welfare" orientation.

TABLE 8-1 COMPARATIVE VOLUNTARY GROUP MEMBERSHIP IN EDGEWOOD AND RIVERVIEW

Type of organization	Proportion belonging* Edgewood	Riverview
Social	42 (253)	43 (355)
Service	39† (258)	30 (246)
Patriotic	22 (108)	21 (144)
Labor	15† (56)	26 (181)
Professional	11 (25)	8 (62)
Political	7 (32)	7 (46)
Business	5 (22)	3 (30)

* This figure is the proportion of members in the total community sample.
† Significant at .01 level.

A significant difference between the communities is also found in labor organization membership. Over twice as large a proportion of union members is found in Riverview, which reinforces our preliminary observations about its relatively stronger union character. Although not shown here, the divergent industrial structures of the communities are revealed by the membership distribution, e.g. the highest proportion of Riverview members are in railroad unions, while in Edgewood the machinists, who mainly serve her two large manufacturing plants, are dominant. There are no important differences in membership rates among the remaining types of voluntary organizations.

PATTERNS OF MEMBERSHIP

We now look at group membership from the more discriminating vantage point of the social characteristics of members compared with nonmembers. The interesting question of the relationship between social class and group participation is considered first. These data indicate the extent of multi-group membership and suggest the distribution of influence in the community, insofar as influence is associated with membership.

In any community, social status is usually positively associated with group membership. Table 8-2 supports this generalization.

TABLE 8-2 CLASS AND MEMBERSHIP IN "POLITICALLY RELEVANT" COMMUNITY ORGANIZATIONS, EDGEWOOD, IN PER CENT

Class*		_Number of organizations_					
		0	1	2	3+	NA	
I	(29)	3	14	10	66	7	(100)
II	(54)	13	19	11	57	0	(100)
III	(145)	20	15	22	41	2	(100)
IV	(179)	16	32	18	32	1	(100)
V	(80)	33	36	16	13	3	(100)

* "Not classifiable" cases have been deleted.

There is a steady relationship here between membership and class status. Two-thirds of Edgewood class I respondents are active in three or more voluntary organizations, compared with less than one-seventh of class V. Almost one-fifth of those in classes IV and V belong to no organizations and over one-third of them belong to only one, not including church membership.

Table 8-3 presents the same analysis for Riverview.

The distribution is similar to Edgewood, with several noteworthy exceptions. Almost four-fifths of class I respondents in Riverview belong to three or more organizations, compared with two-thirds of those in Edgewood. Further analysis reveals that the large difference between class I respondents in the two communities is partly due to the somewhat larger proportion of Riverview respondents who are members of social, veterans', and patriotic organizations. Another interesting finding is the relatively higher proportion of social class V respondents in Edgewood who belong to no organizations. However, just over two-thirds of those in this stratum in both communities belong to none or only one voluntary organization, not including church affiliations.

TABLE 8-3 CLASS AND MEMBERSHIP IN "POLITICALLY RELEVANT" ORGANIZATIONS, RIVERVIEW, IN PER CENT

Class*		0	1	2	3+	NA	
I	(19)	0	11	11	79	0	(100)
II	(55)	11	13	0	76	0	(100)
III	(122)	19	25	16	38	2	(100)
IV	(299)	18	33	18	29	1	(100)
V	(169)	25	41	9	19	6	(100)

Number of organizations shown in columns 0, 1, 2, 3+.

* "Not classifiable" cases have been deleted.

An analysis of membership in all classes at the critical 3+ level shows that Edgewood has an advantage, 36 per cent vs. 33 per cent. One explanation may be that the community has a significantly larger number of upper- and middle-class citizens who are more likely to participate at this level. An additional fillip to pluralism is that 3+ rates of membership in Edgewood are spread more evenly throughout the entire community compared with Riverview, which has a striking gap between its hyper-active upper class and its middle- and lower-class strata. A crucial aspect of this finding will be the extent to which *organizations* in each community participate in the major decisions, and thereby provide a means of access for their members.

CLASS AND MEMBERSHIP PREFERENCES

A further analysis of the distribution of group membership provides some generalizations. We are concerned here to find out whether there is an association between class and membership in certain types of organizations. This matter was raised in Chapter 6 where we hypothesized that divergent patterns of membership among both the leaders and the rank and file in the two communities could be explained in part in terms of class. In addition, however, we would expect the factor of social support to result in somewhat different distributions of membership among the same class in both communities. Tables 8-4 and 8-5 provide data that generally support these hypotheses.

TABLE 8-4 CLASS AND ORGANIZATIONAL MEMBERSHIP IN EDGEWOOD[*]

Proportion belonging

		Church	Religious	Service	Professional	Social	Veterans	Political	Business	Labor
I	(21)	100	81	67	62	48	14	14	5	0
II	(39)	95	44	72	33	77	49	18	5	5
III	(89)	96	67	44	16	69	35	17	8	12
IV	(89)	94	62	52	9	56	30	8	10	20
V	(22)	100	64	45	0	91	23	0	0	18

[*] This table is based upon those having three or more memberships.

The association between class and membership is patent. Although there is a remarkable continuity in the area of church membership, there are striking variations in the remaining organizational contexts. The most extreme differences are found for professional and social organizations. From the data in this and the following table, we can generalize that in these two communities, at least, membership increases as class status decreases in two, and perhaps three, types of organization: veterans groups and labor unions, with social organizations in Edgewood also serving to differentiate on class lines. Business organizations, such as the Grange, Chamber of Commerce, and Farm Bureau, attract very few members from any class, and membership in general reveals no consistent pattern with the exception of class V, which has no members represented.

TABLE 8-5 CLASS AND ORGANIZATIONAL MEMBERSHIP IN RIVERVIEW*

Proportion belonging

		Church	Religious	Social	Service	Professional	Veterans	Political	Business	Labor
I	(17)	100	76	71	47	24	24	18	12	12
II	(42)	83	55	81	60	55	17	19	17	0
III	(62)	95	66	74	48	10	34	24	10	19
IV	(133)	90	32	71	49	5	35	12	5	49
V	(42)	98	38	64	40	0	67	0	0	55

* This table is based upon those having three or more memberships.

In Riverview (Table 8-5), we find similarly discrete associations between class and certain types of memberships. Church membership is again stable regardless of class affiliation, although there is a curious drop-off among class II respondents. In general, membership increases as class status decreases in veterans' and labor organizations.

Some interesting comparative differences appear in the middle range of organizations. For one, in Edgewood, service, professional, and social categories ranked 3, 4, and 5, while in Riverview these ranks are occupied respectively by social, service, and professional. The different ranks of service and social organizations have implications for the effectiveness with which the two communities meet their major problems. From this standpoint, membership in service organizations, which include PTA, United Fund, Red Cross, Cancer, and Heart Societies is especially vital for the community. Edgewood has a somewhat larger proportion of its class I and II citizens in these kinds of activities, and exceeds Riverview in every class category, except III.

With regard to social organizations, the position is generally reversed, with Riverview having a significantly larger proportion ($p = .10$) of its class I and II respondents in social organizations. Only among class V respondents does Edgewood significantly ($p = .05$) exceed Riverview in this respect. In most cases, however, the proportions of each class belonging to each discrete type of organization are similar. One interesting exception is business organizations, where the direction of the distributions is reversed: in Edgewood membership was inversely associated with class status, while in Riverview it is positively and much more strongly associated.

A final question here concerns the specification of membership, i.e. do respondents with membership in only one organization tend to focus upon a certain type. The answer, which has already been suggested by the two preceding tables, is that such "monomembers" confine themselves almost exclusively to *church* membership. The tables also indicate that "multimembers" concentrate their group activities among church, religious, service, and social types of organizations. In effect, since class status is highly correlated with multiple membership, to answer this question, we need only note the types of organizations preferred by upper-class members of the community.

SOCIAL DETERMINANTS OF MEMBERSHIP

To further differentiate membership, we next analyze three social variables that characterize membership in voluntary organizations. To secure an adequate sample, only the three most popular types of organizations are included here: service, social, and patriotic organizations. Membership will be run against three variables: education, occupation, and political affiliation.

TABLE 8-6 EDUCATIONAL STATUS OF MEMBERS IN SERVICE ORGANIZATIONS

	Proportion belonging	
	Edgewood (185)	Riverview (194)
Grade school or less	8	9
High school	55	61
College	36	30

Table 8-6 shows that a somewhat higher proportion of service club members in Edgewood than in Riverview have some college work. That is, insofar as college-educated members may provide better leadership, Edgewood is somewhat advantaged by having relatively more of them.

A related facet of service club membership is more important. Comparative rates of total participation are significantly different ($p = .01$) with 39 per cent of our sample active in Edgewood against only 30 per cent in Riverview. This difference has important implications for community identification in the sense that service organizations, e.g. United Fund, Red Cross, Cancer Society, often attract individuals who are highly motivated by welfare ideals. Unlike many other local organizations with more restricted objectives, service organizations focus on community improvement programs, and their viability may provide a rough index of community identification. Thus the greater appeal of this kind of organization in Edgewood may be important in explaining differences between the two communities.

Table 8-7 shows again that Edgewood is advantaged by having a significantly higher proportion of social club members with some college training. A similar disproportion occurs at the grade school level, with similar implications. These conditions are probably a reflection of the discrete class structures of the two communities, and suggest again that conditions of participation in Riverview are less favorable. Over-all, however, the communities are identical, both having about 40 per cent rates of participation.

TABLE 8-7 EDUCATIONAL STATUS OF MEMBERS IN SOCIAL ORGANIZATIONS

	Proportion belonging	
	Edgewood (200)	Riverview (283)
Grade school or less	5	23
High school	61	58
College	34†	19

† Significant at .01 level.

The main generalization to be drawn from Table 8-8 is that Riverview is disadvantaged in the educational make-up of its patriotic groups. The difference is significant at the crucial college level. In Edgewood, fully one-third of the members have some college training while in Riverview only one-sixth do. Riverview has a larger proportion of members at the grade school level. In sum, Riverview's membership in patriotic organizations is skewed toward the lower educational levels, whereas Edgewood tends to have a larger share of those with more education. Note also that whereas the relative distribu-

TABLE 8-8 EDUCATIONAL STATUS OF MEMBERS OF PATRIOTIC ORGANIZATIONS

	Proportion belonging	
	Edgewood (105)	Riverview (138)
Grade school or less	17	27
High school	49	57
College	33†	16

† Significant at .01 level.

tion of educational achievement in all three types of organization has been very consistent in Edgewood's case, it has varied widely in Riverview.

TABLE 8-9 OCCUPATIONAL STATUS OF MEMBERS IN SERVICE ORGANIZATIONS

	Proportion belonging	
	Edgewood (185)	Riverview (194)
Professional	16	13
Managerial	12	7
White collar	18	14
Skilled worker	11	8
Unskilled	4	3
Housewives	39†	55

† Significant at .01 level.

In Table 8-9 we find that housewives provide the highest proportions of membership in both communities, followed by white-collar workers. Excepting housewives, proportions of each occupational type are quite similar in both communities. Edgewood, however, is advantaged by having a larger proportion of members from higher status occupations. When this table is compared with the two following, we find that service organizations include a substantially higher proportion of professional members, compared with social and patriotic organizations.

Compared with service groups, Table 8-10 shows that a much higher proportion of managers and unskilled workers belong to social organizations. Housewives again provide the largest occupational category. The proportions of each occupational group are very similar in both communities. The only significant difference is between skilled workers, where Riverview enjoys an advantage. The high proportion of unskilled members, some three times as great compared with service organizations, and the considerable decrease in Riverview housewives are also noteworthy.

TABLE 8-10 OCCUPATIONAL STATUS OF MEMBERS IN SOCIAL ORGANIZATIONS

	Proportion belonging	
	Edgewood (200)	Riverview (283)
Professional	7	8
Managerial	22	19
White collar	18	16
Skilled	8††	15
Unskilled	10	10
Housewives	35	31

†† Significant at .05 level.

In Table 8-11, the fairly consistent relationship found earlier between given occupational statuses and memberships disappears. In Edgewood, the highest proportion of membership is white-collar workers; in Riverview, housewives. We also find differences in the relative proportions of white-collar and unskilled workers. Edgewood enjoys a much larger proportion of the former and a significantly smaller proportion of the latter. After being minimally represented in service clubs, managerial types retain about the same proportion as they did in social clubs.

TABLE 8-11 OCCUPATIONAL STATUS OF MEMBERS IN PATRIOTIC ORGANIZATIONS

	Proportion belonging	
	Edgewood (105)	Riverview (138)
Professional	8	8
Managerial	16	18
White collar	26	17
Skilled	21	17
Unskilled	8††	18
Housewives	21	22

†† Significant at .05 level.

An interesting question is the extent to which intervening variables may affect these findings about skill level and membership. For example, is some other social factor, such as age or length of residence, more important than occupation in determining membership? Since education would seem to be among the most crucial of such factors, we will test it against the managers, an important occupational group whose educational achievement ranges across every level.

TABLE 8-12 MEMBERSHIP IN SOCIAL ORGANIZATIONS BY MANAGERIAL AND NONMANAGERIAL OCCUPATIONS AND EDUCATION, EDGEWOOD, IN PER CENT

	Managerial (90)		Nonmanagerial (393)	
	Belong	Not belong	Belong	Not belong
Grade school	14	86	11	89
High school	55	45	47	53
College	52	48	49	51
NA	0	0	6	9

Educational status at the grade level has more effect than occupation. Fully 86 per cent of those managers who have had only a grade school education, for example, are inactive. Among those nonmanagers with only grade school education, the proportions are very similar; this suggests again that at this level education is more important than occupation in determining participation. At the other end of the scale, we find a somewhat different pattern.

An interesting contrast occurs at the high school and college levels where a larger proportion of nonmanagerial types do not belong, compared with managers who show the expected positive association between education and membership. At these levels, it seems, occupation has an independent effect on participation. In sum, insofar as these occupational groups are concerned, education exerts its most important effect at the lowest level.

An interesting question is the extent to which political affiliation is associated with membership in our three representative types of organizations. We turn first to service organizations.

TABLE 8-13 PARTY AFFILIATION OF MEMBERS IN SERVICE ORGANIZATIONS

	Proportion belonging	
	Edgewood (185)	Riverview (194)
Republican	69†	47
Democrat	26	48
Independent	1	—
Liberal	—	1
None	4	4

† Significant at .01 level.

In Table 8-13, nicely reflecting the political complexion of the community, a significantly higher proportion of service club members in Edgewood are Republicans, compared with those in Riverview. Indeed, in both communities, the relative proportions of members are quite comparable with existing party divisions. A glance at the next two tables indicates that, for Riverview, the highest proportion of Republican membership occurs in service clubs, compared with social and patriotic clubs. Since we saw earlier (Tables 8-4 and 8-5) that service clubs attracted a high proportion of class I members, we assume that class is probably at work in Table 8-13. Service organizations such as United Fund, Red Cross, and PTA draw a high proportion of middle- and upper-class members, most of whom would espouse the Republican ideology. When this judgment is checked, we find that 28 per cent of Republican service club members in both communities are in classes I and II, compared with only 10 per cent of Democratic members.

We now turn to political party and membership in social organizations.

Although the distributions in Edgewood are not very different from those found for service organizations, there are significant differences between the two communities with regard to Republican membership. In Riverview, social clubs attract a larger proportion of Democrats, compared with service clubs, suggesting that they have somewhat less of a community-wide, "welfare" appeal and more of a fraternal one.

TABLE 8-14 PARTY AFFILIATION OF MEMBERS IN SOCIAL ORGANIZATIONS

	Proportion belonging	
	Edgewood (200)	Riverview (283)
Republican	69†	42
Democrat	28	50
Independent	1	2
Liberal	—	1
None	2	4

† Significant at .01 level.

Finally, we look at party affiliation and membership in patriotic organizations.

TABLE 8-15 PARTY AFFILIATION OF MEMBERS IN PATRIOTIC ORGANIZATIONS

	Proportion belonging	
	Edgewood (105)	Riverview (138)
Republican	60†	34
Democrat	30	58
Independent	3	1
Liberal	—	1
None	6	5

† Significant at .01 level.

Here, some changes occur. In Riverview, the small Democratic margin found earlier increases considerably and differences in the relative proportions of Democratic and Republican members become much larger. We saw earlier (Tables 8-4 and 8-5) that patriotic organizations were less likely than other organizations to draw high-status members. Insofar as Democrats tend to be of somewhat lower class status than Republicans, the relatively higher proportion of Democratic members in Riverview is not unexpected. In Edgewood, the same class factor may explain the somewhat larger proportion of Democrats and smaller proportion of Republican members, compared with social and service organizations.

Rank-and-File Participation in Community Decisions

Our second concern is the extent to which members of each community participated in the major decisions. This is perhaps a more vital facet of pluralism than organizational membership, since it concerns *direct* individual participation. The specific indicators used here were membership on relevant boards or committees, voting, contributing time or money to the decision, attending a public meeting, or discussing a given decision with a friend. With the exception of committee or board membership, all these media of participation are theoretically accessible to all adult citizens in our sample.

One prefatory admonition is required. We are not trying to show how limited individual participation is. Because political activity has a low priority with most Americans, we should not be surprised to find that rather small proportions of our sample are involved in these major decisions.[10] *The main objective of this part of the analysis is to determine empirically the comparative levels of pluralism in the two communities.* There is little profit in demonstrating again that relatively few citizens play an active role in political affairs, and that voting is their major form of participation.

[10] Dahl, for example, found in his New Haven sample that an average of 25 per cent of 525 registered voters participated in one or more of four kinds of "action in political affairs," *Who Governs?* p. 279; using a national sample of 8000, Woodward and Roper found similarly that only 27 per cent could be called "politically active," using a 5-item index, "Political Activity of American Citizens," 44 *American Political Science Review* (December, 1950), p. 876.

EDGEWOOD

Table 8-16 summarizes the findings on individual participation.

TABLE 8-16 RANK-AND-FILE PARTICIPATION IN EDGEWOOD DECISIONS (479)

	Proportion participating* Decisions				
	1 Flood control	2 Community bldg.	3 Hospital	4 New industry	5 School bond
Voted on referenda**	0	26	0	0	45
Contributed work or money	0	0	38	1	0
Discussed with friend	1	1	1	0	1
Attended public meeting	5	5	0	0.5	10
Member of committee	0	0	7	0	0
Other	4	1	4	2	0.5
Not a participant	93	72	58	97	52

* Some columns total more than 100 because some individuals used more than one medium of participation.
** Available only in decisions two and five.

Here, the sum of all media of individual participation ranges from a low of 3 per cent in the new industry decision to a high of 48 per cent in the school bond issue. As expected, we find that (along with contributions of work or money) voting provides the major form of participation. The school bond issue, it will be recalled, provoked considerable public attention and involved two referenda. An opposition group (three of whom are members of the Edgewood power structure) was formed to fight the first bond issue, which was defeated on the grounds of extravagance and the economic uncertainty of the community. Certainly, this decision meets pluralistic expectations, including the ability of an opposition group to defeat the first proposal.

The next highest rate of participation is found in the hospital decision, with 42 per cent of the adult community active in one way or another. Access occurred mainly through the opportunity afforded citizens to contribute time and money, and to become part of a network of committees charged with fundraising. Unlike the school issue, however, there was no procedural mechanism to ensure widespread direct support or disapproval of the initial decision. Much of the community activity was of a ministerial kind, undertaken only *after* the decision to raise money for a new hospital had been made by a few community leaders centered in the Hospital Board and the Rotary Club. We feel certain, for example, that the generous sums pledged by several wealthy families were a prerequisite to the decision to go ahead. In this sense, community participation was a *post hoc* form of activity. No doubt, judgments about the community's reactions to their decision were among the relevant considerations influencing the leaders. And, no doubt, they knew that the community possessed the energy, commitment, and wealth necessary to ensure the campaign's success. But even when we calculate only ministerial types of participation, the decision seems to have evoked an unusual measure of participation, compared with those remaining.

The community building decision achieves a total participation rate of 28 per cent, due almost entirely to voting in the bond referendum. Comparatively, this decision falls at the midpoint on the continuum. Beyond the referendum vote, participation was quite limited. We have the evidence of the two political leaders who maintained that they pushed the decision through, despite some opposition. As one of them, who could name only two other men as participants in the issue, said, "We organized and ran the meetings. It makes me mad to think of some of the dumb objections people made." The light vote on the referendum, which included 26 per cent of the electorate, suggests the existence of some opposition and considerable apathy. Moreover, only 5 per cent, some two dozen individuals, of our sample of 494 adult citizens attended public meetings to discuss the proposal. Only a half-dozen more talked about the issue with a friend or neighbor.

The two remaining decisions—flood control and new industry—have participation rates of 7 and 3 per cent respectively. No referenda were available in these decisions. Only in the sense that the flood control decision was made by elected officials could it be assumed to have entailed even indirect community participation. In this decision, some two dozen citizens attended public meetings. In the new industry program, about 30 to 40 citizens,[11] including mainly those directly concerned in making the decision, attended a meeting to discuss the issue. According to our direct observations, the principal function of the meeting was to explain a decision already arrived at. Here again, and like the hospital decision, local leaders were able to say that local banks had already pledged themselves to buy a substantial portion of the bond issue required to finance the venture.

In conclusion, the five Edgewood decisions vary considerably in the extent to which they approximate the criteria of pluralism outlined earlier. The school bond decision is the most pluralistic of the decisions, next is the hospital decision. Although in the first instance the community had little effect on the initial decision to launch a voluntary fund drive, about 42 per cent participated in subsequent implementary stages. The mean rate of participation for all five Edgewood decisions was 26 per cent.

RIVERVIEW

Table 8-17 summarizes individual rates and modes of participation in Riverview.

The range of participation here varies from a low of 1 per cent in the housing authority decision to a high of 33 per cent in the school bond decision. Here again, a referendum provides the major form of access, followed in this same case by public meetings, which provided access for another 3 per cent. One-

---

[11] This is an estimate of the number attending a public meeting observed during our research. It is not based upon our community sample.

third of the community voted in the referendum and 3 per cent served on committees directly concerned with the decision. Compared with the Edgewood school decision, the Riverview school issue lies in the middle range of the pluralist continuum. There was no organized opposition to the decision, which might have sparked additional participation, and perhaps even a second referendum, as in Edgewood's case.

TABLE 8-17 RANK-AND-FILE PARTICIPATION IN RIVERVIEW DECISIONS (655)

	Proportion participating* Decisions				
	1 Flood control	2 Housing authority	3 Hospital	4 New industry	5 School bond
Voted on referenda**	0	0	7	0	33
Contributed work or money	0	0	0	3	0
Discussed with friend	0	0	0	0.5	0
Attended public meeting	1	0	0	0	3
Member of committee	0	0	0.5	0	0.5
Other	2	1	1	0.5	0.5
Not a participant	97	99	92	97	67

* Some columns total more than 100 because some individuals used more than one medium of participation.
** Available only on decisions three and five.

Yet, even if this decision is less pluralistic than its Edgewood counterpart, it is by far the most lively issue in Riverview. The hospital decision, which ranked next, had a total participation rate of only 8 per cent, despite a referendum, which galvanized into action 7 per cent of the community. Another one-half of 1 per cent served on boards or committees directly concerned with the decision, while the remaining 1 per cent was involved under the "other" category. For a public decision, which was ranked as the "most important" of the five issues by fully 60 per cent of our respondents, this seems a rather low rate of participation. Perhaps this is one of those cases where apathy must be viewed as a surrogate for approval.

The housing authority, flood control, and new industry decisions together evoked participation from 7 per cent of our community sample.

With the exception of the school bond issue, Riverview decisions tend to cluster around the low end of the pluralist scale. The high school decision engaged a noteworthy portion of the community, namely, one-third of our sample. A comparison of voting patterns in similar communities on the same type of issue in New York State indicates that this figure is quite similar to that for communities of similar size. Each of the remaining decisions engaged 10 per cent or less of the adult community, with the housing authority decision falling at the extreme low end of the continuum. The average rate of participation in Riverview was only 10 per cent, compared with 26 per cent in Edgewood.

SUMMARY

As Figure 8-1 indicates, individual rates of participation in the various decisions vary widely in the two communities. Some interesting continuities appear, however, in terms of the distribution of specific decisions along the continuum. The two school bond issues, along with the Edgewood hospital decision, evoked the highest rates of participation. The lowest rates of participation occur in the housing authority and the new industry decisions, respectively. Comparatively, both flood control decisions and the Riverview hospital decision also rank rather low. This point is stressed because it is often assumed that "public" types of decisions are characterized by higher participation than "private" ones.

In sum, by the index of rank-and-file participation, it is clear from Figure 8-1 that Edgewood and Riverview fall at different points along the pluralist continuum. It should be noted, however, that the two referenda required for the school bond issue inflate Edgewood's participation somewhat. In relative fre-

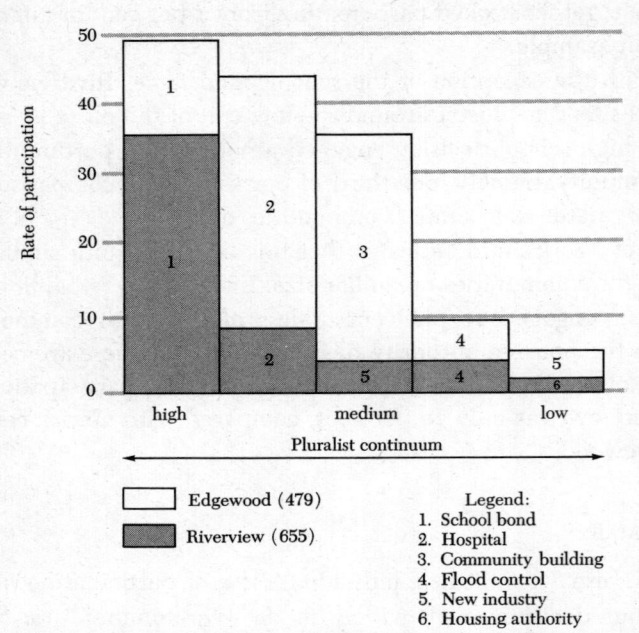

FIGURE 8-1 COMPARATIVE RATES OF RANK-AND-FILE PARTICIPATION,
EDGEWOOD AND RIVERVIEW, IN PER CENT

quency, voting and the opportunity to work for or contribute money to the Edgewood hospital fund drive provide the major forms of access. Most of the other media were used by less than 10 per cent of the participants, although public meetings did reach this level in the Edgewood school bond issue.

Organizational Participation in Community Decisions

As noted earlier, the pluralist thesis holds that voluntary, extra-governmental organizations provide a necessary counterpoise to the power of the state. Such organizations provide an alternative to solutions presumably imposed from above, and enable private citizens to enjoy the benefits of responsibility and independence in handling their own affairs. This division of labor provides better solutions because of the citizen's knowledge and interest in problems that directly affect him. Moreover, his resourcefulness inhibits the growth of big government, ensuring a society in which power is widely dispersed, and civic virtue and substantive rationality work hand in hand.

Pluralism maintains that individuals in our complex society typically make their will felt through membership in groups with access to those with political and economic power. Pluralists recognize that man has been collectivized to some extent, but he is saved from personal impotence through the influence wielded on his behalf by the elites who direct the groups to which he belongs. A central assumption here, of course, is that such elites indeed represent the interests of their members and are in fact capable of making good this interest in the political arena.

If these assumptions are viable, we should find a considerable amount of participation by voluntary organizations *qua* organizations in the ten decisions analyzed here. We will confine ourselves to the role played by the organization as a collective unit in the several decisions. However, to provide some basis for explaining any differences found in participation among organizations, and between organizational leaders and community decision-makers, the SES of the leaders of a sample of organizations will be presented too. We assume that the effectiveness of any organization is mainly a function of the skill, experience, and education of its members, and particularly of its leaders. We also assume that the leaders of an organization are probably among its most competent members in terms of such criteria. In a word, the social status and attending resources of its leaders are regarded as one indicator that can help explain the level of an organization's participation.

Here again, the concept of participation includes both the initial and implementary stages of the decisions, which has the effect of inflating organizational participation somewhat. Participation is defined as active involvement in a decision, using one or more of the following media: the organization passed a resolution supporting or opposing the decision; it formed a special committee to study the issue; or it donated a sum of money or contributed some other type of active support, such as time or equipment.

In this context, we turn to an analysis of participation by our sample of 52 voluntary organizations. Table 8-18 indicates the total extent of *all types of participation* by voluntary groups in both communities.

TABLE 8-18 PARTICIPATION OF VOLUNTARY ORGANIZATIONS IN COMMUNITY DECISIONS

Edgewood (23) Decision	Number of participations*	Riverview (29) Decision	Number of participations
New hospital	10	New hospital	6
School bond issue	2	School bond issue	3
New industry	1	New industry	3
Flood control	1	Flood control	1
Community building	1	Housing Authority	0
Number of organizations participating**	12	Number of organizations participating**	9
Per cent of all organizations	52††	Per cent of all organizations	31

* Because several organizations participated in more than one decision, the total number of organizations participating is less than the total number of participations.

** "Participation" is determined by three criteria: the organization passed a resolution for or against the decision; it formed a special committee to study or work on the issue; or it donated money, time, or some other type of support.

†† Significant at .10 level.

Using our three criteria of participation, we find that about half of Edgewood organizations and a quarter of those in Riverview were active in one or more of the ten major community decisions. As might be expected, the two hospital decisions had the highest measure of participation. Their nonpolitical, humanitarian quality, as well as the voluntary fund drive in Edgewood, inspired several community groups to work together. We have seen that the hospital decisions were ranked as the "most important" of the ten decisions by a majority of respondents in both communities. Also, the need for the new hospitals, especially in Riverview, was so obvious and compelling that there was a clear consensus in their favor. This may be a case in which limited participation reflects widespread community acceptance of a policy, with a resulting tendency to remain inactive.

When we turn to the other decisions, it is striking that so few organizations participated at any stage. In fully half the decisions only *one* local organization played an active role. Here again we find the "anomaly" that a private type of decision, i.e. the Edgewood hospital, evoked the highest measure of participation. Despite the fact that seven of the 10 issues are governmental, private types of decisions have a total of 14 participations as against 14 for public decisions. Comparing over-all rates of participation in the two communities, we find that Edgewood has a significant advantage, 52 per cent of her organizations having been active, over against 31 per cent of those in Riverview.

It is important to distinguish further among kinds of organizational participation, since some are more important than others. Passing a resolution in favor of a decision (designated "X"), for example, is a minimal form of participation. Indeed, several organizational leaders, after saying, "Oh, we had nothing to do with that," would add that they had passed a resolution supporting the decision. On the other hand, contributions in the form of time, equipment, or money (designated "Z"), are probably the most important form of activity. In the following tables, we have differentiated types of organization and participation in the five decisions in each community. In each case only the highest level of participation is shown.

TABLE 8-19 PARTICIPATION BY VOLUNTARY ORGANIZATIONS IN EDGEWOOD

	Flood control	Community building	Decisions Hospital	School bond	New industry
Chamber of Commerce	o*	Z****	Z	X**	Y***
Masons	o	o	Z	o	o
Lions	o	o	Z	o	o
Rotary	o	o	Z	o	o
Exchange Club	o	o	Z	o	o
Moose	o	o	Z	o	o
Legion	o	o	Z	o	o
V. F. W.	o	o	Z	o	o
Business and Professional Women's Club	o	o	Z	o	o
Country Club	Z	o	o	o	o
PTA	o	o	o	Z	o
County Ministerial Assn.	o	o	Z	o	o

* "o" refers to no participation in the decision.
** "X" refers to participation in the form of a resolution supporting or opposing the decision.
*** "Y" refers to establishing a special committee to work on the issue.
**** "Z" refers to participation in the form of contributions such as money, work, or equipment.

Here, a total of 12 organizations are found to have participated in one or more of the five issues at various levels of intensity, but mainly at the optimal "Z" level. *However, fully 90 per cent of active organizations participated in only one decision, namely the hospital fund drive.* Indeed, two-thirds of *all* organizational participations were accounted for by the hospital decision. The Chamber of Commerce, which participated in four decisions, is in a class by itself. The next table provides comparable data for Riverview.

TABLE 8-20 PARTICIPATION BY VOLUNTARY ORGANIZATIONS IN RIVERVIEW

	Flood control	Housing authority	*Decisions* Hospital	School bond	New industry
Moose	X**	o*	X	X	X
Rotary	o	o	X	o	o
Kiwanis	o	o	Z****	o	o
Chamber of Commerce#	o	o	o	o	Z
PTA	o	o	o	Z	o
Women's Federation	o	o	X	X	o
Riverview Athletic Club	o	o	o	o	Z
Ministers Assn.	o	o	X	o	o
Sorority Council	o	o	Z	o	o

* "o" refers to no participation in the decision.
** "X" refers to participation in the form of a resolution supporting or opposing the decision.
**** "Z" refers to participation in the form of contributions such as money, work, or equipment.
# The respondent, newly elected to head the organization, gave "don't know" answers to the first four decisions, but we have changed these on the basis of conclusive evidence as to the extent of the organization's activities.

Although the major conclusion is one of limited activity in both communities, gross levels of participation are quite different. In Edgewood, 48 per cent of our sample participated in none of the five decisions; 90 per cent of those who did participate were involved in only one decision. In Riverview, 70 per cent were not active in any decision, and 87 per cent of those who were active were involved in only one decision. The Moose Lodge was uniquely active, participating in four decisions by passing resolutions supporting them. One noteworthy difference is in the intensity of participation. Whereas all twelve of the Edgewood organizations were active at the optimal "Z" level, in Riverview just over half participated at this level of intensity.

Another contrast is seen in the new industry decision where organizational participation was considerably higher in Riverview. Despite this, we can safely conclude that voluntary groups were considerably more active in Edgewood.

In both communities, participation is scattered among several kinds of organizations, with the Chambers of Commerce and social organizations being the most active. The Edgewood Chamber of Commerce, however, is considerably more lively than its Riverview counterpart, with four decisions to one. The larger degree of participation in Edgewood may be explained in part by the simple fact of greater *opportunity*. The data show that Edgewood organizations concentrated mainly on the hospital program. Defined as a "private" venture, with a humanitarian appeal, this issue understandably evoked widespread participation in a community that prides itself on self-reliance. Although the hospital issue was also the single largest vehicle of participation in Riverview, had it been privately rather than publicly financed, the number of organizations involved would probably have been higher.

In both communities, four "political" decisions which involved subsidies from higher levels of government (i.e. the housing authority,[12] the hospital in Riverview, and the two flood control issues) inspired the least participation. In Edgewood, only one organization was involved in the flood control and municipal building decisions. In Riverview, this phenomenon is even sharper; no community organizations were involved in the public housing decision and only one in the flood control issue. With the single exception of the Edgewood Chamber of Commerce and the Riverview Moose Lodge, the differences among all types of organizations in scope of participation are

---

[12] Given the current importance of urban renewal, it is noteworthy that the Riverview housing authority issue, which included replacing some areas of marginal housing in the city center with parking lots, failed to evoke participation by any organization in our sample (Table 8-20).

small, but there are some interesting comparative differences in the intensity of participation.

In sum, most community organizations in our sample are relatively passive as measured by their participation in the ten critical decisions. While they are apparently quite active in their specific areas of interest, they have been little concerned with the major aspects of community life symbolized by our panel of decisions. In both communities, only 6 per cent of 52 organizations were active in more than one decision. In view of the pluralist image of intense group activity and participation in community projects, how is this finding to be explained?

Although low levels of individual participation were to be expected, and while membership in voluntary groups has typically been exaggerated, the limited extent of organizational participation in major community decisions raises serious questions about this element in the pluralist equation. In effect, even this most "reasonable" indicator of pluralism suggests that organizations have apparently not been very active in carrying out their ascribed function of representing the interests of their members. In the next section, some possible explanations are considered.

EXPLANATIONS FOR LOW ORGANIZATIONAL PARTICIPATION

The reasons for limited organizational participation include their limited special-purpose goals. As the head of one lodge said, "We stick pretty close to fraternal affairs." Some are prohibited by their constitutions from investing their funds in such ventures as the new industry project. Others defined most of the decisions as essentially "political," an area said to be outside their terms of reference. Some ideological dissonance appears here. For example, the president of one organization explained the lack of participation in a given issue by the fact that it was "political," while another president in discussing the same issue explained, "We limit ourselves only to political things and this was *not* political."

Another explanation, mentioned earlier, is that several of the decisions were *external,* in the sense that the final disposition of critical resources remained in the hands of, or at least were broadly shared with, outsiders such as state and federal governments. Certainly, this was true of the flood control decisions in both communities, and of the housing and hospital decisions in Riverview.

To some extent, Tables 8-16, 8-17, and Figure 8-1 support this explanation. Decisions involving local initiative and the use of immediate community resources, i.e. those falling within the financial and organizational capabilities of the community, tend to evoke a higher level of participation. On the other hand, in those "political" decisions in which local politicians negotiated for funds, enabling legislation, or administrative approval from state and federal officials (e.g. flood control, housing, and publicly financed hospital in Riverview), participation is relatively limited. As one leader of a group with almost 500 members said in discussing his organization's failure to participate in the flood control and housing authority decisions, "Nobody has contacted the heads of various organizations about either of these. It is more or less a cut-and-dried affair. When it's all over with, then we hear about it."

Another possible explanation of the low participation of local organizations may be the caliber of their leaders, who may not have the necessary organizing skills, knowledge, or interest. Insofar as interest in *national* political affairs is a valid index of a generalized political interest and sophistication, the following data are useful.

TABLE 8-21 INTEREST OF DECISION-MAKERS AND ORGANIZATIONAL LEADERS IN NATIONAL POLITICAL AFFAIRS, IN PER CENT

	Decision-makers (71)		Organizational leaders (52)	
	Edgewood	*Riverview*	*Edgewood*	*Riverview*
High interest	88	97†	82	70

† Significant at .01 level.

These data show that politics is much more salient for decision-makers, particularly those in Riverview. It is interesting to speculate why the latter are so much more interested in political affairs than their Edgewood counterparts. Perhaps this orientation reflects a lesser degree of identification with the immediate community, although this is pure speculation.

Since we know that SES is positively associated with participation in community affairs, we next compare decision-makers and organizational leaders on this basis.

TABLE 8-22 SES OF DECISION-MAKERS AND ORGANIZATIONAL LEADERS IN EDGEWOOD AND RIVERVIEW, IN PER CENT

	Decision-makers (71)	Organizational leaders (52)
Education: 16 or more years	48††	25
Time in community: over 20 years	82	67
Fathers' occupation, white collar or higher	75	60
Respondents' occupation, white collar or higher	94††	73
Income: over $10,000	70†	31
Political affiliation: Republican	70	56

† Significant at .01 level.
†† Significant at .05 level.

It is clear from Table 8-22 that decision-makers enjoy very much higher class status than organizational leaders. They are also highly advantaged in terms of income, and to a somewhat similar extent in their own occupational status and Republican political affiliation. An important advantage is in length of education which, with the exception of specialist leaders, we have found to be more important than expected. When we consider that organizational leaders are, on the average, 11 years younger than members of the elite (comparative averages, 44 and 55 years), the educational differences are even more impressive, since the younger men would have typically enjoyed more opportunity for higher education. In sum, the failure of organizations to play as active a role as expected may be due in part to the generally lower status and prestige of their leaders, compared with the decision-makers.

The judgments of organizational leaders as to who is powerful in the community may tell us something more about differences between them and decision-makers, as well as about the low level of participation of their organizations. If, for example, a reasonably accurate knowledge of local power configurations is required for participation, such perceptions of organizational leaders become germane. The underlying assumptions here are several. Some sophistication about community power and politics seems necessary if one is to influence local affairs. At the very least, one must know how organizations and individuals are aligned on a given issue. As will be shown in Chapter 10, one must also *believe* that he can in fact exert influence on such issues. A synthesis of knowledge and faith is required. Such requirements tend, one suspects, to be underestimated by individuals whose class status and experience make such knowledge seem obvious. In any case, the ability of organizational leaders to identify local power figures should tell us something about their own and their organization's potential influence.

In general (Table 8-23), such leaders do very well in identifying those in the power structure. We must reject the hypothesis that the inactivity of their organizations is due to their own naïveté about power relations in the community. Some discontinuity, however, exists between the nominations of the two groups. In Edgewood, some of the organizational leaders' nominations seem quite naïve. For example, John Wainwright, probably the most powerful influential in the community, is not included. Four other nominees are definitely not members of the local power structure; they tend to be younger, politically-oriented men, who play an active but implementary role in community affairs. On the other hand, Edgewood organizational leaders recognize the power of the mayor and rank him higher than did the decision-makers.

TABLE 8-23 INFLUENTIAL NOMINATIONS OF DECISION-MAKERS AND OF ORGANIZATIONAL LEADERS

\	Edgewood			Riverview	
Chosen by decision-makers	Chosen by organization leaders	Over-lap	Chosen by decision-makers	Chosen by organization leaders	Over-lap
Jonathan Davis	Harold Carter	Yes	Ted O'Brian	Richard Cavenaugh	Yes
Don Remington	R. G. White	Yes	Richard Cavenaugh	Ted O'Brian	Yes
R. G. White	Jonathan Davis	Yes	Robert Carr	Dick Mason	Yes
Bob Williams	Robert King	Yes	Dick Mason	Dr. Frank Baxter	Yes
John Wainwright	George Wilson	No	Kenneth Armstrong	Ted Johnson	Yes
Henry Turner	Don Remington	Yes	Dr. Frank Baxter	Robert Carr	Yes
R. F. Prince	George Parker	Yes	Fred Schwartz	Fred Rivers	Yes
John Dunn	Clinton Woods	No	John Riley	John Riley	Yes
George Parker	Frank Diehle	No	Fred Rivers	Fred Morrow	Yes
Robert King	Tom Metzger	No	Ted Johnson	Kenneth Armstrong	Yes
Harold Carter	Walter Stouffer	No	Fred Morrow	Mrs. Anna Heymann	No
Anthony Hadwen	Anthony Hadwen	Yes	Kenneth Swanson	Frank King	No
Allen Kimbrough	Henry Turner	Yes	Frank O'Connor	Walter Schumacher	No
Proportion of overlap: 61%			*Proportion of overlap: 77%*		

By comparison, Riverview organizational leaders are more accurate. The explanation for this difference relates to our general conclusion about power in the two communities. In Riverview, power is more concentrated in fewer hands and more visible. Whereas Edgewood's elite includes several behind-the-scenes leaders who dominate local finance and industry and are marginally active in some of the major decisions, in Riverview there is no comparable division of labor between overt decision-makers and potentially powerful influentials. Only one member of the Riverview elite falls in the latter category. As a result, one would expect organizational leaders in Riverview to identify more accurately those with power.

Explanations of lower organizational participation include the fact that most organizations have rather specific objectives, often limited to activities of immediate interest to their members. Such activities, which honor the *raison d'être* of the organization, must be kept within their limited financial resources. Voluntary organizations, in a word, often have interests that are too specialized and resources that are too limited to encourage direct participation in large-scale, community-wide decisions. There are, of course, exceptions to this generalization, most prominently in the case of the Rotary Club's role in Edgewood's hospital decision. But in the main, as the following data suggest, organizations have either more limited or more diffuse goals. The items included in Tables 8-24 and 8-25 are either verbatim quotes or paraphrased responses of organizational

TABLE 8-24 OBJECTIVES OF SELECTED EDGEWOOD ORGANIZATIONS

Organization	Type of objective or activity
American Legion	"To take care of veterans and their families."
V. F. W.	"We sponsor quite a lot of things like Little League."
Rotary	Club, vocational, international and community service.
Lions	"To create world friendship and take an active interest in local community affairs."
Country Club	"Golf and social affairs."
Chamber of Commerce	"To promote all community affairs."
Exchange Club	Law enforcement and scholarship interest.
Bus. & Prof. Women's Club	"Bind working girls together."
PTA	"We are only interested in children."
Republican Committee	"To seize control of village government."
United Fund	"To consolidate charity drives."
Masons	"Fellowship and brotherly love."
Moose	"To provide a home for widow and children of any member who dies."
D. A. R.	"Erection of monuments to the American Revolution."
Eastern Star	"To promote good will and brotherly love."
Catholic Women	"To help the neighborhood Catholic school."
Elks	"We are a charitable organization."
Ministerial Association	"To schedule morning devotionals for radio; to get ministers together for social visits."

leaders to the question, "In as specific terms as possible, could you tell me the major purpose of [organization]?"

TABLE 8-25 OBJECTIVES OF SELECTED RIVERVIEW ORGANIZATIONS

Organization	Type of objective or activity
V. F. W.	"We send a local boy to Boy's State."
Women's Federation	Contribution of funds to public library.
PTA	"We help the school buy things they need"; "also interested in bringing new industry here."
Rotary	Formed a committee to bring new industry in.
Athletic Club	Donations to affiliated church activities.
American Legion	"Our biggest thing is our Americanism activities."
Chamber of Commerce	"We are supporting bringing St. Lawrence electric power here."
Home Demonstration Unit	"We supported the school bond issue on an informal basis."
Moose	Donations to Red Cross, Cancer Fund, etc.
Lions	"We've had speakers on flood control and new hospital."
Council of Churches	United Fund, UNICEF, and local youth programs.
Republican Committee	"We are strictly political, nominate candidates, etc."
Kiwanis	"Bring local problems before our members; and promote recreational appeal of the community."
Country Club	"We allow service clubs, etc. to use our facilities."
Democratic City Club	Participation in local politics.
Elks	"We do what we can."
United Church Women	"Very interested in community decisions as individuals, but as a group, I hardly know how to answer that."

From these data one must conclude that with only five or six exceptions, voluntary organizations in Edgewood and Riverview restrict themselves to rather specific kinds of activities, most of which are of a different order than the panel of decisions analyzed here. On the other hand, some of their objectives are so diffuse and abstract that they do not include the major kinds of decisions that occurred during the time of this study.

Community Organizations and the Recruitment of Elites

Despite the evidence of low participation, community organizations are symbiotically related to the local power elite to the extent that they can play a crucial role in the recruitment of its leaders. This aspect of their activity arose frequently during the interviews. Although our data are somewhat impressionistic, this judgment is supported by the responses of decision-makers to the following question, "Suppose a man wanted to become a leader in this community. Could you give me your ideas as to what he would have to do?" When all responses are analyzed, we find that 42 per cent of 71 leaders specifically included "joining local service and civic organizations" in their answer. Although many others spoke similarly in general terms, such as "he would have to take part in many activities," or "he would have to work hard in the community's interest," only those responses that specifically mentioned participation in organizations are included here.

But not all organizations serve as instruments for the "circulation of elites." Different organizations, as we have seen, attract different kinds of members, some of whom have more leadership resources than others. In the main, "civic" or "service" clubs such as Rotary, Lions, and Kiwanis, and the Chamber of Commerce provide the major bases of recruitment. Yet, some of these are more equal than others, and in Edgewood the Rotary club is the most prestigeful organization. As one decision-maker said in explaining this group's role in the hospital decision, "You have older, seasoned businessmen in Rotary, which makes them different from the Exchange and Lions."

In Riverview, the recruitment function was not fulfilled to the same extent by these long-established organizations. Other *ad hoc* coalitions shared this function. Perhaps because the Chamber of Commerce was moribund, an informal "Tuesday Coffee" organization was established, which brought together young business leaders who planned for industrial and business development and operated independently of both political and some organizational leaders. The Industrial Development Corporation was another center for recruiting and mobilizing leadership. In the main, however, the channels of recruitment were blurred, as suggested by the fact that a young unknown businessman became the successful Republican candidate for mayor in 1961; as well as by Reverend Baxter's quick access into the power structure.

The recruitment function of organizations is often latent, but the essential concept is that one "works his way up" through organizational activities, in this way qualifying for roles of increasing importance. Some sort of testing process is apparently occurring, as suggested by one respondent, who said, "We are always looking for new leaders here."[13] The following quotations suggest that the search is carried out largely in voluntary organizations:

> In the first place, he's got to be a successful businessman or professional. Most of them have come up through office in various service clubs . . . A lot of young fellows jump in and if they make a success, chances are they'll go on. They start small and come up.
> In this community the way to go about it is to get in the service clubs and Chamber of Commerce. And after that, and taking some committee assignments—often the fund raising drives serve this purpose—getting themselves well known.
> I started off as chairman of a Chamber of Commerce committee. From there I became president of the Chamber, where you learn how to meet with lots of people. It does you a lot of good to get mixed up with the various drives—be a director of some-

---

[13] Parenthetically, this suggests that the community leadership system is always "open," provided of course that the candidates meet the criteria set down by those who co-opt them into the local power structure.

thing like Polio, United Fund—it gets your name in the paper, and helps you meet people.[14]

First thing he would have to prove he was a damn good man in his job or business. Number two, he'd have to be a mixer—stay the hell out of politics; join the key clubs—Kiwanis or Rotary. Take an interest in hospital or schools and be an eager beaver in our drives here. Membership in those clubs would open doors for him.

Conclusions

In this chapter we have attempted to test the relative viability of pluralism in Edgewood and Riverview. Rather than try to find absolute quantitative criteria, we have ranked participation in the various decisions along a pluralist continuum. In both communities, certain types of decisions tended to cluster around either the "high" or "low" end of this continuum. Both school bond issues were toward the high end, whereas the new industry and flood control decisions clustered around the low end.

Three major criteria were used to measure pluralism in the two communities: organizational membership, individual participation in the major decisions, and participation by voluntary organizations *qua* organizations in these decisions.

Regarding organizational memberships, we find that Edgewood ranks just a bit more toward the high end of the continuum. Thirty-six per cent of its citizens belong to three or more organizations, compared with 33 per cent for Riverview. Edgewood, moreover, enjoys one noteworthy advantage. In service club memberships which are crucial for community development, 39 per cent of her respondents belonged to one or more such organizations, compared with 30 per cent for Riverview. This difference is significant at the .01 level.

---

[14] For a related analysis of the association between career mobility and philanthropic community work, see A. E. Ross, "Philanthropic Activity and the Business Career," 32 *Social Forces*, pp. 275-8.

Insofar as "rank-and-file" participation in the major decisions is concerned, Edgewood has a mean rate of participation of 26 per cent, compared with about 10 per cent for Riverview, which is again a significant difference. Finally, with regard to participation by organizations, comparative rates are 52 per cent for Edgewood and 31 per cent for Riverview. Almost 90 per cent of these organizations, however, were found to have been active in only one decision. It is well known that individual participation in political affairs, beyond voting, is limited to a small minority of the population, and that membership in voluntary organizations in the United States has typically been overstated. The limited activity of organizations *qua* organizations is, however, surprising. Since such organizational access is often regarded as the most feasible instrument of pluralism in our complex society, our findings have important implications. We conclude tentatively that the role of voluntary organizations in ensuring pluralist forms of political decision-making has been somewhat overstated.

In the next two chapters, some explanations for differences in participation in the two communities will be considered. One explanation concerns differences in their political structure and behavior, and particularly in the extent to which their citizens possess the political interest and skills required for participation. The hypothesis here is that different rates of interest, identification, apathy, and alienation inhibit the development of equally lively political communities. Yet another is that the communities are characterized by different levels of consensus upon certain basic American values. Combined with the structural and environmental properties analyzed earlier, such attitudinal factors may help explain the different levels of pluralism found in the two communities.

9
COMMUNITY SOCIAL STRUCTURE AND POLITICAL BEHAVIOR

Further explanation for the different rates of participation in the two communities must now be sought. Political structure and behavior, social integration, and value consensus seem to be among the major conditions affecting participation. Explanatory variables probably include party structure, voting, political interest, knowledge, and traditions. These are immediately relevant to power structure analysis, for they provide the framework within which leaders must act and they determine the limits of citizen participation. In large measure the ability of leaders to enlist community-wide support in major decisions depends on the political structure of the community and the extent to which citizens use their political resources.[1]

Although political theory is often disengaged from political facts, the two can be brought together by an analysis of the relationship between the decision-making systems in each community and the political actions and values of their members.

---

[1] Perhaps the most obvious example is the extent to which mayors King and O'Brian were dependent upon sustained electoral support for their position in the power structure.

Our theoretical base is provided by Robert Michels's conception of the requirements of democratic participation, which are merely the antitheses of the oligarchic conditions he found in German Social-Democratic political parties.[2] Such conditions include an educated, knowledgeable membership, possessing the political interest which makes participation possible. Although Michels's conceptions were applied to the organizational aspects of political parties, "he who says organization says oligarchy," they are relevant to community decision-making which is concerned essentially with the organization of political power and with the relationships between leaders and the led. The community, in effect, may be characterized as a political organization, against which Michels's prescriptions about the conditions of democracy and elitism may be analyzed. Although the members of the power structure in Edgewood and Riverview do not comprise a closed, monolithic elite, the decision-making process does indeed resemble the elitist model which Michels claimed was inevitable in all types of organizations.

Michels noted that elite rule was made possible by the political incapacity of the rank and file; by the complexity of decisions which excluded most members from participation; by the apathy of the majority; by the need for professional leadership; and by the desire of leaders to perpetuate themselves in office. Such conceptions are useful in explaining participation and pluralism in Edgewood and Riverview. We can ask, for example, to what extent do the rank and file meet his conditions of democratic participation and the avoidance of elitism? To what extent do citizens possess the resources necessary for participation in the decisions that affect them? Is the majority characterized by apathy? Electoral behavior provides some answers to these questions, but other kinds of political evidence and action must also be analyzed.

[2] *Political Parties: A Sociological Study of the Oligarchical Tendencies of Modern Democracy* (New York: Hearst International Library, 1915).

In political structure and behavior the communities are quite different. In Edgewood over 70 per cent of the electorate is registered Republican: in 1956, 76 per cent of the voters cast their ballots for Eisenhower. In Riverview, registered Republicans comprise only 47 per cent of the electorate, and even in the Eisenhower landslide of 1956, only 56 per cent of voters supported him. If Edgewood follows the historic pattern of Republican dominance in upstate New York communities, Riverview is an isolated Democratic enclave surrounded by an overwhelmingly Republican county, but joined ideologically with the state's Democratic oriented metropolitan centers. This political diversity is based demographically on the fact that whereas 75 per cent of Edgewood's citizens, age 20 or over, are Protestant and 83 per cent are of Northern European ethnic origin, in Riverview only 53 per cent of the community is Protestant and 65 per cent of its members are of Northern European origin.

To provide an overview of the social structure of the two communities in relation to their political behavior, we first present detailed trend information on selected demographic characteristics and party affiliation. These data also provide a comparative picture of the kinds of human resources upon which community leaders can draw.

In the main, Table 9-1 replicates existing generalizations about socioeconomic status and party affiliation. Whereas about two-thirds of Protestants tend to be members of the Republican party, a similar proportion of Catholics tend to prefer the Democratic. A much higher proportion of college-educated citizens are Republicans. A similar generalization holds regarding occupation and party in Edgewood; those in higher status occupations (excepting managers) tend to vote Republican. (This generalization does not, however, hold in Democratic Riverview.) Similarly, a much larger proportion of those at the highest income level in Edgewood are members of the Republican party, but again this is not so in Riverview.

TABLE 9-1 SOCIAL STRUCTURE AND PARTY AFFILIATION, IN PER CENT*

Demographic variables	Edgewood Rep.	Dem.	Other**	Cases	Riverview Rep.	Dem.	Other**	Cases
Sex								
Male	54	35	11	(207)	40	48	12	(275)
Female	67	27	6	(269)	39	50	11	(378)
Age								
21-29	35	49	16	(69)	31	52	17	(85)
30-39	54	40	6	(70)	40	47	13	(116)
40-49	62	29	9	(101)	34	60	6	(113)
50-59	75	22	3	(100)	40	52	8	(150)
60+	67	24	9	(135)	47	41	12	(189)
Religion								
Protestant	75	19	6	(35)	61	29	9	(337)
Catholic	21	70	9	(111)	17	71	12	(300)
Other	50	17	33	(12)	0	67	33	(9)
Education								
Grade school	72	19	9	(97)	35	52	13	(201)
High school	52	40	8	(245)	38	52	10	(351)
Some college	69	22	9	(90)	52	34	14	(56)
College graduate	73	20	7	(44)	52	37	10	(48)
Skill level								
Professional	60	31	9	(35)	50	43	7	(46)
Managerial	48	35	17	(90)	44	37	19	(90)
White collar	57	36	7	(44)	53	44	3	(66)
Service workers	65	30	5	(43)	43	43	14	(21)
Skilled	57	37	6	(63)	26	64	10	(74)
Semi-skilled	52	45	3	(31)	33	58	9	(66)
Unskilled	36	64	0	(14)	50	29	21	(24)
Housewives	75	18	7	(156)	36	53	11	(258)
Income								
Under $3000	54	32	14	(118)	42	43	15	(116)
$3000-4999	62	37	1	(81)	40	54	6	(166)
$5000-9999	62	31	7	(199)	37	51	12	(280)
$10,000+	82	15	3	(60)	56	38	6	(32)
NA	28	39	33	(18)	36	45	19	(58)

* Total N's may differ slightly because respondents did not answer all questions.
** This category includes Independents, Liberals, and "no party" affiliation.

Although they run in the same direction, these relationships vary significantly (p = .01) between the two communities; this factor suggests again that the dominant characteristics of the underlying sociopolitical structure and resulting psychological climate strongly affect the distributions. Along all these dimensions, the differences are smaller in Riverview, i.e. college-educated citizens, those in higher occupational statuses, and those who are well-off economically show a relatively smaller rate of Republican affiliation. The strength of Republican loyalties in Edgewood is perhaps best seen in the fact that 72 per cent of those with only a grade school education vote Republican, a proportion almost as high as that found among college graduates.

Two noteworthy exceptions occur. In the case of unskilled workers, the direction is reversed: one-half of Riverview workers in this category are members of the Republican party compared with about one-third in dominantly Republican Edgewood. The other exception relates to age: in the 21-29 category a higher proportion of individuals in both communities are members of the Democratic party. But here again demographic factors assert themselves to mold political affiliations in expected directions. In Edgewood, the relationship between youth and Democratic affiliation reverses itself in the next age category (30-39), and Republican affiliation increases sharply as age increases. In Riverview, however, the nexus between age and Democratic loyalties continues until the 60-and-over category.

A major question is the differences between the rank and file who have little power and leaders who have considerable power. This question is partly answered in Table 9-2, where we find that leaders are a highly unrepresentative segment of both communities. Most of those in the power structure possess larger amounts of the resources that are highly valued in our culture, including high class status, high income, and high edu-

TABLE 9-2 COMPARATIVE SOCIAL CHARACTERISTICS OF COMMUNITY
LEADERS AND RANK AND FILE, IN PER CENT

	Edgewood Leaders	Edgewood Community	Riverview Leaders	Riverview Community
Sex				
Male	86 (36)	43 (211)	95 (37)	43 (294)
Female	14 (6)	57 (279)	5 (2)	57 (394)
Age				
21-29	None	14 (69)	None	13 (88)
30-39	5 (2)	20 (97)	3 (1)	19 (130)
40-49	29 (12)	20 (101)	31 (12)	17 (117)
50-59	43 (18)	20 (100)	36 (14)	22 (150)
60+	24 (10)	26 (126)	31 (12)	29 (199)
Class				
Upper	90 (138)	17 (83)	78 (30)	11 (74)
Middle	10 (4)	66 (324)	15 (9)	64 (421)
Lower	0	16 (80)	0	24 (169)
Party				
Republican	81 (34)	60 (297)	62 (24)	40 (282)
Democrat	17 (7)	30 (148)	35 (14)	49 (345)
Other	2 (1)	10 (49)	3 (1)	11 (77)
Religion				
Protestant	76 (32)	73 (352)	64 (25)	52 (342)
Catholic	17 (7)	24 (116)	33 (13)	47 (306)
Others	7 (3)	3 (15)	3 (1)	1 (9)
Education				
Grade school	None	20 (99)	8 (3)	29 (191)
High school	24 (10)	51 (247)	46 (18)	55 (361)
Some college	17 (7)	20 (97)	15 (6)	8 (56)
College graduate	60 (25)	9 (44)	31 (12)	8 (53)
Skill level				
Professional	38 (16)	11 (39)	18 (7)	12 (49)
Managerial	48 (20)	28 (90)	62 (24)	22 (90)
White collar	12 (5)	14 (44)	13 (5)	17 (67)
Service workers	None	14 (43)	None	7 (27)
Skilled	2 (1)	19 (63)	3 (1)	19 (76)
Semi-skilled	None	10 (33)	5 (2)	17 (67)
Unskilled	None	5 (16)	None	6 (26)

TABLE 9-2 (cont.)

Income								
Under $3000	None		25	(122)	3	(1)	16	(116)
$3000-4999	2	(1)	16	(81)	3	(1)	24	(168)
$5000-9999	10	(4)	41	(202)	44	(17)	40	(284)
$10,000-19,999	48	(20)	9	(45)	33	(13)	4	(25)
$20,000-29,999	24	(10)	3	(14)	13	(5)	1	(4)
$30,000+	17	(7)	1	(1)	5	(2)	1	(2)
NA	None		6	(29)	None		15	(105)

cational achievement. It is noteworthy that 60 per cent of the Edgewood leaders are college graduates, compared with 31 per cent of those in Riverview.

Highly valued properties of leadership may be compared with less valued properties as follows:

TABLE 9-3 PROPERTIES OF COMMUNITY LEADERSHIP

Property	Valued	Less valued
Sex	Male	Female
Age	40+	21-40
Religion	Protestant	Catholic
Education	College graduate	Less
Party	Republican	Democrat
Skill level	Professional-managerial	All others
Class	I and II (upper)	Less
Income	$10,000+	Less

With the exception of age (which in their case covered 35-64 years), these findings replicate those of Freeman and his colleagues in Syracuse.[3] They indicate that the qualities required for leadership are those in relatively short supply in terms of class, income, and skill. They suggest that less tangible

[3] *Local Community Leadership*, p. 7: see also, Woodward and Roper, who conclude on the basis of a national sample that "only 12% of the persons of 'D' [low] economic level are 'politically active,' as against 69% of the 'A's. A person with a college education is five times as likely to be 'very active' as one with a grade school education only," 44 *American Political Science Review* (December, 1950), p. 877.

properties such as interest and the desire to use available resources are somewhat peripheral bases of community power and participation. Obviously, all of those who possess highly valued properties do not use them, but the more important generalization is that active leaders possess disproportionate amounts of them. Undoubtedly, some men who do not possess most of them can exert power; Mayor O'Brian is an excellent example. But such cases are the exception, which, however dramatic and vital in a given context, do not vitiate the generalization.

It is important to compare leaders and followers on another resource dimension—the extent of their political interest and knowledge, as well as the sense of community involvement which each group disposes. Even though such resources, considered alone, are to some extent "subordinate" attributes of power, it is useful to compare the extent to which leaders and rank-and-file members share them. In Table 9-4, "political interest" is based upon responses to a single questionnaire item on interest in national political affairs; "political knowledge" is based upon a set of three questions regarding the names of local, state, and federal officials; and "involvement" is based upon scaled responses to the statement, "Even though this community may not be perfect, it offers just about everything a person could want."

The data suggest that rank-and-file members of both communities generally possess fewer of these kinds of political resources, compared with leaders. The two groups compare quite favorably with regard to political knowledge, but there is a significant difference between them regarding political interest. Only regarding involvement is there a significant difference between the two communities, with both leaders and followers in Riverview ranking much lower on this value.

The data in Table 9-4 provide one answer to the questions raised by Michels concerning the difficulties of achieving democratic participation. Another useful index of community political activism is the extent of voting. We next compare the

TABLE 9-4 COMPARATIVE LEVELS OF POLITICAL INTEREST, KNOWLEDGE, AND COMMUNITY INVOLVEMENT BETWEEN LEADERS AND RANK AND FILE

	Proportion ranking "high"					
	Edgewood			Riverview		
	Interest	Knowl-edge	Involve-ment	Interest	Knowl-edge	Involve-ment
Leaders (81)	88	98	83†	88	99	56
Rank and file (1198)	58	79	71†	54	81	47

† Significant at .01 level.

communities on this basis. First, however, an important theoretical assumption must be mentioned, namely, *that electoral participation per se is a valid index of a broader capacity for and involvement in local political affairs.* As Campbell and his associates maintain, "Voting can be conceived as one act located on a more extended dimension of participation that might be defined, if we wanted to broaden our view, to include a variety of participation forms."[4] To test this proposition and explain our emphasis on electoral participation in this chapter, we analyzed the relations between voting and individual participation in our major decisions, with the following results:

TABLE 9-5 VOTING IN THE 1960 PRESIDENTIAL ELECTION AND PARTICIPATION IN COMMUNITY DECISIONS, IN PER CENT*

	Proportion participating			
	Voters		Nonvoters	
	Edgewood (418)	Riverview (535)	Edgewood (65)	Riverview (106)
Participants	65	45	41	22
Nonparticipants	35	55	59	78

* N.A.'s and "don't remembers" are excluded.

[4] *The American Voter*, p. 92; for a psychological analysis of the differences between voters and nonvoters, see P. Hastings, "The Voter and the Non-Voter," 62 *American Journal of Sociology* (November, 1956), pp. 302-7.

Among the Edgewood respondents who voted in 1960 we find a positive association between voting and participation in the major decisions; two-thirds of those who voted also participated. In Riverview, however, the majority of voters failed to participate. Among nonvoters, the hypothesis is clearly sustained. Participation is relatively lower among them in both communities. Once again, Riverview suffers by comparison, with only one-half as large a proportion being active. From these data, we conclude tentatively that voting is a valid indicator of citizen participation in political activities other than voting. The data, moreover, provide additional confirmation of the different levels of participation in the two communities.

We next compare voting participation levels in national and state elections. In the northeast, about 80 per cent of the electorate voted in the 1960 presidential election; local elections customarily draw around 30 to 40 per cent of the electorate, while state elections fall midway between the national and local levels.[5] Table 9-6 compares the communities for selected years on these standards.

Comparable historical data for local elections are not available. However, by averaging turnout in each community in three elections during the past decade, we found comparable rates to be 48 per cent in Riverview and 40 per cent in Edgewood. Looking at national and state elections in Table 9-6, comparative average rates were 57 per cent for Edgewood and 61 per cent for Riverview. In presidential elections, even smaller differences appear, with 68 per cent for Edgewood and 65 for Riverview. From these data, we conclude that the communities have very similar degrees of political interest and participation. However, insofar as *local* turnout is a valid indicator, Riverview has a considerable advantage. Since its rate of participation in the major decisions is somewhat lower, we must conclude that the relationship between voting and par-

[5] V. O. Key, *Politics, Parties, and Pressure Groups* (New York: Crowell, 1952), p. 568.

ticipation shown in Table 9-5 does not hold true for the community. Riverview's higher local voting rate may be due to its partisan election system in which feeling in recent years has been rather intense.

TABLE 9-6 VOTING PARTICIPATION IN EDGEWOOD AND RIVERVIEW FOR SELECTED YEARS IN NATIONAL AND STATE ELECTIONS*

	Proportion voting**	
	Edgewood National and State	Riverview National and State
1900	39	40
1920	54	58
1928	75	74
1932	77	69
1938	61	63
1942	59	49
1946	54	62
1950	56	69
1956	77	72
1958	55	65
1960	84	78

* These data from official sources are not comparable with data in subsequent tables which are based upon our community sample.
** This percentage includes votes for all parties, and blank and void votes.

In Edgewood, on the other hand, there is a long-standing nonpartisan tradition and a record of individuals voting on a personal rather than on a party basis. (Since 1961, however, local elections have been carried out under party labels.) In 1963, for example, despite the fact that over 70 per cent of voters are registered Republicans, 1100 of 1850 voters cast their ballot for the Democratic candidate for mayor. Since our calculations cover both these periods, and there was little change in total electoral participation, the change to a partisan system does not seem to explain the difference. Perhaps the overwhelmingly Republican character of Edgewood dampens political intensity with the result that a smaller proportion of individuals votes, compared with Riverview where the parties are more evenly matched.

In order to indicate the historical voting patterns in both communities, we next present some trend statistics on party voting in national and state elections.

TABLE 9-7 PARTY VOTING IN EDGEWOOD AND RIVERVIEW, IN PER CENT*

Year	Edgewood Republican	Democrat	Riverview Republican	Democrat
1900	53	47	54	47
1904	64	36	60	40
1908	59	41	49	51
1916	64	37	50	50
1920	71	29	57	43
1924	71	29	50	50
1928	70	30	51	49
1932	62	38	43	57
1936	61	39	46	54
1938	69	31	51	49
1942	71	29	61	39
1946	73	27	57	43
1950	69	31	51	49
1956	76	11	57	25
1958	74	26	50	50
1960	68	27	45	46

* These data are based on official election statistics and will not therefore be comparable with voting data presented in subsequent tables, which are from our community samples.

These data indicate that in both communities the two major parties were split rather evenly at the turn of the century. Both voted somewhat more heavily Republican in 1900 and 1904, when participation was rather low compared with post-World War I elections. In Edgewood, after some variable years between 1900 and 1912, Republican strength grew steadily and the electorate became and remained Republican by about a

3-to-1 margin. Even during the New Deal period this margin remained the same.

In Riverview, we find less stability. In 1908, a slight Democratic edge appears, continues for eight years, and then disappears in 1918. The next decade is characterized by a thin Republican margin, which is overcome by the Democratic revival during the depression of the 1930's. By 1938, however, Republicanism has reasserted itself and this trend continues through the 1940's and early 1950's. In 1956, as we have seen, the vote is split equally, although in 1960 Kennedy carried the city by a fairly secure plurality.

In effect, whereas Edgewood has grown increasingly more Republican over the past half-century, political loyalties in Riverview have fluctuated rather widely, at least until 1950. These historical differences in political stability in the two communities provide important conditions for leadership. In Riverview, the changing balance has probably contributed to a somewhat greater lack of integration in the community. At the same time, such competition may explain the higher rate of participation in its local elections. Yet, this competition for office and the rhetorical combat between the "ins" and "outs" seem to have given Riverview politics a partisan intensity that limits political leaders in their ability to appeal to all citizens on a "community-welfare" basis. The last ditch effort in 1962 of the Democratic "lame-duck" city council to tie the hands of its Republican successors by severe budget cuts symbolizes this partisan milieu.

In Edgewood, on the other hand, the nonpartisan system which was apparently in effect until 1961 when a group of young Republican politicians won office on a party basis, has probably given local politics more continuity and less conflict. If "politics" in Riverview has been almost too prominent in the local consciousness, in Edgewood it has been a relatively less important calculus in local decision-making. Edgewood's "Square-Deal" administration, in power during the period of our research, was not an exceptional departure from the norm of Republican dominance and consensus. Insofar as most of its leaders are concerned, this nonpartisan condition provides a generally desirable basis for decision-making. It ensures, they say, a sense of unity and community service, which in part rests upon the large majority of citizens who share Republican political values, even though they will not always agree on specific values or issues. Yet, despite the nonpartisan political culture, Edgewood citizens were more active in the five decisions. Here again, we note the paradox that Edgewood, which is less "pluralistic" than Riverview, has more participation in political affairs other than voting.

Having traced historical patterns of voting in the two communities, we next differentiate those who are most active politically from those who are less active. We would expect such variables as class, income, and age to be the critical factors affecting electoral behavior. Social class, based upon occupation and education, will be considered first.

TABLE 9-8 SOCIAL CLASS AND VOTING PARTICIPATION*

	Proportion voting in 1960			
	Edgewood		Riverview	
Upper	88†	(83)	92	(74)
Middle	88†	(324)	85	(421)
Low	71	(80)	63	(169)

* "No answer" and "can't remember" responses were coded as "not voting."
† Significant at .01 level.

Since it is well known that voting is positively correlated with class status, we should expect to find steady and significant decreases in participation as we descend the class ladder. However, only in Riverview do we find such a linear relationship; and only between upper and lower classes, and middle and lower, are the differences very great. The largest difference between the communities occurs at the lower-class level, where the proportion of those voting in Riverview dropped to the national average, about 64 per cent, which includes the South and combines all classes. In Edgewood, a substantially larger proportion of the lower-class group voted. The much smaller variation in voting participation at all class levels suggests again that Edgewood is a somewhat more integrated community than Riverview.

In view of the utility of economic determinism in political analysis, and because income is not included as an index of class status, it seems useful to analyze income and electoral participation, as measured by the presidential election of 1960.

TABLE 9-9 INCOME AND PARTICIPATION IN 1960 PRESIDENTIAL ELECTION, IN PER CENT

	Proportion voting	
Income	Edgewood	Riverview
$10,000+	100 (60)	100 (31)
$5000–$9999	88 (204)	85 (283)
$3000–$4999	94†† (81)	83 (168)
Under $3000	80†† (120)	75 (118)

†† Significant at .05 level.

Perhaps the most striking finding here is the high rate of participation in both communities at all income levels. Both communities exceed the average rate of participation (about 80 per cent) in the 1960 presidential elections in Northern states. With the exception of Edgewood citizens in the $3000–$4999 category, voting shows the expected linear correlation with income. Participation is significantly lower in Riverview among those who earn $5000 and less per year.

Social Support and Political Behavior

Some of the variations that appear in voting behavior in the two communities may be explained in terms of the concept of "social support."⁶ The more pervasive a given political ideology or party in a community, the more likely it is to remain so. In other words, political majorities tend to remain major. In psychological terms, people seem to seek "consensual validation" of their own views and often modify them to achieve consistency with those held by a majority of their acquaintances.

Evidence for the social support hypothesis is apparent in Table 9-10 in the fact that, with very few exceptions, college-educated respondents in Edgewood are more likely to be Republicans than those in similar age categories in Riverview. In Edgewood, which is 72 per cent Republican, it also follows that more young Democrats will over time defect to the dominant party, in even larger proportions than the "normal" expected loss.

There is a general tendency for older voters in both communities to gravitate toward the Republican party. At the 50-and-over age level, with the exception of Riverview respondents with college degrees or with only grade school education, a majority of adults in *both* communities are Republicans. Once they are over 50, those with some college education show a marked preference for the Republican party.

In Riverview, which is more equally divided between the two major parties, we would expect this aspect of social support to have less effect. At the same time, it should increase the stability of both Republican and Democratic affiliation, since each group is large enough to provide considerable psychic support for its members. A similar but less pronounced tendency exists for people to desert the dominant Democratic party as they grow older, but the explanation is probably mainly a matter of increased conservatism associated with age. However, the "respectability" of Democratic affiliation in Riverview undoubtedly has some influence, as suggested by the smaller proportion of college respondents (with the exception of those at the 50-and-over age level) who vote Republican,

---

[6] This concept was developed by B. Berelson, *et al.*, *Voting* (Chicago: University of Chicago Press, 1954), pp. 122-7.

compared with Edgewood. There is an interesting difference between the party affiliations of those with *some* college, who are more closely aligned with the majority party in both communities, and those who have graduated, who are somewhat less so. Perhaps the latter group is less subject to community expectations by virtue of its higher educational achievement, but this is only speculation.

TABLE 9-10 RELATION OF AGE AND EDUCATION TO PARTY AFFILIATION, IN PER CENT

	\multicolumn{3}{c}{Edgewood (476)}	\multicolumn{3}{c}{Riverview (653)}
	Rep.	Dem.	Other	Rep.	Dem.	Other
21-29						
Grade school	60	40	0 (5)	33	58	9 (12)
High school	33	53	14 (30)	34	47	19 (64)
Some college	26	52	22 (23)	0	100	0 (4)
College graduate	45	36	19 (11)	0	60	40 (5)
30-39						
Grade school	33	33	33 (6)	22	44	34 (9)
High school	55	40	5 (40)	39	48	13 (95)
Some college	60	40	0 (20)	50	50	0 (6)
College graduate	50	50	0 (4)	67	33	0 (6)
40-49						
Grade school	55	9	36 (11)	32	60	8 (25)
High school	56	37	7 (75)	33	60	7 (72)
Some college	100	0	0 (8)	25	75	0 (8)
College graduate	100	0	0 (7)	50	50	0 (8)
50-59						
Grade school	85	15	0 (20)	35	57	8 (63)
High school	59	41	0 (41)	52	33	15 (33)
Some college	88	0	12 (25)	88	12	0 (16)
College graduate	86	14	0 (14)	44	44	12 (16)
60+						
Grade school	76	20	4 (55)	38	46	16 (92)
High school	49	36	15 (59)	52	45	3 (65)
Some college	100	0	0 (14)	53	21	26 (19)
College graduate	75	13	13 (8)	77	15	8 (13)

Results quite similar to these appear in Table 9-11 when age and party are compared, with occupational status held constant.

TABLE 9-11 RELATION BETWEEN AGE, OCCUPATION, AND PARTY AFFILIATION, IN PER CENT

	Edgewood (476) Rep. Dem. Other				Riverview (645) Rep. Dem. Other			
21-29								
Professional & Managerial	28	33	39	(18)	0	50	50	(10)
White collar	0	100	0	(6)	56	44	0	(9)
Blue collar	38	62	0	(16)	42	42	16	(26)
Housewives	45	41	14	(29)	26	58	16	(38)
30-39								
Professional & Managerial	0	100	0	(4)	33	67	0	(12)
White collar	74	13	13	(15)	29	42	29	(7)
Blue collar	40	53	7	(30)	16	65	19	(31)
Housewives	71	29	0	(21)	48	40	12	(60)
40-49								
Professional & Managerial	53	47	0	(30)	37	54	9	(24)
White collar	60	20	20	(5)	42	58	0	(19)
Blue collar	51	38	11	(37)	36	64	0	(25)
Housewives	86	0	14	(29)	27	64	9	(45)
50-59								
Professional & Managerial	80	20	0	(35)	52	40	8	(52)
White collar	42	58	0	(12)	57	43	0	(21)
Blue collar	83	17	0	(24)	35	51	14	(49)
Housewives	76	14	10	(29)	14	82	4	(28)
60+								
Professional & Managerial	39	32	29	(38)	61	16	23	(38)
White collar	100	0	0	(6)	80	20	0	(10)
Blue collar	67	31	2	(49)	37	56	7	(54)
Housewives	87	13	0	(48)	44	45	11	(87)

With the occasional exceptions among housewives, blue-collar workers in Riverview, and professional-managerial types in Edgewood, there is a general tendency for all skilled groups to become more Republican with age. As expected, the trend is most pronounced in Republican Edgewood. In both communities, however, there is a sharp and inexplicable deviation from Republican affiliation among professional-managerials in the 60+ category. Most of this prestigeful group switches to the "independent" category. In Riverview, it is anomalous to find so much higher a proportion of them Republican, compared with their counterparts in Edgewood. White-collar people in Edgewood are another variable group, who change from being 100 per cent Democrat at the 21-29 age level to 100 per cent Republican at the 60+ level. Blue-collar workers and housewives (particularly in Edgewood) are, on the whole, somewhat more consistent than other groups at most age levels.

We next consider the association between voting, party, and class status. For example, higher rates of nonvoting in Riverview are probably due to its larger proportion of working-class citizens.

TABLE 9-12 SOCIAL CLASS, PARTY VOTE, AND PARTICIPATION IN 1960 PRESIDENTIAL ELECTION, IN PER CENT

| | | | Class status | | | |
| | Upper | | Middle | | Lower | |
Party vote	Edgewood	Riverview	Edgewood	Riverview	Edgewood	Riverview
Republican	57	54	50	27	34	20
Democratic	31	38	38	58	37	43
Nonvoting	10	5	11	14	26	31
NA	2	2	1	2	3	6
	100	100	100	100	100	100
	(83)	(74)	(324)	(421)	(80)	(169)

Here a positive linear association between class status and electoral participation appears. Once again, note that participation is remarkably high, except at the lower-class level. Our earlier speculation that Riverview's somewhat lower rate of voting was largely a function of her class structure is borne out by the difference in the relative proportions of her middle- and lower-class citizens who vote. This finding seems to be reinforced by the high rate of "no answers" among the latter group, which is probably as much an indication of nonvoting as of reluctance to reveal whether or not one has voted. In terms of Michels's criteria of political *interest* as a requirement for democratic rule, this segment of Riverview ranks lower than its Edgewood counterpart. Moreover, insofar as *knowledge* is associated with education, which in turn is a determinant of class status, the significantly larger proportion of Riverview citizens in this stratum further disadvantages the community.

Party and Voting Change as Conditions of Political Leadership

An aspect of community political behavior that is relevant for leadership analysis is the phenomenon of party and voting change. As noted earlier, voting change is very important in local elections, since citizens are more likely to cross party lines than in state and national contests. For example, in the Riverview mayoralty election in 1961, when Mayor O'Brian was defeated after five consecutive terms, his opponent's plurality was 452 votes of a total of 3418. Since only 47 per cent of the local electorate registered Republican in 1961, this indicates that a considerable number of Riverview Democrats also voted for the Republican candidate.

The power of political leaders such as Mayor O'Brian rests mainly on a single major resource—political office. If they are to remain powerful, they must be able to command sustained majorities. We have also seen that Mayor O'Brian's power in the local arena has been greatly augmented by his ability to deliver Democratic majorities in state and national elections. Obviously, changes in party affiliation and in party vote among their constituents are vital for political leaders. The direction of such changes is particularly important in Riverview where the parties are rather evenly matched and small changes can provide the necessary margin for one or the other party. We assume that social support would probably inspire a somewhat greater rate of party change in solidly Republican Edgewood, compared with Riverview which has faithfully supported Mayor O'Brian and state and national Democratic candidates during the past decade.

We turn first to comparative rates of change, by which we mean a change in *party* affiliation, rather than a temporary switch of vote during a given election. When such rates are compared in Table 9-13, we find that Riverview is only slightly less constant than Edgewood. Eighteen per cent of its citizens have changed party, compared with 16 per cent in Edgewood. Table 9-13 indicates that the directions of change are toward the majority party in each community, by precisely the same margins among men, but by a much larger pro-Republican movement among women in Edgewood, compared with those in Riverview.

These data provide several rough generalizations about those who change from their fathers' affiliation. Women tend strongly to change in the direction of the majority party, which reinforces the thesis that majority parties tend to retain their advantage in a given community or state. Men, too, move toward the majority party, but by only a small margin.

Regarding age, we see the usual trend in Edgewood of young people (21-29) moving toward the Democratic party. In Riverview, surprisingly, they change mainly in a pro-Republican direction. In both communities, however, after 40 the main drift is in the direction of the majority party. Over-all results are as expected, with Republicans receiving a net gain in Edgewood, and Democrats enjoying one in Riverview.

Religion shows more consistency, with a much higher proportion of Protestants moving to the Republicans and Catholics

TABLE 9-13 DEMOGRAPHIC CHARACTERISTICS AND DIRECTION OF CHANGE
AMONG THOSE WHO CHANGED PARTY, IN PER CENT*

	Edgewood (78)		Riverview (124)	
	Pro-Republican	Pro-Democratic	Pro-Republican	Pro-Democratic
Sex				
Male	52	48 (42)	48	52 (48)
Female	64	36 (36)	41	59 (76)
Religion				
Protestant	62	38 (60)	45	55 (71)
Catholic	44	66 (18)	40	60 (52)
Age				
21-29	33	67 (9)	63	37 (16)
30-39	68	32 (19)	54	46 (13)
40-49	29	71 (14)	21	79 (14)
50-59	91	9 (11)	40	60 (47)
60+	60	40 (25)	44	56 (34)
Education				
Grade school	52	48 (21)	38	62 (24)
High school	56	44 (36)	40	60 (70)
Some college	67	33 (11)	67	33 (18)
College graduate	70	30 (10)	42	58 (12)
Skill level				
Professional	38	62 (8)	46	54 (13)
Managerial	47	53 (17)	44	56 (9)
White collar	100	0 (6)	71	29 (21)
Blue collar	43	57 (23)	40	60 (35)
Housewives	60	40 (15)	33	67 (46)
Income				
Under $3000	67	33 (9)	41	59 (17)
$3000-4999	67	33 (15)	43	57 (23)
$5000-9999	59	41 (41)	43	57 (69)
$10,000+	87	13 (7)	100	0 (6)
NA	0	100 (6)	13	87 (8)

* Total N's in each category may differ slightly, because respondents did not answer all questions.

defecting to the Democrats in Edgewood. In Riverview, on balance, both Catholics and Protestants are pro-Democratic.

Here again, social support is apparent since the relative proportions of gains for each party are highest in those communities in which they enjoy a majority.

The same influence is generally apparent when education is considered. However, we again see the phenomenon of those respondents with *some* college disrupting the trend; a high proportion of them defect to the Republican party in Riverview. In Riverview, college graduates are obviously more influenced by the political milieu, for contrary to most generalizations about educational level and party, those who change are distributed almost equally between the two parties.

We remarked earlier about the unexpected tendency of professionals to divide their new allegiance more equally than one would have expected, and to be mainly pro-Democratic in both Edgewood and Riverview, despite their high educational level. The same generalization holds for managers, but this is less surprising since they are of somewhat lower class status. Surprisingly, we find white-collar workers in both communities much more likely than professionals and managers to switch to the Republican party. This may reflect the status sensitivity of this group, inspired by its well-known desire to set itself apart from the blue-collar group. Insofar as white-collar workers tend to have work milieus in which status differentials can be marked off and preserved, and in which they are more subject to socialization by higher-status managers and professionals, such influences may also be at work.[7] Housewives who, in effect, represent the political values of *all* skill groups through their husbands, provide evidence for the social support thesis. In both towns, they change in expected directions.

Income data reveal no surprising results. The usual association between income and Republican affiliation is apparent in the fact that almost 90 per cent of those in the $10,000 category

---

[7] For a complete analysis of white-collar structure and psychology, see C. Wright Mills, *White Collar: The American Middle Classes* (New York: Oxford University Press, 1951).

in Edgewood have changed toward the Republican party, while among the same group in Riverview all changers have moved in the expected Republican direction. These data support the well-known generalization that upper-income groups are rather more sophisticated and economically determined in their political alignments than those in lower-income strata.

THE 1956 AND 1960 PRESIDENTIAL ELECTIONS

We have noted the importance of religion in the political culture of Riverview, and the degree to which Mayor O'Brian's power was related to his support from the strong Democratic-Catholic element. The dynamics of this support are suggested by the degree of influence which religion had in the 1960 presidential election. Unlike Edgewood voters who remained nonpartisan in local elections, Riverview voters tended during the period of O'Brian's administration to vote along party lines, until the 1961 election when many Democrats crossed party lines to defeat him. In the opinion of local politicians, the voters had concluded that "it was time for a change." Table 9-14 suggests again the effect of a community's ethnic and religious structure on its political behavior. The influence of social support is again

TABLE 9-14 RELIGION AND PARTY VOTING IN THE 1956 AND 1960 PRESIDENTIAL ELECTIONS, IN PER CENT

	Edgewood (468)				Riverview (648)			
	Rep.	Dem.	D.V.*	N.A.	Rep.	Dem.	D.V.*	N.A.
1956								
Protestant	76	5	19	1 (352)	70	11	16	3 (342)
Catholic	47	25	27	1 (116)	40	36	18	6 (306)
1960								
Protestant	64	23	13	0 (352)	52	31	14	2 (342)
Catholic	8	81	10	2 (116)	3	74	19	4 (306)

* Did not vote.

confirmed. Finally, the data may be considered in the context of voting change in the 1956 and the 1960 presidential elections. The table compares the voting of respondents with their religious affiliation, and then determines the degree of cross-party voting in 1960, compared with that in 1956. The results suggest the extent to which religion influenced voting in 1960 in the two communities.

These data show that a majority of Protestants voted for the Republican candidate in both elections. Catholics, on the other hand, split their votes widely or failed to vote in 1956, but voted overwhelmingly for Kennedy in 1960. In 1956, nonvoting is highest in Edgewood, particularly among Catholic voters. In 1960, however, nonvoting is highest in Riverview, again among Catholic respondents. However, unlike Edgewood, it is at almost the same general level as in 1956, suggesting that neither election was as stressful for Riverview voters as the 1956 election proved to be for Edgewood voters, who have characteristically had somewhat lower nonvoting rates. When the Riverview Catholic nonvoter group is analyzed, we find a partial explanation for this figure. Fully 76 per cent fall in classes IV and V and 53 per cent are women. It is well known that Catholic voters, along with young people, women, and members of the lower class, are quite unstable in their political involvement and are less likely to vote than men, the middle-aged, and higher status respondents.[8]

Although a great deal of switch voting obviously occurred in both communities in 1960, Protestants were considerably more consistent than Catholics. The ambivalence of many Catholic voters toward Stevenson in 1956, concerning such matters as his divorce, and aggravated no doubt by their conviction that he could not win, is suggested by the extremely high rate of nonvoting (27 per cent) among them in Edgewood, compared

---

[8] Among others, see W. N. McPhee and W. A. Glaser, *Public Opinion and Congressional Elections* (New York: Free Press, 1962), p. 44, Chap. 1 *passim*.

with 1960 (10 per cent).[9] The data may also be a commentary on the importance of personality in American presidential elections, which may be inversely associated with the failure of our major parties to differ much on substantive issues.

We now turn more specifically to voting change by religion in the two elections.

TABLE 9-15 COMPARISON OF VOTING CHANGE AMONG PROTESTANTS AND CATHOLICS IN THE 1956 AND 1960 PRESIDENTIAL ELECTIONS, IN PER CENT

| | *Edgewood 1956* | | | |
| | Vote Republican | | Vote Democratic | |
	Protestant (268)	Catholic (69)	Protestant (17)	Catholic (29)
1960				
Rep.	79	13	6	3
Dem.	15	86	82	90
D.V.	6	1	12	6
	Riverview 1956			
	Protestant (239)	Catholic (123)	Protestant (36)	Catholic (111)
1960				
Rep.	66	8	11	—
Dem.	28	79	81	97
D.V.	5	13	8	3

As Table 9-15 indicates, when consistency in the two elections is compared, striking differences appear. Of the 268 Prot-

[9] There is no consensus on the question of the over-all effect of religion on the 1960 election. For analyses, see P. E. Converse, *et al.*, "Stability and Change in 1960: A Reinstating Election," 55 *American Political Science Review* (June, 1961), pp. 276-79; and V. O. Key, "Interpreting the Election Results," in P. David (ed.), *The Presidential Election and Transition, 1960-1961* (Brookings Institution: Washington, D. C., 1961), pp. 150-75. However, Campbell, *et al.*, on the basis of the 1954 congressional and 1956 presidential elections, have shown that Catholic voters do shift their vote to Catholic candidates and will cross party lines to do so. A. Campbell, P. Converse, W. Miller, and D. Stokes, *The American Voter* (New York: John Wiley, 1960), pp. 319-21.

estants who voted Republican in 1956, over three-fourths voted the same way in 1960. However, the 69 Catholic Republicans in Edgewood showed much less consistency in 1960. In fact, less than one-seventh voted the same way. In general, the picture is the same for Riverview Republicans.

Among Democratic voters in 1956, there was little shift in either community in 1960. However, among these voters, Catholics were somewhat more consistent than Protestants (90 per cent versus 82 per cent in Edgewood; 97 per cent versus 81 per cent in Riverview). With a Catholic presidential candidate running on the Democratic ticket, Catholic Republicans were the group most likely to change. If we assume that the winning candidate represented both a political party and a religious grouping, it is possible to conclude from these data that religion is a more powerful factor in voting than is political affiliation, since many fewer Republicans in general and few Protestant Republicans in particular switched their vote to the Democratic party. There was, moreover, a greater pro-Democratic shift in Riverview which was already more Democratic in 1956, again reinforcing the social support hypothesis. This was particularly—and surprisingly—true among Protestant Republicans. Catholic Republicans, however, showed a tendency to go into conflict in Riverview, as evidenced by a higher percentage of nonvoting.

To further differentiate voters who remained loyal from those who changed their vote in 1960, we next compare the social characteristics of the two groups.

Several findings are noteworthy here. First, Democrats in both communities were generally more loyal to their party than Republicans in the 1960 election. However, Republicans in dominantly Republican Edgewood were as a rule more likely to be loyal than their counterparts in Riverview. Whereas the "mean change rate" for Edgewood Republicans in all demographic categories was 17 per cent, it rose to 25 per cent among

TABLE 9-16 SOCIAL CHARACTERISTICS OF "LOYAL" AND "DEVIANT" VOTERS IN THE 1960 PRESIDENTIAL ELECTION, IN PER CENT*

	Edgewood (398)				Riverview (495)			
	Republicans Loyal Deviant		Democrats Loyal Deviant		Republicans Loyal Deviant		Democrats Loyal Deviant	
Sex								
Male	85 15 (104)		93 7 (61)		76 24 (90)		96 4 (116)	
Female	81 19 (163)		93 7 (70)		74 26 (127)		91 8 (162)	
Religion								
Protestant	89 11 (238)		91 9 (56)		84 16 (182)		80 20 (84)	
Catholic	22 78 (23)		95 5 (73)		24 76 (34)		99 2 (185)	
Education								
Grade school	82 18 (60)		100 0 (17)		69 31 (49)		85 15 (81)	
High school	80 20 (117)		92 8 (85)		76 24 (116)		98 2 (163)	
Some college	90 10 (58)		90 10 (20)		81 19 (27)		100 0 (16)	
College graduate	78 22 (23)		100 0 (9)		72 28 (25)		83 17 (18)	
Age								
21-29	72 28 (18)		94 6 (34)		80 20 (20)		91 9 (33)	
30-39	78 22 (32)		100 0 (22)		83 17 (42)		91 9 (47)	
40-49	76 24 (58)		82 18 (22)		68 32 (37)		95 5 (64)	
50-59	85 15 (72)		100 0 (22)		76 24 (49)		95 5 (66)	
60+	89 11 (87)		90 10 (31)		71 29 (69)		91 9 (68)	
Income								
Under $3000	85 15 (53)		86 14 (35)		74 26 (38)		90 10 (41)	
$3000-4999	71 29 (45)		100 0 (29)		81 19 (57)		99 1 (76)	
$5000-9999	85 15 (115)		93 7 (56)		74 26 (89)		89 11 (131)	
$10,000 and over	82 18 (49)		100 0 (9)		65 35 (17)		100 1 (12)	
Skill level								
Professional	86 14 (21)		82 18 (11)		81 19 (21)		85 15 (20)	
Managerial	95 5 (40)		100 0 (24)		74 26 (34)		90 10 (31)	
White collar	84 16 (25)		100 0 (15)		67 33 (33)		100 0 (26)	
Service	71 29 (24)		78 22 (9)		86 14 (7)		100 0 (7)	
Skilled	81 19 (32)		100 0 (23)		68 32 (19)		95 5 (42)	
Semi-skilled	87 13 (15)		71 29 (14)		67 33 (12)		100 0 (35)	
Unskilled	100 0 (4)		100 0 (7)		100 0 (6)		75 25 (4)	
Housewives	78 23 (106)		96 4 (28)		75 25 (79)		91 9 (113)	

* To reduce the complexity of this table, all "not ascertained," "none," and "other" categories have been eliminated. Only 29 cases fell in these categories.

those in Riverview. Among Democrats the comparative rates were only 7 and 6 per cent respectively.

The highest rates of deviation occur among the following (overlapping) groups in rank order: Catholic Republicans, Riverview Republicans making $10,000, white-collar, skilled, and semi-skilled Republican workers in Riverview, Republican voters in Riverview in the 40-49 age category, Republicans with grade school educations in Riverview, Riverview Republicans in the 60 age group, Republican service workers in Edgewood, and Edgewood Republicans in the $3000-$4999 income category. One-quarter or more of those in each of these groups defected. Among them, Catholic Republicans in both communities were two-and-one-half times more likely than other groups to have changed their vote. This suggests the importance of the religious issue among these groups, since we can assume that they voted Republican in 1956.

Differences in the political culture of the two communities are suggested by a comparison of the class make-up of those in the Republican party. Such differences, which may be hidden by traditional party labels, also tell us something about the comparative political resources of the communities. From what we know of Riverview, we would predict that its Republican ranks contain a much larger proportion of lower-class members. Such differences, if they exist, tend to make political opinion in the community less "typically" Republican in its attitude concerning government participation in the economy, welfare programs, and the like. They would also help explain the willingness of Republican economic leaders, such as Cavenaugh and Armstrong, to join O'Brian in federally-sponsored programs that might offend their personal preferences for "private" solutions to community problems. In effect, they could count on considerable local support among Republican citizens. No similar substratum of opinion exists in Edgewood where "political" decisions were monopolized by political leaders.

To this extent, formal party distributions in the community

are an unreliable guide to its dominant ideological complexion. Table 9-17 presents the class distribution of the major parties.

TABLE 9-17 CLASS STATUS OF REPUBLICANS IN EDGEWOOD AND RIVERVIEW, IN PER CENT

Class status	Edgewood	Riverview
Upper	21	17
Middle	69	58
Lower	10	23
NA	0	2
	100 (291)	100 (259)

As expected, over twice as high a proportion of lower-class citizens are members of the Republican party in Riverview, compared with Edgewood. Moreover, there is a substantially smaller proportion of middle-class Republicans in Riverview. The implications of these findings for the role of leaders include the need for economic elites to dampen their appeals for "private" solutions to community problems, self-reliance, etc.; at least, this must be done if they hope to make programmatic as distinct from rhetorical gains. The lack of private wealth and a philanthropic tradition in Riverview, which reflects and reinforces its class structure, means that the entire power structure will be obliged to turn to a greater extent to external, governmental resources in solving community problems. One consequence is that the luxury of indulging their ideological preferences enjoyed by Edgewood Republican leaders is denied their Riverview counterparts.

Some Community Differences in Political Values

It seems useful to compare the communities on a number of sensitive political issues, since these again tell us something about the attitudinal context within which leaders must function. They also have some direct implications for the viability of the two communities. For example, community attitudes toward labor unions undoubtedly play a part in the ability of the two communities to attract new industry. In Edgewood, where most Republicans (who constitute almost three-fourths of the community) believe that unions are of questionable value (see Table 9-19), leaders have been able to bring into the community at least one company wishing to escape labor troubles and high labor costs experienced in a neighboring state. There is apparently no local sentiment that questions this practice. In Riverview, by contrast, at least one new industry has been disqualified because local labor leaders, some of whom were either decision-makers themselves or closely aligned with the local Democratic city administration, believed that it intended to pay substandard wages. In both cases, leaders were constrained by the differing contextual properties of public opinion in this area.

Tables 9-18 through 9-23 (N = 1023) are based upon individual items which tap generalized attitudes about contemporary political issues. Although they are obviously less reliable than the scales we have used elsewhere, they provide additional data about value differences in the communities.

The data show significant differences in opinion. Twice as high a proportion of Edgewood Republicans feel pessimistic

TABLE 9-18 PARTY AND ATTITUDE TOWARD CHANGE, IN PER CENT

"We have moved too far away from those principles that made America great."

	Agree Edgewood	Agree Riverview	Disagree Edgewood	Disagree Riverview	Don't know Edgewood	Don't know Riverview	NA*
Republican	52†	38	31††	40	17	18	5
Democratic	26†	28†	49	37	25	30	2

* NA's have been combined for this and the following four tables.
† Significant at .01 level.
†† Significant at .05 level.

about the course of events, compared with Democrats. In Riverview, the difference between members of the two parties is not so extreme. Since this point of view, which regards the guidelines of the past as preferable to those of the present, can be defined as "conservative" we may say that Republicans in Edgewood tend to be more conservative on this value than those in Riverview. A significantly smaller proportion of Democrats in both communities agree with the generalization, although there is little difference between them. However, when the "disagree" column is checked, we find that a significantly higher proportion (p = .01) of Edgewood Democrats, compared with those in Riverview, reject the statement. This may reflect some difference between the communities in political commitment.

A variable which often serves to differentiate individuals and groups on a "liberal-conservative" continuum is their attitude toward labor unions. The following table compares the major parties on this dimension.

TABLE 9-19 PARTY AND ATTITUDE TOWARD UNIONS, IN PER CENT

"On the whole, labor unions are doing a lot of good in the country."

	Agree Edgewood	Agree Riverview	Disagree Edgewood	Disagree Riverview	Don't know Edgewood	Don't know Riverview	NA*
Republicans	21†	49	49†	32	29	18	3
Democrats	55††	65†	26†	15†	17	19	1

† Significant at .01 level.
†† Significant at .05 level.

As noted a moment ago, significant differences of opinion exist here. Republicans in both communities tend to question the role of unions much more than Democrats. This opinion is most strongly held by Edgewood Republicans. Note that in Riverview, essentially a working-class community, a much higher proportion of Republicans are sympathetic toward unions than in Edgewood. Social support again appears: the great difference found between the Republican parties in the two communities suggests that the dominant tradition of a community has a considerable leavening effect on the opinions of its members, regardless of party, ideology, and other social characteristics.

An issue of singular importance and some controversy has been American support of the United Nations. The following data indicate how party members in the two communities feel about this matter.

TABLE 9-20 PARTY AND INTERNATIONAL AFFAIRS, IN PER CENT

"On the whole, American participation in the UN has been a good thing."

	Agree		Disagree		Don't know		
	Edge-wood	River-view	Edge-wood	River-view	Edge-wood	River-view	NA*
Republican	84	83	1†	7	14	8	3
Democratic	91††	87	3†	12	5	2	1

† Significant at .01 level.
†† Significant at .05 level.

Although Democrats in both communities are somewhat more favorably inclined toward the UN, there is a remarkable unanimity on the desirability of U.S. participation. A much larger proportion of both Riverview Republicans and Democrats disagree, compared with Edgewood, but both communities are overwhelmingly favorable to the organization.

The major thrust of the U.S. foreign aid programs in underdeveloped countries has been in the form of military equipment and instruction. Some individuals have felt that this emphasis should be modified in the direction of more "welfare" programs, including education, public health, and economic development. The following table associates party and attitudes toward such a change.

TABLE 9-21 PARTY AND INTERNATIONAL AFFAIRS, IN PER CENT

"We should give more of our foreign aid to social welfare projects."

	Agree Edgewood	Agree Riverview	Disagree Edgewood	Disagree Riverview	Don't know Edgewood	Don't know Riverview	NA*
Republican	51	46	18††	27	30	24	4
Democratic	52	55††	20	22	26	22	3

†† Significant at .05 level.

On this issue, a bare majority of citizens in both parties in both communities agree that more social welfare programs ought to be built into our foreign aid programs. The highest proportion of agreement is found among Democrats in Riverview, and the highest proportion of disagreement among Riverview Republicans. The somewhat higher proportion of "don't knows" among all respondents indicates a greater degree of ambivalence (or perhaps, lack of knowledge) about this issue, compared with preceding ones.

Another general issue concerning international perspectives is the extent to which Americans should be concerned about the way people in other countries evaluate the United States. Symbolic of this issue are such themes as "You can't buy friendship," and "Other nations respect power and its forthright use." In 1962, for example, the Kennedy Administration's strong stand against Russia in the matter of the latter's missile site bases in Cuba was widely interpreted as enhancing U.S. prestige abroad. The following data reveal community opinions on this general value.

Whereas half or more of the members of both parties in both communities disagree that the United States should be less concerned with foreign opinion, in Riverview the proportion of "don't knows" is a bit higher on this judgment. Some one-third of both parties in both communities agree that a "tough" posture is preferable. Riverview Democrats, by contrast, rank lowest on disagreement with this item. Given the fact that a more "internationalist" posture has been characteristic of their party since World War II, this more tenuous concern with foreign opinions toward the United States is somewhat unexpected.

TABLE 9-22 PARTY AND ATTITUDES TOWARD INTERNATIONAL AFFAIRS, IN PER CENT

"The United States should be less concerned about what other people think of us."

	Agree		Disagree		Don't know		
	Edge-wood	River-view	Edge-wood	River-view	Edge-wood	River-view	NA*
Republican	33	30	54	59	12	9	2
Democratic	32	32	53	49††	13	19	0

†† Significant at .05 level.

Regarding the relative agreement characterizing attitudes of Republicans and Democrats in each community, we find the greatest disparity in Edgewood, on the items concerning the assumed decline of traditional principles and the contribution of labor unions. Republicans are much more pessimistic on both counts. On the remaining three items, the responses are quite uniform in both communities, with the exception of a significant difference between Riverview Democrats and Republicans on the issue of interlarding our foreign aid with more "social welfare" types of programs. As might be expected, Democrats are more favorable toward this policy. In general, the findings illustrate again the differences in the political cultures of the two communities, with Riverview leaning much further toward a "welfare liberalism" ideology than Edgewood. On international matters, however, they are quite similar, and in tune with the apparent national consensus on the issues raised here.

One final item provides insight into the general political

complexions of the communities, as indicated by their toleration of minority political views.

TABLE 9-23 TOLERANCE OF MINORITY POLITICAL VALUES IN EDGEWOOD AND RIVERVIEW, IN PER CENT

"An atheist or a socialist should have as much right to make a public speech in [Edgewood or Riverview] as anyone else."

	Agree		Disagree		Don't know	
	Edgewood	Riverview	Edgewood	Riverview	Edgewood	Riverview
Leaders (81)	76	72	10	23	14	5
Rank and file (1098)	45	49	35††	20	20	29

†† Significant at .05 level.

As expected, leaders are more permissive than followers in both communities. However, the economic liberalism of Riverview leaders is not matched by their political liberalism; one quarter would deny a socialist or an atheist the right of free speech. Riverview followers are more permissive than Edgewood's. A higher proportion agree, and the proportion who *disagree* is significantly less. Insofar as rank-and-file opinion is concerned, Riverview is again shown to be a somewhat more "liberal" community. At the same time, however, the fact that half or more of citizens in both communities either "don't know" or "disagree" that those holding minority views should be allowed to express them publicly, provides support for Michels's conclusion that a lack of political sophistication among the rank and file encourages elitism.

Conclusions

A useful theoretical framework for explaining the different degrees of participation in the two communities is provided by Robert Michels, whose theory suggests several conditions required for democratic as opposed to elitist rule. Essentially, he maintained that the rank and file must be interested, knowledgeable, and politically skillful. One index of these qualities is voting participation. In general, we found that Edgewood's citizens possessed somewhat more of these qualities. One important exception, however, is that Riverview had a higher rate of participation in *local* elections.

Community integration and political viability are partly revealed by the extent of participation in elections. In some of these respects, we find that Edgewood is somewhat more favored than Riverview. For example, two-thirds of Edgewood's citizens are Republicans; in Riverview Democrats enjoy a small margin. Whereas the former has an over-all range of only 8 percentage points in voting participation among its three class strata, the latter has a dispersion of 29 points. Average participation in the presidential elections of 1956 and 1960 was somewhat lower in Riverview, which had a significantly larger proportion of nonvoters in 1960. However, in local elections which are of more direct concern to power structure analysis, Riverview has had higher rates of participation. We believe this reflects the social diversity and intensity of political feeling in the community, compared with the nonpartisan, political tradition and social uniformity of Edgewood. The paradox here is that in Riverview higher local turnouts and more political diversity and competition (i.e. pluralism) do not culminate in greater citizen participation in the decisions considered.

From such findings, we conclude that political structure and behavior in Riverview and Edgewood provide somewhat different conditions for viable leadership. As shown in Chapter 6, taken as a whole the members of the Riverview power structure possess somewhat fewer of the resources typically required for leadership; however, we find the community itself has a more lively political culture. This conclusion is based on the assumption that local voting participation is a valid indicator of a generalized political interest. The act of voting seems to be part of a larger tendency toward political activism. Tentative confirmation of this assumption is provided in Table 9-5 which shows a positive relation between voting in the 1960 presidential election and individual participation in one or more of the major decisions. However, despite a higher degree of local voting participation in Riverview, there is a lower degree of participation in the five decisions. We must therefore conclude that the relationship between voting and other political activities does not hold. The paradox remains that Riverview fulfills more of the social and political conditions of pluralism, yet remains less pluralistic in the major decisions and somewhat less effective in meeting the problems which inspired the decisions.

The social aspects of political structure in the two communities are found to be quite different. Edgewood is predominantly Republican, while in Riverview the Democratic party has a slight edge. This reflects the historical political evolution and the ethnic and religious structures of the communities. By the end of World War I, Edgewood had become a Republican stronghold, in which only about one-third of the voters were Democratic. This condition has persisted since that time. In Riverview, on the other hand, with the exception of the depression years during the 1930's, the proportionate strength of the two major parties remained roughly equal until 1950. Since then, however, the Democratic party has been dominant. The existence of a small contingent of the left Liberal party in Riverview suggests its greater political diversity, compared with Edgewood.

The communities are also different in class terms, which affects their over-all electoral behavior and the "followership potential" upon which leaders may draw. Edgewood has a somewhat higher proportion of voters among its middle- and lower-class respondents, compared with Riverview. The latter, however, has a significantly higher proportion of voters among its small upper-class stratum, and a larger proportion of working-class citizens, who normally vote Democratic. Riverview also has a larger proportion of Catholics, who tend to vote Democratic. These two conditions explain to a great extent Mayor O'Brian's long term in office and his leadership in most of the major decisions.

The influence of religion in the 1960 presidential election was analyzed in an effort to illustrate the effects of ethnic and religious factors in the local political culture. An analysis of change in party voting from 1956 to 1960 indicated that, among Republican voters, a remarkably higher proportion of Catholics compared with Protestants switched to Kennedy in 1960. Nonvoting in 1960, moreover, was highest among Catholic Republicans in Riverview, which suggests that this election may have provoked unusual psychological tension among this group. Insofar as Mayor O'Brian's political tenure and his access to the power structure rest upon the support of Riverview's strong Catholic-Democratic element, its political behavior is immediately relevant to an understanding of community decision-making during the period covered by our research.

The influence of "social support" appears in many contexts, the generalization being that, over time, most members of both communities tend to accommodate themselves to dominant local political values. Expected differences resulting from party and socioeconomic characteristics are modified accordingly. Republicans in "Democratic" Riverview, for example, are less likely to have social characteristics customarily regarded as Republican. The "typical" associations between class, wealth, and party are less pronounced, as shown for example by the relatively higher proportion of lower-class members in the Riverview Republican party. One consequence is that her Republican economic leaders are obliged to temper their preferences for private initiative and limited government in line with the more pragmatic, "welfare" expectations of their constituents.

10
COMMUNITY VALUES AND CONSENSUS

The different rates of participation and pluralism that characterize Edgewood and Riverview probably reflect the extent to which leaders and followers share certain bench-mark values, as well as the extent to which the communities themselves share common assumptions about politics, economics, and society. Certainly, democratic political theory assumes that a broadly shared pattern of values is necessary to bind the social system together. Such values provide a rationale for community action; political and economic conflicts are mediated by its ground rules. To some extent, leaders must work within this context. As V. O. Key concludes, "The leadership structure exists on a foundation of popular consent, which reflects itself in consensus on specifics as well as in a generalized support of the political system."[1]

Despite its importance, "consensus" is rarely defined. In this

[1] After a careful analysis of the conceptual difficulties of the "magic word" consensus, Key concludes that the concept remains useful: "On the American scene it may be supposed that a compatibility exists between the modal expectations, values, opinions, and attitudes of the population generally and ways of behavior of the political activists." *Public Opinion and American Democracy*, p. 53, Chap. 2, *passim*.

analysis, the concept is used to mean merely the *extent of agreement* that exists. It does not presume any quantitative criterion, such as 90 per cent of the community must share a view before one may say that consensus exists. In keeping with our comparative orientation, we will try to determine the relative amounts of agreement existing within and between the two communities.

Sociologists often stress the advantages of value consensus, which, in their terms, plays a "functional," integrative social role.[2] This formulation derives from the biological world, in which organisms are maintained in equilibrium by the homeostatic operation of their parts. The biological analogy is transferred to the social system. The very term "system" is symptomatic, for systems are composed of functionally interdependent parts; hence the "functionalist" mode of analysis which asks of each part in a given system: What is its function or purpose in a given social unit? What, for instance, is the function of religious rites or political ceremonials?

In some such context, it has often been argued that "consensus" about certain basic values is the critical variable in democratic political systems. Such values probably include the acceptance of evolutionary as opposed to revolutionary change; religious and racial tolerance; the principle of free expression as a prerequisite of peaceful, rational change; limited government; pluralism as opposed to an all-powerful state; social mobility to prevent rigid, explosive class stratification; and participation in the political process for those who desire it. Obviously, some of these values are inconsistent with reality, as seen in the conflict between the ideal of racial equality and the position of the American Negro. Nevertheless, they are often

---

[2] For an analysis of "functionalism," see R. Merton, *Social Theory and Social Structure* (revised ed.) (Glencoe: Free Press, 1957), pp. 19-84; for a critique of this orientation, see K. Davis, "The Myth of Functional Analysis as a Special Method in Sociology and Anthropology," 24 *American Sociological Review* (December, 1959), pp. 757-73.

strongly held in principle and there is little doubt that they influence a great deal of behavior.

In an attempt to determine whether the two communities vary in terms of value consensus, which in turn may affect their collective political efficacy, we included relevant questions in our interviews. Some of the questions are generalized attitudinal items taken from well-known scales; others are directed specifically to attitudes about political effectiveness and participation.

From what we have learned about participation in the two communities, we will hypothesize that a higher degree of consensus exists between the leaders and the community, as well as within the community, in Edgewood compared with Riverview. Edgewood should prove to be somewhat more politically "conservative" than Riverview. We should expect to find a somewhat higher degree of alienation in Riverview. Finally, in line with the "law" of social support, we should expect to find somewhat higher rates of participation among Edgewood citizens, regardless of class, income, or ideology.

Table 10-1 considers the ideological perspective of Edgewood and Riverview leaders with regard to "conservatism."[3] "Conservatism" has been measured by responses to several questionnaire items. These include certain attitudes toward government, labor unions, American principles, the equation of democracy with free enterprise, and the decline of the Protestant ethic, particularly the veneration of hard work. We assume that individuals expressing *more* faith in governmental solutions to problems of health, welfare, etc. are less conservative than those who advocate private solutions to such problems. Individuals who believe that long-established political and moral "principles" have been abandoned are often more conservative than those who feel otherwise. Similarly, rejection of

[3] Unfortunately, the items used to define "conservatism" did not form a scale; hence the findings are presented as being suggestive, but not as measuring a unidimensional quality.

the statement that labor unions have generally done considerable good for the country is usually regarded as an index of conservatism.

We would expect to find that *political* leaders, both Republican and Democratic, would tend to endorse governmental solutions to community problems more frequently than their economic counterparts, and perhaps more often than the specialist groups. As noted earlier, the two communities seem different in their preferences for governmental versus "private" solutions to their major problems. Since Riverview has drawn more heavily upon state and federal aid, we would assume that, compared with Edgewood, a higher proportion of its elite group would exhibit pro-governmental values. It will be recalled that only one of the five decisions in Riverview was a "private" type, whereas Edgewood's decisions included two essentially "private" ones. The following table shows the perspective of the two elites toward "conservatism."

TABLE 10-1 "CONSERVATISM" AMONG EDGEWOOD AND RIVERVIEW ELITES

	Proportion agreeing	
	Edgewood	*Riverview*
	(42)	(39)
1. "That government which governs least governs best."	60	46
2. "We have moved too far away from those fundamental principles that made America great."	48	49
3. "One of the biggest problems with the world is that people don't work hard enough any more."	48	54
4. "Democracy depends fundamentally on the existence of free enterprise."	90	82
5. "On the whole, labor unions are doing a lot of good in this country."	45	59

Somewhat greater faith in government among Riverview leaders is suggested by responses to item one which evokes a generalized attitude toward government. Only 46 per cent of Riverview's leaders accepted this *negative* statement about government, as opposed to 60 per cent of the Edgewood group. The important point here is the difference between the degrees of rejection in each community. This difference is entirely consistent with the judgment one would make after analyzing decisions in the two communities with their peculiar socioeconomic structures. It is also consistent with the well-known tendency of less favored groups in our society to endorse government activity more highly than those who enjoy larger shares of what is available.

Another striking difference between the leaders is in their evaluations of labor unions. Riverview leaders are considerably more favorable toward them. The only other item upon which the two leader groups exhibit any substantial difference is the equation of free enterprise and democracy. Although both groups strongly endorse this value, the difference indicates a somewhat greater ideological diversity in Riverview, reflecting in turn its ethnic, economic, and religious diversity. Since this value, which joins free enterprise and democracy, is deeply engrained in American society and rather systematically fostered by the mass media, one would expect to find it more firmly held by a community such as Edgewood which more closely fits the dominant Anglo-Saxon, Protestant model.

The data in Table 10-1 obscure differences between the respective types of elites in both communities, which are probably quite substantial for some values. Table 10-2 supports this judgment.

Regarding the "anti-government" value, we find that Edgewood political leaders rank almost twice as high as their Riverview counterparts, and considerably higher than economic leaders in both communities. The relatively more "liberal"

TABLE 10-2 INTERCOMMUNITY VARIATIONS IN LEADERS' "CONSERVATISM"

	Proportion agreeing			
	Edgewood		Riverview	
	Political (9)	Economic (14)	Political (10)	Economic (19)
1. "That government which governs least governs best."	78	57	40	53
2. "We have moved too far away from those fundamental principles that made America great."	33	57	50	53
3. "One of the biggest problems with the world is that people don't work hard enough any more."	55	57	60	63
4. "Democracy depends fundamentally on the existence of free enterprise."	89	93	80	84
5. "On the whole, labor unions are doing a lot of good in this country."	44	50	80	47

values of Riverview politicos are also apparent in the fact that almost twice as high a proportion of them endorse unions, compared with politicians in Edgewood. Yet, the latter group ranked much lower than all others on the "conservative" item concerning the alleged abandonment of first principles. The explanation may be that this item taps a more generalized "conservative" attitude than the first "anti-governmental" item, which may be viewed as more narrowly "political." However, this is pure speculation. On the whole, Edgewood leaders seem to be somewhat more conservative, particularly its political leaders who rank much higher on the free enterprise-democracy alliance and, as noted, quite low on approval of unions. It is noteworthy that whereas economic leaders in both communities respond rather similarly to all items, political leaders differ widely on three of the five values. The explanation probably lies in social support, which means that even Democratic politicians in conservative, dominantly Republican Edgewood will be more likely to exhibit conservative values than their counterparts in "liberal" Riverview. Also, it should be noted that two-thirds of Edgewood's political leaders are Republicans, compared with only half of those in Riverview. The same demographic influence, however, does not seem to be at work among economic leaders; Riverview leaders rank somewhat higher on three of the five items, but the differences are not nearly as large as those found between political leaders.

These "conservatism" items can also be used to measure agreement between the decision-making elite and rank-and-file members of each community. If our earlier hypothesis is valid that the effectiveness of leaders is related to the degree of continuity in values between them and the community, and since Edgewood has been somewhat more successful in meeting its problems, we would expect to find a higher degree of consensus in Edgewood. A related hypothesis may be stated in terms of community *integration:* the ability of a community to solve its problems is a function of its relative homogeneity in terms of income, class, politics, ethnicity, and religion. Value consensus, which may be viewed as the product of a community integrated along these lines, would provide a barrier against divisive cleavages based upon one or several social discontinuities. Let us turn first to a comparison of conservatism within and among the two communities. Table 10-3 compares Edgewood's elite and rank and file along this dimension.

In Edgewood, we have a situation in which agreement among the leaders is not remarkably high. Given their social homogeneity, this finding is somewhat unexpected. Only in the case of what may be called an anti-government value (item 1) and the equation of free enterprise with democracy (item 4) do over half of the leaders converge in support of an essentially "conservative" point of view. Moreover, less than half of them agree with the "liberal" value that labor unions on the whole have done a lot of good for the country. As noted in the preceding table, in both communities the conservatism of the economic leaders is balanced by the left-to-middle-of-the-road posture of the political leaders. Nevertheless, a higher rate of positive agreement on conservative values among the entire elite group would have been expected.

TABLE 10-3 "CONSERVATISM" AMONG EDGEWOOD ELITE AND RANK AND FILE

	Proportion agreeing Leaders	Rank and file
	(42)	(494)
1. "That government which governs least governs best."	60†	24
2. "We have moved too far away from those fundamental principles that made America great."	48	40
3. "One of the biggest problems with the world is that people don't work hard enough any more."	48	41
4. "Democracy depends fundamentally on the existence of free enterprise."	90†	68
5. "On the whole, labor unions are doing a lot of good in this country."	45	32

† Significant at .01 level.

Given their greater social diversity, it is not surprising that the community sample exhibits even less acceptance of the conservative items. Only one-quarter of this dominantly Republican community believe that government is best when weak. This is ironic in view of the fact that fully 75 per cent of Edgewood's voters supported Eisenhower in 1956. Perhaps it reflects the extent to which voters differentiate between campaign rhetoric and political reality. Another somewhat anomalous finding is that only 32 per cent of the community sample, substantially less than that among the leaders, agree with the statement that labor unions have generally been beneficial for the country. This datum supports earlier findings that community leaders are more liberal than their fellow citizens.

Only on the equation of free enterprise and democracy does over half of the community agree. These findings suggest that on matters of positive government, the community is less conservative than its dominantly Republican leaders.[4] Not only do they reject the view that good government is weak government, but they are considerably less sure, although still a firm majority, that there is any necessary connection between free enterprise and democracy. In sum, while neither the leaders nor the rank and file in Edgewood are as "conservative" as might have been expected, there is considerable difference among them.

TABLE 10-4 "CONSERVATISM" AMONG RIVERVIEW ELITE AND RANK AND FILE

	Proportion agreeing	
	Leaders	Rank and File
	(39)	(704)
1. "That government which governs least governs best."	46†	17
2. "We have moved too far away from those fundamental principles that made America great."	49††	32
3. "One of the biggest problems with the world is that people don't work hard enough any more."	54††	38
4. "Democracy depends fundamentally on the existence of free enterprise."	82†	61
5. "On the whole, labor unions are doing a lot of good in this country."	59	51

† Significant at .01 level.
†† Significant at .05 level.

Comparing Table 10-4 with 10-3, the over-all impression one receives is that Riverview leaders and followers are somewhat

[4] This finding is consistent with that of H. McClosky, et al., who concluded that ideological differences between leaders and followers were much greater between Republican leaders and followers than among Democrats, and that Republican "leaders are uniformly more conservative than their followers." Among Democrats, on the other hand, leaders are "slightly more 'progressive' than their followers on most of the issues on which differences appear." "Issue Conflict and Consensus Among Party Leaders and Followers," 44 American Political Science Review (June, 1960), pp. 422-3.

less conservative than those in Edgewood, and that, with the exception of the union item, somewhat greater differences exist between them. Almost half of Riverview leaders accept the value that limited government is best, compared with only 17 per cent of the community. There is also a sharp difference between leaders and followers on the "principles" item. A similar disparity exists concerning the problem of a declining interest in hard work. With one exception then—the belief that labor unions are of limited value—the Riverview elite is significantly more conservative than its followers. On the matter of the benefits of unionism, however, Riverview leaders are substantially more "liberal" compared with those in Edgewood.

Concerning the two community samples, the same generalization may be made: Riverview citizens are somewhat less conservative than those in Edgewood. On the anti-government item, for example, only 17 per cent of the Riverview sample agree that good government is weak government, compared with 24 per cent in Edgewood, a significant difference. This is the base upon which O'Brian and Morrow rested their recourse to higher levels of government for the solution of Riverview's problems. Also, on the equation of democracy with free enterprise, the former community is less sure (although a majority does agree) than Edgewood that such a nexus is necessary. On the benefits of labor unions, Riverview is significantly higher in agreement than Edgewood. Riverview citizens are also less likely to believe that we have abandoned those principles that made America great or that people no longer work hard enough.

In sum, there appears to be a somewhat lower degree of agreement between Riverview leaders and followers upon dominant conservative values. *Leader-community differences are significant in four of the five items in Riverview, compared with only two in Edgewood. Such evidence provides support for our hypothesis that consensual validation is probably higher in Edgewood.*

Given the somewhat greater tendency of Riverview to use

governmental aid to solve its problems, the larger proportion of Democrats among its citizens, and its class structure, the large difference between leaders and followers on the anti-government item is unexpected. At the same time, relatively speaking, there is more agreement between them than found in Edgewood on this item. Such extreme differences may help us explain the low rates of *individual* participation found in both communities. Not sharing to the same extent some of the major values of their leaders, citizens may feel less inclined to support their programs.

More direct evidence on the question of relative consensus is evoked by the judgment, "While it may not be perfect, I think this community offers about everything that a person could want." To some extent, this question also measures *identification*, but it also seems to measure consensus upon this variable among leaders and between them and the community.

TABLE 10-5 ELITE AND RANK-AND-FILE ATTITUDES TOWARD THE COMMUNITY

	Proportion agreeing	
	Edgewood	Riverview
Elite (81)	83†	56
Rank and file (1198)	71†	47

† Significant at .01 level.

The data in Table 10-5 are suggestive along two dimensions. First, we find a significantly higher degree of agreement on the attractiveness of the community among leaders and followers in Edgewood compared with Riverview. However, the difference between leaders and followers in each community is roughly similar. This is contrary to the other values analyzed. The major conclusions here are two: leaders and followers in the two communities vary sharply in their perceptions of the attractiveness of their towns as places to live, and both sets of leaders are more positive than their followers. In addition to factors of class and community wealth, the comparatively lower rate of individual participation in Riverview is probably associated with the fact that less than half its citizens regard the city as a good place to live. The small difference between elite and rank and file is unexpected, mainly because individuals who participate actively in local affairs are often much more closely identified with the community than their inactive fellow citizens. Despite this, Riverview (and Edgewood) leaders are not much more identified with the community than the rank and file.

Political Alienation

Having looked at some data relating to consensus, we will now analyze the two communities in terms of value dissonance. The extent of "alienation" provides an index of dissonance. Whereas consensus may reflect a lack of concern with specific issues because of common acceptance of underlying values, political alienation seems to reflect more conscious reactions of rejection of dominant norms and programs or cynical withdrawal from political action. Alienation is likely to be accompanied by feelings of political ineffectiveness, of an inability to influence community decisions. We therefore expect it to affect participation adversely.

An explanation for differential levels of participation between decision-makers and the community may thus be made in terms of alienation. There is some evidence that political participation is associated with faith in one's ability to influence events. Studies of political alienation, for example, suggest that individuals who feel relatively deprived in terms of income, status, and prestige often exhibit feelings of political disengagement and a negative attitude toward community projects.[5] Such

[5] J. E. Horton and W. E. Thompson, "Powerlessness and Political Negativism: A Study of Defeated Local Referendums," 47 *American Journal of*

attitudes may be accompanied by feelings of powerlessness and a mild paranoia, which expresses itself in suspicion that certain community programs, e.g. fluoridation, are part of huge, generalized subversive political movements.[6] They may also be regarded as evidence of a massive effort on the part of big government and big business to manipulate individuals into accepting ever greater encroachments upon their freedoms.

At a less extreme level, we may find an association between a belief in elite leadership and disengagement. In self-fulfilling prophecy, citizens who believe that control of community affairs is restricted to a few insiders may not attempt to participate. The alienation phenomenon is also apparent in bureaucratic, highly organized, mass-production kinds of work.[7] Lack of personal control over bureaucratized work seems to encourage the displacement of values and energy to off-work activities such as leisure and travel.

Some evidence on comparative attitudes toward political effectiveness and the degree of integration among leaders and rank and file is provided by responses to three individual items. Even though leaders in neither community "scaled" on these items, they may still offer useful comparative evidence.

A noteworthy finding in Table 10-6 is the significant disparity between the responses of community leaders and followers. As

---

Sociology (March, 1962), pp. 485-93. For a general discussion of the "sense of political efficacy," which is regarded here as the opposite of alienation, see A. Campbell, G. Gurin, and W. E. Miller, *The Voter Decides* (Evanston: Row, Peterson, 1954), pp. 187-94. The authors conclude, "Education is highly related to the efficacy scale; one half of those respondents who attended college rank high on this scale, as compared with only 15 per cent of those who have completed no more than grade school. The other two socioeconomic variables, income and occupation, are also highly related to political efficiency," pp. 190-91.

[6] Arnold L. Green, "A Signpost for Research on Fluoridation Conflicts: The Concept of Relative Deprivation," 17 *Journal of Social Issues* (1961), pp. 26-36.

[7] Robert Presthus, *The Organizational Society* (New York: Knopf, Inc., 1962).

TABLE 10-6 COMMUNITY ATTITUDES TOWARD POLITICAL EFFECTIVENESS, IN PER CENT

"Anyone in [Edgewood or Riverview] who wants to, gets a chance to have his say about important issues."

	Agree	Disagree*	NA
Edgewood leaders (42)	95†	5	0
Edgewood community (494)	60‡	35	4
Riverview leaders (39)	84†	11	5
Riverview community (704)	56	34	9

* In this and the two tables following, "don't know" responses have been combined under "disagree."
† Significant at .01 level.
‡ Significant at .10 level.

might be expected, the major proportion of leaders tend to feel that anyone in the community can influence decisions if he wants to. Many of them feel, no doubt correctly, that apathy is a major deterrent to participation among many citizens.[8] On the other hand, the rank and file tend to have more reservations about equality of access to the decision-making process. Another finding is the difference between communities, which shows a significantly greater tendency ($p = .10$) among Edgewood citizens to believe that they can have a voice in community decisions. In the context of integration, the disparity between the views of leaders and followers might cause some tension, which may be reflected in the small proportion of citizens who participated in the major decisions, as shown in Chapter 8.

A second item regarding political efficacy concerns perceptions about the structure of leadership in the communities, and in effect measures attitudes toward elitism and pluralism.

Significant differences are found here between rank-and-file members in the two communities. Although the highest agreement is found among Riverview followers, a small majority of

[8] Aaron Wildavsky finds a similar attitude among leaders in his forthcoming study of Oberlin.

TABLE 10-7 COMMUNITY ATTITUDES TOWARD LEADERSHIP STRUCTURE, IN PER CENT

"Most decisions in [Edgewood or Riverview] are made by a small group that pretty well runs the city."

	Agree	Disagree	NA
Edgewood leaders (42)	55	45	—
Edgewood community (494)	52†	45	3
Riverview leaders (39)	46‡	52	3
Riverview community (704)	60	32	8

† Significant at .01 level.
‡ Significant at .10 level.

both groups believe that a small group does in fact "run" the city. In Riverview, there is a significant difference between the attitudes of leaders and followers, with a much higher proportion of the latter maintaining that a small clique dominates most of the important decisions. Riverview leaders, by contrast, rank lowest on acceptance of this point of view; a much smaller proportion of them, compared with Edgewood leaders, accepts the elitist hypothesis. This finding suggests again that there is a somewhat greater ideological disparity between leaders and followers in Riverview than in Edgewood. It also provides another bit of evidence that Riverview citizens feel less politically effectual than their Edgewood counterparts.

A final item regarding attitudes toward political efficacy and local politics concerns citizen beliefs about their ability to oppose local government.

Here again, we find significant differences between the attitudes of leaders and rank-and-file members in both communities. Leaders, who are relatively more powerful, quite naturally feel more able to make their will felt vis-à-vis local government. As our data on class show, they possess more of the resources that typically characterize those who are more likely to achieve their ends. As a result they have an objective basis for feeling that they can counteract governmental power.

It may be, too, that some rationalization is going on, in the sense that leaders may unconsciously tend to justify their present influence. As Dahl shows, leaders tend to mirror the dominant themes of pluralism and group participation in local affairs; such democratic rhetoric is often part of the symbolic stock in trade of leaders, both political and economic.[9]

TABLE 10-8 COMMUNITY ATTITUDES TOWARD GOVERNMENTAL POWER, IN PER CENT

"The old saying, 'You can't fight city hall,' is still basically true."

	Agree	Disagree	NA
Edgewood leaders (42)	23†	77	0
Edgewood community (494)	44	53	3
Riverview leaders (39)	16†	80	3
Riverview community (704)	45	47	8

† Significant at .01 level.

Regarding community integration, the large and significant attitudinal difference between leaders and followers in the two communities is noteworthy. Compared with the elite, almost three times as high a proportion of followers in Riverview accept the jaundiced view of governmental power. In Edgewood, the disparity though still great falls to approximately 50 per cent. Combining both communities, we find that almost 80 per cent of the leaders reject the generalization, whereas only 50 per cent of followers do. In sum, although we find con-

[9] "Members of the political stratum . . . are more familiar with the 'democratic' norms, more consistent, more ideological, more detailed and explicit in their political attitudes, and more completely in agreement on the norms" (p. 319). Again, "Because a democratic creed is widely subscribed to throughout the political stratum, and indeed throughout the population, the public or overt relationships of influence between leaders and subleaders will often be clothed in the rituals and ceremonies of "democratic" control, according to which the leaders are only the spokesmen or agents of the subleaders, who are representatives of a broader constituency." *Who Governs?* p. 102.

siderable dissensus between all leaders and followers, the differences are again somewhat greater in Riverview.

The data in the three preceding tables provide only random evidence, but they do show (with one exception) that significant differences exist between leaders and followers on items that seem to be related to feelings of political efficacy or, on the contrary, of political alienation. We can now turn to some more systematic evidence, namely, the extent of alienation in the communities as measured by an alienation scale.

The gross extent of alienation in Edgewood and Riverview is indicated in the following tables, which are composed of responses to a four-item alienation scale.[10]

TABLE 10-9 SOCIAL CLASS AND ALIENATION IN EDGEWOOD, IN PER CENT

			Class status	
		Upper	Middle	Lower
		(83)	(324)	(80)
1	Low	34	18	9
2		51	32	27
3	Medium	8	22	20
4		2	17	20
5	High	2†	10	23
NA		2	2	2

† Significant at .01 level.

Alienation is nicely correlated here with class status. Although alienation increases steadily as class status declines, it reaches significantly higher proportions at the lower-class level where the proportion who rank high on this value is over ten times as great as those who rank high among the upper-class

[10] This Guttman scale is composed of the following items: 1) "Most decisions in Riverview-Edgewood are made by a small group that pretty much runs the community"; 2) "Anyone in [Edgewood-Riverview] who wants to, gets a chance to have his say about important issues"; 3) "The average man doesn't really have much chance to get ahead today"; 4) "The old saying, 'You can't fight city hall,' is still basically true."

category. Another way of stating this difference is to note that whereas over 80 per cent of upper-class citizens rank low on alienation, only 36 per cent of lower-class citizens do. Edgewood's leaders, who are mainly of upper-class origin, rank very low on alienation; by inference they have a well-developed sense of political efficacy.

Given the extent of religious, ethnic, and political homogeneity in Edgewood, it is rather surprising to find such differences along this dimension. One would expect to find some variation among social strata, but perhaps not to the degree revealed here. But in the sense that leadership is probably the major requirement for community viability, the low alienation-high political efficacy ranking of Edgewood leaders suggests one reason why it is possible to have considerable lower-class alienation without vitiating a community's ability to meet its problems.

We now turn to the evidence concerning alienation in Riverview.

TABLE 10-10 SOCIAL CLASS AND ALIENATION IN RIVERVIEW, IN PER CENT

		Upper	Class status Middle	Lower
		(74)	(421)	(169)
1	Low	26	14	8
2		54	34	28
3	Medium	14	26	15
4		3†	17	25
5	High	4	6	15
NA			2	8

† Significant at .01 level.

Although the major trends are similar to those in Edgewood, there are some differences. Generally, we find the expected nexus between alienation and class status. Lower-class citizens are significantly more likely to be highly alienated than those in the upper class. However, Riverview citizens on the whole are somewhat more homogeneous on this dimension than are those of Edgewood. Upper-class citizens, for example, are somewhat *more* likely to be alienated than their Edgewood counterparts, but citizens at the lower end of the social scale are slightly less likely to rank at the 3, 4, and 5 levels, compared with the same group in Edgewood. Certainly, our hypothesis that Riverview as a community would prove to be significantly more alienated than Edgewood is not sustained by these particular data. The explanation may rest in the fact that, class differences notwithstanding, people in Riverview generally tend to share more fully the values tapped by the alienation scale. Opinion about the character of the community seems more uniform, as shown in Table 10-5. The somewhat higher rates of alienation (levels 3, 4, and 5) among the Riverview *upper-class* group, which would normally provide its greatest leadership potential, may partially explain the community's relatively greater difficulty in meeting problems. However, here again, the difference falls short of being statistically significant.

Other Correlates of Alienation

It may be useful to differentiate further among other social variables related to alienation. Table 10-11 tests education, which considered alone may give us additional information about alienation and political efficacy in both communities.

We find a remarkable symmetry here in the relationship between education and alienation in the two communities. At the high end of the scale, there is a significant difference between those at the college and grade-school levels. Alienation increases steadily as education decreases. At the grade-school level, the relative distributions are virtually identical for both communities. However, Riverview college-trained individuals are significantly more alienated (.05 level) than those in Edgewood. Since college education is a critical element in community leadership, this is a suggestive finding. On the other hand, a somewhat higher proportion of Edgewood citizens with high school training rank high on the alienation scale. We conclude that education, by itself, is a vital factor in alienation, but that the demographic character of the community has some effect upon those at the high school and college level. It is of course entirely reasonable that individuals with higher levels of education should feel less alienated, i.e. somewhat more effectual regarding their ability to influence community decisions.

TABLE 10-11 EDUCATIONAL ACHIEVEMENT AND ALIENATION, IN PER CENT

		College Edgewood	Riverview	High school Edgewood	Riverview	Grade school Edgewood	Riverview
		(141)	(109)	(247)	(361)	(97)	(212)
1	Low	30	25	18	14	7	7
2		50	45	34	45	14	13
3	Medium	16	21	21	21	22	21
4		.5†	6†	18	14	30	28
5	High	2	0	10	3	23	22
NA		2	3	0	3	4	9

† Significant at .01 level.

Age is another variable that one would expect to be associated with alienation. It is often assumed that the élan, sense of personal effectiveness, and naïveté characteristic of youth diminish as one grows older and becomes more aware of social and personal limitations to mobility. Mental depression, for example, apparently occurs most frequently among those 40 years of age and over, when the hope of fulfillment of idealized career aspirations can no longer be sustained. There is also evidence that, although electoral participation increases steadily with age, the belief in one's capacity to affect political events declines after the age of 55. One careful study using a national sample, for example, found that both the sense of political efficacy and of "citizen duty," which are negatively related to alienation as defined here, fell off sharply among those 55 years of age and over.[11] In this general context, let us turn to the evidence in Edgewood and Riverview.

TABLE 10-12 AGE AND ALIENATION, IN PER CENT

		Under 30 Edgewood	Under 30 Riverview	30-49 Edgewood	30-49 Riverview	50-59 Edgewood	50-59 Riverview	60 and over Edgewood	60 and over Riverview
		(76)	(88)	(171)	(247)	(100)	(150)	(139)	(199)
1	Low	18	18	26	14	29	13	4	12
2		49	38	36	45	33	37	26	19
3	Medium	18	22	20	19	22	21	17	24
4		8	14	10	11	11††	21	29‡‡	24
5	High	7	9	8	5	5††	9	20‡‡	12
NA		0	0	0	6	0	0	4	9

†† Significant at .02 level.
‡‡ Significant at .05 level.

Here, the major conclusion is that until the age of 50 and over, age is not significantly associated with alienation, but after this time there is a significant increase in alienation and attending feelings of political inefficacy. There is a particularly sharp rise at the high (4-5) end of the scale among Edgewood citizens of 60 or over. In Riverview, for reasons including the fact that our sample overrepresents the 50-59 age group by over 4 per cent (see Appendix), high alienation begins early. In the 50-59 group, the proportion of individuals who feel disenchanted about community affairs is significantly higher than in Edgewood. Surprisingly, as noted, the position is reversed at the 60-and-over level, where a significantly higher proportion of Edgewood citizens rank at the high end of the scale.

Another social factor often regarded as relevant to alienation and political effectiveness is income.

[11] Campbell, Gurin, and Miller, *op. cit.*, pp. 191-8.

TABLE 10-13 INCOME AND ALIENATION, IN PER CENT

		\$10,000-and-over Edge-wood	\$10,000-and-over River-view	\$9999-7500 Edge-wood	\$9999-7500 River-view	\$7499-5000 Edge-wood	\$7499-5000 River-view	\$5000-and-less Edge-wood	\$5000-and-less River-view
		(60)	(31)	(70)	(85)	(134)	(198)	(200)	(284)
1	Low	37	16	33	22	22	18	10	12
2		30	65	30	40	42	36	29	35
3	Medium	20	6	30	21	14	21	20	21
4		12†	0†	3	14	11	18	24	19
5	High	1†	13†	4	0	11	7	16	12
NA		0	0	0	2	0	0	1	1

† Significant at .01 level.

With the exception of some discrepancies among those at the $10,000 level in Riverview, we find a steady increase in alienation as income declines. The largest proportion of those at the high (4-5) end of the scale are found among those who earn $5000 and less per year. The exceptionally large proportion of Riverview citizens at the $10,000+ level who rank high (5) on alienation is explained in part by their low educational level, for over half have only high school or less education. This finding suggests why income, by itself, is not a reliable index of class, although of course it is often positively associated with class status.

Although these data provide interesting evidence about the distribution of alienation, a more important question is its impact upon *participation* in community affairs. What are the political consequences of ideological disenchantment? In the following table, our community sample has been divided into two categories, participants and nonparticipants. Since it is virtually impossible to assign meaningful weights to the various media of participation (voting, contributing money, discussing a decision with a friend, etc.), we have merely separated those who participated in *any* way from those who were not active in any major decisions.

TABLE 10-14 ALIENATION AND POLITICAL ACTIVISM, IN PER CENT

		Participants Edgewood	Riverview	Nonparticipants Edgewood	Riverview
		(285)	(270)	(167)	(388)
1	Low	27†	19†	9	11
2		32	40	35	32
3	Medium	18	25	24	20
4		13††	10†	18	23
5	High	9††	4†	13	12
NA		2	1	0	1

† Significant at .01 level.
†† Significant at .05 level.

Looking first at the low and high ends of the alienation scale, we find significant differences between participants and nonparticipants in both communities. At the high end (4-5), Riverview nonparticipants are sharply differentiated (p = .01) from their more active fellow citizens. At the low end (1) of the scale, a similar difference exists between both groups in both communities. In Edgewood, three times as many participants compared with nonparticipants are likely to reject *all* four of the items in the scale. Although the difference is much less extreme in Riverview, we again find a significant difference in alienation between those who were active in some way in some of the issues and those who were not active in any.

We should also expect to find an inverse association between alienation and membership in voluntary groups. Since group membership is a major element of pluralist theory, we have analyzed the two communities from this standpoint.

In both communities, an inverse association is found between alienation and voluntary group membership. Individuals who feel politically ineffectual and less identified with the community and its major values are typically less likely to belong to such groups. Undoubtedly, social class is an intervening variable here, since alienation is inversely associated with class while membership is positively associated with it.

TABLE 10-15 ALIENATION AND GROUP MEMBERSHIP, IN PER CENT*

		Proportion belonging to one or more groups	
		Edgewood	Riverview
		(470)	(652)
1	Low	84	93
2		85	80
3	Medium	73	72
4		68	64
5	High	56	60

* Memberships in church and religious organizations are excepted.

One other dimension, not shown in the two previous tables, is of interest. Whereas only 37 per cent of Edgewood's adult citizens were completely inactive in the five issues, in Riverview this group includes fully 59 per cent of the community. This difference is significant at the .01 level. Since we have used a very low criterion for "participation," namely, *the use of any one of five possible media of participation in any one of the major decisions,* and since our research covers their most important decisions during the past decade, these findings provide a striking commentary on the political viability of the two communities. By this criterion, Edgewood ranks much further toward the "high" end of the pluralist continuum.

TABLE 10-16 RELATIONSHIP BETWEEN ALIENATION AND PARTICIPATION IN 1960 PRESIDENTIAL ELECTION, IN PER CENT

		Edgewood and Riverview	
		Voters	Nonvoters
		(953)	(161)
1	Low	19	6
2		35	33
3	Medium	21	23
4		17	20
5	High	8†	17
NA		5	2

† Significant at .01 level.

Since we would hypothesize from political theory that nonvoting is in part the result of alienation and feelings of ineffectiveness with regard to politics, we now compare nonvoters with voters on this dimension.

The expected differences are found between voters and nonvoters, with the latter ranking considerably higher on alienation. At the high end (5) of the scale, we find a significant difference between the two groups, with over twice as high a proportion of nonvoters at this level. Moreover, three times as many voters, compared with nonvoters, rank low (1) on the scale. We next determine whether comparative rates of alienation are similar between *nonvoters* in the two communities.

TABLE 10-17 COMPARATIVE RATES OF ALIENATION AMONG NONVOTERS, IN PER CENT

		Edgewood (58)	*Riverview* (103)
1	Low	12	2
2		38	30
3	Medium	16 ⎫	27
4		14 ⎬ ††	22
5	High	17 ⎭	17
NA		3	2

†† Significant at .02 level.

A significantly higher proportion of Riverview nonvoters tend to cluster around the medium-to-high end of the alienation scale. For example, fully two-thirds of Riverview nonvoters fall within points 3, 4, and 5 on the scale, compared with less than half of those in Edgewood.

Such differential rates of alienation and participation may be a function of the discrete socioeconomic structures of the two communities. We saw a moment ago that class was positively and strongly associated with these variables. To some extent the total reservoir of potential participants is a function of the class distribution of the community. Sixteen per cent of Edgewood's citizens are in classes I and II, compared with only 10.5 per cent in Riverview. Conversely, whereas just over half of Edgewood's population is in the two lowest classes, IV and V, fully two-thirds of Riverview's falls in this category. This indicates a substantial difference in the proportion of educated, interested citizens who are most likely to demand progress and have the political resources needed to bring it about. Edgewood has a considerably higher proportion of college graduates; and when those from both communities who have *some* high school education are compared, we find a striking difference favoring Edgewood of 27 to 15 per cent. Riverview, in sum, suffers from a smaller share of leadership skill, but it seems even more disadvantaged by its relatively smaller proportion of talented followers whose co-operation is often necessary to make good the aspirations of its leaders.

Elite and Rank-and-File Authoritarianism

We now turn to the relationship of authoritarianism to participation and the extent to which current hypotheses about "working class" authoritarianism are sustained by our data.

An interesting speculation has long been the extent of so-called "authoritarian" values among elite groups. Research among business leaders, for example, has found that an easy acceptance of the authority of supervisors, accompanied by a detached view of subordinates, characterizes successful executives.[12]

[12] "People with high F-scores [authoritarianism] are more strongly identified with top management (authority) and are more ready to acquiesce with a top management decision," T. W. Costello, *et al.* "Attitudes Toward a Planned Merger," 8 *Administrative Science Quarterly* (September, 1963), p. 248; W. Henry, "The Business Executive: The Psychodynamics of a Social Role," 54 *American Journal of Sociology* (January, 1949), pp. 286-91; T. Leary, *Interpersonal Diagnosis of Personality* (New York: Ronald Press Co., 1956), Chap. 20; and B. Gardner, "What Makes Successful and Unsuccessful Executives," 13 *Advanced Management* (September, 1948), pp. 116-25.

Miller and Swanson have suggested that typical child-training patterns of middle- and of working-class parents have different effects on the child's ability to function effectively in our society.[13] Middle-class children are taught to accept authority, to turn aggression inward. Other research has found that dominance "traits" are common among certain types of leaders.[14] Some of the values of those who rank high on the California "F" scale have been suggested as being consonant with upward mobility in a typical bureaucratic structure.[15] Even in our democratic society, leadership has certain elitist connotations, based upon assumptions about the natural distribution of ability and the social and educational conditions that foster it.

On the other hand, both theoretical considerations and empirical evidence suggest that leaders, who tend to come from socially advantaged classes, are less likely to be authoritarian than the majority of citizens. As experts in compromise and the winning of consent, they must avoid the rigidity often characteristic of authoritarians. If they want power, it must often be obtained by permissive methods. Some commentators do not believe that power is highly valued by political leaders. Lasswell, for example, has speculated that for modern political leaders power is a "coordinate or secondary value" and that intensely power-centered persons tend to be relegated to comparatively minor roles in the political system.[16] Stouffer's re-

---

[13] D. R. Miller and G. E. Swanson, *The Changing American Parent* (New York: Wiley & Co., 1958).
[14] For a survey of the literature, see G. Lindzey, *Handbook of Social Psychology*, Vol. 2 (Cambridge: Addison-Wesley Pub. Co., 1954).
[15] T. W. Adorno, et al., *The Authoritarian Personality* (New York: Harper and Bros., 1950); R. Presthus, *op. cit.*
[16] Harold D. Lasswell, "Effect of Personality on Political Participation," in R. Christie and M. Jahoda, *Studies in the Scope and Method of the Authoritarian Personality* (Glencoe: Free Press, 1954) pp. 221, 222, 197-225 *passim;* similarly, Lane concludes that the American political arena is little used to indulge individual needs for power; however, a *"moderate desire to impose one's views and wishes on others"* is said to contribute to political activism, R. E. Lane, *Political Life* (New York: Free Press, 1959), pp. 124-28.

search using a national sample concluded that community leaders were likely to be less authoritarian than the rank and file.[17]

On a theoretical basis, however, there seems some reason to assume that those who rise to the top in bureaucratized political and economic roles have certain attitudes toward authority and power that approximate some of the values commonly attributed to "authoritarian personality" types.

An attempt was made to clarify such opposing theories and research by including several items from the Adorno "F" scale in our design.[18] However, even though the community sample

[17] S. A. Stouffer, *Communism, Conformity, and Civil Liberties* (New York: Doubleday and Co., 1955).

[18] T. Adorno, *et al.*, *The Authoritarian Personality* (New York: Harper and Bros., 1950). We are aware of the severe criticisms of the methodology of the Adorno research and the "F" scale, perhaps the most comprehensive example being H. H. Hyman and P. B. Sheatsley, "The Authoritarian Personality: A Methodological Critique," in R. Christie and M. Jahoda, *Studies in the Scope and Method of* The Authoritarian Personality (Glencoe: Free Press, 1954). Nevertheless, despite sampling inadequacies, inadequate use of statistical tests, and psychodynamic explanations which strain their findings, the essential *theory* behind the analysis has not been seriously challenged, and the book has inspired a great deal of subsequent research. As Christie says, "despite some methodological weaknesses in the original research, subsequent findings have been predominantly confirmatory," *ibid.*, p. 196. For a summary of some of this research, see R. Christie, "Authoritarianism Revisited," in R. Christie and M. Jahoda, *ibid.*, pp. 123-96; and E. Frenkel-Brunswick, "Further Explorations by a Contributor to 'The Authoritarian Personality,'" *ibid.*, pp. 226-75. The utility of the "authoritarianism" hypothesis and attending research for political analysis is demonstrated in S. M. Lipset, *Political Man* (Garden City: Doubleday and Co., 1959), Chap. 4. In the present study, some of the difficulties of the "F" (authoritarian) scale are eased by the use of the Guttman method which ensures a *unidimensional* scale, i.e. a respondent who accepts one scale item must accept the rest. In our research, responses of the community-wide sample to the following items provided such a scale: 1) "The most important thing to teach children is absolute obedience to their parents"; 2) "There are two kinds of people in the world: the weak and the strong"; 3) "No decent man can respect a woman who has had sex relations before marriage"; 4) "Any good leader should be strict with people under him in order to gain their respect."

did scale on four such items, *an analysis of the leaders' responses revealed that in neither community were they uniform enough to provide a scale.* The conclusion, therefore, is that our community leaders do not respond to these items as a unidimensional syndrome. Despite this result, it seems worthwhile to inquire further into the question. By scoring the combined responses of each leader to the same four items that did scale for the entire community, we can provide comparative data which may differentiate the two groups of leaders, even though such results do not measure a unidimensional "authoritarianism" property. The following table uses the same items and the same scoring procedure as the community sample.

TABLE 10-18 COMPARATIVE RESPONSES OF COMMUNITY LEADERS TO FOUR DISCRETE "AUTHORITARIANISM" ITEMS, IN PER CENT*

	Edgewood (42)	Riverview (39)
Low	33	10
Medium	53	54
High	15	36

* To determine "high," "medium," and "low," the scores of all leaders were calculated and the proportions of responses in each category of a 0.4 scale were percentaged. Categories 3 and 4 were defined as "high"; categories 1 and 2 became "medium"; and the "0" (no affirmative responses) category was designated as "low."

These data suggest that among Riverview leaders there is a larger proportion of individuals who respond affirmatively to individual authoritarianism items. This judgment is consistent with our findings (Table 10-20) on class and authoritarianism in which the Riverview upper-class group, which includes a substantial proportion of community leaders, ranks somewhat higher on authoritarianism than its Edgewood counterpart.

When we turn to the community as a whole, the authoritarianism items do scale.[19] This enables us to deal with an inter-

[19] Recent evidence indicates that "acquiescence set," i.e. the tendency of less-educated respondents to agree with affirmatively-stated items, results

esting theoretical question, namely, the extent to which authoritarianism is mainly a "working-class" phenomenon. Some observers have argued that the tendency to seek arbitrary solutions to frustrating social and economic problems is especially characteristic of members of the working class.[20] This thesis is based mainly on recent history in Western Europe where the rise of totalitarianism apparently occurred with the active support of *Lumpenproletariat* segments of both German and Italian society. In the United States, as noted earlier, Stouffer has suggested that community leaders, who are often of middle- or upper-class origin, are more "liberal" on civil rights, free speech, etc., than lower status members of the community.[21] While one immediately thinks of contrary European evidence, including elite military, intellectual, and capitalist support of Hitler and Mussolini,[22] and while positive support for civil

---

in spurious findings on working-class authoritarianism. A. Campbell, *et al.*, *The American Voter*, pp. 512-15. Unfortunately, this evidence was not yet available when we prepared our questionnaire. As a result, we can only note that in considering our findings, this reservation must be added to the usual qualifications of F-scale research findings. It is noteworthy, however, that when Campbell, *et al.* removed the influence of "response set," they found that a "residual relationship with education remains, the more poorly educated being once again the more authoritarian," p. 514. Since education is a basic factor in class, and low educational achievement is in turn associated with lower-class status, our major finding that authoritarianism is highest among lower-class respondents remains convincing.

[20] For a summary and analysis of evidence relating to the "working-class authoritarianism" hypothesis, see S. M. Lipset, *Political Man*, Chap. 4; also, Hannah Arendt, *The Origins of Totalitarianism*, 2nd ed. (New York: Meridian Books, 1958), Chap. 10.

[21] Stouffer, *op. cit.*

[22] As Arendt says, "It would be rash indeed to discount, because of artistic vagaries or scholarly naïveté, the terrifying roster of distinguished men whom totalitarianism can count among its sympathizers, fellow-travelers, and inscribed party members," *op. cit.*, p. 326. Karl Polyani says similarly, "Moreover, there was a striking lack of relationship between its [European fascism] material and numerical strength and its political effectiveness. The very term 'movement' was misleading since it implied some kind of enrollment or personal participation of large numbers. If anything was characteristic of fascism it was its independence of such popular manifestations.

rights for Negroes and labor unions in the U. S. has hardly been a going concern of conservative, upper-class groups, it may be that marginal, lower-class individuals have more objective reasons for seeking scapegoats and for endorsing violent solutions in an effort to ease their disadvantaged situation. It is certainly true, moreover, that lack of education makes one less sensitive to philosophical justifications of free speech and democratic processes, as well as to the benefits of tolerance for those who disagree with majority opinion.[23] At the same time, it must be remembered that highly educated middle- and upper-class groups are rather more subtle about expressing socially disapproved attitudes. Anti-semitism, for example, is often carefully masked, and will tend to be expressed, if at all, only among the in-group. In this sense, there is a danger of exaggerating lower-class authoritarianism because the socialization of its members has made them less ingenious in concealing some of its characteristic values.

We begin by showing the distribution of authoritarianism in the two communities.

It is apparent that Riverview has a significantly larger proportion of individuals who rank at the high end (4-5) of the scale. Moreover, twice as high a proportion of its citizens rank at the high point compared with the lowest point of the scale. In Edgewood, on the other hand, respondents are more evenly distributed along the scale. At the same time, these differences are not impressive; only that at the low end is significant at the rigorous .01 level.

Though usually aiming at a mass following, *its potential strength was reckoned not by the number of its adherents but by the influence of the persons in high positions whose good will the fascist leaders possessed,* and whose influence in the community could be counted upon to shelter them from the consequences of an abortive revolt, thus taking the risks out of revolution," *The Great Transformation* (New York: Beacon Paperback ed., 1957) p. 238. Italics added.

[23] The positive connection between education, occupation and class (which are highly interrelated) and tolerance is shown in many studies, including V. O. Key, *op. cit.*, Chap. 6; and Stouffer, *op. cit.*

TABLE 10-19 AUTHORITARIANISM IN THE TWO COMMUNITIES, IN PER CENT

		Edgewood (494)	Riverview (704)
1	Low	12†	6
2		19	20
3	Medium	27	24
4		26††	30
5	High	13	13
NA		3	7

† Significant at .01 level.
†† Significant at .10 level.

Although small differences characterize the communities when they are compared *en bloc,* we would expect greater discontinuities to appear when they are compared on such variables as class, income, age, and religion. We turn first to the relation between social class and authoritarianism.

TABLE 10-20 CLASS AND AUTHORITARIANISM, IN PER CENT

		\multicolumn{6}{c}{Class distribution}
		Upper Edgewood	Upper Riverview	Middle Edgewood	Middle Riverview	Lower Edgewood	Lower Riverview
		(83)	(74)	(324)	(421)	(80)	(169)
1	Low	18	20	11	5	11	3
2		35	31	16	24	16	9
3	Medium	19	19	30	24	21	27
4		16†	24†	29	30	31	39
5	High	10†	5†	12	15	17	14
NA		2		2	2	3	7

† Significant at .01 level.

Considered as a whole, the data reveal the expected linear association between class and authoritarianism. In general, authoritarianism rises as class status falls, and there are no significant differences between the classes in both communities. At every class level, however, Riverview citizens tend to be slightly more authoritarian than their Edgewood counterparts. Possible explanations include the relatively lower rate of educational achievement among Riverview citizens. However, since education is to some extent standardized within each class group, the explanation must lie in part elsewhere.

Our findings provide impressive support for the "working-class authoritarianism" thesis. Authoritarianism is clearly highest among the lower-class group, and there is a significant difference between upper- and lower-class members of both communities. It will be recalled, moreover, that our authoritarianism items did not scale among our leadership group of 81 upper- and middle-class leaders in both communities, thereby providing further support for Stouffer's finding that community leaders are more "liberal" than their fellow citizens.

We look next at the relationship between income and authoritarianism, mainly because income is not included as a determinant of social class, although it is, of course, closely associated with both education and occupation.

TABLE 10-21 INCOME AND AUTHORITARIANISM, IN PER CENT

		$10,000+ Edgewood	$10,000+ Riverview	$9999-7500 Edgewood	$9999-7500 Riverview	$7499-5000 Edgewood	$7499-5000 Riverview	$5000— Edgewood	$5000— Riverview
		(60)	(31)	(70)	(85)	(134)	(198)	(200)	(284)
1	Low	15	0	13	15	20	6	7	4
2		15	30	37	24	13	31	18	16
3	Medium	30	19	29	20	34	24	22	27
4		28††	26	10††	33	20	21	36	40
5	High	12††	26	11††	6	13	18	15	13
NA		0	0	0	2	0	0	1	1

†† Significant at .05 level.

Here a variable but dominant tendency appears for authoritarianism to rise as income falls. On the other hand, there are striking differences between the two communities. At the second highest income level ($9999-7500), Riverview has a significantly higher proportion of individuals at the high end (4-5) of the scale. At the $10,000 level, a similar difference exists. When these individuals are further analyzed, we find that for so high an income group, they include a rather large proportion of noncollege graduates, namely, 56 per cent, which would partially account for their high ranking. Moreover, 53 per cent of them are aged 45 and over, which again increases the probability of high authoritarianism. At the two lower income levels, however, the differences vanish and members of both communities are equally inclined to endorse values commonly regarded as authoritarian. Another striking fact is that whereas approximately the same proportion of citizens rank high on this value at the lower ends of the income scale, there are sharp differences at higher levels. At the $10,000 level, for example, over twice as high a proportion of Riverview respondents rank at the high end (5) of the scale. Here, as with the similar finding on alienation, we assume that differences in educational achievement provided an explanation.

When Table 10-21 is compared with the preceding one on class and authoritarianism, some interesting differences appear. Whereas the distributions in the class table are linear, here we find a curvilinear pattern. Authoritarianism is quite pronounced at the upper level, declines in the middle range, and then climbs again to a peak among those at the lowest income level. In the class table, by contrast, with the exception of the Riverview upper-class group at the 4-level, we find a steady increase in authoritarian values as we move from upper to lower class.

There has been a great deal of speculation and some research about the association of religion with authoritarianism. It has been found that those of Roman Catholic faith tend to rank higher on this value than their Protestant fellow citizens.[24] This

---

[24] Among others, see T. W. Adorno, *et al., op. cit.;* L. W. Moss, *et al., An Exploratory Study of Psychiatric Aides at a Home and Training School for the Mentally Retarded* (Detroit: Wayne State University, 1956); D. J. Levinson and P. Huffman, "Traditional Ideology and Its Relation to Personality," 23 *Journal of Personality* (1955), pp. 251-73.

tendency is assumed to rest upon such attributes as the collectivist philosophy of Catholicism and the honoring of a patriarchial family structure, as well as upon the Church's insistence on a monopoly of truth in ecclesiastical matters. The following table illustrates the association between religion and authoritarianism in the two communities.

TABLE 10-22 RELIGION AND AUTHORITARIANISM, IN PER CENT

		Protestant		Catholic	
		Edgewood	Riverview	Edgewood	Riverview
		(352)	(342)	(116)	(306)
1	Low	13	6	15	6
2		19	18	19	25
3	Medium	26	23	31	28
4		30†	34†	23	29
5	High	12†	18†	12	10
NA		1	1	0	3

Religious affiliation (column span header)

† Significant at .01 level.

The hypothesis raised above is obviously not sustained by these data. Indeed, in Riverview a significantly larger proportion of Protestants are found at the high level (4-5) on the scale. It is noteworthy, moreover, that in Riverview *both* Protestants and Catholics tend to rank higher on authoritarianism than do those in Edgewood. There is a significant difference between Protestants in the two communities.

We next consider the effect of other intervening variables on authoritarianism, such as educational achievement and age. In order to control its influence, education is held constant in the next table.

Although these data are not as consistent as those in earlier tables, some generalizations can be made. With the exception of those at grade-school level in Edgewood, a larger proportion of Protestants rank higher (4-5) on the authoritarianism scale, regardless of education. There is a general although not linear tendency for authoritarianism to decline as one ascends the educational ladder. Riverview Protestants ranked highest on authoritarianism in the preceding table, and here again we find them ranking somewhat higher at the grade-school and college levels, and similarly, although less high, at the high-school level. Insofar as authoritarianism in both communities is concerned, Riverview has a significantly higher proportion ($p = .10$) of individuals ranking high (4-5) at the grade-school level.

TABLE 10-23 RELIGION AND AUTHORITARIANISM WITH EDUCATION HELD CONSTANT, IN PER CENT

	College				High school				Grade school		
	Edgewood		Riverview		Edgewood		Riverview		Edgewood		Riverview	
	Prot.	Cath.	Prot.	Cath.	Prot.	Cath.	Prot.	Cath.	Prot.	Cath.	Prot.	Cath.
	(92)	(43)	(65)	(44)	(183)	(59)	(176)	(176)	(77)	(14)	(121)	(86)
1 Low	22	30	20	16	10	7	5	5	6	0	0	3
2	30	30	26	25	19	15	23	33	6	0	4	8
3 Medium	23	21	14	34	25	37	24	27	32	36	21	27
4	15	14	26	16	34	24	28	28	35	50	41†	36
5 High	10	5	9	9	11	17	15	7	17	14	24†	20
NA	1	0	5	0	0	0	5	0	3	0	10	6

† Significant at .10 level.

Another variable often assumed to be associated with authoritarianism is age. We saw earlier that alienation was more pronounced among older members of our community sample. It is useful to determine if a similar pattern characterizes authoritarianism and age, particularly since Riverview contains a somewhat higher proportion of individuals at the upper age levels.

The effects of age upon authoritarianism appear to be relatively small, although in the expected direction, until one approaches 60. At that point, a sharp increase in the proportion ranking high on this value occurs. Moreover, in each age cate-

TABLE 10-24 AGE AND AUTHORITARIANISM, IN PER CENT

		Under 30 Edgewood	Under 30 Riverview	30-50 Edgewood	30-50 Riverview	50-60 Edgewood	50-60 Riverview	Over 60 Edgewood	Over 60 Riverview
		(76)	(88)	(171)	(247)	(100)	(150)	(139)	(199)
1	Low	21	7	13	9	21	4	1	3
2		29	32	20	23	23	25	9	8
3	Medium	26	33	37	26	25	19	17	24
4		21	26	19	26	23	32	43	38
5	High	3	2	11	9	8	21	25†	20
NA		0	0	0	6	0	0	4	8

† Significant at .10 level.

gory up to 60, there is a tendency for Riverview to have a higher proportion of its members falling at the high end (4-5) of the scale. This disparity begins with the lowest age group and continues to rise disproportionately until the over-60 category is reached, after which a significantly larger proportion (p = .10) of Edgewood's older citizens rank high on authoritarianism. This change is so striking that the Edgewood group was analyzed separately in an effort to explain it. The group was found to include a high proportion of individuals with limited education. Fully 86 per cent had only high-school education and less, while only 2 per cent were college graduates. In fact, the entire Edgewood over-60 group included only 6 per cent of college graduates. However, the Riverview over-60 group had similar proportions of 82 per cent high school and less education, and only 8 per cent college graduates, yet its members ranked lower on authoritarianism. This means that something other than education and age must explain the high ranking of the Edgewood over-60 group.

Two other explanations suggest themselves—class and religion. If the Edgewood over-60 group included a much larger proportion of class IV and V members, we could explain its higher authoritarianism on this basis, since authoritarianism is apparently highest at these levels. However, when we compare both groups, we find that Riverview has 60 per cent of its oldest citizens in these class categories whereas Edgewood has only 54 per cent. We must, therefore, discard this hypothesis. The other explanation is more fruitful. We have seen that Protestants appear to be somewhat more authoritarian than Catholics. If there is a significantly higher proportion of Protestants among the Edgewood group that ranks high on authoritarianism, we have a partial explanation. We find indeed that 76 per cent of this group is Protestant in Edgewood, compared with only 36 per cent in Riverview.

This leads us to further consideration of what is probably the most critical single variable affecting authoritarianism, namely, education. We saw earlier that when religion is controlled for education, the influence of the former is sharply modified. In the next table the association between education and authoritarianism is analyzed.

TABLE 10-25 EDUCATION AND AUTHORITARIANISM, IN PER CENT

		College Edgewood	College Riverview	High school Edgewood	High school Riverview	Grade school Edgewood	Grade school Riverview
		(141)	(109)	(247)	(361)	(99)	(212)
1	Low	23	18	9	5	5	1
2		29	26	19	27	5	5
3	Medium	23	22	27	26	32	27
4		14	22	31	30	34	39
5	High	8†	9†	13	10	20	22
NA		2	3	0	2	4	7

† Significant at .01 level.

The data show a linear relation between education and authoritarianism. A glance at the high and low ends of the scale indicates that as education decreases, authoritarianism increases steadily. In both communities, those with grade-school education are about twice as likely to rank high (4-5) on authoritarian values as those with some college education. This difference is significant at the .01 level. One or two interesting differences characterize the communities. We find a somewhat higher proportion of Riverview citizens with grade-school education at the high end of the scale. Among those with high school education, the distribution of authoritarianism is virtually identical, but when we turn to the college group, we find a significantly higher proportion ($p = .10$) of Riverview citizens at the high end of the scale. From this and earlier evidence, there seems to be a tendency for Riverview citizens to rank somewhat higher than their Edgewood counterparts on authoritarianism, regardless of class, income, education, or religion. Here again, social support seems useful as an explanatory variable, in the sense that the discrete structural characteristics and historical experience of Riverview seem to provide a psychological climate that shapes the opinion and behavior of its members in such distinctive ways.

The question remains as to possible effects of authoritarianism on participation. We saw earlier that individuals who ranked high on alienation were less likely to have participated in the ten major decisions. While the logical relation between authoritarianism and participation is less patent, it may be that authoritarianism also breeds a certain cynicism about the political system and its underlying pluralist assumptions. Those who participate actively in it may have an unusual affinity for power. Certainly, some of the most bizarre manifestations of power, such as the Nazi persecution of the Jews, Russian collectivization of agriculture, or, for that matter, American decimation of the Indian, have been carried out under political aegis. Since there is often an association between occupation and personality, we may assume theoretically that politics attracts individuals who have an unusual need or desire for power. Such participation can fulfill the need for self-esteem by giving one feelings of shared power, inside information, and the opportunity to borrow prestige from powerful figures.[25]

[25] For an analysis of the psychological attractions of political participation, see R. E. Lane, *op. cit.*, pp. 115-31.

On the other hand, it may be that authoritarianism *reduces* political participation because it may be attended by cynicism and withdrawal. The rewards of a political career (save at the very top) are not highly regarded in the United States, and the endless needs for compromise and bargaining probably prove highly frustrating to the individual who wants to dominate. It may be too that lower-class authoritarians accept the elitist notion that only the anointed, the "chosen few" and the "experts," should lead. Since authoritarianism is more likely to occur among lower-class citizens, who are relatively disadvantaged in the resources typically required for participation (education, income, interest, expertise, prestige, etc.), it is difficult to regard their authoritarianism as an independent variable affecting political participation. In this sense, social class would seem to provide a better explanation of individual levels of participation, since it accommodates this condition.

One way of analyzing any effects of authoritarianism on participation is to compare the relative rankings of political activists (those who participated in the major decisions) with those who did not. The next table does this for both communities.

TABLE 10-26 AUTHORITARIANISM AND PARTICIPATION, IN PER CENT

		Participants		Nonparticipants	
		Edgewood	Riverview	Edgewood	Riverview
		(285)	(270)	(167)	(388)
1	Low	14	9	13	5
2		23	27	17	17
3	Medium	28	27	26	25
4		22††	25†	28	37
5	High	12††	11†	16	17
NA		2	1	0	0

† Significant at .01 level.
†† Significant at .05 level.

The data show that nonparticipants rank significantly higher on authoritarianism than those who participate. And once again, there are differences between the communities. Well over half of Riverview's nonactives rank at the 4 and 5 end of the scale, compared with just over one-third of its more active citizens. In Edgewood, the differences are considerably less, although they run in the same direction and are still significant. Looking at the other side of the coin, it is apparent that Riverview citizens are less likely to cluster around the low end (1) of the scale; indeed, the proportion of them ranking at the 1 level is only half that of Edgewood citizens.

An interesting finding is that over-all participation differs significantly in the two communities. Whereas about 60 per cent of Edgewood's adult citizens were active, i.e. they used one or more media of participation in one or more of the five major decisions, in Riverview only 40 per cent were active in five such decisions.

An intriguing question is whether participation in specific types of organizations is associated with authoritarianism. In effect, do certain kinds of voluntary groups attract those who rank high on this value? Something more may also be learned about social support by analyzing differences between the communities in this regard, as shown in Table 10-27.

By averaging the proportions of members ranking high in both communities, we can design a scale of "organizational authoritarianism" in which professional and service organizations rank lowest with 28 per cent and labor unions rank at the top with 49 per cent. Undoubtedly, social class and particularly its educational component are critical intervening variables here.

When the communities are compared, we find that Riverview has a higher combined "plus" score on authoritarianism for six of the seven organizations, although the differences are very small in service and patriotic organizations. The most striking difference, significant at the .05 level, occurs in business memberships, where Riverview has a "plus" score differ-

TABLE 10-27 COMPARATIVE LEVELS OF AUTHORITARIANISM BY ORGANIZATIONAL MEMBERSHIP, IN PER CENT

	Type of organization												
	Business		Political		Professional		Union		Social		Service		Patriotic	
	Edge-wood	River-view	Edge-wood	River-view	Edge-wood	River-view	Edge-wood	River-view	Edge-wood	River-view	Edge-wood	River-view	Edge-wood	River-view
Low	50 (10)	28 (7)	49 (16)	31 (15)	55 (29)	51 (27)	16 (9)	30 (52)	36 (72)	33 (94)	42 (77)	35 (68)	31 (33)	32 (46)
Medium	25 (5)	16 (4)	27 (9)	31 (15)	24 (13)	15 (8)	30 (17)	26 (44)	28 (57)	23 (65)	32 (60)	36 (69)	27 (28)	25 (36)
High	25†† (5)	56 (14)	24 (8)	38 (19)	21 (11)	34 (18)	54 (30)	44 (75)	36 (73)	44 (125)	26 (48)	29 (57)	42 (44)	43 (62)
Direction	+31		+14		+13		+10		+8		+3		+1	
Totals	100 (20)	100 (25)	100 (33)	100 (49)	100 (53)	100 (53)	100 (56)	100 (171)	100 (202)	100 (284)	100 (185)	100 (194)	100 (105)	100 (144)

†† Significant at .05 level.

ence of over 30 points. Political organizations provide the next greatest disparity. Since high authoritarianism connotes rigidity and a tendency to personalize opposition, and because many leaders are included in these organizations, perhaps these differences help explain the greater intensity and dysfunctional consequences of the competition between political and economic leaders in Riverview compared with that between Edgewood leaders.

Finally, we consider another suggestive correlate of participation—social class. Do comparative rates of community participation differ when class is held constant?

TABLE 10-28 CLASS AND PARTICIPATION, IN PER CENT

Proportion active in one or more decisions					
Upper class		Middle class		Lower class	
Edgewood	Riverview	Edgewood	Riverview	Edgewood	Riverview
(83)	(74)	(324)	(421)	(80)	(169)
57††	50††	67†	42	43	32

† Significant at .01 level.
†† Significant at .05 level.

In both communities, significant differences exist between upper- and lower-class participation. We also find additional evidence of a somewhat higher degree of activism in Edgewood, where participation drops below 50 per cent only among those in the lower-class category. In Riverview, by contrast, participation *reaches* this level only in the upper-class group. A striking finding is the significantly different rates of participation between middle-class groups in the two communities: sixty-seven per cent of Edgewood's citizens were involved in some way in one or more decisions, compared with only 42 per cent in Riverview. Mean rates of participation work out at 57 per cent for Edgewood and only 41 per cent for Riverview. Another comparative index of participation is found by ascertaining the total proportion of citizens who participated in each community, minus N.A.'s. When this is done, as noted earlier, we get the following proportions: Edgewood 63 per cent and Riverview 41 per cent. Both these differences are significant. However, this latter figure is inflated somewhat in Edgewood's case by the fact that two school bond referenda provided an opportunity for participation not available in Riverview. In any event, Edgewood again falls in the middle ranges of the pluralist continuum, whereas Riverview falls in its lower ranges.

Conclusions

An analysis of community values and consensus (defined as the extent of agreement on certain values without reference to any absolute criterion) and their relation to participation in the ten decisions indicates that political consensus among leaders and community is probably somewhat higher in Edgewood than in Riverview. Insofar as community integration and consensus on certain basic values are required for effective political action, Edgewood seems to have an advantage. On the whole, Riverview exhibits somewhat more "liberal" values, insofar as these are measured by our "conservative" items. In this context, rank-and-file members in both communities are significantly more inclined than leaders to exhibit "pro-government" values. It will be recalled, for example, that whereas an average of 86 per cent of leaders in both communities endorsed the democracy-free enterprise value, only 72 per cent of the rank and file did. However, it is noteworthy that the responses of leaders and community did not scale on these "conservative" items, which raises doubt about their unidimensionality, i.e. whether the discrete attitudes are really shared as part of a common dimension. At best, the findings on conservatism-liberalism are suggestive; they are certainly not conclusive.

Regarding attitudes toward the community as a good place to live, there is remarkably greater consensus in Edgewood, where 77 per cent of leaders and community *combined* endorse this value. In Riverview, only 52 per cent agree with this point of view. Additional evidence on this question is provided by our findings on alienation. Whereas upper-class citizens in Edgewood rank somewhat lower on alienation than those in Riverview, at the lower social levels the opposite is true. Edgewood's less privileged citizens rank somewhat higher on the scale. Even though none of these differences is significant, they are unexpected in view of the evidence that Edgewood is somewhat more socially and politically homogeneous than Riverview. When we differentiate participants from nonparticipants in the two communities (Table 10-14), Riverview exhibits a slightly *larger* proportion of nonparticipants who rank high on alienation. Perhaps the most noteworthy conclusion here is that Edgewood is fortunate in having less alienation among its upper-class stratum, where there is the greatest leadership potential.

When age is correlated with alienation, we find little effect until the age of 60, after which alienation rises rapidly. This is partly because of educational differences, since only a very small proportion of individuals in this age group have had college experience, which often has the effect of reducing the feelings of political ineffectuality and normlessness that characterize alienation. Income, too, is found to be associated with alienation; as income rises, there is a steady decrease in alienation.

The most important finding about alienation is its relation to political activism, as measured by individual participation in the ten decisions. Significant differences exist between those who are active and those who are not, the generalization being that those who rank low on alienation are more likely than those who rank high to have participated in important community decisions. This finding is especially strong in Riverview where, compared with participants, *over three times as large a proportion of nonparticipants ranked high on alienation.* The proportion in Edgewood runs in the same direction, but falls to 70 per cent.

Finally, the question of authoritarianism in the two communities was considered. Although we hypothesized that both leaders and rank and file would be characterized by authoritarianism, the leaders' responses did not scale on this dimension. This finding supports earlier research which found leaders to be more "liberal" than their fellow citizens. One research-based hypothesis that did not survive the analysis was that authoritarianism is associated with Catholicism. Indeed, with the exception of Edgewood Catholics with grade-school educations, high authoritarianism was more characteristic of Protestants than of Catholics, even with education held constant. Another interesting replication was that "working-class" authoritarianism seems to be characteristic of both communities. Significantly larger proportions of respondents ranking high on this value were found among those at lower socioeconomic levels.

The major social variable affecting authoritarianism seems to be education. Although income, age, religion, and class are also related, education seems to be the primary single factor differentiating those who rank high from those who rank low. Relationships similar to those found for alienation were found between authoritarianism and age, as well as between this variable and participation. However, intervening variables of education and religion have an important effect on these associations.

One finding which seems useful in explaining the relatively greater degree of tension and conflict between Riverview political and economic leaders compared with Edgewood is that a significantly higher proportion of members of Riverview business and political organizations rank high on authoritarianism. Such ideological differences and attending differential rates of participation found in the two communities probably rest to some extent upon differences in their social structures. As noted earlier, Edgewood enjoys a larger measure of leadership and economic resources. Its class structure contains a higher proportion of those with potential political resources. More important, more of its citizens use their resources. One significant difference emphasizes this point: whereas the over-all rate of *individual* participation in Edgewood decisions is just over 60 per cent, in Riverview it falls to 40 per cent. One-third more of Edgewood's citizens participated in some empirically differentiable way in one or more decisions.

Equally noteworthy is the fact of different rates of participation *within* each class, which provides additional evidence of a discrete civic psychology within each community. Regardless of class differences, Edgewood citizens are more committed to participation. In all class strata, a significantly higher proportion of them are politically active, as measured empirically by their participation in one or more of the critical issues. Such findings emphasize again the importance of social support in community decision-making and whatever pluralism it achieves.

11

POWER STRUCTURE AND ORGANIZATIONAL EFFECTIVENESS

The leadership structure of any community is an important element in the environment of local organizations. Our basic theoretical assumption in this chapter is that the operational capability of certain types of organizations is largely a function of the degree to which they are tied into the local power structure, since the allocation of the major resources required by these organizations rests largely in the hands of those who make up this elite. We shall now attempt to demonstrate this proposition, using the two local hospitals in Edgewood and Riverview.

Some organizations may be able to dictate to the community at least some of the terms under which they will maintain operations locally, and some can spell out in detail what must be "given" to them as a condition for their continued functioning. Whether this is because they enjoy a virtual monopoly in providing a basic service to the community, because the centers of authority and resources crucial to their survival are remote from the local arena, or because of some combination of these, they enjoy an autonomy which is denied to small hospitals like Edgewood Memorial and Riverview District.[1]

Such organizations have an immediate, short-run dependence upon their communities for resources and customers, and their success in gaining such support is vital to the achievement of their objectives. The more adequate the support, the greater their *potential* for goal achievement. In turn, their ability to get such support may depend in large part upon their relations with community leaders. Differences in the support achieved by these two hospitals in the past dozen years may be partially attributable to differences in their relationships with the leadership structure and the role of these leaders in hospital affairs. Thus goal achievement for organizations of this type seems to be partially dependent upon the nature of the community power structure and their relations with it.

Certain objective conditions define the working environment of both hospitals. As "community" institutions and as the only hospitals within a twenty-mile radius of their respective communities, they must make their facilities available to all segments of the community. Moreover, while business organizations can, within limits, set their prices in the name of "economic rationality" and may refuse their products or services to those who cannot afford to pay for value received, this is not true of a humanitarian organization like the hospital. These two facts of hospital life mean that the hospital is not entirely free to charge

---

[1] As with any power relationship which is maintained primarily by the pure dominance of one partner over the other, this situation of autonomy is unstable and subject to change. Examples of this type of "domineering" relationship are, however, not hard to find. Perhaps the organized medical profession stands in this type of position in the community, as the "doctors' strike" in Saskatchewan suggests. See, for example, "When Doctors Strike," 39 *Medical Economics* (Sept. 10, 1962), pp. 77-110. The major employer in a "one-industry" community may be in a similar position as are some of the new industries which communities in dire economic straits seek to attract. For a general theoretical discussion of this subject see J. D. Thompson and W. J. McEwen, "Organizational Goals and Environment," 23 *American Sociological Review* (February, 1958), pp. 23-31.

what the "traffic will bear," and that it typically loses a considerable amount of money each year from bad debts and uncollected bills.

In addition, these two hospitals have had to obtain large sums of money, new equipment, and buildings to enable them to meet the rising expectations of the community for better care. While a number of programs including increased governmental payments for welfare cases, prepaid, voluntary insurance, and federal Hill-Burton aid have been developed to ease such problems, the local hospital is still extremely dependent upon its community to provide necessary additional resources.

To the extent that such resources and support are of a distributive nature, hospitals are in direct competition with other health and nonhealth organizations in the community. This is most clearly the case where monetary resources are at stake; in a very real, if indirect, way the hospital is competing with the Main Street merchant or the local movie house for a share of the limited capital available. Other community resources like land, time, and energy are similarly limited, and, as Everett Hughes has observed, "To survive, an institution must find a place in the standards of living of people, as well as in their sentiments."[2]

Community leaders are in a position to influence the allocation of such scarce resources and thus affect the support position of the hospital for several reasons. This fact is most obvious in the instance of financial resources. As is frequently the case, leaders, their families, and their friends may possess a great deal of personal wealth, a portion of which may be given to the hospital.[3] Even without personal wealth, they may direct an

[2] "The Ecological Aspect of Institutions," 1 *American Sociological Review* (April, 1936), p. 186.
[3] While it may represent only a fraction of the *total* wealth in the community, this fraction is often concentrated in a few hands. For examples see R. S. Lynd and H. M. Lynd, *Middletown in Transition*, Chap. 11, and H. Scoble, "Leadership Hierarchies and Political Issues in a New England Town," in *Community Political Systems* (Glencoe: Free Press, 1961), pp. 136-8.

organization which controls a major part of the community's capital, or they may be chief officials in large, voluntary organizations like trade unions which could contribute substantially to the hospital or other community enterprises. Their organizational and social skills and knowledge are also vital, since lively community-wide participation is often the difference between a successful and an unsuccessful fund drive.

In addition to such direct influence, community leaders may also be able to affect the support level of an organization through what might be called the process of *legitimation*. Because of the increased complexity of modern society and the specialized activities of organizations like the hospital, the average citizen is hardly able to judge the quality of their services or to evaluate the various claims which each makes upon him for attention, time, and energy.[4] Under such conditions the legitimacy of these claims may be enhanced by community leaders who lend their prestige to the organization or, more importantly, become directly involved in its activities. These individuals serve as links between the general community, the various other community institutions to which they belong, and the organization. They are in a position to focus the community's attention—or at least the portion of it which they represent—upon discrete institutional areas of communal life.

Patterns of Community Support

In a capitalistic economy the availability of funds is the key to the many other resource requirements of any organization, regardless of its goals. With money the hospital is able to secure more and better physical resources such as land, buildings, and equipment. It can attract better physicians because it can provide them with newer, more expensive equipment and better facilities for the treatment of their patients. It can afford to hire more experienced administrators and send them to various pro-

[4] C. Perrow, "The Analysis of Goals in Complex Organizations," 26 *American Sociological Review* (Dec., 1961), esp. pp. 857-8.

fessional conferences. In short, the most important support a community can give to its hospital is money. This being the case, we will first ask whether the hospitals in Edgewood and Riverview differ in respect to the amount and kind of monetary support they receive? Does each community support its hospital equally well in this regard? The data in Table 11-1 show that there are substantial differences between them.

TABLE 11-1 FUNDS RECEIVED BY THE TWO HOSPITALS FROM ALL EXTERNAL COMMUNITY SOURCES, JANUARY 1, 1949, TO DECEMBER 31, 1960

Source of funds	Edgewood Memorial (75 beds in 1960) Amounts received	Per cent of total	Riverview District (51 beds in 1960) Amounts received	Per cent of total
Governmental appropriations	215,000	18	305,349	72
Bond issues and notes	0	—	79,000	19
Voluntary fund drives	724,231	60	0	—
Contributions and increase in endowments	265,378	22	38,144	9
	$1,204,609	100.0	$422,493	100.0

As can be seen, one hospital clearly received less from its community than the other. On a "dollars per bed" basis, Edgewood Memorial received almost twice as much ($16,063) as Riverview District ($8304). The disparity becomes even greater when total funds received are calculated on a per capita basis. Here we find that the Riverview hospital received only $28.44 while its counterpart received $145.53. On these bases Edgewood has been most generous in the money contributed to its hospital.

The data reveal several other interesting facts. *Over 80 per cent of the funds received by Edgewood Memorial have come from private, voluntary donations.* Even though this hospital is legally owned by the village and operated by a board of managers appointed by the mayor, the money provided by the community has come mainly from voluntary fund drives and private donations, i.e. from nongovernmental channels. This does not mean, of course, that the hospital has never considered the alternative of supporting itself through public financing or that this alternative is, for some reason, ruled out. At one point, before the construction of the new building, the village board had agreed to raise additional funds through a bond issue. A supplementary fund drive made this unnecessary. It is quite possible that future construction may be paid for in this fashion, but the dominant pattern of monetary support in this case has been one of voluntary contributions and bequests.

Contrast this with Riverview District, over 90 per cent of whose funds have come from public sources. In 1950 the hospital established a memorial fund to which people could donate money in memory of friends or relatives who had died in the hospital. With these gifts it purchased several pieces of equipment, including a $20,000 X-ray unit. In 1955 a representative of a fund-raising organization visited the community at the request of the hospital board and several civic leaders and assessed the chances of a voluntary fund drive. As a member of the board reported, "He said the most we could raise was $300,000. He had assurances of a $50,000 gift from three families." However, as the table makes clear, the usual means of monetary support has been some form of public financing.

It might seem that the explanations for such differential patterns of support are obvious. Edgewood has been able to provide generously for its hospital without major reliance upon the tax powers of local government simply because it is wealthy. Riverview, by contrast, is poorer and, lacking any great local wealth, has had to turn to public financing as the only means for supporting its hospital, paying for expenditures out of tax monies collected from local property owners and industries. While this is certainly a partial explanation, it clearly does not account for the entire difference.

If differences in "what is available" in Edgewood and Riverview were sufficient to explain why one hospital has received less in the way of financial support than the other, we would expect that total community support for the hospital in Riverview would be at least equal to or greater than the community effort in Edgewood. The hospital competes with other local organizations and businesses for a share of the citizen's dollar, and it could be that Riverview District has, in fact, received a share comparable to Edgewood Memorial. However, as shown in Table 11-2, this has not been the case.

TABLE 11-2 COMMUNITY MONETARY SUPPORT INDEX: TOTAL MONETARY SUPPORT OF THE HOSPITAL AS A PROPORTION OF TOTAL VOLUME OF RETAIL SALES, 1949-1960

	Total retail sales* (Col. 1)	Total monetary support of hospitals**	(Col. 2 ÷ Col. 1)
Edgewood	$170,669,000	$1,204,609	.71%
Riverview	$137,429,000	$ 422,493	.31%

* *Sales Management*, "Survey of Buying Power," 1949-60.
** *Ibid.*, Table 1, p. 9.

The total volume of retail sales in the two communities for the years 1949-1960, which gives us one measure of family expenditures for nonhospital goods and services, is shown in the table. By dividing this figure into the total monetary support received by the two hospitals, we can compare the relative financial effort of each community. As can be seen, Riverview has an index number of .31 while Edgewood's is .71. In sum, when expenditures on the hospital are expressed as a proportion of expenditures on other goods and services in the community, Edgewood has made over twice the financial effort to support its hospital that Riverview has made.

Another way to approach this same problem is to ask: What about those people in Riverview who do have money? Have they been as willing to contribute to the hospital as their counterparts in Edgewood? Addressing himself specifically to this question, a former member of the hospital board and a key figure in most of the major community decisions of the past twelve years observed:

> It has been most unfortunate that the people who had money in the community—well, in most communities you have families who have or have had money, but [Riverview] has never had many families like that. The few who have had it have never been interested in leaving memorials, money, or helping their community in any way. . . .
>
> We had one fairly wealthy, influential man a few years ago, Representative Harris who got the big state highway for us, and he left a lot of money to the community including the hospital. The Hunter family are probably millionaires, but when the old man died he didn't leave any money to anybody at all, not even his church. Dr. Lofgren lived in the community most of his life and when he died he left several thousand dollars behind. He didn't leave a nickel to the hospital he had been connected with all his life. . . .
>
> But I don't want to leave the impression that it is just these people themselves who are at fault in acting this way. Nobody has ever thought of trying to cultivate such people. I suggested to Cavenaugh (president of the hospital board) that we set up a committee to contact the wealthy people and to try to get them to leave memorials and money for the hospital, and such a committee was established about a year ago with Reverend Baxter as the presumed head, and I haven't heard anything about it since then. I've tried to get them to get the Moose, the Elks, and the other clubs interested in giving to the hospital and so far there has been nothing on that. They haven't even had publicity or brochures distributed to the community asking for aid. . . .
>
> It's not only the hospital—this cuts across the whole community. The churches don't get any sizeable donations around here. There's not a single memorial in this town. Most towns have a few statues or a library or a few plaques around with the names of different people on them, but there's not a single, solitary memorial around this place. There just isn't a tradition of giving. . . . And the doctors haven't contributed anything to this hospital, not five cents. I suggested to the board one

time that the doctors give the first $50,000 toward a new hospital, and the board practically threw me out of the room. . . .

An analysis of contributions to the hospitals in the two communities lends support to this judgment. Using reported family income in 1960, the number of individuals in the family age 20 and over in 1961, and home ownership to construct a scale of economic well-being, respondents were compared in terms of voluntary donations to the hospitals. The results are summarized in Table 11-3.

TABLE 11-3 RELATIONSHIP BETWEEN ECONOMIC WELL-BEING AND VOLUNTARY CONTRIBUTIONS TO THE HOSPITALS IN EDGEWOOD AND RIVERVIEW, IN PER CENT

Economic well-being	Voluntary contributions Edgewood		Riverview	
Lowest	28	(40)	9	(23)
Low	43	(81)	40	(101)
Medium-low	41††	(87)	28	(170)
Medium-high	45†	(143)	31	(204)
High	74	(69)	61	(79)
Highest	91†	(45)	43	(23)

† Significant at .01.
†† Significant at .05.

At every economic level, respondents in Riverview were less likely to report a donation to the hospital than were those in Edgewood. Furthermore, the difference between these two groups, significant at the .01 level, is greatest for those at the highest end of the economic well-being scale. In comparison with their counterparts in Edgewood, those with the most to give in Riverview have been least likely to do so. However, the table also makes clear that within each community a few individuals in every economic range have contributed voluntarily to their hospital.

It might be argued that everybody has given less voluntarily in Riverview because they are giving comparatively more to the hospital through taxes. While there is no way to test this view conclusively with the available data, there are some figures which suggest that at least *objectively* this is probably not so. (Subjectively, of course, people in Riverview may *think* they give more to the hospital in taxes than do people in Edgewood.) All governmental appropriations for the hospital in Edgewood have come from the village, with a population of 5967 in 1960. These appropriations come to $35.97 per capita. By contrast, the per capita tax contribution of the Riverview hospital district (pop. 14,892) was only $25.81. In other words, on a tax base that was about three times that of Edgewood, tax contributions during this 12-year period were still about $10 less per capita in Riverview. It seems clear that the differences between these two hospitals insofar as monetary support by each community is concerned cannot be attributed simply to differences in their wealth alone.

What about community support of the hospitals through volunteer services? Auxiliaries and other types of volunteer organizations can perform a number of important hospital services. In addition to contributions of money and equipment, such groups frequently perform numerous duties in the hospital, e.g. wrapping bandages, serving meals, cleaning up the hospital's grounds, etc., which leave the regular staff free to concentrate on more vital work.

In terms of the major goal of a hospital, some of this volunteer work may be viewed as a "frill." Opening mail for patients, writing letters for them, maintaining a coffee shop, selling magazines, making dolls for children, etc., may seem to have little to do with the formal objectives of this organization. However, there is some evidence that laymen tend to evaluate the quality of a community hospital more in terms of its "friendly, homelike atmosphere" and hotel-like characteristics than in terms of its medical excellence. Furthermore, a hospital auxiliary is a public relations asset. Not only do its members help to legitimate the hospital to other organized groups to which they belong, but, on occasion, they may act as an organized pressure group by championing its interests before local governing bodies or health and welfare agencies.

Until 1960 Riverview District hospital had no organized volunteer services of any kind. In that year, due mainly to the efforts of Reverend Baxter, who was then a new board member, the Red Cross chapter finally organized a unit of the Gray Ladies. A year later they had 47 members, each of whom was expected to work 100 hours a year at the hospital. Commenting upon some of the problems encountered in organizing the group, its president observed:

> . . . They [hospital personnel] really appreciate us now, but we had a lot of trouble over there at first. The nurses accepted us, but the aides were afraid we would do them out of a job and the administrator was *very* hesitant about the whole thing from the first. . . .
>
> I can't tell you, though, what a time I have had trying to get volunteers for this work. Several of us have had experience with the Gray Ladies in other hospitals, and we seem to be the ones who do most of the work. I don't know, I just can't seem to find people who are willing to do this sort of work here. I can't understand it either. I guess they're just not progressive in this town or something. . . . Those I get all come from right here in [Riverview], too, and only one or two come from [other communities which are part of the hospital district].

While there have been instances when organized groups such as Rotary, King's Daughters, or the Polish-American Club have contributed either money or time to the hospital in the past twelve years, these have been few. Only three civic organizations out of 28 interviewed were able to cite specific instances where their organizations had contributed support for the hospital in the previous three years.

During the past few years the Edgewood Hospital Auxiliary has contributed an estimated $70,000 and uncounted hours of volunteer service to the hospital. Organized into fourteen

"Twigs," auxiliary members are drawn from the community and surrounding rural townships. In 1961 there were 270 dues-paying members and at least an additional 50 women who worked but who were not members of the auxiliary. Nor is this the extent of direct community support for the hospital through volunteer activities. The heads of eight of 21 civic organizations contacted in the community were able to recall instances when they had made contributions or provided some form of volunteer service.

In addition, the annual hospital fair, sponsored by the hospital auxiliary, is one of the main community events. Most civic organizations sponsor booths, the proceeds from which are turned over to the hospital. Editorial comments in the local paper note with pleasure the attendance figures at each year's fair. Commenting on the community's response, the president of the auxiliary said:

> This will show you what kind of a community [Edgewood] is. Last year when we got over to the VFW Hall to set up the booths, we found that it was black as pitch in there. So we got on the 'phone and called the [Maxwell Corporation] people and they sent their whole electrical crew over to the Hall—just pulled them off their regular work and sent them over to help us. They spent the whole afternoon stringing lights for us, the whole afternoon. That gives you some idea of the way people help out on this thing.

As can be seen from Table 11-4, there is a significant difference in the relative amounts of volunteer work received by each hospital. Comparatively few people in Riverview, when asked, "Have you ever worked in the [community] hospital in any capacity?" spontaneously reported that they had done volunteer work of some kind. In Edgewood over 13 per cent of those interviewed mentioned that they had contributed volunteer service of some kind to their hospital. The small number of cases, particularly in Riverview, makes it impossible to do any detailed analysis of these responses, but these figures lend additional weight to earlier qualitative observations. People and organizations in Riverview have been much less likely to give their time and money to the community hospital than has been the case in Edgewood.

TABLE 11-4 PER CENT OF THOSE INTERVIEWED WHO SPONTANEOUSLY MENTIONED THAT THEY HAD DONE VOLUNTEER WORK IN THE HOSPITAL

Edgewood (494)	Riverview (704)
13†	2

† Significant at .01.

An important test of a community's support of its hospital is the extent to which citizens are willing to use its services as patients, assuming that they have some alternative. From this point of view, there is little difference between the two hospitals. As shown in Table 11-5, comparative per-bed admissions during this time period have not differed markedly. For each year per-bed admissions in Edgewood have almost always been slightly higher than in Riverview, and there has been a slow, if fluctuating, increase in the number of admissions during these years in each hospital. The over-all average for Edgewood Memorial was 34, compared with 33 for Riverview District.

An equally important question, however, is whether or not all groups in the two communities have shown an equal willingness to become patients in their respective hospitals. When people in the community go to the hospital, do they usually go to the local hospital or do they go elsewhere? Other hospitals are available within thirty minutes' driving time from both communities. Given this fact, plus the economic opportunity to be able to make such a choice, how do the hospitals compare in this respect?

The data indicate that those who can afford to have been much more likely to go outside of the community for hospitalization in Riverview than have those with similar incomes in Edgewood. Looking at those who are "native" to each commu-

TABLE 11-5 PATIENT ADMISSIONS PER BED IN EDGEWOOD AND RIVERVIEW, 1949-60

Year	Edgewood	Riverview
1949	33	31
1950	33	31
1951	33	31
1952	36	33
1953	34	34
1954	33	33
1955	30	36
1956	33	34
1957	37	35
1958	34	36
1959	36	32
1960	38	36

nity, and thus most likely to have faced a choice between the local and a nonlocal hospital, we find in Table 11-6 that there is little difference between the two communities at the bottom ends of the economic well-being scale. As might be expected, a very high proportion of those in the low or medium-low categories who have had any hospitalization experience have had it locally. When we move to the high end of the scale in Edgewood, the proportion of natives who have been patients in the community hospital remains at the same level. This does not, however, hold for Riverview; in the high category only about 60 per cent of the respondents picked Riverview District as compared with 90 per cent of this same group in Edgewood who have chosen to go to their own hospital.

In brief, the more financially advantaged a person in Riverview is, the more likely it is that he will go outside the community when he has to be hospitalized. Proportionally speaking, support through patient usage of Riverview District has tended to come from those at the bottom of the economic ladder. No such situation has occurred in Edgewood, where almost all of those who have been most likely to have faced a choice between "their" hospital and one outside the community have picked the local hospital, regardless of their economic status.

TABLE 11-6 HOSPITALIZATION EXPERIENCE OF COMMUNITY NATIVES
CONTROLLED FOR ECONOMIC SECURITY, IN PER CENT

	Local hospital experience			
Economic well-being	Edgewood		Riverview	
Low	90	(17)	82	(30)
Medium-low	92	(22)	94	(67)
Medium-high	90†	(18)	79	(69)
High	90††	(18)	59	(19)

† Significant at .05.
†† Significant at .10.

Hospitals and Community Leaders

These two hospitals clearly have a different priority in the eyes of their respective communities; in effect, one has indeed been more successful than the other in finding a place in the standard of living of its community. We will now show that the reasons for this include differences in the roles played by community leaders in each hospital and in the manner in which these hospitals are tied into the power structures of Edgewood and Riverview.

In Edgewood the hospital has been largely the private preserve of wealth and "society" in the community. In spite of its governmental status, its partial reliance upon taxes as a method of financing, and the fact that board members are appointed by local political officials, the hospital has never become "politicized" in the partisan sense of the word. It began as the bequest of a member of Edgewood "society," and upper-class elements in the community have since been highly identified with the hospital. They have lent it their prestige and given it their money. They have stamped it with the mark of "respectability."

Hospital board membership in Riverview is certainly not the mark of social prestige that it is in Edgewood. In Edgewood the *de facto* tenure of board members has averaged over 15 years; in Riverview, turnover has been very high; in 1961, for example, only two of twelve members had been active for as long as 11 years, while the majority were relatively new. More important, most of them were of middle- and lower-middle-class backgrounds and represented a social stratum quite different from their Edgewood counterparts.

Table 11-7 shows the occupations of those who were on both boards in 1961, or, in the case of women members, the occupations of their husbands. As can be seen, the Edgewood board is composed exclusively of businessmen (or wives) and profession-

TABLE 11-7 OCCUPATIONAL COMPOSITION OF HOSPITAL BOARD MEMBERS
IN EDGEWOOD AND RIVERVIEW

Edgewood		Riverview	
Mrs. Reed	— Civil Engineer and Bus. Exec. (hus.)	Dick Hysan	— County Clerk (elective)
Tom Mason	— Engineer	Herman Harris	— Farmer
Mrs. Pamela Thomas	— Stock Broker (hus.)	Fred Rivers	— Businessman
		Alex Schmidt	— Physiotherapist
George Wilson	— Businessman	Richard Cavenaugh	— Bank President
William Rogers	— Engineer	Ian Black	— Pharmacist
Mrs. George Parker	— Lawyer (hus.)	Frank Baxter	— Minister
		Herb Tarpey	— Small Businessman
Frank Thomas	— Business Executive	John Wolchak	— Chief Clerk (R.R.)
R. G. White	— Bank Vice-President	Harold Plank	— Personnel Mgr.- City Councilman
Tom Hughes	— Businessman		
		Mrs. Floyd Luther	— State Govt. Official (appointed) (hus.)
Don Remington	— Business Executive*	Mrs. Frank King	— Business Executive (hus.)
Scott Maxwell	— Bank President**		

* Remington is not actually a member of the board *per se,* but only the legal requirement that all board members come from the village proper has kept him from this position. As a member of the advisory board, however, he attends all meetings, exerts a major influence on the proceedings, and has been very active in hospital affairs including directing the fund drive for the new building.

** One month before the present study began, Maxwell resigned as a board member, a position he had held for seventeen years, and became president of a larger bank in another community. His position on the board was taken by R. G. White.

als. In Riverview, there is a greater representation of different occupations on the board, including three individuals, Hysan, Plank, and Wolchak, who have clerical-managerial positions in local industry or government.

Differences in the socioeconomic make-up of the two boards are further demonstrated in Table 11-8.

TABLE 11-8 FAMILY INCOME IN 1961, SOCIAL CLASS, AND FATHER'S SOCIAL CLASS OF HOSPITAL BOARD MEMBERS, IN PER CENT

	Edgewood (9)	Riverview (12)
Family income (1961):		
Under $5000	0	0
$5000-$9999	0	58
$10,000-$19,999	67	33
$20,000 and over	33	9
Social class:		
I	33	33
II	67	34
III	0	33
Father's social class:		
I	11	0
II	0	16
III	78	42
IV	11	25
V	0	17

In terms of family income, Riverview board members are clearly less fortunate than those in Edgewood. Almost 60 per cent of them are in the $5000-$9999 category while none of the Edgewood members reported earnings of less than $10,000 in 1961. Insofar as social class is concerned, all board members in Edgewood were in either class I or class II and only one of them came from a family of lower-middle or lower-class status. In contrast, one-third of those on the board of Riverview District were in class III and over 40 per cent of them came from lower-middle or lower-class family backgrounds.

Furthermore, in the recent past appointments to the Riverview board have been in the hands of mayors and councilmen who, insofar as education, occupational status, and income are concerned, are less advantaged than the community members who usually make up such a body.[5] Lacking other resources of wealth and social status, and not unconscious of their inferiority in these respects, local government officials have attempted to capitalize on the one resource which they do have—political power. Thus appointments to the board have sometimes become "politicized," in the partisan sense of the word.

One woman, class IV and a member of the board at the time the hospital authority was established, was appointed mainly because of her past work in the Democratic Club in the city. Another such member, also class IV, was a postal clerk. His major qualification as an appointee was his activity in Democratic politics in Riverview. A third former board member, a small businessman in the community and a "most nominated" influential, was a power in the local Democratic party. Sharing the common aversion of local businessmen to partisan controversy, he shortly resigned his position because he was afraid his identification with the hospital might "hurt his business."[6] Mrs. Frank King, a socially prestigeful member of the present board, was appointed primarily because her husband had once been Democratic mayor of the city. As a final example of the role of partisan politics in hospital affairs, one board member observed that:

. . . Senator Peterson, who was a wealthy man, used to be on the hospital board about twenty years ago. Then the Democrats came in and Judge Roberts, who was head of the Democrats, had him kicked off. Peterson was so mad that he never gave the hospital anything.

[5] T. Burling, Edith M. Lentz, and Robert N. Wilson, *The Give and Take in Hospitals* (New York: Putnam's Sons, 1956), esp. Chap. 4; and N. Babchuck, *et al.*, "Men and Women in Community Agencies," 25 *American Sociological Review* (June, 1960), pp. 399-403.

[6] John Riley, class III, is an undertaker. As has been noted elsewhere, local businessmen seem to have less of an aversion to politics *per se*, than a fear of losing or, at least in Riverview, of becoming identified with an unpopular or controversial cause, which may result in the loss of customers.

TABLE 11-9 OVERLAPPING DIRECTORSHIPS OF EDGEWOOD MEMORIAL BOARD, PATED IN THREE

Names	Occupation	Social Class	Citizens Bank	First Trust Co.
Hospital Board:				
R. G. White*	Banker	II	X	—
Frank Thomas	Business Executive	I	—	—
Tom Hughes	Businessman	II	—	X
Mrs. Reed	(hus.) Engineer	I	—	—
George Wilson	Businessman	II	X	—
Tom Mason	Engineer	I	—	—
William Rogers	Engineer	I	—	—
Mrs. Pamela Thomas	(hus.) Stock Broker	II	—	—
Mrs. G. Parker	(hus.) Lawyer*	I	—	—
Don Remington*	Business Executive	II	—	—
(Scott Maxwell)[1]	Banker	I	X	—
Sub Total			3	1
*Influentials:**				
Jonathan Davis	Business Executive	II	—	X
Harold Carter	Bank Clerk-Mayor	III	—	—
Robert King**	Small Businessman-Ex-Mayor	II	—	—
Allen Kimbrough	Business Executive	II	—	X
Henry Turner	Business Executive	II	—	X
Bob Williams	Business Executive	I	—	X
John Dunn	Banker	I	—	X
Ben Eberhart	Businessman-Town Supervisor	III	—	—
Anthony Hadwen	Banker	II	—	X
G. Parker	Lawyer	I	X	—
R. F. Prince	Newspaper Editor	II	—	—
John Wainwright	Business Executive	I	X	—
Sub Total			2	6
*Decision-makers:***				
Clinton Woods	City Attorney-Politician	I	—	—
Joseph Wells	Businessman-Accountant	I	—	—
Sub Total			0	0
TOTALS			5	7

* Most nominated influentials
** Decision-makers who participated in 3 or more of the 5 decisions studied

"MOST NOMINATED" INFLUENTIALS, AND DECISION-MAKERS WHO PARTICI- OR MORE DECISIONS

		Organizations							
GEI	United Fund	Chamber of Commerce	Country Club	Rotary Club	Mental Health Assn.	County Demo. Comm.	Epis- copal Church	1st Cong. Church	Total Score
	X	X	—	—	—	—	—	—	4
—	X	—	—	X	X	—	—	X	4
—	—	—	—	—	—	—	X	—	2
—	—	—	X	—	—	—	—	—	1
—	—	X	—	X	—	—	—	—	3
—	—	—	—	—	—	—	—	—	0
—	—	—	—	—	—	X	—	—	1
—	—	—	X	—	—	—	—	—	1
—	—	—	X	—	—	—	—	—	1
X	—	—	—	—	—	—	—	—	1
X	X	—	—	X	—	—	—	—	4
3	3	2	3	3	1	1	1	1	22
X	X	—	X	—	—	—	—	—	4
X	—	—	—	—	—	—	—	—	1
X	—	X	—	X	—	X	—	—	4
—	—	—	—	—	—	—	—	—	1
X	X	—	—	—	—	—	—	—	3
—	—	—	—	—	—	—	—	—	1
X	—	—	—	—	—	—	—	—	2
X	—	—	—	X	—	X	—	—	3
X	—	X	—	—	—	—	—	—	3
X	X	—	X	—	—	—	—	—	4
X	X	—	—	X	—	—	X	—	4
—	—	—	—	—	—	—	—	X	2
9	4	2	2	3	0	2	1	1	32
—	—	—	—	—	X	X	—	—	2
—	—	—	—	—	—	—	—	—	0
0	0	0	0	0	1	1	0	0	2
12	7	4	5	6	2	4	2	2	

[1] Maxwell was on the Hospital Board for 17 years until he left the community in Feb. 1961.
[2] For each directorship or office held by a board member or leader, a score of "1" was assigned. These were then totaled. These scores include only organizations in which there is an overlap between board members and leaders.

Further differences between the two boards appear when we look at the memberships which their members share in common with other influentials in the communities. With one exception, as Table 11-9 shows, every hospital board member in

TABLE 11-10 OVERLAPPING DIRECTORSHIPS OF RIVERVIEW DISTRICT AND DECISION-MAKERS WHO

Names	Occupation	Social class	Riverview Trust Co.
Hospital Board:			
Frank Baxter* **	Minister	I	—
Richard Cavenaugh* **	Banker	I	X
Mrs. F. King	(hus.) Business Executive	II	—
Harold Plank	Personnel Mgr.-Politician	II	—
John Wolchak	Chief Clerk (R.R.)	III	—
Fred Rivers* **	Businessman	II	—
Alex Schmidt	Physiotherapist	II	—
Sub Total			1
*Influentials:**			
Fred Schwartz	Small Businessman	II	—
John Riley	Small Businessman	III	X
Ted O'Brian**	Mayor-Stock Clerk	IV	—
Ted Johnson	Business Executive	II	X
Kenneth Armstrong**	Newspaper Editor	I	—
Robert Carr	Businessman	II	—
Dick Mason	Banker	II	—
Fred Morrow**	Lawyer	I	—
George McGuire	Supermarket Manager	III	—
Kenneth Swanson	Business Executive	II	—
Frank O'Connor	Lawyer	I	—
Sub Total			2
TOTALS			3

* Most nominated influentials
** Decision-makers who participated in 3 or more of 5 issues studied
[1] For each directorship or office held by a board member or leader, a score of "1" was assigned. These were then totaled. These scores include only organizations in which there is an overlap between board members and leaders.

Edgewood is a director or chief official in an organization with one or more other community leaders. Three members, R. G. White, Scott Maxwell, and Frank Thomas, have held more key positions in other organizations (four each) than any other

BOARD (CITY OF RIVERVIEW ONLY), "MOST NOMINATED" INFLUENTIALS, PARTICIPATED IN THREE OR MORE DECISIONS

Riverview Savings & Loan Assn.	United Fund	Chamber of Commerce	Episcopal Church	County Demo. Party	City Council	Red Cross	School Board	Peterson Furniture	Total Score
–	X	–	–	–	–	–	–	–	1
X	–	X	X	–	–	–	–	X	5
–	–	–	–	–	–	X	–	–	1
–	–	–	–	X	X	X	–	–	3
–	X	–	–	X	–	–	–	–	2
–	–	–	–	–	–	–	X	–	1
–	–	–	–	–	–	–	–	–	0
1	2	1	1	2	1	2	1	1	13
–	–	–	–	–	–	–	–	–	0
–	–	–	–	–	–	–	–	–	1
–	–	–	–	X	X	–	–	–	2
–	X	X	–	–	–	–	–	X	4
X	X	X	X	–	–	–	–	–	4
–	–	X	–	–	–	–	–	–	1
–	X	–	–	–	–	–	X	–	2
–	–	–	–	–	–	–	–	–	0
–	–	X	–	–	–	–	–	–	1
–	–	X	–	–	–	–	–	–	1
–	X	–	–	X	–	–	–	–	2
1	4	5	1	2	1	0	1	1	18
2	6	6	2	4	2	2	2	2	

member. The overlapping directorships of the three women members of the board have been limited to one organization, the Country Club, while one member, Tom Mason, has not held a key position in any other organization in the community.[7] The average number of key positions held by Edgewood board members is 2.00, slightly less than the average score of the community leaders (2.43).

Both banks in Edgewood are directly represented on the hospital board as is GEI, a key organization in the community. The United Fund provides another point of overlap as do the Chamber of Commerce and the Rotary Club. In short, there are a number of spots where one or more members of the hospital board hold key positions in organizations with one or more community leaders.

Another striking feature of the data presented in Table 11-9 is the extent to which decision-makers, both those on the board like White, Remington, and Maxwell, and nonhospital board members, are integrated in terms of their directorships in certain organizations. All but three of the "most nominated" leaders (N = 14) belong to GEI, and six of them are also directors of the First Trust Company. Two of the "most nominated" influentials, Allen Kimbrough and Bob Williams, are not officials in GEI, but they are on the board of First Trust and their sons are directors of GEI. Moreover, of the four leaders who may be classified as politicians and local government officials, Harold Carter, Robert King, Ben Eberhart, and Clinton Woods, three are directors in GEI, a focal point in the community.

When we look at Riverview hospital board members in terms of their membership in key positions, a somewhat different picture emerges, as Table 11-10 shows. Only one member of this

[7] Both engineers on the board, but especially Mason, were somewhat marginal in terms of their influence in hospital affairs and their acceptance by community influentials. As further evidence of this, Mason resigned from the board shortly after this study was completed, a unique event on this board of "old timers."

board, Richard Cavenaugh, holds a key position in the economic institutions in the community. Not only is he on the board of directors of the largest bank in Riverview and of the small savings and loan association, but he is also a director of the largest manufacturing company. He holds more key positions (5) than any other individual on either board. The other bank in Riverview is not directly represented and two of the board members, Mrs. Frank King and Alex Schmidt, share no directorships in common with the community leaders shown here. A third, Reverend Baxter, shares only his position in United Fund. The average score of the members of the hospital board in Riverview is 1.86 and compares with an average score of 1.78 for the leaders shown in the table.

Furthermore, when we look only at community leaders, the degree of integration through overlapping directorships found in Edgewood is missing. The greatest area of overlap has been the Chamber of Commerce and the United Fund, but several of the "most nominated" influentials, e.g. Rivers, Riley, and O'Brian, are not directors nor officials of either. The two men who were most active in the major decisions, Ted O'Brian and Fred Morrow, were not associated with any of the other leaders as directors of these organizations. In short, leaders as well as leaders and board members in Edgewood have more of an opportunity to influence each other through mutual organizational memberships than is the case in Riverview.

Evidence that these connections reflect a deeper and closer social network is presented in Table 11-11. Almost everyone in Edgewood who was active in one or more of the five decisions and/or was nominated as an influential, reported knowing one or more of the hospital board members socially. That is, an overwhelming majority of the community leaders in Edgewood exchange home visits with various members of the board. The data also show that these social contacts are not limited to only two or three members of the board. *All* board members have

TABLE 11-11 SOCIAL CONNECTIONS (EXCHANGE OF HOME VISITS) BETWEEN

Community Leaders**	Social class	Mrs. Reed	Wilson	Mason	Rogers	Mrs. Thomas	Hughes	Mrs. Parker	White	Thomas	Remington
1	II	—	Self	—	—	—	—	—	X	—	—
2	I	X	—	—	—	X	—	X	X	—	X
3	I	—	—	—	—	X	—	—	—	—	—
4*	II	—	—	—	—	—	—	—	—	—	—
5	II	—	—	—	—	—	—	—	X	X	X
6*	II	X	—	X	—	X	X	X	—	X	Self
7	I	—	—	—	—	—	X	X	—	Self	X
8*	I	—	—	—	—	—	—	—	—	—	—
9	I	—	—	—	—	—	—	—	—	—	—
10*	III	—	X	—	X	X	X	—	—	X	X
11	II	—	—	X	—	X	X	X	—	—	X
12	II	—	X	—	—	—	—	—	—	—	—
13*	II	—	X	X	—	X	X	X	—	X	X
14	II	—	—	X	—	—	—	—	—	—	X
15	I	—	—	X	X	X	X	X	X	X	X
16*	II	—	—	—	—	—	X	—	—	—	X
17	I	X	—	X	—	—	X	X	—	X	—
18	II	X	—	—	—	—	X	X	—	X	—
19	I	—	—	—	—	—	—	X	X	—	X
20	II	—	—	—	—	—	—	X	—	—	—
21	I	—	—	—	X	—	—	—	—	—	—
22	I	—	—	—	—	—	—	—	—	—	X
23*	I	X	—	—	—	X	X	X	—	—	X
24	II	—	—	—	—	—	Self	X	—	X	X
25	I	—	—	—	—	—	—	X	—	—	—
26	II	X	—	—	—	X	X	X	X	X	X
27	II	X	—	—	—	X	X	—	—	—	X
28	II	X	X	X	X	X	X	X	—	X	X
29	I	—	—	—	X	X	—	—	X	—	X
30*	I	X	—	—	—	X	X	Wife	—	X	X
31	III	—	—	—	—	—	—	—	—	—	—
32	III	—	—	—	—	—	—	—	—	—	—
33	II	—	—	—	—	X	X	X	—	X	—
34	III	—	—	—	—	—	—	—	—	—	X

HOSPITAL BOARD MEMBERS AND COMMUNITY LEADERS IN EDGEWOOD

Community Leaders**	Social class	Mrs. Reed	Wilson	Mason	Rogers	Mrs. Thomas	Hughes	Mrs. Parker	White	Thomas	Remington
35	III	—	—	—	—	—	—	—	—	—	—
36	III	—	X	—	—	—	—	X	X	—	—
37	II	X	—	—	—	X	X	X	X	X	X
38	II	X	—	X	—	—	—	X	—	—	—
39	III	—	—	—	—	—	X	X	X	—	X
40	III	X	—	X	—	X	X	X	—	—	X
41	I	—	—	X	X	—	—	—	—	—	—
42	I	X	—	—	—	—	X	X	X	X	X
43	I	—	—	—	—	—	—	—	—	—	—
44	I	Self	—	—	—	X	—	X	—	—	X
45	I	—	—	—	—	—	—	—	X	—	X
46	I	X	—	—	—	X	X	Self	—	X	X
47*	I	X	—	—	—	X	X	X	—	X	X
48*	III	—	—	—	—	—	—	X	X	—	—
49*	II	—	—	—	—	—	—	—	—	—	—
50*	II	—	—	—	—	—	X	X	X	X	X
51*	II	X	X	—	—	X	X	X	X	X	X
52*	II	—	X	—	—	—	—	—	Self	—	—
TOTALS		16	7	10	6	20	23	27	15	18	29

* Most nominated influential
** The total number of community leaders in this and the following table is higher than that in earlier chapters because the leadership criteria used here included formal membership in boards or commissions associated with a given decision. As explained in Chapter 2, this criterion was not used in the major part of the study.

close social ties with some of these leaders and there is considerable overlap among these ties. Almost 60 per cent of the leaders listed in Table 11-11 reported knowing three or more board members socially. The two members who are best known socially by community leaders are D. Remington, one of the "most nominated" influentials, and Mrs. George Parker, whose husband was another of the "most nominated" leaders.

The data demonstrate again the relatively greater homogeneity and integration of the board and the community leadership network in Edgewood. Almost all of the decision-makers, over 80 per cent, are in either class I or class II, and all of the board members are in one of these two classes. Many of the community leaders socialize with hospital board members, and, by implication, with each other. Finally, we saw earlier that a considerable overlap of directorships in community organizations exists between board members and the "most nominated" leaders, and within this leadership group itself. In sum, there is a socially homogeneous, integrated group of leaders in Edgewood who are, in turn, closely tied in with members of the hospital board.

The comparative lack of institutionalized connections between the hospital board and the leadership structure in Riverview is accompanied by an even more marked paucity of close social ties between these two groups. As Table 11-12 shows, only 36 per cent of all Riverview leaders reported knowing *any* of the board members socially. The comparable proportion of Edgewood leaders who knew at least one board member socially was 85 per cent.

TABLE 11-12 SOCIAL CONNECTIONS (EXCHANGE OF HOME VISITS) BETWEEN HOSPITAL MEMBERS AND COMMUNITY LEADERS IN RIVERVIEW

Community Leaders	Social class	Wolchak	Plank	Schmidt	Mrs. King	Baxter	Rivers	Cavenaugh
1*	IV	—	—	—	—	—	—	—
2	III	—	—	X	—	—	—	—
3	II	—	—	—	—	—	—	—
4	III	—	—	—	—	—	—	—
5	III	—	—	—	—	—	—	—
6*	II	—	—	—	—	—	X	X
7	III	—	—	—	—	—	—	—
8	III	—	—	—	—	—	—	—
9*	I	—	—	—	—	—	X	X

	Social class	Wolchak	Plank	Schmidt	Mrs. King	Baxter	Rivers	Cavenaugh
10	III	—	—	—	—	—	—	—
11*	II	—	—	—	X	—	Self	—
12*	I	—	—	—	X	—	—	Self
13*	I	—	—	—	—	Self	—	—
14	II	—	—	—	Wife	—	X	X
15	II	—	—	—	—	—	—	—
16	I	—	—	—	—	—	X	X
17	III	—	—	—	—	—	—	—
18	II	—	—	—	—	—	X	X
19*	I	—	—	—	—	—	—	—
20	III	Self	—	—	—	—	—	—
21	II	—	—	—	—	—	—	—
22*	III	—	—	—	—	—	X	X
23	III	—	—	—	—	—	—	—
24	II	—	—	—	—	—	—	—
25	I	—	—	X	—	—	X	X
26	II	—	Self	—	—	—	—	—
27	IV	—	—	—	—	—	—	—
28	III	—	—	—	—	—	—	—
29	II	—	—	—	X	—	X	X
30	V	—	—	—	—	—	—	—
31	IV	—	—	—	—	—	—	—
32	III	—	—	—	—	—	—	—
33	IV	—	—	—	—	X	X	—
34	IV	—	—	—	—	—	—	—
35	II	—	—	—	—	—	—	—
36	II	—	—	—	—	—	—	—
37	III	—	—	—	—	—	—	—
38	III	—	—	—	—	—	—	—
39	II	—	—	Self	—	—	—	—
40	IV	—	—	—	—	—	—	—
41	I	—	—	—	—	X	X	X
42	II	—	—	—	—	—	—	—
43*	II	—	—	—	X	—	X	X
44*	II	—	—	—	X	X	X	X
45*	II	—	—	—	X	—	X	—
46*	III	—	—	X	—	—	—	—
47*	I	—	—	—	—	—	—	—
TOTALS		0	0	3	6	3	13	11

* Most nominated influential

Even more striking is the fact that these social acquaintances are almost completely limited to two members of the Riverview board, Richard Cavenaugh and Fred Rivers, two of the "most nominated" influentials on the board. The third "most nominated" leader on the board, Reverend Baxter, is known socially by only three of the other community leaders. In addition, there are no community leaders who acknowledge a close social acquaintance with two other board members, John Wolchak and Harold Plank. Nor can these differences between Edgewood and Riverview be explained completely in terms of differences in the social class composition of the power structures in the two communities. Social support appears to be at work again, for, regardless of social class, leaders in Riverview are less likely to know any board member socially than are their counterparts in Edgewood.

Turning to a brief consideration of more direct types of involvement of community leaders in hospital affairs, there is, in one sense, little difference between the communities. Three board members in Riverview were also "most nominated" influentials while Edgewood has only one such individual, R. G. White, on its board along with the wife of another. Don Remington, another leader, is not a member of the board, although he attends its meetings regularly in an "advisory" capacity.

However, these similarities between the two communities in the direct participation of leaders in the hospital board mask some rather important differences in the actual roles which they have played as board members in the respective communities. Richard Cavenaugh, president of the board in Riverview, has served on it for over twenty years. Son of one of the most prominent men of the past in the community, he is also president of the city's largest bank. In addition to being a "most nominated" influential, he was active in three of the five major decisions, the flood control project, the new industry issue, and the hospital decision.

His participation in these decisions as well as his performance in meetings of the hospital board reveal several important characteristics of his leadership role. He was not an *initiator* of any decision. Even in the case of the establishment of the hospital authority, the main impetus came from the mayor, the city attorney, and the editor of the newspaper, who was, at that time, president of the Chamber of Commerce. As far as these three issues and the hospital itself are concerned, Cavenaugh's main contributions appear to be largely of a technical nature. As the city's leading banker and a member of the board of the federal reserve bank, he has access to and knowledge of financial institutions outside of the community. He is a man who "knows money" in the sense that he knows how to go about making financial arrangements.

Despite his personal wealth, his formal position in the community, and his long association with the hospital, he has apparently never made any real attempt to contact others in the community and to persuade them to help the hospital financially. While he has made his technical knowledge available to the hospital and the community, he has not used for the benefit of the local hospital the influence inherent in his position in the community. His conservatism and traditional way of "doing things" have sometimes inhibited innovation and change both in the community and in the hospital.

Reverend Baxter, a newcomer to the Riverview board, has established himself solidly in the relatively short ten years he has lived in the community. A highly motivated, "community-minded" man, he was minimally involved in bringing the new industry to the community and also participated in the citizens' advisory committees for the new high school and the hospital. His main contribution to both the community and the hospital has been his skill as a manipulator of verbal and written symbols. He was chief publicist on the two citizens' committees in which he was active, and he has served for two years as chairman of the community relations committee of the hospital board. It was largely through his efforts that the local chapter of the Red Cross finally established a Gray Ladies unit (volunteer service) in the hospital in 1960.

An incident which occurred during one meeting of the hospital board illustrates the role which he has played. Until this meeting and in the ones which followed, he rarely participated in any way in the board's discussions. Furthermore, he was not often consulted by his colleagues on the board. As a member of the state "social action" committee of his church, as well as several other "liberal" organizations, many of his views are at variance with those of other board members. At the beginning of this particular meeting, a letter of resignation from the hospital administrator was read, and Dr. Baxter was asked if he would write a reply. During the balance of the meeting he composed a letter which he read to the board shortly before adjournment. The members listened in awed silence to his nice prose and well-turned phrases. In the process, Reverend Baxter talked longer than at any other time during the four board meetings covered in our research.

The third "most nominated" member of the board, Fred Rivers, is a local contractor and businessman who has served for a number of years on the school board and was active in the flood control decision. Prior to his appointment to the hospital board two years earlier, he had never had any connection with the hospital, and, like Cavenaugh, has never contributed any money or equipment to it. Commenting on the reasons for his own appointment to the board, he observed:

> . . . The mayor came down to me around Christmas time and wanted me to resign from the school board so I could go on the hospital commission. I told him I would serve on both of them. A lot of people like to magnify the time they spend being on boards. That's what we have well paid principals and superintendents for—to do the work. Anyway, there's no secret about it. The only reason they appointed me [to the hospital board] was because I was in construction work, and they felt better having someone like me around when they were building a new hospital.

Turning now to leaders who are on the board of Edgewood Memorial, R. G. White, a recent appointee, is a vice president of one of the two banks in the community. White is a "home town boy" who has worked his way up through various positions at the bank to his present spot. At both the hospital and bank, he has taken the place of the same man.[8] Prior to his appointment, his only involvement in the hospital was as a contributor and a minor member of one of the fund-raising committees which conducted the drive for the new hospital. During his time on the board, he has served as chairman of the finance committee and, in addition, handled most of the work involved in selecting and hiring a new administrator for the hospital. "In fact," the new administrator said later, "I hardly saw any of the other board members. All my arrangements and contacts were through Mr. White." In short, although he has been on the board for only one year, he appears to be assuming a leading role in its affairs.

The man who receives most of the credit for the new hospital building and another decision-maker on the board is Don Remington.[9] President of a locally owned oil company, a director of GEI, and a member by marriage of one of the oldest families in Edgewood, Remington has access to the social and economic elite of the community. As noted earlier, his role in the community power structure has been that of the "fund raiser." Besides being a member of the civic committee of the Rotary, which instigated the move for a new hospital, he organized and was head of the drive which raised some $750,000 for the building. More recently, he was head of the drive to raise the $100,000 necessary to bring the new industry to Edgewood. As might be expected, he has great influence in board deliberations, especially where matters of money or relation-

[8] See page 383, Table 11-7 above. This is a nice example of the synthesis between occupational and philanthropic roles.
[9] See page 383, Table 11-7 above for a description of his official relation to the board.

ships between the hospital and other community organizations are concerned.

Mrs. George Parker, one of the three women members of the board and wife of a "most nominated" influential, is a representative of Edgewood "society." Like the other women members, she devotes a good deal of her time to church and hospital activities, and, in fact, their presence at board meetings frequently give them the atmosphere of a "ladies' sewing circle." Considerable time is spent discussing subjects like the need for chintz curtains in the nurses' dressing room or the dustiness of closets. For this reason, most of the key decisions are made and carried out on an informal basis by White, Remington, and George Wilson, another board member and a representative of Main Street business interests. Mrs. Parker's husband, a charming, cultured man, is legal counsel for one of the local banks, a member of its board of directors, and was chairman of the county Republican committee for over 25 years.

In addition to their board membership, there are a number of other possible ways in which decision-makers in the two communities could have played some direct part in hospital affairs. They could, of course, have made financial contributions to the hospital or have been members of various volunteer groups like the auxiliary which have done work for or at the hospitals. The data presented in Table 11-13 indicate that community leaders in Edgewood are much more likely to have been directly involved in actions affecting the hospital than is the case in Riverview. Almost all of the leaders in the former community reported making a voluntary contribution to the hospital at some time, while less than half of those in Riverview have done so. Similarly, leaders in Edgewood are considerably more likely to have given some of their time and attention to hospital affairs than their counterparts in Riverview. Even when such factors as social class, family background, income, or length of residence are controlled, community leaders in Edgewood make a much better showing in these respects. In short, relationships between the hospital and the leadership structure in Edgewood have been much closer and more widespread, and the decision-makers as a group have been more likely to take an active interest in and feel some commitment toward the hospital than has been true in Riverview.

TABLE 11-13 INVOLVEMENT OF COMMUNITY LEADERS IN THE HOSPITALS THROUGH COMMITTEE MEMBERSHIPS, GOVERNMENTAL OFFICES, OR PERSONAL FINANCIAL CONTRIBUTIONS, IN PER CENT

	Edgewood		Riverview	
Active on committees or in official positions involving hospital	60	(32)	39	(17)
Voluntary contributions to the hospital	92†	(48)	46	(21)

† Significant at .01.

Conclusions

An organization's ability to achieve its objectives is a function of many things, one of the most important being its success in getting the resources and clientele it requires. Edgewood Memorial has been considerably better supported in terms of money and volunteer activities and the organization has been slightly more successful in getting patients than has Riverview District. Furthermore, the hospital is truly a "community" hospital in the sense that support for it has come from a cross-section of Edgewood. It is well integrated with the power structure of the community, a leadership system which itself is integrated and fairly homogeneous. This fact has made it relatively easy for the hospital to secure the support it needs from the community.

Not only has the hospital in Riverview not enjoyed such close ties with community leaders, but the leadership system itself is less well integrated and is thus less able, so to speak, to deliver the goods. Any accomplishment, including building support for the hospital, too often depends upon a handful of individuals and their ability to overcome the parochialism and passivity of large segments of the community, as well as of some men in formal positions of power. The active minority relies upon persuasion, entreaty, prayers, and, in the end, is too often successful only when it can point to concrete sanctions which some external center of power will invoke if the community fails to act. When, for example, it became evident that the state was about to close the hospital as a health and fire hazard, Riverview leaders were forced to act or lose the hospital altogether. Badly needed administrative and medical reforms followed only after banks in Buffalo City had refused to lend money for the new hospital building until such changes were made. In the new school decision, we saw that pressure from state officials and the fear of losing state building aid were among the incentives. In brief, the power system is fragmented and disjointed, potential leaders are sometimes alienated from the community and, as a consequence, the hospital and the rest of the community have difficulty in solving their problems.

The explanation of differences in the relationships between the power structures and the hospitals in Edgewood and Riverview, with their discrete consequences for the support level of the hospitals, lies in the wider differences between the power structures and the communities themselves. The hospital in Riverview has become "politicized" in a community where, as shown in earlier chapters, political differences tend to follow class and religious lines and feelings of partisanship run deep. As noted earlier, Riverview is a community in which political power has often been exercised by individuals who are socially and economically marginal, the type of individual who is not always tolerant, receptive to change and new ideas, and who feels socially insecure. Not only does the upper- or upper-middle-class person who wishes to take an active part in hospital affairs have to cross class lines, but he exposes himself to the suspicion and antagonism of such marginal groups in the community. Middle-class values of "civic mindedness" and "civic responsibility" provide little incentive to action and decision in this socially and politically fragmented community.[10]

The process, moreover, feeds upon itself. Problems are seldom resolved until further inaction becomes prohibitively expensive, and then, when something is done, it leaves behind a residue of mistrust and suspicion which serve to sharpen underlying tensions and the lack of integration. The more such differences become rigidified, the greater the emotional costs of "doing something," and the more difficult it becomes for elements in the power structure to work together. Like other organizations, the hospital gets caught in the middle and its ability to gain the support it requires to meet its objectives is impaired. In a nice demonstration of the self-confirming prophecy, this fact is then defined by the rank and file as further evidence of the ineptness of its leaders.

In Edgewood a similar circularity occurs, but it often works to the benefit of the hospital and the community. One does not have to defend the extreme position that all leaders think alike on all problems and always work in concert for their own personal gain to point out that Edgewood's power structure functions effectively because it is well integrated, is able to evoke the value of "civic responsibility," and is composed of political and economic leaders who share many values and class qualities.

Differences and antagonisms do exist in Edgewood, and, as in the controversy over the school bond issue, occasionally break out into the open. Generally, however, conflict is submerged, partially because leaders in Edgewood have more in common with each other than is the case in Riverview, and partially because they are able to make meaningful appeals to do "what is best for Edgewood." Such appeals strike the pro-

---

[10] For similar conclusions about the role of "civic mindedness" as a motivator in community leadership consult F. A. Stewart, "A Sociometric Study of Influence in Southtown," 10 *Sociometry* (1947), esp. p. 381.

verbial responsive chord in the hearts of this middle-class community. Organizations like the hospital, which are demonstrable "successes," reinforce the altruistic claims of leaders that they are acting in the best interests of the community, thus increasing the likelihood that they will be listened to, and followed, the next time around. Their formal positions of power in the major communication, political, economic, and social institutions in the community, their shared values, and the concomitant lack of any organized basis around which effective opposition might rally, ensure that their definitions of community problems and solutions will usually persist.

12

CONTINUITIES IN POWER STRUCTURE THEORY AND RESEARCH

Our conclusions can be summed up under three broad categories: substantive, methodological, and normative. Wherever possible, major continuities (as well as discontinuities) found in all three spheres will be noted, including similarities between Edgewood and Riverview, and those found between this and earlier community power structure research. Under the normative category we will speculate briefly about the meaning of our findings and the future of pluralism in small communities.

Substantive Continuities

Regarding the structures of power found in the two communities, some 80 citizens (.005 per cent of the total populations) play the central, active role in initiating and directing major community decisions. This is similar to findings in some half-dozen other community studies. Within the power structures reported here there is some specialization. In effect, two discrete decision-making systems were found. One of these is essentially "political," in the narrow sense of the term. It is based upon local electoral support and the co-optation of state and federal offices and resources through political associations resting mainly upon the ability of local politicians to get into office and to deliver majorities to higher level politicians. Mayor O'Brian's administration is an obvious example of this system, and to a lesser extent so is Mayor King's although he resisted the appeals of the state Democratic organization to bring his "Square-Deal" party into its fold. The second decision-making system is essentially economic, comprising leaders whose power resources rest on high formal positions in industry, finance and business, and superior class status, and who draw essentially upon "private" local resources to carry out their programs. Contrasted with political office, which is the major power base of political elites, economic leaders enjoy greater continuity in the power structure. Their bases of power are likely to be more extensive, constant, and durable than those of their political counterparts.

Economic leaders, in sum, tend to dominate essentially "private" types of decisions that entail the use of nongovernmental resources. Political leaders generally control what we have called "public" issues, i.e. those requiring the expenditure of public funds, legitimation in the form of referenda, negotiations with politicians at higher levels of government, and meeting the conditions prescribed by these centers of power and largesse. There is some evidence that such issues are not very salient for economic leaders. Still, there is some sharing of participation in "public" decisions, resulting from competition and co-operation between the two elites, as well as from the efforts of political leaders to co-opt the superior prestige and status resources of economic leaders, in this way legitimating public decisions by the resulting patina of political nonpartisanship and disinterest.

Such a division of labor is expected, given the political values, resources, and interests possessed by each group. Like the rest of us, active community elites use the resources they have, and their activities are guided by their ideologies and the spheres of interest legitimated by them. A third elite, the specialists, are a residual category of "welfare-oriented" leaders, distinguished from others in the elite structure by their marginal power and prestige. From the community point of view, they probably enjoy considerable prestige, since they are often highly educated, have professional statuses, and play active, highly visible roles in community affairs. However, in a power structure context, they are rarely nominated as "influentials," nor do they characteristically prove to be active in more than one major decision.

By a combined use of reputational, decisional, and *Verstehen* modes of analysis, we found that economic leaders enjoyed somewhat more power than political leaders in Edgewood in contrast to Riverview where political leaders proved to be more powerful than their economic counterparts. But each elite does not simply play the same role in its community, for political leaders exercised *relatively* greater initiative and control in Riverview than did economic leaders in Edgewood. However, in both communities, there was some competition between the two elites, and between them and the specialists. In Edgewood, this competition was generally functional because each group contributed to the solution of local problems. In Riverview, competition was more intense but less utilitarian. With only a few exceptions, economic leaders tended to withdraw. Their inefficacy was partly the result of internecine conflict among them, centered mainly on the divergent policies that characterized an "old economic guard" and a "young Turk" element. Theirs was less an ideological conflict than a strategic one, based upon differing perspectives of the most effective ways of developing the city and halting its gradual decline as a trading center. In Edgewood, by contrast, the economic group was quite cohesive, with the exception of the school bond issue, where some members fought the first issue while others supported it.

Three indicators of individual and organizational participation were used to test the relative degree of pluralism in each community. The evidence indicated that Edgewood decisions ranged along the "middle" of the pluralist continuum, whereas those in Riverview clustered around the "low" side. By these measures, Edgewood citizens were found to be more active in the decisions chosen for analysis. We are unable to conclude from this, however, that decision-making in Edgewood is "pluralistic," if this term is defined to mean a viable competition among many groups and widespread community participation in important decisions. Moreover, if one defines pluralism as the existence of multiple competition among leaders, i.e. little overlapping among the local elites in terms of their participation in major issues, we cannot say that this was the case. The concept of oligopoly seems more germane. In Edgewood, two-fifths of the leaders were active in two or more decisions, each of which was substantively different; in Riverview, it was one-third. Similar degrees of overlapping were found by other researchers in three other communities of roughly the same size. *It appears that there is an inverse association between overlapping (elitism) and size.* For example, in Madison and New Haven (100,000+) overlapping rates were 19 and 6 per cent respectively; in Bennington and Edgewood (10,000+), they were 39 per cent. One may conclude tentatively that size per se is an important variable in determining the degree of pluralism found in local power structures.

Regarding the traditional pluralist expectation[1] that citizens will exercise some direct influence on major decisions through periodic elections, referenda, public meetings, and contributing time and money to campaigns or programs, we found very low rates of participation. This finding is consonant with many others showing that most citizens exercise little direct influence

[1] Obviously, this expectation has been undercut by research in political behavior; nevertheless, a normative residue of pluralism seems to be that everyman can and should have some influence on political affairs.

on community affairs. They may exert some indirect influence on specific decisions through periodic elections, etc., but no one has yet demonstrated precisely how this process works. Referenda provide the most used means of participation, ranging from 7 per cent of the adult community in the Riverview hospital issue to 45 per cent in the Edgewood school bond issue which comprised two referenda.

Since most observers agree that very few citizens play a direct role in specific issues, we also tested *organizational* participation as an index of pluralism. The going rationale here is that this medium provides a surrogate for individual participation in a highly organized society. Since pluralism also assumes that a multiplicity of such organizations make their will felt in political decisions, such a test seems equitable and relevant. Here, evidence from a sample of 52 representative voluntary organizations indicates that an average of 40 per cent were concerned in some way with the major decisions. Of this entire group, however, 90 per cent were active in only one decision. In total organizational participation, Edgewood again enjoys some advantage over Riverview: comparative rates of participation are 53 and 31 per cent.

In terms of total individual *memberships* in organizations, the communities are quite similar. However, in such organizations as service clubs, which are especially strategic for community development, Edgewood again has some advantage. It also has a slightly higher proportion of citizens belonging to three or more organizations. Although we find something less than the full-blown picture of membership suggested by de Tocqueville, the Beards, and some contemporary pluralists, membership rates compare favorably with the national averages cited in Chapter 9. Excluding church memberships, some one-third of respondents in both communities belong to three or more organizations: the respective proportions were Edgewood 36 per cent and Riverview 33 per cent. About one-half belong to none or only one organization.

The explanations for these differences are multiple. From the standpoint of both class and industrial resources, Edgewood enjoys considerable advantage. Moreover, these conditions are related to the domination of local decision-making by different elements of the power structure in each community. In Edgewood, economic leaders dominate access to essentially private resources *within* the community. As the new industry decision illustrates, they can mobilize substantial financial resources through their control of local banks.[2] They can pledge the support of their corporations to such programs as the voluntary fund drive for the new hospital. They can delegate active roles to their subordinates, as well as assume an active role themselves. Since they generally have the highest social status and prestige within the community, they can also bring to bear these kinds of resources. In this context, they are "locals," whose span of attention and scope of influence is focused on the immediate community.

On the other hand, political leaders in Riverview have more "cosmopolitan" perspectives. Their peculiar skills and ideology are functionally suited to an environment in which internal community resources of most kinds are generally less promising. As a result, they turn to external, essentially political, power centers for the resources required to handle most local problems. In some cases, such as the housing authority, it may be that the actual need was less relevant than the opportunity to do something positive as an alternative to doing nothing. The community's dependence upon political resources placed a premium on the skills and interests of the mayor and his legal aide, who provided the initiative in four of the five Riverview decisions. *From this, we hypothesize that in communities with limited leadership and economic resources the power structure*

---

[2] The crucial role of banks in local politics is noted in Kammerer, *et al.*; in five of eight small and medium-sized cities, they "provided the leadership or foci for coherent political cliques." *The Urban Political Community* (Boston: Houghton Mifflin Co., 1963), pp. 200-201.

will be more likely to be dominated by political leaders, whereas in those with more fulsome internal resources it will probably be dominated by economic leaders.

However, from our evidence, it seems that over an extended period of time economic leaders will probably dispose the most powerful role in community affairs. This is because their characteristic bases of power are relatively more stable than those of political leaders who must often depend upon *office* as the major basis of their power.[3] In addition, economic leaders in both communities typically enjoy higher SES rankings, which means that they possess more of the resources typically required for the exercise of power, including more education and income, higher class and prestige status, and Republican political affiliation. These attributes, combined with their access to the financial and economic resources of local banks and corporations, provide them greater *continuity* of leadership. Even though political leaders also depend upon business as their major source of income, they are more likely than their economic counterparts to be "Main Street" store owners or employees. This latter distinction, however, is more relevant to Edgewood than Riverview, where several of the less powerful economic leaders were also small businessmen.

Another conclusion related to pluralist assumptions may be mentioned. It is often assumed that diversity and constrained conflict are functional attributes of the political system, and no doubt this premise is often well-founded. In essence the idea seems to be that the ventilation of disparate views and the hammering out of consensus culminate in a higher synthesis.

[3] For a useful comparative analysis of the relative proportions of community leaders representing several institutional areas (different bases of power) which found economic leaders at the top with 57 per cent and professionals next, but with only 13 per cent, see W. V. D'Antonio, *et al.*, "Institutional and Occupational Representatives in Eleven Community Influence Systems," 26 *American Sociological Review* (June, 1961), pp. 440-46. The authors' rankings of seven institutional areas corresponded exactly with those of Freeman, *et al.*, in Syracuse.

In the process governmental power is fragmented and the citizen gains the opportunity for active participation in the policies that affect him. If this thesis were valid for our communities, we should expect that Riverview would prove more viable than Edgewood, as measured by participation in major decisions. It is more diverse in political, ethnic and religious structure, and class distribution. Political values are strongly held and variable; the community includes a small enclave of the New York Liberal party. Edgewood is a more integrated community, in terms of political and class structure, ethnic and religious characteristics. Yet, as we have shown, there tends to be a somewhat higher rate of participation in Edgewood, civic morale (measured by service club memberships and identification with the community) is somewhat higher, and integration and value consensus among the community and its leaders are also somewhat higher. A relatively high degree of social uniformity and value consensus seems to be more functional than great diversity along these lines. *From this evidence, we hypothesize that there is a positive relation between the degree to which a community is socially integrated and the manner in which it solves its problems, i.e. through some citizen participation in crucial local decisions, or through more centralized control and action by a few hyperactive leaders.*

One unexplored facet of community power structure research concerns the extent to which the capability of organizations is associated with their integration in the local power elite. It is well known that organizations must draw upon local resources for the support necessary for their activities, but no empirical testing of the support hypothesis has yet been attempted. Using two local hospitals, the research sought to throw some light on this theoretical perspective. By establishing quantitative indexes of support and by determining the degree to which members of the governing board of the hospitals were "tied into" the local power structure through social, organizational, and class liaisons, *it was found that the hospital which enjoyed the closest ties with the members of the power structure received greater support and operated at a higher level of competence.*

It is useful to determine the extent of continuity between our findings and various "hypotheses on political participation in American communities" set down by political scientist Robert Lane following a review of several landmark community studies.[4] Our relevant findings will be inserted after each hypothesis. They are presented with the general assumption that power is somewhat more concentrated, and participation (as measured by the major decisions) is somewhat lower in Riverview compared with Edgewood.

1. Political participation increases with (a) the proportion of commercial, as contrasted to industrial, occupations in the community, (b) the proportion of occupations, such as civil service positions, with high political relevance, (c) the smallness of the proportion of lower-lower class members in the community.

(a) *Comparative occupational profiles of the communities (Table 6-10) show that Edgewood has a significantly higher proportion ($p = .01$) of managers and proprietors than Riverview. Moreover, Riverview has a significantly higher proportion ($p = .01$) of "operatives." If one accepts these data as valid indicators of the relative degree of "commercial" and "industrial" occupations, Edgewood's somewhat higher rate of participation in the major decisions is consistent with the hypothesis. However, Riverview also has a significantly higher proportion of "sales and clerical" occupations, which seems to controvert the hypothesis.*

(b) *Riverview has a somewhat smaller proportion of lawyers, whom we would rank high on the scale of "political relevance." The proportion of civil servants in both communities*

[4] *Political Life*, p. 261; Chap. 18, *passim*.

is about 1 per cent. These findings tell us little about the hypothesis. In general, however, and despite its being more politically conscious, Riverview was less politically active, insofar as community-wide participation in the major decisions was concerned.

(c) *Edgewood has a significantly smaller proportion ($p = .01$) of lower-lower class (class V) members (16 per cent compared with 24) in the community, which supports the hypothesis.*

2. Political participation decreases with the concentration of power in an elite group because (a) the elite itself fails to participate openly in political life, and (b) the elite discourages effective participation by members of the working class, lower-status ethnics, and residents of slum and low-status political districts.

(a) *Although the differences would be easy to exaggerate, some members of the Riverview economic elite, at least, failed completely to participate in the major issues, whereas some of those in Edgewood participated marginally, although not enough to qualify as "decision-makers."*

(b) *We found no evidence in either community that members of the power structure consciously discouraged effective participation by lower-status groups. Such disqualifications seem instead to have been mainly self-imposed, or they were the result of inadequate political resources.*

3. Concentration of power in a local community tends to exaggerate the discrepancies between national and local turnout. Because power is more concentrated in smaller communities than larger communities, larger communities tend to have higher participation [voting] rates among those of lower status than do smaller communities.

Contrary to the hypothesis, the discrepancies between participation in local and national elections are greater in Edgewood than in Riverview. Although Riverview is one-third larger than Edgewood, its power structure and decisional process proved to be more concentrated, and there was a lower rate of voting participation among its lower-class members (pp. 295 and Table 9-12). However, the size difference between the communities may not be great enough to sustain such comparisons.

4. The better organized a social stratum (class, ethnic group, residential area) is under its own leadership, the more politically effective it will be . . . Metropolitan areas offer greater opportunities for pluralistic patterns of organization than smaller communities.

Our findings in part support the hypothesis. As Tables 6-12 and 6-13 indicate, members of the power structure in Edgewood were more closely tied together through group memberships than those in Riverview. Moreover, upper-class economic leaders in Edgewood tended to be somewhat more closely-knit through more prestigeful organizations than their Riverview counterparts. However, we did not find, insofar as multiple membership is a valid test, that the structure and process of group behavior in the two communities provided any fewer opportunities for "pluralistic patterns of organization" than those offered in metropolitan areas. Indeed, membership rates were quite comparable with those found in the latter. The problem, instead, was that the organizations qua *organizations were not very active. One of our most important findings may be that there is little positive association between the level of voluntary group membership in a community and the degree of pluralism existing in the kinds of decisions analyzed in this study.*

5. Among "nonpolitical" associations, upper middle-class associations are more likely to focus attention on civic and political affairs than those of any other class (at least this is true where unions are weak).

Our findings generally support the hypothesis. Business, social, and service clubs such as Chambers of Commerce, Rotary, Moose, Kiwanis, and PTA, were among the most active organizations (measured by our decisions) in both communities. No labor organizations (despite the strength of labor in Riverview) and only two patriotic organizations (both in Edgewood) were active. These organizations may be roughly divided on class lines (Tables 8-4 and 8-5) with service and social types tending generally to have larger proportions of upper- and middle-class members, whereas labor and veterans' organizations attract a larger proportion of working-class members. A major exception is, however, professional organizations which include a high proportion of upper-class members but were not active in the major issues.

6. Associational structures, organized separately from the main body of community associations, may lead to high political interest and activity, but politically oriented "gatekeeper" leaders must serve as links between the community and the separated association members.

Here, the reference is to specialized religious and ethnic groups, such as athletic clubs, or religious organizations such as Knights of Columbus. Only one active organization of this kind was found in the two communities, the Main Street Athletic Club in Riverview, which contributed money in the new industry decision. The "gatekeeper" phenomenon was observed in Riverview, but it occurred in a broad ethnic or religious context rather than with respect to a single organization. However, insofar as such associations do represent discrete groups, they may serve as a medium through which leaders in the power structure tap local resources in the larger community interest.

Turning to hypotheses and conclusions of more recent studies, we begin with a study by R. Agger and D. Goldrich of two small Western cities.[5] They concluded:

1. "There is a positive and substantial relationship between SES and Republican Party affiliation."
   Our findings generally substantiate this conclusion (Tables 9-1 and 9-12) although "social support" results in less "typical" Republican party and class status relationships in Riverview.
2. "There is a positive and substantial relationship between SES and participation in community organizations."
   Our research strongly confirms this conclusion (Tables 8-2 and 8-3).
3. Democrats in general achieved leadership through party and governmental channels, and not through the voluntary organizational structure.
   Our findings generally support this conclusion; Democratic leaders were usually political officials. Republican leaders were usually in strategic economic positions and were more likely to gain access to the power structure and to work through "civic" organizations.
4. "Economic dominants" and "top leaders" (i.e. reputational nominees) were two different groups.
   Our findings differ. We found instead that economic dominants were in most cases among the most powerful members of the power structure, and were most likely to be identified by the reputational method. This was particularly true in Edgewood whose more affluent industrial structure pro-

[5] "Community Power Structures and Partisanship," 23 *American Sociological Review* (August, 1958), pp. 388-9.

vided the basis for a larger proportion of such economic types.

Two conclusions from R. Schulze's and L. Blumberg's research in "Cibola," a city of 20,000, are now compared with our findings.[6]

1. Techniques focused upon formal status in local economic, political, and civic organizations and reputational nominations produced sharply disparate results.
Contrary to this finding, our use of two instruments, the decisional and the reputational, produced an average overlap of 52 per cent. Moreover, whereas our "reputational" technique isolated many leaders with high formal status in local political and economic organizations, the "decisional" instrument identified many subsidiary "leg-man" types of leaders. Although the "decisional" technique is obviously not the same as Schulze's "formal status" technique, his is one of the few attempts to compare the results of two different methods of identifying community leaders.
2. There was a widespread reluctance on the part of economic dominants to become involved in local political decisions.
Generally, and assuming a fairly narrow definition of "political" to mean governmental types of decisions, our findings support this hypothesis. This was especially so in Edgewood where political leaders completely dominated such decisions. In Riverview, even though economic leaders were equally ambivalent about political action, Mayor O'Brian's policy of co-optation brought several of them into governmental types of decisions, such as flood control, housing, and the hospital issue. Nevertheless, the generalization holds that economic leaders are reluctant to participate in political affairs and decisions.

[6] "The Determination of Local Power Elites," 53 *American Journal of Sociology* (Nov., 1957), pp. 290, 292, 296.

Next, we turn to conditions found by R. Pellegrin and C. Coates in a Southern city of 200,000, dominated by four huge corporations.[7]

1. Corporation executives of absentee-owned corporations play "pre-eminent roles" in "Bigtown" life.
   Our findings differ. In Edgewood, the community most influenced by powerful, nationally-owned plants, corporation executives were more active; at least one executive from each of four such corporations was a decision-maker. In Riverview, three administrators from the four largest absentee-owned corporations were decision-makers, but they were less powerful than their Edgewood counterparts. In neither town, however, did they as a group play "pre-eminent roles." Bank executives in both communities were relatively more powerful.
2. Local governmental officials are relatively powerless figures, who secure their position through working-class votes.
   Our findings again differ, probably in part because of the small size of Edgewood and Riverview, compared with "Bigtown." In both communities, several local political officials were members of the power structure and their scope of influence was wide (Table 6-11). In Riverview, two of them were probably the most powerful men in the community. Mayor O'Brian certainly depended to a large extent upon working-class support. In Edgewood, political leaders were in active competition with economic leaders for control of local affairs. However, political leaders suffered in such competition by their lack of continuity, and lack of the "hard" resources of class, education, control of organizational resources, and wealth upon which community leadership is primarily but not exclusively based.

[7] "Absentee-owned Corporations and Community Power Structure," 51 *American Journal of Sociology* (March, 1956), pp. 413-14.

Finally, we set our findings against some of the major conclusions of Dahl's study of New Haven.[8]

1. Community leadership has changed from a system in which resources of influence were highly concentrated in patrician hands to one in which they are highly dispersed among many groups, including "ex-plebes" who lack the most salient resources possessed by their predecessors: hereditary social status, wealth, business prominence, professional achievement, and formal education beyond high school.[9]

   Our findings indicate (Figure 6-1, Tables 9-2 and 9-3) that, although a few political leaders without the resources listed above exercised power, leaders are characterized by a virtual monopoly of typical "influence resources," compared with the community rank and file. In Edgewood and Riverview at least "traditional" influence resources remain decisive in community power.

2. (a) ". . . A leader in one issue-area is not likely to be influential in another."

   (b) "If he is, he is probably a public official, and most likely the mayor."[10]

   (a) *Insofar as overlapping among issue areas is concerned, we found an average overlap rate of 35 per cent in the two communities (Tables 4-1 and 5-1). Moreover, analysis of overlap rates in nine communities produced an average of 29 per cent (p. 95). It is noteworthy that overlapping appears to be inversely associated with size, ranging from only 6 per cent in New Haven (164,000) to a high of 39 in Edgewood (5,800).*

   (b) *Our data partially confirm this conclusion. The mayors of both communities were at the top in terms of gross participation (four and five issues respectively) as well as in*

---
[8] *Who Governs?*
[9] *Ibid.*, pp. 227-8.
[10] *Ibid.*, p. 183.

aggregate power attributions (Table 6-11). In Riverview, economic leaders were more likely than political ones to experience overlapping, 58 to 40 per cent respectively. In Edgewood, however, political leaders were much more likely to overlap, almost 90 per cent of them were active in two or more decisions, compared with 56 per cent of their economic counterparts.

3. (a) "The Social and Economic Notables of today . . . are scarcely a ruling elite such as the patricians were."

(b) "They are, however, frequently influential on specific decisions, particularly when these directly involve business prosperity."[11]

(a) *Social and Economic Notables tend, in Edgewood and Riverview at least, to be important members of the power structure. One may not want to categorize them as a "ruling elite," but they constituted a vital segment of the 1 per cent of the community who were directly active in the initiation and control of the major community decisions in our sample.*

(b) *Our findings support this conclusion. The new industry decisions, which were dominated by economic leaders in both communities, are a case in point. However, economic notables also participated in "welfare" types of decisions, particularly in the Edgewood hospital issue.*

Methodological Continuities

A major issue in community power research is the relative utility of the reputational and decisional methods of identifying those individuals and groups who dispose power. We began this research assuming that the decisional method would prove to be superior to the older reputational method, which seemed to measure the form rather than the substance of power and to be unduly subject to sociometric bias. Perhaps, too, we felt it was too simple a method. However, given the rudimentary

[11] *Ibid.*, p. 84.

stage of community power research and the tentative state of its methods, we decided to compare the results obtained by each approach.

As our findings were analyzed it became increasingly apparent that both methods had something to contribute. Each had its peculiar weaknesses and strengths. The reputational method tended to isolate those with high "positional" status which gave them a high power *potential*, even though they had not always used this power overtly. It was useful to be made aware of these "behind-the-scenes" leaders, particularly because the resources (both human and financial) of the organizations they controlled were frequently brought into the major decisions. Although such individuals did not always appear on the decisional list, their appearance on the reputational scale directed our attention to the question of why men who were judged to be powerful by the most sophisticated members of the community failed to manifest their power overtly, or at least to be identified by the decisional method. We are satisfied that our analysis of power in Edgewood and Riverview would have been less penetrating had we accepted uncritically the findings of the decisional instrument, and relied exclusively upon them.

On the other hand, by asking the question the other way around, we were able to make judgments about the relative power of some individuals who appeared on the decisional list but were not identified by the alternative method. For example, some active (i.e. decisional) leaders played essentially ministerial, implementary, or formal roles in several decisions. When these individuals were not named as powerful by other decision-makers, we were, in effect, given a clue that their high power rating might be an artifact of the decisional method. In several cases, further analysis showed that these inflated ratings were often a function of official positions which wired their holders into several decisions, even though their participation was minimal.

However, the advantages of the decisional method are indicated by the corroborative evidence provided in the cases just mentioned by the requirement that all respondents name the two or three "most influential" decision-makers in each issue in which they participated. By the use of a rating system (Table 6-11) which ascribed varying weights for different *intensities* of participation, we were able further to differentiate between leaders in terms of their relative power.

More broadly, the decisional method has the advantage of focusing on *behavior,* enabling one to differentiate better between overt and potential power. Even here, however, in the sense that the researcher must always reconstruct past events and must rely heavily upon the recollections and judgments of respondents, the method still uses some techniques that are quite similar to those of the reputational approach. Another serious limitation is that the selection of decisions may provide for a built-in tendency to structure power into certain configurations. In effect, decisions may be chosen which inadvertently result in overlapping among the leaders or, on the other hand, in considerable specialization among them. As long as research resources are limited, so that only a sample of decisions can be analyzed, this possibility remains. Another problem of the decisional method is that it tends to overlook the more subtle manifestations of power whereby certain individuals with impressive resources play a quiet role in decisions, often through their "leg-men." In such cases, the anomalous result follows that the latter are deemed to be overtly, i.e. "really" powerful, while those who employ, direct, advise, and influence them are said to be merely "potentially" powerful. This condition raises questions about the validity of the very distinction between "overt" and "potential" power.

For such reasons, the use of both methods gave us a more systematic differentiation among members of the power structure. From this experience, and the economy of the reputational method, which can easily be incorporated into the study design, it seems desirable to use both the reputational and decisional methods in community power analysis. Here, we share the view of those sociologists who have tested the validity of the reputational method and found it imperfect but effective. It appears to identify over half of the most overtly powerful individuals in the community, as well as certain leaders who are "indirectly" powerful, such as Davis, Wainwright, and Turner. These leaders, who usually have extensive organizational resources at their command, often play a decisive role in community affairs through their "leg-men" and their ability to commit their prestige and financial resources to various kinds of decisions.[12]

On the other hand, we do not believe that the reputational method should be used independently to identify power. It provides an excellent starting point of analysis, but used alone, it will probably fail to identify individuals whose interest, energy, and sense of community responsibility propel them into decisions despite their comparative lack of rather more concrete and durable attributes of power. Our specialist groups provide several examples of such individuals, who are rarely nominated to the reputational list, but who nevertheless dispose some power in community affairs.

In order to illustrate this point more precisely, the results of the two methods are again compared, with somewhat differing results in the two communities. Similar to our earlier findings,

---

[12] This aspect of community power has been systematically demonstrated by L. Freeman, *et al.*, *Metropolitan Decision-Making: 1962*. "This new analysis was suggested by the close correspondence between reputation for leadership and organizational participation . . . This correspondence implies that when persons are asked to name the top leaders, their responses are—to a large degree—colored by organizational ties. For example, when John Jones is named as a top leader, he may not be named as John Jones, participant in public affairs, but as John Jones, head of the Ace Corporation, and that the *corporation* is active in the resolution of community issues. In other words, the individual would not be the proper unit of study," p. 19; pp. 18-26. This emphasis is in line with our theoretical emphasis upon power as a *social* and *institutional* phenomenon, rather than an individual one. The reputational instrument is especially useful in revealing this aspect of community power.

the following table indicates that decisional and reputational power is highly correlated in Riverview, but less so in Edgewood.

TABLE 12-1 INVOLVEMENT IN DECISIONS AND INFLUENTIAL NOMINATIONS, EDGEWOOD AND RIVERVIEW, IN PER CENT*

Participation**	Reputed influence						
	High		Medium		Low		
	Edge-wood	River-view	Edge-wood	River-view	Edge-wood	River-view	
High	47 (8)	64 (9)	24 (4)	21 (3)	29 (5)	14 (2)	100
Medium	12 (2)	31 (4)	53 (9)	23 (3)	35 (6)	46 (6)	100
Low	41 (7)	6 (1)	24 (4)	44 (7)	35 (6)	50 (8)	100

* This table is taken from an analysis (based on the present research) of the comparative utility and characteristics of the reputational and decisional methods, see L. V. Blankenship, "Community Power and Decision Making: A Comparative Evaluation of Measurement Techniques," (forthcoming).
** After assigning each participant a score for participation and a score for reputed influence, each list was simply divided into thirds with the first third being called High, the second third Medium and the final third Low. $X^2 = 12.287$, significant at the .05 level.

The data show that participation and reputed influence are significantly associated in Riverview. Almost two-thirds of the active leaders rank high in reputational power. One of the two men who ranked low has recently retired; had the study been carried out a few years earlier, when he was actively involved in the flood control issue, he would probably have been included among the leaders. Generally speaking, however, "real" power is nicely associated with reputational power.

In Edgewood, the picture is less clear. Almost half of the decision-makers are ranked high on reputed power, but almost 30 per cent of those who were most overtly active are ranked low. These findings probably reflect differences in the two power structures. As noted earlier, in Riverview, power is more concentrated and hence more visible, for there is less difference between overt and reputed power. In Edgewood, power is shared to a great extent, and there are more reputational leaders who have highly visible and important organizational statuses, but do not play an active role personally. These factors may account in part for the greater disparity between overt and reputed power found in Edgewood.

Normative Continuities

How are we to explain the fact that the two communities occupy rather different positions on the pluralist continuum? Why does Edgewood have a somewhat more "pluralist" decisional process and power structure than Riverview? We noted earlier that the pattern of community decision-making and the internal operations of the power structure in Edgewood cluster around the middle range of the continuum, whereas in Riverview they are found in the lower range. If, for example, we average the sums of the three major indexes of community pluralism, namely, group membership, individual participation, and organizational participation, we find that Edgewood falls approximately at midpoint on the continuum, while Riverview clusters around the 25 per cent level.

Within the power structure, moreover, despite the somewhat larger ratio of overlapping found in Edgewood, we found greater concentration, i.e. more elitism, in Riverview. Two political and three economic leaders tended to monopolize the major decisions. (See Table 6-11 for aggregate power distributions of community leaders.) In Edgewood, competition between political and economic elites was lively and generally functional, whereas in Riverview such competition and the politicization of issues tended to result in withdrawal or disenchantment on the part of some potentially powerful economic leaders.

The explanation for these variations seems to lie in the structural and behavioral properties of the two communities.[13] In Riverview sharper class and economic differences and resulting disparities in expectations, values, and consensus seem to have placed a premium on more centralized, imperative leadership. As organizational theory and studies of group behavior suggest, social support, shared values, and common expectations make possible the minimization of overt power and authority. When community consensus is limited, leaders tend to function in a more unilateral manner. In sum, Riverview more nearly approximates the fragmented "mass society" type of political community which encourages elitism. As many observers have noted, communities composed of unorganized, atomistic individuals provide the most fertile ground for elitist political systems.

Within the two power structures, these conditions produce similar divergencies in leadership style. As our comparative analyses of overlapping social and organizational memberships suggest (Tables 6-12 and 6-13), integration among Riverview leaders is less fully developed than among their Edgewood counterparts. Fewer opportunities for personal interaction and the attending development of shared activities and sentiments are available through these media. Leadership, in effect, tends to be highly personalized and to depend upon the almost frenetic activity of a few individuals, in contrast to the more institutionalized and permissive patterns of power and influence possible in a more *Gemeinschaft*-type of community.

Differences in the economic structure and affluence of the communities also shape the form and behavior of their leadership groups. Greater community wealth and a more viable tradition of philanthropy and private initiative provide a sym-

---

[13] *It is important to emphasize here that we are describing differences of degree, not of kind, between the two communities.* Total organizational membership, for example, was not much different in the two communities. Opposition was visible in both, although in Riverview opposition tended to be latent, diffused, and unorganized.

pathetic framework in which Edgewood's economic leaders can use their particular kinds of resources to make good their particular normative preferences for self-reliance and "private" initiative over against governmental solutions to local problems. Even though these preferences remain partly rhetorical, they legitimate vigorous private action by economic leaders.

In Riverview, on the other hand, both a less affluent economic base and a less viable conservative ideology inhibit a similar major preference for "private" solutions. Instead, the community is more obliged to rely upon external political resources for the means to solve its problems. Internecine tensions and the immobilization of some potential economic leaders contribute to this condition, and a major result is an opportunity for leaders with political skills to maintain the initiative in four of the five major decisions. In the event, two political leaders, possessing widely different, but nicely complementary bases of power, dominated the local power structure. Their alliances with the larger political system; their ability to command Democratic majorities in local, state, and national elections; their resourceful use of legal and political skills in the state and national arena enabled them to secure comparatively large resources from state and federal governments, and in some cases, such as the housing authority project, almost to force the community to accept them. (The extent to which the conditions affecting local communities are now influenced by higher levels of government and industry is clearly apparent in this experience.)

A related structural property underlying these diverse patterns of leadership is that whereas local political organization and ideology are well-developed in Riverview, Edgewood politics function under a somewhat jejune nonpartisan system. Domination of the local power structure by political leaders seems more likely in communities such as Riverview where party machinery and political modes of operation are honored by tradition and community expectation. In nonpartisan milieux, in contrast, elites with other bases of power (which, of course, should not from an analytical standpoint be called nonpolitical) have greater opportunity to affect the local decision-making process. In such communities, either economic dominance or a broadly diffused pattern of influence may characterize local power configurations.

The Future of Pluralism

Comparing our findings with the traditional assumptions of pluralist theory, we did not find the expected measure of individual or organizational participation in major decisions. Multiple group membership, however, compared very favorably with national norms. Edgewood was somewhat advantaged in each of these sectors, but neither community demonstrated what may be called a lively degree of pluralism. This judgment is made in terms of a somewhat traditional definition of pluralism which retains its historic emphasis upon individualism as well as its contemporary assumptions about group membership, competition, and access. We accept the practical modification that in a complex society it is visionary to expect very much individual *qua* individual participation in political affairs. This expectation has been proved untenable in countless studies. However, the alternative propositions that pluralist communities are characterized by multiple memberships and viable competition among groups representing most major interests remain part of contemporary pluralist theory. Against these bench-marks, our findings are not highly supportive.

A final word is needed in the context of the definition of pluralism currently used by some power structure researchers. It will be recalled that pluralism is now said to exist when community decision-making is characterized by competition or specialization among an admittedly small constellation of local elites. If no single elite dominates all types of community decisions, pluralism remains viable. Research findings, however, indicate that in cities of 150,000 and less, the proportion of decisional overlapping among members of the power structure will average about 30 per cent. This figure is found by averaging overlap rates in Madison, Syracuse, New Haven, Green Bay, Racine, Kenosha, Edgewood, Bennington, and Riverview.

From this, we conclude that whereas some specialization of leadership surely occurs, a "significant" amount of overlapping of decisional power is characteristic of members of power elites in cities of these sizes. One explanation is that certain individuals develop local reputations for skill in one or another of the activities typically required in any major decision. Such skills include fund-raising, public relations, "organizing" ability, political contacts, and access to financial resources. As a result, those who possess them tend to be drawn into various decisions, regardless of their substantive nature. Again, the heads of some large corporations designate certain executives to "represent" the organization in community affairs, with similar effects.

In sum, our findings in Edgewood generally support earlier research of sociologists who found a tendency toward elitism in community power structures which were usually dominated by economic elites. In Riverview, the decision structure remains highly concentrated, but political leaders play the major role. Regarding the restriction of active participation to the few, the more recent findings of political scientists are quite similar. Differences regarding the nature of the political system may lie in the interpretation of the data. *To some extent, where the sociologists found monopoly and called it elitism, political scientists found oligopoly but defined it in more honorific terms as pluralism.* This conclusion, as we have tried to show, rests upon a restrictive, although eminently realistic, definition of pluralism, in which its historical emphasis upon individualism and a rough equality of bargaining power among groups has been subjugated to the assumption that pluralism exists if specialization and competition characterize groups of leaders who constitute some one-half of 1 per cent of the community. Certainly this definition meets prevailing conditions of group organization and political access, but it seems to omit some of the conditions and normative by-products traditionally associated with pluralism.

Some of the implications of our power structure findings are disturbing. One of these is the paradox found in Edgewood and Riverview, where an inverse association exists between pluralism and participation. Riverview is a closer approximation to the traditional pluralist model. It has a more diversified socioeconomic structure; far more active political competition; its organizational membership rates are very similar to those of Edgewood; and participation in state and national elections is not greatly different from that in Edgewood while in local elections it is higher. Yet, by the criteria of participation in the major decisions, there is less community interest and activism. Edgewood, on the other hand, is much more integrated socially and politically; its local political system was, until 1961, apparently nonpartisan. There is less controversy and sharp conflict on basic values within the community. Despite these conditions, which oppose those of traditional pluralism, with their assumed advantages, it has been somewhat more effective in meeting change and participation has been higher, as measured by the five major decisions.

Our results suggest that there may be some incompatibility between economic affluence and pluralist democracy, despite recent findings that democracy is associated with a high level of economic stability.[14] In Edgewood, industrial strength and major control of decisions by economic leaders make possible considerable self-reliance and effective decision-making by those in its power structure; both its political and economic leaders tend to share dominant "free enterprise" values. They

[14] Among others, see J. Coleman and G. Almond, eds., *The Politics of Developing Areas* (Princeton, N. J.: Princeton University Press, 1960), and S. Lipset, *Political Man*.

believe in doing things by themselves and for themselves, and even when government largesse is accepted, this fact is muted. But decisions are not the result of truly widespread participation (even though participation was more "pluralistic" than in Riverview). There is instead a quiet consensus on most matters, with a belief that leaders know best and will work, as they do, in the community interest. All this results in effective, expeditious decision-making, but it often occurs without the active citizen participation implied by pluralist theory.

The tendency for the major conditions of community decision-making to be set down by higher levels of government and industry is another crucial finding. In this way the periphery of local autonomy is becoming more restricted. Our evidence indicates that participation both within the power structure and the community tends to be positively related to the degree to which decisions involve the use (as well as the rhetoric) of essentially local rather than "external" resources. In both communities, participation was highest in decisions such as schools, hospitals, and new industry, where a good proportion of the resources were of local origin. Essentially external, "political" decisions, such as Riverview's housing authority and the two flood control issues, evoked little participation. From this, we may hypothesize that if the trend toward reducing the scope of local decision-making continues, pluralism at the community level will probably become even less lively. Since integration, easy access to the political apparatus, and "grass-roots" democracy have been historically associated with small communities, it is ironic that the decline of pluralism seems to be occurring precisely at this level. The nation-wide centralization of both political and economic decisions on behalf of greater rationality and control probably includes such among its unanticipated consequences.

A final, somewhat disturbing continuity is that despite high levels of popular education, economic stability, a fair degree of social mobility, a marvelously efficient communication system, and related advantages usually assumed to provide sufficient conditions for democratic pluralism, the vast majority of citizens remains apathetic, uninterested, and inactive in political affairs at the community level. Most political scientists and sociologists who have analyzed community behavior accept this generalization. Some who believe in the cult of expertise or share a Burkian conception of political representation, honor it. But whether this condition is attributed to majority apathy or to minority desires for power, status, and prestige, it remains an awkward reality for those who take democracy seriously.

APPENDIX

1. Sampling Procedure

The technique used for selecting respondents in our community sample was based on methods devised by Leslie Kish.[1] After a survey of our resources, it was decided to interview a total of 600 individuals in the two communities and to limit interviews to those who were aged 20 and over on their last birthday. The total sample size was divided between the two communities in proportion to the number of people of this age category according to the 1960 *U. S. Census of the Population*.[2] On this basis, the total sample size in Riverview was 352 and 248 (both unweighted) in Edgewood.

A list of names and addresses was drawn at random from city directories compiled in 1959. These were used to locate the households in which each interview was to be conducted.[3]

---

[1] "A Procedure for Objective Respondent Selection Within the Household," 44 *Journal of the American Statistical Association* (Sept. 1949), pp. 380-87.

[2] The number in Riverview was 5448 and in Edgewood, 3836. *U. S. Department of Commerce, U. S. Census of Population: 1960, General Population Characteristics (New York)* (Washington, D. C.: U. S. G.P.O., 1961).

[3] If the house was listed as "vacant," it was still included in the sample with instructions for the interviewer to conduct an interview if someone now lived there. If the family listed in the directory no longer lived at a given address, the interviewers conducted an interview with one of the new occupants. If the household was "vacant" at the time of the first contact and if no one was moving in, a substitute name and address were selected at random from a special list.

APPENDIX 435

Once the interviewer had ascertained the number of adults in the household, he consulted a table reproduced on the front of each questionnaire. This table indicated which individual was to be interviewed.[4]

Following the technique suggested by Kish, each interview, after being punched on IBM cards, was "weighted" (reproduced) according to the number of adults in the household. This was to avoid the necessity of doing more than one interview in each household or having the interviewers make futile calls on households where no interview was taken. While such weighting may increase the sampling error,

> . . . in the present instance this increase is not great because of the concentration in two adult households. About 60 per cent of the households have two adults, about 10 per cent have more than three adults and about one per cent more than five . . .[5]

In Edgewood, 64.5 per cent of the sample was in two adult households and in Riverview 66.8 per cent. Ten per cent of the Edgewood sample was in three adult households and 3.6 per cent was in households with four or more adults. In Riverview 10.2 per cent of the sample was in three adult households and 3.1 per cent was in households of four or more adults. When weighted, the size of the sample in Edgewood was 494 (13 per cent of the adult population) and in Riverview, 704 (also 13 per cent of the adult population).

The interviews, which were between an hour and an hour-and-a-half in length, were conducted during the months of August and September 1961, by locally-hired individuals. All interviewers were given a two-day instruction period on the study itself and the techniques of interviewing, including sev-

[4] The adults in the household were listed from oldest to youngest, males first and females second. Each was then assigned a number in the order listed. The table on the front of each questionnaire, which was taken from Kish, *op. cit.*, p. 384, indicated which "number" was to be interviewed, depending on the number of adults in the household.

[5] Kish, *op. cit.*, p. 383.

eral supervised, practice interviews with people in the community.

The interviews in Edgewood were completed in just over two weeks with minimum difficulty. In Riverview, however, the story was somewhat different as the figures below indicate.

PER CENT OF OVER-ALL REFUSALS AND REFUSALS TO SELECTED QUESTIONS

	Edgewood (N=494)	Riverview (N=704)
Complete	2.4	6.4
Family income in 1960*	5.8	14.7
Political affiliation*	2.4	9.7
Religion*	2.4	6.8

* Includes complete refusals as well as refusals on this particular item. The over-all refusal rate in Riverview, while not high, was 6.4 per cent, almost triple that in Edgewood. In addition, the refusal rate on certain selected questions, particularly total family income in 1960, was consistently higher in Riverview than it was in Edgewood.

There are a number of factors which, together, probably account for the higher refusal rate in Riverview. In the first place, the quality and motivation of the interviewers in Riverview was, without exception, lower than that of the Edgewood interviewers.[6] In fact, it would have been impossible to have completed the interviews in Riverview without the help of four of the Edgewood interviewers who did over half of the interviews.

[6] An identical ad was placed in the local newspapers in Riverview and Edgewood, describing the job and the qualifications desired of potential interviewers. In Edgewood the response was enthusiastic, and almost thirty people appeared to apply for a job as interviewer. The ten individuals selected for the job were, with one exception, either school teachers or the wives of teachers. Considerable *esprit de corps* developed among these interviewers.

In Riverview, in contrast, only twelve people appeared to apply for the job, at least half of whom were unqualified. Of the five finally hired as interviewers, one was a teacher, two were housewives (or nonprofessionals), and two were college students. At no time did they evince the same interest or commitment shown by the Edgewood interviewers.

Secondly, there was some unfavorable publicity in Riverview about the community survey. Several housewives telephoned an Opinion Please program on the local radio station to voice complaints about the length of the interview, its purpose, and some of the questions asked. It was several days before we could answer these complaints over the air. Finally, due to the difficulties already mentioned, the interviews dragged on longer than anticipated and were not completed until the end of the first week in September.

A comparison of selected items from the survey with data from the 1960 Census shows that, on these factors, the sample does not differ markedly from the known characteristics of the population.

A COMPARISON OF THE COMMUNITY SAMPLES WITH CENSUS DATA ON SEX, AGE DISTRIBUTION, FOREIGN BORN, AND MEDIAN EDUCATION, IN PER CENT

	Edgewood Survey	Edgewood Census	Riverview Survey	Riverview Census
Sex: (1960)				
Male	43.1	45.6	42.8	47.8
Female	56.9	54.4	57.2	52.3
Age: (1960)				
20-29	15.6	15.9	12.8	14.6
30-39	14.4	17.6	19.0	20.1
40-49	20.7	18.2	17.1	18.7
50-59	20.5	18.3	21.9	17.5
60-69	13.1	14.3	17.8	16.0
70 and over	15.4	15.5	11.3	12.9
Birth: (1960)				
Foreign born	3.6	2.9	6.9	3.7
Education: (1960)				
Median	11.8 yrs.	12.1 yrs.	10.6 yrs.	10.5 yrs.

In both communities women appear to be slightly overrepresented in the sample, especially in Riverview. Likewise, younger people in both communities (those under 40) are underrepresented, and those people of middle age (40-59) are overrepresented, especially the 50-59 age group in Riverview. Those of foreign birth are overrepresented in the Riverview sample. All of these differences, however, are within the limits allowed by sampling variation, and there is no reason to believe that they are due to any systematic bias in the sampling techniques or error on the part of the interviewers.

2. Questionnaires

COMMUNITY DECISION-MAKERS

The following questionnaire concerns several important decisions in your community. We have been told that you were active in one or more of these decisions. We are trying to determine how these decisions were made and something about the individuals who participated in them.
All answers to this questionnaire are absolutely confidential. Any results will be presented in an anonymous or a statistical form.

Code No.: _____
Interviewer: _____
Date of Interview: _____

1. Name: _____

2. Place of Interview: _____

PART I:

A.

1. We have prepared a list of some of the issues which have come up in the community in the past five years or so. Some of these will be familiar to you, some of them less so. (Hand numbered "issue" cards to respondent.) Would you look through these cards, select out those issues in which you participated, regardless of whether you were in favor of them or against them, and give me the numbers printed on the cards. (Indicate issues in which he participated below with a check [√].)

Issue No.: I. _____
II. _____
III. _____
IV. _____
V. _____

2. There are undoubtedly some of these issues which you feel were more important than others. In terms of their effect upon the whole com-

APPENDIX 439

munity, which two of them do you think were most important, whether or not you participated in them?
    a. _____ Don't know, couldn't say, all of them the same, etc.
    b. _____ Number of most important issue
    c. _____ Number of second most important issue
AD HOC COMMENTS: (Write down any comments made by respondent during the selection process.)

3. Of the issues in which you participated, did you generally *support* all of them?
    a. _____ Yes
    b. _____ No
    c. _____ Don't know, Can't say, etc.
(If *no:*) Which ones did you actively oppose? (List number of issues below.)
    a. _____
    b. _____
    c. _____
    d. _____
    e. _____
AD HOC COMMENTS:

B.
1. Of those issues in which you participated, would you give me the names of several other people in the community that you know of firsthand who participated in them and were generally in favor of them? Let us begin with _____ (Insert name of the issue, beginning with the lowest numbered one in which respondent participated.)
Issue No.:
a. _____
   _____
   _____

b. Was this support organized in any way? That is, did those who actively participated in and supported the issue either organize themselves into a group for that purpose or were they concentrated in one or two community organizations?
(If *yes:*) Could you tell me a little bit more about that?
(If not clear: PROBE) Which organizations were these?
c. (If not already clear:) At what *stage* did you become involved in it and how did that come about?
(If not clear: PROBE) Do you remember who first contacted you about it?
d. (If not clear:) What *part* did you personally play in the issue?
e. (If not clear:) Do you remember any people that you contacted about it?

f. Could you give me the names of three or four people who actively *participated in* and *opposed* this issue?

_____   _____
_____   _____

g. Was this opposition organized in any way or concentrated in one or two community organizations?
(If *yes:*) Could you elaborate a bit on that?
(If not clear: PROBE) Which organizations were these?
h. Who would you say were the two or three people who you feel were *most influential* in determining the outcome of the issue?
i. Do you think that the outcome would have been different if they had *not* participated?
Why is that?

2. Let us take the next issue which you stated that you participated in, the _____ (Insert name of the issue, using the next lowest number in which the respondent participated.) Who are several other people that you know of first-hand that participated in it and were generally in favor of it?
Issue No.:
a. _____   _____   _____
              _____   _____
              _____

b. Was this support organized in any way? That is, did those who actively participated in and supported the issue either organize themselves into a group for that purpose or were they concentrated in one or two community organizations?
(*If yes:*) Could you tell me a little bit more about that?
(If not clear: PROBE) Which organizations were these?
c. (If not already clear:) At what *stage* did you become involved in it and how did that come about?
(If not clear: PROBE) Do you remember who first contacted you about it?
d. (If not clear:) What part did you personally play in the issue?
e. (If not clear:) Do you remember any people that you contacted about it?
f. Could you give me the names of three or four people who actively *participated in* and *opposed* this issue?

_____   _____
_____   _____

g. Was this opposition organized in any way or concentrated in one or two community organizations?
(If *yes:*) Could you elaborate a bit on that?

(If not clear: PROBE) Which organizations were these?
h. Who would you say were the two or three people who you feel were *most influential* in determining the outcome of this issue?
i. Do you think that the outcome would have been different if they had *not* participated?
Why is that?

3. The third issue which you mentioned that you participated in was _____ (Insert name of the issue, using the next lowest number of the issue in which he participated.) Who are several other people that you know that participated in it and were generally in favor of it?
Issue No.:
a. _____

b. Was this support organized in any way? That is, did those who actively participated in and supported the issue either organize themselves into a group for that purpose or were they concentrated in one or two community organizations?
(If *yes:*) Could you tell me a little bit more about that?
(If not clear: PROBE) Which organizations were these?
c. (If not already clear:) At what *stage* did you become involved in it and how did that come about?
(If not clear: PROBE) Do you remember who first contacted you about it?
d. (If not clear:) What *part* did you personally play in the issue?
e. (If not clear:) Do you remember any people that you contacted about it?
f. Could you give me the names of three or four people who actively *participated in* and *opposed* this issue?

g. Was this opposition organized in any way or concentrated in one or two community organizations?
(If *yes:*) Could you elaborate a bit on that?
(If not clear: PROBE) Which organizations were these?
h. Who would you say were the two or three people who you feel were *most influential* in determining the outcome of the issue?
i. Do you think that the outcome would have been different if they had *not* participated?
Why is that?

4. You mentioned that you participated in _____. (Insert name

of issue.) Would you name five or six other people who were active participants and were in favor of the issue?
Issue No.:
a. _____ _____ _____
   _____ _____
   _____ _____

b. Was this support organized in any way? That is, did those who actively participated in and supported the issue either organize themselves into a group for that purpose or were they concentrated in one or two community organizations?
(If *yes:*) Could you tell me a little bit more about that?
(If not clear: PROBE) Which organizations were these?
c. (If not already clear:) At what *stage* did you become involved in it and how did that come about?
(If not clear: PROBE) Do you remember who first contacted you about it?
d. (If not clear:) What *part* did you personally play in the issue?
e. (If not clear:) Do you remember any people that you contacted about it?
f. Could you give me the names of three or four people who actively *participated in* and *opposed* this issue?

_____ _____
_____ _____

g. Was this opposition organized in any way or concentrated in one or two community organizations?
(If *yes:*) Could you elaborate a bit on that?
(If not clear: PROBE) Which organizations were these?
h. Who would you say were the two or three people who you feel were *most influential* in determining the outcome of this issue?
i. Do you think that the outcome would have been different if they had *not* participated?
Why is that?

5. How about the _____? (Insert name of issue.) Who are several other people that you know of first-hand that participated in it and were generally in favor of it?
Issue No.:
a. _____ _____ _____
   _____ _____
   _____ _____

b. Was this support organized in any way? That is, did those who actively participated in and supported the issue either organize themselves into a group for that purpose or were they concentrated in one or two community organizations?
(If *yes:*) Could you tell me a little bit more about that?

(If not clear: PROBE) Which organizations were these?
c. (If not already clear:) At what *stage* did you become involved in it and how did that come about?
(If not clear: PROBE) Do you remember who first contacted you about it?
d. (If not clear:) What *part* did you personally play in the issue?
e. (If not clear:) Do you remember any people that you contacted about it?
f. Could you give me the names of three or four people who actively *participated in* and *opposed* this issue?

_____   _____

_____   _____

g. Was this opposition organized in any way or concentrated in one or two community organizations?
(If *yes:*) Could you elaborate a bit on that?
(If not clear: PROBE) Which organizations were these?
h. Who would you say were the two or three people who you feel were *most influential* in determining the outcome of the issue?
i. Do you think that the outcome would have been different if they had *not* participated?
Why is that?

PART II:

A.
1. I would now like to get some idea from you about the general nature of leadership and decision-making in this community. Suppose a major project were before the community, one that required decision by a group of leaders whom nearly everyone would accept. Which people would you choose to make up this group—regardless of whether or not you know them personally? (List names in spaces below.)

a. _____   b. _____
c. _____   d. _____
e. _____   f. _____
g. _____   h. _____
i. _____   j. _____

2. Suppose that you decided to run for public office here in the community. Who are the people you would be most likely to contact in order to get their backing and support so that you would have a good chance of winning?

a. _____   b. _____
c. _____   d. _____
e. _____   f. _____
g. _____   h. _____
i. _____   j. _____

3. If a decision were to be made in Albany that affected this community, who would be the best contact man to get in touch with state officials besides local members of the legislature?
a. _____ b. _____

4. Who, besides local members of Congress, would be the best man to get in touch with federal officials in Washington on some local problem?
a. _____ b. _____

5. Suppose a man wanted to become a leader in this community. Could you give me your ideas about what he would have to do?

B.
1. As I explained to you earlier, one of the things in which we are interested is the general question of hospital-community relations. Have you ever been a patient in the Edgewood Hospital? (Check one.)
    a. _____ Yes
    b. _____ No
(If *yes:*) How many times?
    a. _____ Once only
    b. _____ Twice
    c. _____ More than twice

2. Have you ever contributed any land, equipment, or money to the hospital? (Check one.)
    a. _____ Yes
    b. _____ No

3. Have you ever served on any committee connected to the hospital, for example, the hospital board, a publicity committee, or a fund raising committee?
    a. _____ Yes
    b. _____ No
(If *yes:*) What kind of a committee was this and when were you on it?

4. Could you tell me the name of a. The hospital administrator: _____
    b. The president of the hospital board. _____

5. Here is a list of the members of the hospital board and the administrator. (Hand respondent prepared list.) Some of these people may be your close friends and others you may know only casually or not at all. To indicate how well you may or may not know them, would you place a check mark at the right of *each* name on the list?

6. Now here is a list of the doctors who are on the staff of the hospital.

(Hand respondent prepared list.) Would you do the same thing opposite each of their names?

7. If you wanted to talk with someone connected with the hospital on, say, a matter related to the hospital budget, charges to patients or just general finances, whom would you be most likely to contact first? (Write in name below.)
a. _____ b. _____

8. What if you had some question about the quality of medical care at the hospital. Whom do you think that you would contact first to ask about it? (Write name below.)
a. _____ b. _____

9. If you had some question about the general administration of the hospital, for example, personnel policies, purchasing practices, or the kind of attention given to patients or visitors, whom would you be most likely to contact about it? (Write name below. If more than one name is given, indicate *which one the respondent would contact for which purpose.*)
a. _____ b. _____
     c. _____

10. During the past month can you remember talking with either a member of the hospital board, a doctor on the staff or a nurse about the hospital (Check as *many as appropriate.*)
a. _____ Yes, one or more doctors.
b. _____ Yes, one or more board members.
c. _____ Yes, one or more nurses.
d. _____ Other (Specify: _____)
e. _____ Didn't talk with anyone in past month about it.
f. _____ Don't know, can't remember, etc.

(If respondent reports at *least one such conversation, ask:*) I wonder if you could tell me the circumstances of your most recent conversation, that is how did it come about and where?

PART III:

Now I would like to ask you a few questions about yourself and your background.
1. How long have you lived in Edgewood?
a. _____ Less than 6 mos.
b. _____ 6 mos.–11 mos.
c. _____ 1–5 years.
d. _____ 6–10 years.
e. _____ 11–20 years.
f. _____ Over 20 years.
g. _____ All my life.

2. Sex: M _____ F _____.

3. How old were you on your last birthday?
   a. _____ Under 21   g. _____ 45-49
   b. _____ 21-24   h. _____ 50-54
   c. _____ 25-29   i. _____ 55-59
   d. _____ 30-34   j. _____ 60-64
   e. _____ 35-39   k. _____ 65-69
   f. _____ 40-44   l. _____ 70 or over
              m. _____ No answer

4. Where were you born?
   _____
   (city)   (state)   (country)

5. Marital status:
   a. _____ single
   b. _____ married
   c. _____ other

6. What was the last grade of school which you completed? (circle) 1 2 3 4 5 6 7 8 9 10 11 12 13 14 15 16 17+

7. Do you rent your present home?
   a. _____ Yes
   b. _____ No

8. What is your present occupation in as precise terms as possible?
   _____

9. Which daily newspapers do you subscribe to?
   a. _____ None
   b. _____
   c. _____
   d. _____

10. What is your political affiliation?
    a. _____ Republican   c. _____ Liberal
    b. _____ Democrat   d. _____ Other
              e. _____ none

11. Do you recall whether you voted for Eisenhower or Stevenson in the 1956 election?
    a. _____ Eisenhower   c. _____ Don't remember,
    b. _____ Stevenson   don't know, etc.
                               d. _____ Didn't vote.

12. In the 1960 election did you vote for Kennedy or Nixon?

a. _____ Kennedy
b. _____ Nixon
c. _____ Don't remember, don't know, etc.
d. _____ Didn't vote.

13. Do you consider yourself very interested, interested, slightly interested or not at all interested in national political affairs?
    a. _____ Very interested
    b. _____ Interested
    c. _____ Slightly interested
    d. _____ Not at all interested
    e. _____ Don't know

14. What is your religious affiliation?
    a. _____ Protestant
    b. _____ Catholic
    c. _____ Jewish
    d. _____ Other
    e. _____ None
    f. _____ No answer

15. How many times would you say that you attended church in the past month?
    a. _____ Not at all
    b. _____ Only once
    c. _____ 2-3 times
    d. _____ Over 3
    e. _____ Don't know

16. If people ask you your nationality or descent, how would you identify yourself?

_____

17. Have you ever been a patient in *any* hospital?
    a. _____ Yes
    b. _____ No
    c. _____ Don't know, can't remember, etc.

18. Have you or a member of your immediate family got someone that you would consider a 'family doctor'? That is, a doctor that you see at least once a year or more?
    a. _____ Yes, one.
    b. _____ Yes, more than one.
    c. _____ No.

19. What was your father's place of birth?

_____
    (city)   (state)   (country)

20. What kind of work did your father do most of his life? (Be specific.)

_____

21. What was the last grade of school completed by your father? (circle)
1 2 3 4 5 6 7 8 9 10 11 12 13 14 15 16 17+

22. Is or was your father highly active in community organizations and affairs?

a. _____ Yes
b. _____ No

23. Is or was your mother among the social leaders of the community?
    a. _____ Yes
    b. _____ No

24. What kind of work did your father's father do most of his life? (Be specific.)
_____

25. What kind of work did your wife's father do most of his life? (Be specific.)
_____

26. (Hand respondent card.) I wonder if you would look at that card and tell me the letter which corresponds to your family's total income from all sources for 1960 before taxes.
    a. _____ under $999   f. _____ $10,000-$19,999
    b. _____ $1,000-$2,999   g. _____ $20,000-$29,999
    c. _____ $3,000-$4,999   h. _____ $30,000-$49,999
    d. _____ $5,000-$7,499   i. _____ Over $50,000
    e. _____ $7,500-$9,999   j. _____ No answer

COMMUNITY INFLUENTIALS

The following questionnaire concerns several important decisions in your community. We have been told that you were active in one or more of these decisions. We are trying to determine how these decisions were made and something about the individuals who participated in them.

All answers to this questionnaire are absolutely confidential. Any results will be presented in an anonymous or a statistical form.

                                    Code No. _____
                                    Interviewer _____
                                    Date of Interview _____

1. Name: _____
2. Place of Interview: _____

PART I:

1. First, in your opinion, what have been the most important issues or problems which this community has faced during the past five years? Anything else?

APPENDIX 449

2. Here are five cards containing the names of five issues with which our study is primarily concerned. (Hand respondent cards.) There are undoubtedly some of these issues which you feel were more important than others. In terms of their effect upon the whole community, which two of them do you think were most important?
    a. _____ Don't know, couldn't say, all of them the same, etc.
    b. _____ Number of most important issue
    c. _____ Number of second most important issue
AD HOC COMMENTS: (Write down any comments made by respondent during the selection process.)

3. Did you personally participate actively in *any* of these five issues?
    a. _____ Yes
    b. _____ No

4. Would you indicate which of the issues you supported and which you opposed?

Supported:	Opposed:
#_____	#_____
#_____	#_____
#_____	#_____
#_____	#_____
#_____	#_____

5. Some studies of other communities have shown that a small group pretty well runs local affairs and makes most of the important decisions. In your opinion is this an accurate description of the way in which things are done here?
Why is that?

PART II:

1. One of the things in which we are interested is the general question of hospital-community relations. Have you ever been a patient in (*RIVERVIEW:* the Riverview District Hospital; *EDGEWOOD:* Edgewood Memorial Hospital)? (Check one.)
    a. _____ Yes
    b. _____ No
(If *yes:*) How many times?
    a. _____ Once only
    b. _____ Twice
    c. _____ More than twice

2. Have you ever contributed any land, equipment, or money to the hospital? (Check one.)
    a. _____ Yes
    b. _____ No

3. Have you ever served on any committee connected with the hospital, for example, the hospital board, a publicity committee, or a fund raising committee?
    a. _____ Yes
    b. _____ No
(If *yes:*) What kind of a committee was this and when were you on it?

4. Could you tell me the name of a. The hospital administrator: _____
    b. The president of the hospital board; _____

5. Here is a list of the members of the hospital board and the administrator. (Hand respondent prepared list.) Some of these people may be your close friends and others you may know only casually or not at all. To indicate how well you may or may not know them, would you place a check mark at the right of *each* name on the list? In some cases you may need to place more than one check mark opposite a name.

6. Now here is a list of the doctors who are on the staff of the hospital. (Hand respondent prepared list.) Would you do the same thing opposite each of their names? Notice that there is a new category at the top of this list: Been treated by him as a patient.

7. If you had some question about the general administration of the hospital, for example, personnel policies, purchasing practices, or the kind of attention given to patients or visitors, whom would you be most likely to contact about it? (Write name below. If more than one name is given, indicate *which one the respondent would contact for which purpose.*)
    a. _____ b. _____
        c. _____

8. What if you had some question about the quality of medical care at the hospital. Whom do you think that you would contact first to ask about it? (Write name below.)
    a. _____ b. _____

9. During the past month can you remember talking with either a member of the hospital board, a doctor on the staff or a nurse about the hospital? (*Check as many as appropriate.*)
    a. _____ Yes, one or more doctors.
    b. _____ Yes, one or more board members.
    c. _____ Yes, one or more nurses.
    d. _____ Other (Specify: _____)
    e. _____ Didn't talk with any one in past month about it.
    f. _____ Don't know, can't remember, etc.

APPENDIX 451

(If respondent reports *at least one such conversation, ask:*) I wonder if you could tell me the circumstances of your most recent conversation, that is how did it come about and where?

PART III

1. I would now like to get some idea from you about the general nature of leadership and decision-making in this community. Suppose a major project were before the community, one that required decision by a group of leaders whom nearly everyone would accept. Which people would you choose to make up this group—regardless of whether or not you know them personally? (List names below.)

a. _____ f. _____
b. _____ g. _____
c. _____ h. _____
d. _____ i. _____
e. _____ j. _____

2. Suppose that you decided to run for public office here in the community. Who are the people you would be most likely to contact in order to get their backing and support so that you would have a good chance of winning?

a. _____ f. _____
b. _____ g. _____
c. _____ h. _____
d. _____ i. _____
e. _____ j. _____

3. If a decision were to be made in Albany that affected this community, who, besides local members of the state legislature, would be the best contact man to get in touch with state officials?
a. _____ b. _____

4. Who, besides local members of Congress, would be the best man to get in touch with federal officials in Washington on some local problem?
a. _____ b. _____

5. Suppose a man wanted to become a leader in this community. Could you give me your ideas about what he would have to do and the qualifications he would need?
(If not clear:) Would he have to belong to any particular organizations or clubs?

PART IV:

Now I would like to ask you a few questions about yourself and your background.

1. How long have you lived in Riverview (Edgewood)?
   a. _____ Less than 6 mos.   e. _____ 11-20 years
   b. _____ 6 mos.-11 mos.   f. _____ Over 20 years
   c. _____ 1-5 years   g. _____ All my life
   d. _____ 6-10 years

2. Sex: M _____ F _____

3. How old were you on your last birthday?
   a. _____ Under 21   g. _____ 45-49
   b. _____ 21-24   h. _____ 50-54
   c. _____ 25-29   i. _____ 55-59
   d. _____ 30-34   j. _____ 60-64
   e. _____ 35-39   k. _____ 65-69
   f. _____ 40-44   l. 70 or over

4. Where were you born?
   _____
          (city)   (state)   (country)

5. Marital status:
   a. _____ single
   b. _____ married
   c. _____ other

6. What was the last grade of school which you completed? (Circle) 1 2 3 4 5 6 7 8 9 10 11 12 13 14 15 16 17+

7. Do you rent your present home?
   a. _____ Yes
   b. _____ No

8. What is your present occupation in as precise terms as possible? (Spell out in detail and be sure to ascertain whether self-employed and/or managerial.)
   _____
   _____
   _____

9. Which daily newspapers do you subscribe to?
   a. _____ None
   b. _____
   c. _____
   d. _____

10. What is your political affiliation?
    a. _____ Republican   d. _____ Independent
    b. _____ Democrat   e. _____ None
    c. _____ Liberal   f. _____ No Answer

APPENDIX

11. Do you recall whether you voted for Eisenhower or Stevenson in the 1956 election or didn't you vote?
    a. _____ Eisenhower
    b. _____ Stevenson
    c. _____ Don't remember, don't know, etc.
    d. _____ Didn't vote.

12. In the 1960 presidential election did you vote for Kennedy or Nixon or didn't you vote?
    a. _____ Kennedy
    b. _____ Nixon
    c. _____ Don't remember, don't know, etc.
    d. _____ Didn't vote.

13. During most of his life did your father consider himself a Republican, a Democrat or something else?
    a. _____ Republican
    b. _____ Democrat
    c. _____ Liberal
    d. _____ Independent
    e. _____ Don't know

14. Do you consider yourself very interested, interested, slightly interested or not at all interested in national political affairs?
    a. _____ Very interested
    b. _____ Interested
    c. Slightly interested
    d. _____ Not at all interested
    e. _____ Don't know

15. What is your religious affiliation?
    a. _____ Protestant
    b. _____ Catholic
    c. _____ Jewish
    d. _____ Other
    e. _____ None
    f. _____ No Answer

16. How many times would you say that you attended church in the past month?
    a. _____ not at all
    b. _____ only once
    c. _____ 2-3 times
    d. _____ over 3
    e. _____ Don't know

17. If people ask you your nationality or descent, how would you identify yourself? For example, German-Irish, Polish, French-Italian, or something else.
    _____

18. Have you ever been a patient in *any* hospital?
    a. _____ Yes
    b. _____ No
    c. _____ Don't know, can't remember, etc.

19. Have you or a member of your immediate family someone that you consider a 'family doctor'? That is, a doctor that you see at least once a year or more?
    a. _____ Yes, one.
    b. _____ Yes, more than one.
    c. _____ No

20. What was your father's place of birth?

_____
    (city)   (state)   (country)

21. What kind of work did your father do most of his life? (Spell out in detail and be sure to ascertain whether self-employed and/or managerial or nonmanagerial.)

_____
_____

22. What was the last grade of school completed by your father? (Circle)
1 2 3 4 5 6 7 8 9 10 11 12 13 14 15 16 17+

23. Is or was your father highly active in community organizations and affairs?
   a. _____ Yes
   b. _____ No

24. Is or was your mother among the social leaders of the community?
   a. _____ Yes
   b. _____ No

25. What kind of work did your father's father do most of his life? (Spell out in detail and be sure to ascertain whether self-employed and/or managerial or nonmanagerial.)

_____

26. What kind of work did your *wife's* father do most of his life? (Spell out in detail and be sure to ascertain whether self-employed and/or managerial or nonmanagerial.)

_____

27. (Hand respondent card.) I wonder if you would look at that card and tell me the letter which corresponds to your family's total income from all sources for 1960 before taxes.

   a. _____ under $999   f. _____ $10,000-$19,999
   b. _____ $1,000-$2,999   g. _____ $20,000-$29,999
   c. _____ $3,000-$4,999   h. _____ $30,000-$49,999
   d. _____ $5,000-$7,499   i. _____ Over $50,000
   e. _____ $7,500-$9,999   j. _____ No Answer

COMMUNITY ORGANIZATIONAL LEADERS

Introduction: We have been given a grant to study the nature of leadership in medium-sized communities such as this one. One aspect of the study involves looking at certain organizations like _____ (insert name)

APPENDIX 455

of which you are _____ (insert proper title). I would like to ask you a few questions about your organization, its activities, and community decision-making. Perhaps I should add that all of the information will be treated in a confidential matter. Any reports of the study will treat the data in a statistical manner and individuals will not be identified.

Code No. _____
Date _____
Interviewer _____
Place of Intvw. _____

1. Name of Organization _____

2. Name and Position of Respondent _____
In order to have a better idea of the nature of your organization and the activities in which it engages, I would like to ask you a few questions about it.

3. First, could you give me the names and positions of the other officers of _____. (Insert name of organization.) (List names and positions below.)

Full Name	Position

4. How many active members do you have at present? _____
(If not clear:) Is this more or less than your usual number of active members?
_____ More   _____ About the same   _____ Less
(If more or less:) What is your usual number then? _____

5. How often do you hold regular meetings? _____

6. What are the qualifications for membership in _____? (Insert name of organization.) NOTE: Be certain to ask about age and sex requirements, residence requirements, whether membership is by invitation only and if so who does the inviting, and whether there are any other special requirements for membership if the respondent does not answer these spontaneously.

7. Would you say that most of the people who are eligible for membership presently belong?
    a. _____ Yes
    b. _____ No
    c. _____ Don't Know

(If no:) Why is that?

8. What are your membership dues, if any? (Be sure to find out if they are monthly, yearly, lifetime, etc.)

---

9. (If not already clear:) Do you have different categories of membership, for example, lifetime, associate, courtesy, family, etc?
    a. _____ Yes
    b. _____ No
(If yes:) Could you tell me what they are and approximately how many people are in each category?

10. In as specific terms as possible could you tell me what the major purpose of _____ (insert name of organization) is?

11. Would you say that _____ (insert name of the organization) is very interested, interested, slightly interested or not at all interested in national and international affairs?
    a. _____ Very Interested   d. _____ Not at all Interested
    b. _____ Interested   e. _____ Don't Know
    c. _____ Slightly Interested
(If interested or very interested:) What activities, if any, has your organization undertaken in this area?

12. Would you say that _____ (insert name of the organization) is very interested, interested, slightly interested or not at all interested in local community affairs?
    a. _____ Very Interested   d. _____ Not at all Interested
    b. _____ Interested   e. _____ Don't Know
    c. _____ Slightly Interested
(If interested or very interested:) What activities, if any, has your organization undertaken in this area?

13. Was _____ (insert name of organization) actively involved in any way in the establishment of the Riverview District Housing Authority?
    a. _____ Yes
    b. _____ No
    c. _____ Don't Know
(If yes:) Did your organization generally support or oppose it or didn't it take any kind of formal position on the issue?
Why was that?
What, specifically, did you do?

14. How about on the School Bond Issue for the new High School, was _____ (insert name of organization) involved actively in that?
    a. _____ Yes
    b. _____ No
    c. _____ Don't Know

APPENDIX

(If yes:) Did your organization generally support or oppose it or didn't it take any kind of formal position on the issue?
Why was that?
What, specifically, did you do?

15. Did _____ (insert name of organization) become actively involved in any way in bringing the Skybolt Fabricating Company to Riverview?
    a. _____ Yes
    b. _____ No
    c. _____ Don't Know
(If yes:) Did your organization generally support or oppose it or didn't it take any kind of formal position on the issue?
Why was that?
What, specifically, did you do?

16. Was _____ (insert name of organization) actively involved in any way in the establishment of the Riverview Flood Control Project?
    a. _____ Yes
    b. _____ No
    c. _____ Don't Know
(If yes:) Did your organization generally support or oppose it or didn't it take any kind of formal position on the issue?
Why was that?
What, specifically, did you do?

17. How about the establishment of the new Riverview District Hospital, was _____ (insert name of organization) involved actively in that?
    a. _____ Yes
    b. _____ No
    c. _____ Don't Know
(If yes:) Did your organization generally support or oppose it or didn't it take any kind of formal position on the issue?
Why was that?
What, specifically, did you do?

18. Has your organization ever had any dealings with the hospital? For example, has it ever taken a formal position supporting or opposing some hospital policy, or been represented on some committee associated with the hospital or made formal representations of any kind to the hospital board, the administrator or the doctors on the hospital staff?
    a. _____ Unqualified no
    b. _____ Don't think so, but not certain
    c. _____ Yes
    d. _____ Don't Know
(If yes:) Could you tell me more about that?

19. If you had some general question about the policies of the hospital, whom would you contact to find out about them? _____

Why? _____

20. Here is a list of the members of the hospital board and the administrator. (Hand respondent prepared list.) Some of these people may be your close friends and others you may know only casually or not at all. To indicate how well you may or may not know them, would you place a check mark at the right of *each* name on the list.

21. Now here is a list of the doctors who are on the staff of the hospital. (Hand respondent prepared list.) Would you do the same thing opposite each of their names?

22. I would now like to get some idea from you about the general nature of leadership and decision-making in this community. Suppose a major project were before the community, one that required decision by a group of leaders whom nearly everyone would accept. Which people would you choose to make up this group—regardless of whether or not you know them personally?

a. _____ b. _____
c. _____ d. _____
e. _____ f. _____
g. _____ h. _____
i. _____ j. _____

23. If a decision were to be made in Albany that affected this community, who would be the best contact man to get in touch with state officials besides local members of the legislature?
a. _____ b. _____

24. Who, besides local members of Congress, would be the best man to get in touch with federal officials in Washington on some local problem?
a. _____ b. _____

24. Some studies of other communities have shown that a small group pretty well runs local affairs and makes most of the important decisions. In your opinion is this an accurate description of the way in which things are done in Riverview?
Why is that?

25. Finally, I would like to ask you a few questions about your own background. How long have you been _____ (insert proper title) of _____ (insert name of organization)?

26. How long have you lived in Riverview?

APPENDIX

a. _____ Less than 6 mos.	d. _____ 6-10 years
b. _____ 6 mos.-11 mos.	e. _____ 11-20 years
c. _____ 1-5 years	f. _____ Over 20 years
	g. _____ All my life

27. Sex: _____ M _____ F

28. How old were you on your last birthday?
    - a. _____ Under 21
    - b. _____ 21-24
    - c. _____ 25-29
    - d. _____ 30-34
    - e. _____ 35-39
    - f. _____ 40-44
    - g. _____ 45-49
    - h. _____ 50-54
    - i. _____ 55-59
    - j. _____ 60-64
    - k. _____ 65-69
    - l. _____ 70 or over
    - m. _____ no answer

29. Where were you born? _____
    (city)   (state)   (country)

30. What was the last grade of school which you completed? (circle) 1 2 3 4 5 6 7 8 9 10 11 12 13 14 15 16 17+

31. Do you rent your present home?
    - a. _____ Yes
    - b. _____ No

32. What is your present occupation in as precise terms as possible? (Spell out in detail and be sure to ascertain whether self-employed and/or managerial or nonmanagerial.)

33. Which daily newspapers do you subscribe to?
    - a. _____ None
    - b. _____
    - c. _____
    - d. _____

34. What is your political affiliation?
    - a. _____ Republican
    - b. _____ Democrat
    - c. _____ Liberal
    - d. _____ Independent
    - e. _____ Other
    - f. _____ None

35. Do you recall whether you voted for Eisenhower or Stevenson or didn't vote in the 1956 election?
    - a. _____ Eisenhower
    - b. _____ Stevenson
    - c. _____ Don't remember, don't know
    - d. _____ Didn't vote

36. In the 1960 election did you vote for Kennedy, Nixon, or didn't you vote?
    a. _____ Kennedy   c. _____ Don't remember
    b. _____ Nixon   d. _____ Didn't vote

37. Do you consider yourself very interested, interested, slightly interested or not at all interested in national political affairs?
    a. _____ Very interested   d. _____ Not at all interested
    b. _____ Interested   e. _____ Don't know
    c. _____ Slightly interested

38. What is your religious affiliation?
    a. _____ Protestant   d. _____ Other
    b. _____ Catholic   e. _____ None
    c. _____ Jewish   f. _____ No answer

39. How many times would you say that you attended church in the past month?
    a. _____ not at all   d. _____ over 3
    b. _____ only once   e. _____ Don't Know
    c. _____ 2-3 times

40. Have you ever been a patient in *any* hospital?
    a. _____ Yes   c. _____ Don't know, can't
    b. _____ No   remember

41. Have you or a member of your immediate family got someone that you would consider a 'family doctor'? That is, a doctor that you see at least once a year or more?
    a. _____ Yes, one   c. _____ No
    b. _____ Yes, more than one

42. What was your father's place of birth?
_____
        (city)   (state)   (country)

43. What kind of work did your father do most of his life? (Spell out in detail and be sure to ascertain whether self-employed and/or managerial or nonmanagerial.)
_____

44. What was the last grade of school completed by your father? (circle)
1 2 3 4 5 6 7 8 9 10 11 12 13 14 15 16 17+

45. Is or was your father highly active in community organizations and affairs?
    a. _____ Yes   b. _____ No

APPENDIX

46. Is or was your mother among the social leaders of the community?
    a. _____ Yes   b. _____ No

47. What kind of work did your father's father do most of his life? (Spell out in detail and be sure to ascertain whether self-employed and/or managerial or nonmanagerial.)

_____

_____

48. What kind of work did your wife's father do most of his life? (Spell out in detail and be sure to ascertain whether self-employed and/or managerial or nonmanagerial.)

_____

_____

49. Finally, I wonder if you would look at that card (hand respondent card) and tell me the letter which corresponds to your family's income from all sources for 1960 before taxes?

    a. _____ Under $999   f. _____ $10,000-$19,999
    b. _____ $1,000-$2,999   g. _____ $20,000-$29,999
    c. _____ $3,000-$4,999   h. _____ $30,000-$49,999
    d. _____ $5,000-$7,499   i. _____ Over $50,000
    e. _____ $7,500-$9,999   j. _____ No answer

50. What would you say have been the most important issues which Riverview has faced in the last 5 years?

51. (Hand respondent cards.) There are undoubtedly some of these issues which you feel were more important than others. In terms of their effect on the whole community, which two would you say were most important?
    a. _____ Don't know
    b. _____ Number of most important issue
    c. _____ Number of second most important issue

COMMUNITY RANK-AND-FILE SAMPLE

Community Sample Questionnaire

How many people age 20 and over live in this household? _____
(If *two* or less, consult table below and select respondent. The male head of the household should be number 1, the female number 2. If *more than two*, complete the following:)

What is the name of the head of the household and his (her) age on his (her) last birthday?

_____ M _____ F _____
(name)   (age on last birthday)

What are the names and ages of all other males in the household 20 and over and their relationship to the head of the household?

_____ No other males (check)

(name)	(age on last birthday)	(Relation to head of house)
(name)	(age on last birthday)	(Relation to head of house)
(name)	(age on last birthday)	(Relation to head of house)

Now, what are the names and ages of all other females in the household 20 and over and their relationship to the head of the household?

_____ No other females (check)

(name)	(age on last birthday)	(Relation to head of house)
(name)	(age on last birthday)	(Relation to head of house)
(name)	(age on last birthday)	(Relation to head of house)

(*INSTRUCTIONS:* Number the people in the household 20 and over (1, 2, 3, etc.) from oldest to youngest, beginning with the males and then select the respondent to be interviewed from the table below.)

If no. of adults in household is

1	2	3	4	5	6 or more

Select adult numbered

1	2	2	3	4	4

RECORD OF CONTACTS:
Initial contact: _____ Second contact: _____
              (date)   (time)   (date)   (time)
                  Third contact: _____
                                (date)   (time)

Code No.: _____
Interviewer No.: _____
Community: _____

APPENDIX

PART I

1. In order to understand how important community decisions are made in Riverview we have selected for more intensive study five issues which have come up in the past few years. Here are the names of these five issues. (Hand respondent cards.) Please select the two which in your opinion have been the most important for the community as a whole.
    a. _____ Don't know, couldn't say, all of them the same, etc.
    b. _____ Number of most important issue
    c. _____ Number of second most important issue

2. A. Beginning with the establishment of the Riverview Housing Authority, were you personally a participant in this issue in *any way* at all? (Check one.)
    a. _____ Yes   b. _____ No
(If *yes*, ask 2B and 2C.)

B. What part did you personally play in it? (Check appropriate categories.)
    a. _____ Served on a committee or board which considered this project. (Specify name of board: _____)
    b. _____ Other (Specify the nature of involvement clearly and in detail:) _____

C. Could you give me the names of two or three people in Riverview who you know were active participants in this issue? (List names and/or comments below.)
a. _____ c. _____
b. _____ d. _____
COMMENTS:
(If *no*, go on to question 2C.)

3. A. Were you in *any way* involved in the Riverview flood control project? (check)
    a. _____ Yes   b. _____ No
(If *yes*, ask 3B and 3C.)

3. B. What part did you personally play in it? (Check appropriate categories.)
    a. _____ Served on a committee or board which considered this project. (Specify name of board: _____)
    b. _____ Attended public hearings on the project
    c. _____ Other (Specify the nature of involvement clearly and

in detail.) _____

(If *no*, go on to question 3C.)

C. Could you give me the names of two or three people in Riverview who you know were active participants in this issue? (List names and/or comments.)

a. _____ c. _____
b. _____ d. _____

COMMENT:

4. A. What about the construction of the new Riverview District Hospital, were you a participant in this issue in *any way*? (check)
    a. _____ Yes   b. _____ No

(If *yes*, ask 4B and 4C.)

B. What part did you personally play in it? (Check appropriate categories.)

    a. _____ Served on a committee or board which considered it. (Specify name of board: _____)
    b. _____ Other (Specify the nature of involvement clearly and in detail.) _____

(If *no*, go on to question 4C.)

C. Could you give me the names of two or three people in Riverview who you know were active participants in this project? (List names and/or comments.)

a. _____ c. _____
b. _____ d. _____

COMMENTS:

5. A. What about the bond issue for the new junior-senior high school? Were you in *any way* involved in that? (check)
    a. _____ Yes   b. _____ No

(If *yes* to question 5A, ask 5B and 5C.)

B. What part did you personally play in it?

    a. _____ Served on a committee or board which considered it. (Specify name of board:) _____
    b. _____ Attended public discussions of the bond issue
    c. _____ Voted on the bond issue
    d. _____ Other (Specify nature of the involvement clearly and in detail:) _____

(If *no*, go on to question 5C.)

C. Could you give me the names of two or three people in Riverview who

APPENDIX

465

you know were active participants in this project? (List names and/or comments.)
a. _____ c. _____
b. _____ d. _____
COMMENTS:

6. A. What about the bringing of the Skybolt Fabricating Company to Riverview? Were you in *any way* involved in that? (check)
    a. _____ Yes   b. _____ No
(If *yes*, then ask 6B and 6C.)

B. What part did you personally play in it? (Check appropriate categories.)
    a. _____ Served on a committee or board which considered it. (Specify name of board:) _____
    b. _____ Bought stock in the corporation
    c. _____ Other (Specify nature of the involvement clearly and in detail:) _____
(If *yes* or *no*, ask question 6C.)

6. C. Could you give me the names of two or three people in Riverview who you know were active participants in this project? (List names and/or comments.)
a. _____ c. _____
b. _____ d. _____
COMMENTS:

7. Now here is a list of names of some people here in Riverview who have been active at one time or another in various community issues and projects. (Hand respondent list of names.) Would you put a check mark opposite *each* name to show us how well you personally know these people. Just check don't know, heard of, or if you exchange home visits with any of them, know socially, etc.

PART II

1. A. We are also studying the general question of hospital-community relations. Have you ever been a patient in the Riverview District Hospital?
    a. _____ Yes   b. _____ No
(If *yes*, ask:) B. How many times?
    a. _____ Once only
    b. _____ Twice
    c. _____ More than twice
(If *no*, go on to question 2.)

2. Have you ever contributed any land, equipment, or money to the hospital? (Check one.)
    a. _____ Yes   b. _____ No

3. Have you ever served on any committee connected with the hospital, for example, the hospital board, a publicity committee, or a fund raising committee? (check)
    a. _____ Yes   b. _____ No

4. (If respondent is a *female*, ask this question. Otherwise, skip to question 5.) Are you presently a member of the hospital auxiliary?
    a. _____ Yes   b. _____ No

5. A. Have you ever worked at the hospital in any capacity? (check)
    a. _____ Yes   b. _____ No

(If *yes*, ask:) B. In what capacity? (Check appropriate categories.)
    a. _____ Janitorial or custodial work (building and ground maintenance)
    b. _____ Registered Nurse
    c. _____ Nurse's Aide or Practical Nurse
    d. _____ Clerical (secretary, telephone operator, typist, billing clerk, etc.)
    e. _____ Other (Specify clearly with brief *job description* and job title:) _____

(If *no*, go on to question 6.)

6. Is the hospital privately owned and operated or is it owned and operated by a governmentally appointed body? (check)
    a. _____ Operated by a governmentally appointed body
    b. _____ Privately owned
    c. _____ Don't know

7. A. Do you think that citizens in this community like yourself have a great deal of say or very little say about the way the hospital is run? (check)
    a. _____ Great deal of say
    b. _____ Little say
    c. _____ Don't know

(If *little say*, ask 7B)

B. Do you feel that you should have *more* of a say in hospital affairs than you do? (check)
    a. _____ Yes   b. _____ No

(If *yes* or *no* to question 7B, ask question 7C.)

7. C. Why do you feel this way? (Write in comments in space below.)
COMMENTS:

(If *great say* or *don't know* for 7d, go on to question 8.)

8. Could you give me the name of the President of the hospital board? (Write in name and/or comments in spaces below.)

_____
(name)

COMMENTS:

APPENDIX 467

9. Here is a list of the members of the hospital board and the administrator. (Hand respondent list.) Would you put a check mark opposite *each* name to show us how well you personally know these people.
10. Here is a similar list of the doctors on the staff of the hospital. (Hand respondent list.) In addition to checking how well you know each of them, would you also put a check mark in the sixth column if you personally have ever been treated by this doctor as a patient.

PART III

Now I would like to get some information about your background.

1. How long have you lived in Riverview?
    a. _____ less than 6 mos.   d. _____ 6-10 years
    b. _____ 6 mos.-11 mos.   e. _____ 11-20 years
    c. _____ 1-5 years   f. _____ Over 20 years
                   g. _____ All my life

2. Sex _____ M _____ F

3. Where were you born?

(city)	(county)	(state)	(country)

4. How old were you on your last birthday? (check one)
    a. _____ Under 21   g. _____ 45-49
    b. _____ 21-24   h. _____ 50-54
    c. _____ 25-29   i. _____ 55-59
    d. _____ 30-34   j. _____ 60-64
    e. _____ 35-39   k. _____ 65-69
    f. _____ 40-44   l. _____ 70 or over
                   m. _____ no answer

5. (If respondent is *not the head of the household,* ask questions 5 and 6. If the respondent *is head of the household,* skip to question 7.)
What was the last grade of school completed by the head of the household?
(circle)
1 2 3 4 5 6 7 8 9 10 11 12 13 14 15 16 17+

6. What is the present occupation of the head of the household in as precise terms as possible? (Spell out in detail and be sure to ascertain whether self-employed and/or managerial or nonmanagerial.)

7. (Ask question 7 of *all respondents.*) What was the last grade of school which you completed? (circle)
1 2 3 4 5 6 7 8 9 10 11 12 13 14 15 16 17+

8. (Ask of *all respondents*.) What is your present occupation in as precise terms as possible? (Spell out in detail.)

---

9. Does your family rent its present home? (check)
    a. _____ Yes   b. _____ No

10. Which daily newspaper does your family subscribe to? (Write in names.)
    a. _____ None (check)   c. _____
    b. _____ d. _____

11. What is your political affiliation? (check)
    a. _____ Republican   d. _____ Independent
    b. _____ Democrat   e. _____ Other
    c. _____ Liberal   f. _____ None

12. Do you recall whether you voted for Eisenhower or Stevenson in the 1956 election, or didn't you vote?
    a. _____ Eisenhower   c. _____ don't remember, don't know
    b. _____ Stevenson   d. _____ didn't vote

13. In the 1960 election did you vote for Kennedy, Nixon, or didn't you vote? (check)
    a. _____ Kennedy   c. _____ Don't remember
    b. _____ Nixon   d. _____ Didn't vote

14. During most of his life, did your father consider himself a Republican, a Democrat, or something else? (check)
    a. _____ Republican   c. _____ Independent
    b. _____ Democrat   d. _____ Other
                e. _____ Don't know

15. Do you consider yourself very interested, interested, slightly interested or not at all interested in national political affairs? (check)
    a. _____ Very interested   c. _____ Slightly interested
    b. _____ Interested   d. _____ Not at all interested
                e. _____ Don't know

16. What is your religious affiliation? (check)
    a. _____ Protestant   d. _____ Other
    b. _____ Catholic   e. _____ None
    c. _____ Jewish   f. _____ No answer

17. How many times would you say that you attended church in the past month? (check)
    a. _____ not at all   c. _____ 2-3 times
    b. _____ only once   d. _____ over 3
                e. _____ Don't know

APPENDIX

18. Have you ever been a patient in *any* hospital?
   a. _____ Yes   b. _____ No
   c. _____ Don't know, can't remember

19. A. Have you or a member of your immediate family someone that you consider your 'family doctor,' that is a doctor that you see at least once a year or more? (check)
   a. _____ Yes   b. _____ No
(If *yes*, ask:) Have you more than one such person that you consider a 'family doctor'? (check)
   a. _____ Yes   b. _____ No
(If *no to question 19A*, go on to question 20.)

20. What was your father's place of birth? (Write in answer.)

_____
     (city)   (state)   (country)

21. (*If respondent has already given you his or her father's education and occupation* in questions 5 and 6, Part III, above, skip to question 23. If not, ask questions 21 and 22.)
What was the last grade of school completed by your father? (circle) 1 2 3 4 5 6 7 8 9 10 11 12 13 14 15 16 17+

22. What kind of work did your father do most of his life? (Spell out in detail and be sure to ascertain whether self-employed and/or managerial or nonmanagerial.)

_____

23. If people ask you your nationality or descent, how would you identify yourself? For example: German-Irish, English, Italian, or something else? (Write in answer.)

_____

24. What is your marital status? (check)
   a. _____ married   b. _____ single   c. _____ other

25. What kind of work did your father's father do most of his life? (Spell out in detail.)

_____

26. Is or was your father highly active in community organizations and affairs? (check)
   a. _____ Yes   b. _____ No

27. Is or was your mother among the social leaders of the community? (check)
   a. _____ Yes   b. _____ No

28. (*If respondent is or was married*, ask question 28. If not skip to question 29.)
What kind of work did your *wife's* father do most of his life? (Spell out in detail and be certain to ascertain whether self-employed or not and whether managerial or nonmanagerial.)

---

29. Now we would like to get some idea of the various organizations in which you have been active in the community. What elective or appointive governmental offices have you held since 1950? For example: mayor, library board member, hospital board member, county supervisor, school board member, etc.
    a. _____ None (check)
TITLE OF OFFICE   DATES OF OFFICE

30. Have you been a member of any committees or commissions created to deal with a local community problem since 1950? For example: a committee to attract industry to the city, a committee on crime and juvenile delinquency, a publicity committee for a school bond issue or a hospital fund drive, etc.
    a. _____ None (check)
TITLE OF COMMITTEE   DATES OF OFFICE

31. Have you been on the boards of directors of any private corporations or banks since 1950?
    a. _____ None
NAME OF ENTERPRISE   OFFICES HELD   DATES OF OFFICE

32. What local and national community service organizations have you been a member of since 1950? For example: PTA, United Fund, Mental Health Association, or anything else connected with health, education or welfare.
    a. _____ None (check)
NAME OF ORGANIZATION   OFFICES HELD   DATES OF OFFICE

33. Have you been a member of any business organizations like the Chamber of Commerce, or the National Association of Real Estate Dealers since 1950?
    a. _____ None (check)
NAME OF ORGANIZATION   OFFICES HELD   DATES OF OFFICE

34. What professional organizations have you belonged to since 1950? For example: the American Medical Association, the American Bar Association, the National Association of Civil Engineers, or something like them.
    a. _____ None (check)
NAME OF ORGANIZATION   OFFICES HELD   DATES OF OFFICE

APPENDIX 471

35. Have you belonged to any labor union organizations since 1950?
   a. _____ None (check)

NAME OF ORGANIZATION   OFFICES HELD   DATES OF OFFICE

36. What clubs and social organizations like the Elks, the Mason, the Rotary Club or the country club have you been a member of since 1950?
   a. _____ None (check)

NAME OF ORGANIZATION   OFFICES HELD   DATES OF OFFICE

37. What churches and religious organizations like the Methodist Church, the Knights of Columbus, the Young Lutheran Men, etc. have you been a member of since 1950?
   a. _____ None (check)

NAME OF ORGANIZATION   OFFICES HELD   DATES OF OFFICE

38. Have you belonged to any political party organizations since 1950? For example: the Young Democrats, the Republican Women's Club, the County Democratic Committee, the League of Women Voters, etc.
   a. _____ None (check)

NAME OF ORGANIZATION   OFFICES HELD   DATES OF OFFICE

39. What veterans' and patriotic organizations like the American Legion Auxiliary, the V.F.W., the American Legion, the D.A.R., etc., have you belonged to since 1950?
   a. _____ None (check)

NAME OF ORGANIZATION   OFFICES HELD   DATES OF OFFICE

40. Finally, I wonder if you would look at this card (hand respondent card) and tell me the letter—a, b, c, etc.—which corresponds to your family's total income from all sources for 1960 before taxes.
   a. _____ Under $999   f. _____ $10,000-$19,999
   b. _____ $1,000-$2,999   g. _____ $20,000-$29,999
   c. _____ $3,000-$4,999   h. _____ $30,000-$49,999
   d. _____ $5,000-$7,499   i. _____ Over $50,000
   e. _____ $7,500-$9,999   j. _____ No answer

PART V:

VALUES AND MEMBERSHIP (THIS QUESTIONNAIRE WAS GIVEN TO RESPONDENTS IN ALL CATEGORIES).

Instructions: Read each of the following statements carefully and then circle the response at the right of each statement that best expresses your feeling about it. *There are no right or wrong answers to these statements.* We are simply interested in your opinions about them.

A. Here are some general statements about family relationships, health, and human nature.

		STRONGLY AGREE	AGREE	DON'T KNOW	DIS-AGREE	STRONGLY DISAGREE
1.	To a large extent, the happiness and development of the world depends upon continued scientific research and experimentation.	SA	A	?	D	SD
2.	Most people are inclined to look out for themselves.	SA	A	?	D	SD
3.	The most important thing to teach children is absolute obedience to their parents.	SA	A	?	D	SD
4.	There isn't really much that one person can do to change the world.	SA	A	?	D	SD
5.	People should be a lot more careful than they are about letting doctors and hospitals use all those new drugs on them.	SA	A	?	D	SD
6.	People should be more careful with their money than they are and save it instead of spend it all.	SA	A	?	D	SD
7.	Human life is not an expression of divine purpose but only the result of chance and evolution.	SA	A	?	D	SD
8.	Prison is too good for sex criminals. They should be publicly whipped or worse.	SA	A	?	D	SD
9.	The average man doesn't really have much chance to get ahead today.	SA	A	?	D	SD
10.	Life as most men live it is meaningless.	SA	A	?	D	SD
11.	One of the biggest problems with the world is that people don't work hard enough anymore.	SA	A	?	D	SD
12.	There are two kinds of people in the world: the weak and the strong.	SA	A	?	D	SD

APPENDIX

		STRONGLY AGREE	AGREE	DON'T KNOW	DIS- AGREE	STRONGLY DISAGREE
13.	Every hospital should try and make its books balance.	SA	A	?	D	SD
14.	Nowadays people make too big a fuss about their health.	SA	A	?	D	SD
15.	No decent man can respect a woman who has had sex relations before marriage.	SA	A	?	D	SD
16.	There is a lot of truth in the statement that 'nice guys finish last.'	SA	A	?	D	SD
17.	Its better to take a good, secure job than to take one where the rewards may be much higher but so are the chances of losing everything.	SA	A	?	D	SD
18.	There is still a lot to be said for the old home remedies when one is sick.	SA	A	?	D	SD
19.	It's hardly fair to bring children into the world with the way things look for the future.	SA	A	?	D	SD
20.	Any good leader should be strict with people under him in order to gain their respect.	SA	A	?	D	SD
21.	A relative or friend who knows you well might be able to help you more with a health problem than a doctor could.	SA	A	?	D	SD
22.	Nowadays a person has to live pretty much for today and let tomorrow take care of itself.	SA	A	?	D	SD
23.	Everybody needs a medical check-up at least once a year.	SA	A	?	D	SD
24.	The welfare of the patient should always come first in any hospital.	SA	A	?	D	SD
25.	Everybody should have a religious faith as a guide for his conduct.	SA	A	?	D	SD

26. What three things or activities in your life do you get the most satisfaction from?

Please write a *1* in the space preceding the most important; a *2* in the space preceding the next most important; and a *3* in the space preceding the third most important.

Rank
Three

_____ Your career or occupation
_____ Family relationships
_____ Leisure-time recreational activities
_____ Religious beliefs or activities
_____ Participation as a citizen in the affairs of your community
_____ Participation in activities directed toward national or international betterment

27. What two qualities on this list do you think really get a young person ahead the fastest today? (Check *two*.)

a. _____ Hard work
b. _____ Having a pleasant personality
c. _____ Brains
d. _____ Knowing the right people
e. _____ Good luck
f. _____ Being a good politician

B. Here are some general statements about local, national and international affairs.

	STRONGLY AGREE	AGREE	DON'T KNOW	DIS- AGREE	STRONGLY DISAGREE
1. That government which governs least governs best.	SA	A	?	D	SD
2. Most of my best friends live right here in Riverview.	SA	A	?	D	SD
3. The old saying that 'you can't fight city hall' is still basically true.	SA	A	?	D	SD
4. On the whole labor unions are doing a lot of good in this country.	SA	A	?	D	SD
5. The only hope for a real, lasting peace is to establish some kind of world government.	SA	A	?	D	SD
6. Democracy depends fundamentally on the existence of free enterprise.	SA	A	?	D	SD

APPENDIX

		STRONGLY AGREE	AGREE	DON'T KNOW	DISAGREE	STRONGLY DISAGREE
7.	On the whole, American participation in the United Nations has been a good thing.	SA	A	?	D	SD
8.	Anyone in Riverview who wants to, gets a chance to have his say about important issues.	SA	A	?	D	SD
9.	We have moved too far away from those fundamental principles which made America great.	SA	A	?	D	SD
10.	We should fight an all-out war to stop the advance of world Communism before it gets any stronger than it is.	SA	A	?	D	SD
11.	An Atheist or a Socialist should have as much right to make a public speech in Riverview as anybody else.	SA	A	?	D	SD
12.	We should give more of our foreign aid for social welfare type projects.	SA	A	?	D	SD
13.	When I have a discussion, I almost always prefer to talk about what's happening around here, rather than about national or international news.	SA	A	?	D	SD
14.	Most decisions in Riverview are made by a small group that pretty well runs the city.	SA	A	?	D	SD
15.	While it may not be perfect, I think this community offers about everything that a person could want.	SA	A	?	D	SD
16.	The United States should be less concerned about what people in other countries think about us.	SA	A	?	D	SD

Read each of the following statements. If you believe it to be true, circle

T and if you think it false, circle F. If you don't know or are uncertain, circle the ?.
1. Ted O'Brian is the mayor of Riverview.   T   F   ?
2. The Governor of New York is Averell Harriman. T   F   ?
3. Adlai Stevenson is the United States Representative
   to the United Nations.   T   F   ?
4. Herbert Lehman is presently a U.S. Senator from the
   state of New York.   T   F   ?

C. Your memberships since 1950.
a. Elective or appointive governmental offices held since 1950. For example, city councilman, county supervisor, hospital board member, city commissioner, etc.
TITLE OF OFFICE   DATES OF OFFICE
b. Committees or commissions created to deal with a local community problem. For example, a committee to attract industry to the city, a publicity committee for a school bond issue or a hospital fund drive, etc.
NAME OF COMMITTEE   OFFICES HELD   DATES OF OFFICE
c. Boards of Directors of private corporations or banks, since 1950.
NAME OF ENTERPRISE   OFFICES HELD   DATES OF OFFICE
d. Local and national community service organizations. For example, any organization concerned with health, education, or welfare, e.g., PTA, United Fund, Mental Health Association, Council of Social Welfare Agencies, etc.
NAME OF ORGANIZATION   OFFICES HELD   DATES OF OFFICE
e. Business organizations. For example, Chamber of Commerce, National Association of Real Estate Dealers, etc.
NAME OF ORGANIZATION   OFFICES HELD   DATES OF OFFICE
f. Professional organizations. For example, the American Medical Association, the American Bar Association, etc.
NAME OF ORGANIZATION   OFFICES HELD   DATES OF OFFICE
g. Union organizations. For example, United Brotherhood of Carpenters and Joiners.
NAME OF ORGANIZATION   OFFICES HELD   DATES OF OFFICE
h. Clubs and social organizations. For example, the Elks, the Shriners, the country club, etc.
NAME OF ORGANIZATION   OFFICES HELD   DATES OF OFFICE
i. Churches and religious organizations. For example, the Methodist Church, the Knights of Columbus, etc.
NAME OF ORGANIZATION   OFFICES HELD   DATES OF OFFICE
j. Political parties, organizations, and clubs. For example, the Young Democrats, the Republican Women's Club, etc.
NAME OF ORGANIZATION   OFFICE HELD   DATES OF OFFICE
k. Veterans' and patriotic organizations. For example, the V.F.W., the American Legion, etc.
NAME OF ORGANIZATION   OFFICE HELD   DATES OF OFFICE

NAME INDEX

Adorno, T., 52, 348
Agger, R., 417
Alford, R., 94
Aristotle, 10, 15
Armstrong, K., 147, 157, 160, 163, 167, 215, 235

Baxter, F., 147, 158-9, 165, 167-9, 171, 216, 378, 394, 397-8
Beard, C. and M., 239, 409
Bensman, J., 59, 227
Blankenship, L. V., 56
Blumberg, L., 418

Campbell, A., 290
Carr, E. H., 11
Carr, R., 147
Carter, H., 123, 389
Cavenaugh, R., 147, 161, 164-5, 169, 215, 389, 392, 395, 398
Coates, C., 419

Dahl, R., 38-41, 44, 50, 94-5, 336, 420
D'Antonio, W., 42
Davis, J., 111, 118-21, 424
de Tocqueville, A., 239, 409
Dooley, Mr., 37, 222
Drake, A. E., 65
Durkheim, E., 12, 35, 45

Eberhard, B., 112, 196, 389
Eisenhower, D. D., 205, 284

Fischer, N., 165, 168, 171
Form, W., 42
Freeman, L., 43, 45, 137, 205n, 288

Goldrich, D., 417

Harriman, A., 85, 224, 226
Hitler, A., 350
Hollingshead, A., 176
Hunter, F., 7, 26, 37, 58, 59, 109-10
Hysan, R., 384

Jackson, A., 30
Johnson, T., 153-4

Kariel, H., 17
Kennedy, J. F., 225, 294, 306, 315, 320
Key, V. O., 18-19, 321
Kimbrough, A., 122, 389
King, Mrs. F., 385, 389
King, R., 112, 196, 211, 213, 220, 228, 232-4, 236, 389
Kish, L., 434-5
Komarovsky, M., 239-40

Lane, R., 413
Laski, H., 14
Locke, J., 14, 35
Lodge, H., 225
Lynd, R. and H., 26, 35

McGuire, G., 154-5
Madison, J., 15
Mannheim, K., 38
Marx, K., 35
Mason, R., 157, 165, 169
Maxwell, S., 388
Merriam, C., 33
Michels, R., 32, 95, 284, 289, 301, 317

NAME INDEX

Miller, D., 42
Miller, D. R., 347
Mills, C. W., 191
Morrow, F., 85-6, 90, 143, 147-8, 150-52, 157, 160, 163-4, 166, 172-3, 198, 201, 210, 214, 216, 224, 226-7, 235, 330, 389
Mussolini, B., 350
Myrdal, G., 62

Nixon, R., 225

O'Brian, T., 85, 142, 143, 147, 151-2, 156-7, 160, 163-6, 170, 172-3, 198, 200, 209-11, 214-15, 223-4, 226-7, 234, 289, 301-2, 305, 310, 320, 330, 389
O'Connor, F., 154, 157

Pareto, V., 11, 51, 205
Parker, G., 112
Parker, Mrs. G., 392, 400
Patriarch, F., 170
Pellegrin, R., 419
Plank, H., 384, 394

Reed, D., 228
Remington, D., 116, 388, 392, 395, 399, 400
Riley, J., 389
Rivers, F., 389, 392, 398

Rockefeller, N., 225
Romney, G., 206
Rousseau, J.-J., 14

Schmidt, A., 389
Schulze, R., 36, 43, 46, 58, 118
Schwartz, F., 149, 155
Scoble, H., 39, 50, 94
Sherman, F., 118
Smith, A., 35
Stevenson, A., 306
Stouffer, S., 347, 353
Sullivan, H. S., 41
Swanson, G., 347

Thomas, F., 388
Tönnies, F., 9, 35
Turner, H., 114, 117, 120, 122-3, 424

Veblen, T., 35
Vidich, A., 59, 227

Wainwright, J., 114-16, 118-22, 181, 274, 424
Weber, M., 4, 5, 9, 35, 42, 61
White, R. G., 123, 388, 395, 399, 400
Williams, R., 181, 220, 389
Wilson, G., 400
Wolchak, J., 164, 384, 394
Wrong, D., 4

SUBJECT INDEX

Absentee-owned corporations
 power of executives in, 119, 119n, 137, 419
Age: of "behind-the-scenes" elite, 123
 of decision-makers, 273
 of organizational leaders, 273
Albany, N.Y., 226-7, 234
Alienation, 332-45
 and age, 341
 and class, 337-8
 and education, 340
 and income, 342
 and membership, 344
 and nonparticipation, 365-6
 among nonvoters, 345
 and political activism, 343
 scale, 337, 337n
 and sense of effectiveness, 332-4, 333n
 and voting, 344
Ambivalence, toward politicians, 133, 159n, 206-10
American Legion, 198, 200, 268, 277
American Medical Association, 12
Anglo-Saxon dominance, 124, 130
"Anticipated reaction" hypothesis, 116-17
Aristocracy, 66
Atlanta, Georgia, 110
Attorney-General, state, 233
Authoritarianism, 346-63, 347n
 and "acquiescence set," 349n
 and authority, 346, 346n, 347-9
 in Edgewood and Riverview, 351-3
 and income, 353-4
 among leaders, 346-9

 in organizations, 361-3
 "organizational authoritarianism" scale, 362
 and religion, 354-6
 "working class," 349-53

Behavior, as critical datum, 110
"Behind-the-scenes" leaders, 114-21 *passim*, 127, 153
Bennington, Vt., 94, 430
"Bigtown," 419
British Parliament, 43

Chamber of Commerce, 12, 80, 194-8, 200, 218, 268, 270, 276, 277, 278, 279
Change: attitudes toward, 312
 in power structure, 50-51
"Changers," of party, 301-5
 characteristics of, 308-10
 by religion, 307
 of vote, 305-10
Cibola, 36, 418
"Circulation of elites," 46, 51, 205
Class
 and authoritarianism, 352
 determination of, 176
 differences in leaders and followers, 176-9
 and membership, 246-9
 and participation, 363, 382-95
 politics, 213-14
 status of Republicans, 311
 and voting, 295, 300, 414
Coalition, strategy, 214-21
"Community viability," 184-5
Consensual validation, 137, 192, 193n, 330

479

Consensus, 112, 321-32 *passim*, 432
  on community desirability, 364-5
  definition of, 332
  role in society, 321-3
"Conservatism," 323-30
Consumer interest, weakness of, 31
Continuities
  methodological, 421-5
  normative, 426-9
  in research, 405-29
  substantive, 405-21
Continuity, of economic power, 29-30, 100, 411
Continuum, elitist-pluralist, 25, 27, 93, 242; *see also* Pluralism
Co-optation, 156, 158, 169-70, 197, 197n, 215, 216, 418
Corporations, role in community, 119-20
Corps of Engineers, 87, 88, 102, 145, 226
Councils, and new industry issue, 104-5
"Countervailing power" thesis, 16
Country Club, 194, 196-201, 268, 276, 277

Decisional method: of identifying leaders, 51-7, 60, 138, 407, 418, 422-5
  shortcomings of, 42, 59-60, 113, 138-9
"Decision-makers"
  aversion to politics, 207
  defined, 55, 56, 135, 150, 153
  "most influential," 99, 113, 163
  "most powerful," 112, 114, 216
  social characteristics, 177, 273
  see also Economic, Political and Specialist leaders
Decisions: criteria, 53, 53n
  as "critical incidents," 91
  participation in "public," 432
  "private," 102, 105, 107-8, 120, 143, 186, 231, 270, 372, 382, 428, 432
  "public," 107, 108, 143, 166, 186, 270
  stages in, 54
  state-federal influence on, 428, 432

"welfare," 129, 131, 145
"Democratic" creed, 24, 334, 335, 336, 336n

Economic affluence, and pluralism, 431-2
Economic dominance, 111, 111n, 205, 205n, 214-21, 410, 410n, 411, 419, 427-8
Economic leaders
  aggregate power, 190-91
  conflict among, 407
  and co-optation, 173
  defined, 50
  and domination of power structure, 411, 411n
  "most influential," 99, 163
  organizational ties, 194-200
  participation, 128, 146, 159, 406, 414, 419
  power of, 134-5, 138, 205, 205n, 410
  rejection of politics, 206-7, 418
  resources, 132-5, 156, 179, 202, 424
  SES, 155, 182, 183, 208
Edgewood
  cohesion among elite, 197, 331
  dependence on state-federal largesse, 227-9
  ethnicity, 67
  flood control issue, 86-8
  hospital issue, 83-4
  industries, 66, 71
  local government, 67
  municipal building issue, 89
  new industry issue, 80-81
  occupational structure, 73
  political structure, 284-8
  population, 66
  power structure, 92-100
  "private" orientation of leaders, 228-30
  religion, 68
  retail sales, 72
  school bond issue, 74-8
  SES, 184
  unions, 70
  wages, 72
Education
  community levels of, 187

SUBJECT INDEX

of Edgewood leaders, 129
and membership, 251-2
and occupation, 253-4
of organizational leaders, 273
and party, 256-7
of Riverview leaders, 155
"Elder statesmen" leaders, 116
Elections
as instrument of pluralism, 233
local, 70, 101, 318
and power structure, 413-14
presidential, 67, 225, 292-3
state, 225, 292-3
Elites
"circulation" of, 51
cohesion among, 191-200, 237
methods of, 24-7
"old-family," 130
power of, 26, 421
properties of, 287-9
ubiquity of, 11
Elitism, 24-7, 30, 31, 429-30
in Edgewood, 413, 426
index of, 27, 94
in Middletown, 35-6
in Riverview, 413, 426-7
see also Michels
Elks, 195, 199, 200, 201, 276, 277
Ethnicity, 67-70
"External" resources, 224-5, 428, 432

F-scale, 347, 347n, 348, 348n; *see also* Adorno
Fascism, 350, 350-51n
Foreign aid, attitudes toward, 315
Formal position: and participation, 55, 55n
and reputation, 110, 424, 424n
"Front-man," 169
Functionalism, 322, 322n

G.E.I., 194, 196
"Gatekeepers," 169-70, 214, 416
Gemeinschaft, relations, 9, 45, 192, 432
and participation, 148, 427
Green Bay, Wisconsin, 95, 430
Group behavior, 98n, 192-3

Hill-Burton Act, 223-4, 229

"Hired-hands," 46, 167; *see also* "Leg-man"
History, impact on social analysis, 35
Hospital boards, 199
class, 387, 392
income, 384
and joint memberships, 386-91
members' occupations, 383
politicization of, 385-6
relations with power elite, 386-96, 412-13
social interaction, 392-6
tenure of, 382-3
Hospital Fund Drive, 195
Hospitals, 83-6
elite involvement in, 401
support levels in, 372-81
and "support" theory, 368-71
see also Hospital boards

Identification: with higher level politicians, 212
with community, 331
Ideology, 8, 35, 105, 108, 148, 149, 271, 407, 428
and "conservatism," 323-31
"private," of Edgewood elite, 227-30
"Inactive influentials," 125-7
Income
of leaders, 129, 156, 208, 286
and leadership, 288
and change of party, 303
and change of vote, 309
and voting, 296
Industry, 69, 71, 175
Interviews: with leaders, 56-7
with rank and file, 434-8
Involvement, in community, 289-90, 331

Kenosha, 95, 430
Kiwanis, 79, 199, 269, 277, 278

Lawyers, among leaders, 187, 413
Leaders
"alienation" among, 334-6
"authoritarianism" among, 346-9
"behind-the-scenes," 114-20, *passim*

Leaders (cont.)
  class status, 176
  cohesion among, 237n
  "conservatism" among, 325-30
  decision-makers, 49, 122, 180
  economic, 49, 98, 100, 103-4, 111, 131, 134, 155, 158, 161, 166-7, 175, 182, 205
  and hospital boards, 386-97
  "hired-hands," 167
  "influentials," 49, 58, 97, 178-82
  involvement in hospitals, 401
  "leg-man," 49, 116-21, 133, 137
  "marginal," 113, 138, 158, 171
  "old-family," 125, 160
  organizational, 49, 275
  political, 49, 131-34, 155, 158, 204-6
  social characteristics, 286-7
  specialist, 49, 97, 100, 107, 121, 127, 130-31, 155, 158, 167-9, 171-4, 219
  toleration, 317
  see also Economic, Political, Specialist leaders
"Leg-man," 49, 54, 116-21, 133, 137, 154, 205, 418
Legitimation, 19, 19n, 60, 133n, 371
Lions, 269, 276, 277, 278
Local government, 67, 70
  power of officials, 419
Long Island, N.Y., 77
Lumber industry, 66, 68
Lumpenproletariat, 350

Madison, Wisconsin, 95, 408, 430
Main Street Athletic Club, 269, 416
Masons, 195, 199, 200-201, 268, 276
Mass democracy, 11
Mass society, Riverview as, 427
Membership
  and class, 203, 246-9
  as index of power, 55, 55n
  in organizations, 244-8, 409
  in U.S., 239-41
  see also Participation
Methods: of research, 47-61
  continuities in, 421-6
  see also Decisional and Reputational methods
Mobility
  defined, 204-5
  politics as instrument of, 211-12, 234-6
Monism, 10n, 14
Moose, 198, 200, 201, 268, 269, 270, 276, 277
"Most influential" leaders, 99, 113, 163
"Most powerful" leaders: criteria, 112, 114, 137
Multiple membership, 239, 246-7, 250, 415
Municipal Building issue, 89
  opposition in, 260

Natural law, and pluralism, 10
"New Deal," 214
New Haven Study, 94, 95, 408, 420, 430
New York City, 20n, 94, 168, 224, 226
New York State
  Agency for Industrial Development, 217
  Attorney-General, 233
  Department of Commerce, 71
  Housing Agency, 90
  Power Authority, 229
  school districts, 185
  State Comptroller, 185n
Newspapers, 215, 222

Oil, 65-6
"Old-family" elite, 125
Oligarchy, 31-2; see also Michels
Opposition, as index of power, 4-5
"Organic" community, 45-6, 412
Organizational interaction
  as index of cohesion, 197, 203
  as index of power, 191-200, 203n, 386-91
Organizations
  and class, 246-50, 416
  effect on participation, 137
  and elite interactions, 191-201, 386-90, 415
  as means of pluralism, 12-14, 17, 19, 22-3, 31, 281, 409
  membership rates, 280
  recruitment of elites, 278-80

SUBJECT INDEX

role in decisions, 266-71
"support theory" of, 289, 368-71, 401-2
"Overlapping"
  in decisional and reputational methods, 110-13, 147-55
  in elite participation, 26-7, 93-7, 141-3, 408, 429-30
  as index of elitism, 35-7, 93, 141
  as index of power, 97-8, 145, 160-61, 176
  in memberships, 193-200; see also Membership

PTA, 78, 79, 268, 277
Participants
  "most influential," 98-100
  "most powerful," 112, 114; see also Leaders
  "rank and file," 263
Participation
  class differences in, 295, 300, 363
  comparative rates of, 263
  criteria of, 55-7, 55n, 266, 408
  defined, 11-12
  electoral, as index, 290
  generalizations on, 413-21
  and income, 296
  by individuals, 258-63, 258n
  levels of, 43-4, 263
  in major decisions, 242-71
  measuring of, 51-61
  by organizations, 264-77, 409-10
  in "political" decisions, 270
  in "private" decisions, 270
  and reputational power, 423-6
  styles of, 100-10, 142-5
Party affiliation, and social structure, 285
Pluralism
  conditions of, 22-4
  criteria of, 242
  decline of, 432-3
  defined, 10, 239
  and economic affluence, 431-2
  in Edgewood and Riverview, 405-12, 426-8
  history of, 12-16
  and individualism, 17-18, 30
  ironies of, 17-21, 411-12, 431
  and level of participation, 415

and research, 3, 21, 27-8, 102, 107, 295, 408
revisions of, 21, 25n, 40-41, 429-30
Riverview as model, 431
tests of, 42-5, 241-71
and voluntary groups, 12-14, 17, 19, 22-3, 31
Polish, ethnic group, 69, 169, 170
Politbureau, 98n
Political efficacy, 332-7, 333n
Political interest, 272, 290, 301
Political knowledge, 301
Political largesse: dependence of Riverview on, 221-7
Political leaders
  aggregate power, 190-91
  as brokers, 223
  class status, 173, 207-8
  defined, 50, 206
  issue participation, 128, 146, 159, 175, 406
  lack of "hard" resources, 419
  means of power, 417
  "most influential," 99, 163
  organizational ties, 194-200
  power of, 134-5, 410
  "private" ideology, 229
  resources, 132-5, 156-7, 202, 237
  SES, 155, 182, 183, 208
  use of coalitions, 214-21
  visibility, 210
Political rivalry, 145-6; see also Politics
Politicization, 145-6, 213, 214, 385
Politics
  as a career, 132, 206
  and change, 301-5
  "class," 213-14
  defined, 34
  and ideology, 212
  and mobility, 211, 234-6
  and nonpartisanship, 109, 213, 292, 294-5, 428
  relevance of, 34n
  and religion, 305-8, 307n
  as study of power, 33
  and tension among leaders, 105, 146, 149
  and visibility, 210-11

Power
  concentration among elite, 190-91
  concentration in Riverview, 174, 413, 427
  defined, 4-5, 32, 37
  disequilibria, 18
  measurement of, 51-61
  as net of social relations, 5-8, 191-2, 386-94
  opposition as index, 4-5, 32, 228, 228n, 260
  of political and economic leaders, 111, 111n, 160-65, 205, 410, 411, 431
  "potential" and "overt," 52-8, 98, 109-11, 422-3
  reluctance to test itself, 124
  specification of, 189-91
  "spill-over" phenomenon, 110-11
  and visibility, 152, 156, 210-11
Power structure, 8, 24, 26, 28, 95
  cohesion in, 197, 415
  concentration in, 413
  economic influence in, 111, 111n, 410, 411, 411n, 417, 421
  in Edgewood, 92-4, 95-109, *passim*, 176-203
  elitism in, 426
  and hospital boards, 386-96, 412-13
  "overlapping" in, 26-7, 93-7, 141-3
  and participation, 413-14
  recruitment into, 278-80
  in Riverview, 140-42, 143-71, *passim*, 176-203
  turnover in, 119-20
Private groups
  internal government of, 20-21
  membership levels in U.S., 239-40
  role of, 12-14, 241
Private interests, 18
Producer groups, power of, 31
Protestants: and authoritarianism, 355-6, 366
  in Edgewood, 68
  in Riverview, 70
"Psychological tone," of community, 146
Public Health Service, 224

"Public interest," 18

Racine, Wisconsin, 95, 430
Railroads, 69
Rank and file
  defined, 49
  participation of, 263, 281
Reference group theory, 116
Referenda
  as means of pluralism, 23-4, 101-2, 233
  in parking lot issue, 233
  in school decision, 259, 262
Religion, 70, 284, 305-8; *see also* Protestants, Roman Catholics
Reputational method, of identifying leaders, 57-61, 98, 109-24, 147-55, 407, 424, 425
  and formal position, 114, 114n
  and organizational role, 424n
  shortcomings of, 60, 422
  as sociometric index, 110, 151
Resolution, as means of participation, 267
Resources, 34n
  of economic leaders, 406, 410, 411, 419, 421
  failure to use, 151, 187n, 397
  of leaders, 176-83, 404, 420
  of legal expertise, 225-6, 235
  of organizational leaders, 272-5, 423
  of politicians, 211, 223, 237-8, 301, 406, 419-20
  and power structure, 175-89
  of rank and file, 176, 187, 283, 286-90, 301, 317, 414
  state and federal, 224-9
Respondent bias, 113, 148-51
Riverview
  cohesion among elite, 197
  dependence on state-federal largesse, 221-7
  ethnic structure, 69-70
  flood control issue, 88-9
  hospital decision, 84-6
  industries, 69-71
  local government, 70
  new hospital dedicated, 224
  new industry issue, 81-3
  occupational structure, 73, 186, 187

SUBJECT INDEX

political structure, 221-6, 284-8
population, 69
power structure, 140-42, 143-71 *passim*, 176-203
public housing issue, 90-91
religion, 70
retail sales, 72
school bond issue, 78-9
SES, 184
unions, 70
wages, 72
Roman Catholics, 14, 70, 169, 214, 309, 310, 320
and authoritarianism, 355-6, 366
and voting, 305-8
Rotary, 79, 106, 195, 268, 278

Sampling procedure, 52, 434-6
School Board, 75-9, 129, 195
Service clubs, role of, 251
SES, 135, 166, 171-84, 202
community differences in, 184
of "influentials," 178-9
and organizational participation, 417
of political and economic leaders, 183
"Significance," tests of, 50
"Situational determinism," 38
Size of community and overlapping, 45, 95, 408
Skybolt Fabricating Co., 81, 83
Social and economic notables, 421
Social integration, and participation, 412
Social interaction, as index of power, 191-200
Social relations, 218, 392-5
"Social support," 296-300, 297n, 320, 323, 395
Social-Democratic parties, 283
Specialist leaders
and co-optation, 173
as "cosmopolitans," 167-8
defined, 50
issue participation, 128-31, 159, 168, 71, 407
marginal status, 138-9, 158, 219
"most influential," 163
resources, 130, 158
SES, 155
and "welfare" issues, 144

Specialization, among leaders, 99-100, 170-71, 430-9
Springdale, 227
"Square-Deal" party, 105, 108, 233, 406
"Support" theory, 48, 368-71, 401-2
Survey Research Center, 103
Syracuse, N.Y., 43-4, 95, 111n, 148n, 430

Tolerance, toward minority values, 317
"Tuesday coffee" group, 279

Unions
CIO-AFL, 16
community attitudes to, 313
in Edgewood and Riverview, 70, 245
United Fund, 194, 199-201, 203
United Nations, 314
Unpolitical man, 30, 432-3
U.S. Congress, 43
U.S. Senate, as power system, 5

V. F. W., 269, 276, 277
Values
and alienation, 337-46
and authoritarianism, 346-63
cohesion in Edgewood, 431
community differences in, 311-17
and conflict in Riverview, 145
"free enterprise" of Edgewood elite, 105, 431
fusion of political and economic, 167-8, 167n
"grass-roots," 108
of leaders, 193
of leaders and community, 323-7
in research, 41-2, 62
Verstehen, 60-61, 97, 121, 407
Vindiciae Contra Tyrannos, 14
"Visibility," and power, 152, 156-7
Voting, and issue participation, 290

Washington, D.C., 227, 234
"Welfare" issues, 107, 144-5, 407
appeals, 257
ideals, 251
Women, as specialists, 97, 129-30, 165
"Working class," 214, 346, 349-54